Jackson State University:
The First Hundred Years—1877-1977

JACKSON STATE UNIVERSITY

The First Hundred Years
1877-1977

Lelia Gaston Rhodes

University Press of Mississippi

Jackson

Reprinted in 2026
Copyright © 1979 by
Jackson State University
Library of Congress Card Catalog Number 77-18107
All Rights Reserved
Distributed by University Press of Mississippi

Publisher: University Press of Mississippi, Jackson, USA
Authorized GPSR Safety Representative: Easy Access System Europe - Mustamäe tee 50, 10621 Tallinn, Estonia, gpsr.requests@easproject.com

Library of Congress Cataloging in Publication Data

Rhodes, Lelia G
   Jackson State University

  Includes bibliographical references and index.
  1. Jackson State University—History. I. Title.
LD2596.J23R48   378.762'51   77-18107

Hardback ISBN 978-1-49686-065-1
Trade paperback ISBN 978-1-49686-066-8
Epub single ISBN 978-1-49686-067-5
Epub institutional ISBN 978-1-49686-068-2
PDF single ISBN 978-1-49686-069-9
PDF institutional ISBN 978-1-49686-070-5

DEDICATED TO

The Founders, Presidents, Alumni, Faculty, Staff,
Students and Supporters
who in the midst of insurmountable odds,
had faith in Jackson State University and its raison d'être.
To Survive and Thrive: From A Century of Service We Go Forward.

Photographs

Endsheets: Aerial View of Jackson State University—1976 University Buildings

Following page 14: H. P. Jacobs, first President of the Mississippi Black Baptist Convention; Historical photographs during the Ayer Administration

Following page 14: Color photographs of University Presidents, Artist, Clara Faye West; University faculty with long tenure; Official Campus Hostesses; Mississippi Black Legislators; Selected Alumni; University Buildings

Following page 46: Early photographs taken during the Barrett Administration

Following page 46: The Hubert Administration: "Highlights"

Following page 78: The Dansby Administration—Photographs taken during the "Lean Years"

Following page 110: The Reddix Years—The State Assumed Control of the Institution in 1940

Following page 142: Selected photographs highlighting The Peoples' Years, 1967-

ACKNOWLEDGMENTS

THE VERY CREATION OF JACKSON STATE UNIVERSITY was an act of faith that all men created by God should have the right to the opportunity to develop to their fullest potential and thus has come a great institution.

The roots of Jackson State University go deeply into the soil of American tradition. The writer is deeply indebted to many persons who contributed to the birth of this presentation. Special acknowledgment goes to President John A. Peoples who commissioned the writer to chronicle the saga of events depicting 100 years in the life of the institution.

The President of the University provided the author with financial assistance, staff, released time, and facilities without which this history could not have been written. What is most important, Dr. Peoples personally supported and encouraged the writer in overcoming the many difficulties which inevitably arise during the research and writing which were done sporadically over a period of six years.

Many thanks to the staff of the National Archives, Washington, D.C.; the Library Staff of Colgate-Rochester Divinity School, Rochester, New York; Dr. Atha Baugh, Deputy Executive Secretary and Mrs. Henrene George, Supervisor, Records Management Center, both from National Ministries Incorporated as The American Baptist Home Mission Society, Valley Forge, Pennsylvania; Mr. Elbert R. Hilliard, State Historic Preservation Officer and the Reference Librarians, Mississippi Department of Archives and History, Jackson, Mississippi; Staff of the Public Library, Natchez, Mississippi; Hinds County and Chancery Clerks' Office; Adams County Court House, Natchez, Mississippi; Baptist Historical Archives, Clinton, Mississippi; President John A. Peoples; Presidents Emeriti Jacob L. Reddix and B. B. Dansby who gave personal interviews; Alumni Presidents; hundreds of Alumni; and faculty. The writer acknowledges the several critics who read portions or all of the various versions and made many valuable suggestions.

Special acknowledgment goes to Dr. Clara Grochowska, Professor of Modern Foreign Languages, who spent long hours critiquing drafts of the manuscript. Also to Dr. Margaret Hutton, Professor of History, Dr. Ancilla Coleman, Professor of English, and Dr. Bennie Reeves, Professor and Head of the History Department.

Several members of the Jackson State University Library staff were most cooperative in many ways in helping to secure data and assist with typing. These included: Mrs. Bernice Bell, Assistant Director; Mrs. Orthella Moman, Coordinator of Technical Services; and Mrs. Lou Helen Sanders, Science/Reference Librarian. Mrs. Victoria List served as an administrative secretary who spent many long hours typing and re-typing drafts to finalize the copy for the publishers. Because of Mrs. List's additional duties as a member of the library staff, she was assisted by other library staff members who included: Mrs. Bennie Kendrick, Administrative secretary, Arthur Taylor, Miss Rosie Griffin, Miss Rubye Griffin and Mrs. Raja Rashied, and other secretaries located in other departments on campus—Mrs. Curties Mary Lewis, Secretary, General Science and Physics; and Miss Aletha L. Almore, Secretary to the Vice President for Student Affairs.

The writer expresses appreciation to Dr. Lee E. Williams, Vice President for Administration, Chairman of the Centennial Celebration, Dr. Estus Smith, Vice President for Academic Affairs who served as her mentors, and Dr. Paul Wayne Purdy, Vice President for Fiscal Affairs who also saw the author through the crisis when the going was roughest.

Commissioned to write the history of Jackson State University in May 1971, the writer not only spent six years of sporadic research and writing, but coordinated the combined efforts of a group of dedicated critics in the midst of other academic responsibilities to produce this document.

Only the author knows it was God who sustained her and brought her through an experience that was challenging, traumatic, painful and yet pleasurable. Her hope is that the reading population will find the pages herein a source document extolling the story of a memorable past and promising an exciting future into the second century: To Survive and Thrive—From a Century of Service We Go Forward.

It is impossible to adequately thank everyone who gave assistance, but special acknowledgment goes to my husband John D. Rhodes who encouraged me to follow through with the manuscript when many times the efforts seemed futile. His love, patience and consideration in competing with an "unusual" schedule deserve my special recognition. Other members of my family, my mother, Mrs. Fred A. Gaston, my children, Marilyn and John Jr., my sisters and my brothers along with my three very young grandchildren have my eternal love for standing by to see the manuscript to realization.

A Brief History of Jackson College by B. B. Dansby and *A Voice Crying in the Wilderness: The Memoirs of Jacob L. Reddix* were invaluable source documents used by the writer. Special editorial assistance was provided by Reverend and Mrs. Theodore C. Simmons.

*Board of Trustees of State Institutions of
Higher Learning
Members with terms beginning May, 1978*

Verner S. Holmes, M.D.,
   PRESIDENT
Bobby L. Chain,
   VICE PRESIDENT
R. C. Cook
Robert W. Harrison, Jr., D.D.S.
Charles C. Jacobs, Jr.
John R. Lovelace, M.D.

Travis E. Parker
N. Denton Rogers, Jr.
Robert L. Shemwell, Jr.
W. M. Shoemaker
Miriam Q. Simmons
Boswell Stevens
Betty A. Williams
E. E. Thrash, ED.D.

CONTENTS

	Acknowledgments	vii
	Foreword by President John A. Peoples, Jr.	xiii
	Preface	xvii
I	The Decision for Greatness *Prologue to the Founding of Jackson State University*	3
II	The Challenge and the Response *the Administration of President Charles Ayer, 1877–1894*	15
III	The Exodus and the Renaissance *the Administration of President Luther G. Barrett, 1894–1911*	34
IV	The Academic Revolution *the Administration of President Zachary T. Hubert, 1911–1927*	50
V	A Charge to Keep *the Administration of President B. Baldwin Dansby, 1927–1940*	75
VI	The Symphony of the Whole Individual *the Administration of President Jacob L. Reddix, 1940–1967*	102
VII	The Advancement of Truth and Freedom *the Administration of President John A. Peoples, Jr., 1967–*	142
VIII	The Conclusion	216
	Appendices	223
	Notes	325
	Index	331

President John A. Peoples, Jr., 1967-

FOREWORD

On September 14, 1976, I had the privilege of making remarks during the Opening Centennial Convocation of Jackson State University. These remarks, "A Story of Faith," made in reference to the consummation of the first century of existence and the beginning of the second century seem particularly appropriate as a foreword to this chronicle of the first century of existence and the first 100 years of this historic institution by Dr. Lelia G. Rhodes.

Dr. Rhodes has traced the history of Jackson State University from its inception, giving considerable detail to its embryonic stages. Her extensive research discloses documents and facts hitherto unknown or unrecognized by previous writers. Using the methods of the biographer as well as the historian, she uses in turn the administration of each of the six presidents as a rubric for developing the 100-year history of Jackson State University. When one considers the sacrifices, the courageousness, the challenges and achievements of those persons whose contributions have brought about the realization of this modern, now highly regarded, University, the faith of the many persons involved in its history indeed becomes manifest. Thus, the excerpt from the Opening Convocation's remarks, "A Story of Faith," here aptly introduces the *First Hundred Years of Jackson State University*.

"... The story of Jackson State University is a story of people with a dream; black people, white people, poor people, rich people; but always people working together for a sacred cause. It is a story of struggle against monumental odds; it is a story of a fight for freedom of mind and thought; it is the story of a quest for the truth and the right to tell the truth; it is a story of love, yes, even of the right to love without regard to color of the skin or the size of the purse; and, it is a story of an abiding faith in God. Yes, a faith; indeed a true belief that Almighty God will deliver his people from the evils of ignorance and hatred, and will provide them with enlightenment and love, and that He will do this either with the help of, or in spite of, those who have the earthly power to give or take material things.

Consider the Founders of Jackson State University, those black men who conceived of it in a prayer meeting, and those white men who had the wherewithal to move the idea to a tangible reality. Did they dare dream that their embryonic Natchez Seminary would metamorphose into a major State university of national reputation, educating men and women to serve in every walk of life throughout this nation? I think they did have such a dream. For if they had not, that spirit which moved this institution forward—on through the white pioneers, Ayer and Barrett—on through the black stalwarts, Hubert, Dansby and Reddix—if they had not had such a dream, then that spirit would not be with us here today. And I can personally testify that that spirit lives here today within me and all of us who are involved in this institution.

And so, my dear friends, what do we here today dare dream for this proud institution, as we look toward its second century of existence? Having been accorded the high honor of serving as sixth president of Jackson State University, I believe that it is the will of all its constituents that I serve as oracle for its second century. Thusly, do I pronounce:

We do here dream and pledge our utmost efforts and those of our posterity that during its second century—

(1) Jackson State University will continue its sacred mission to provide education for persons from deprived conditions, believing it is the function of higher education to teach those who need help most, as well as those who might well learn without help.

(2) Jackson State University will maintain its leadership in eliminating racial, social, sexist and economic barriers to education.

(3) Jackson State University will continue to emphasize excellence in teaching and learning, seeking nothing less than the highest quality in faculty and teaching facilities.

(4) Jackson State University will further advance its position

toward the cutting edge of change in teaching methodology, learning theory, and educational philosophy.

(5) Jackson State University will broaden its academic program to include offerings responsive to the intellectual and career needs of the people at appropriate degree levels, including the doctorate.

(6) And because people want it so, Jackson State University will overcome all impediments to its efforts to serve all the people, be those impediments prejudice, provincialism, petty competition, or politics.

(7) And most importantly, Jackson State University will realize its destiny of becoming a major American University, bringing honor and fame to this State and nation.

These accomplishments for the second century of Jackson State University we do pledge to fulfill as we initiate the last year of the first century. May God grant that these pledges will not have been made in vain."

John A. Peoples, Jr.
PRESIDENT
Jackson State University
Jackson, Mississippi

PREFACE

With its centennial theme "To Survive and Thrive: From a Century of Service We Go Forward," Jackson State University stands at the crossroads of history—its past chronicled; its present in progress; its future significant with great expectations. Jackson State University has had as its mission for the past one hundred years, specifically but not exclusively, to train underprivileged people in advancing to new horizons and new opportunities through education. As the Institution enters its second century, what the future holds for it augurs well for Jackson State. Predicated on the ideals and principles of its founders, the University will survive and thrive because of its commitment to education for all people irrespective of race, sex, and national origin.

For one hundred years, Jackson State University has assumed the responsibility for the education of thousands of black students in the state of Mississippi. The interesting saga of events that took place in this institution warrants a thorough analysis, an evaluation of its mission, its goals, and its objectives in an effort to chart its course for the challenges that lie ahead in the twenty-first century.

To chronicle an account of Jackson State University, which had its origin in Natchez, the first capital of Mississippi, is to narrate the genesis and survival of education for blacks in Mississippi from 1877 to 1977. The writing of this history comes at a time when the United States has concluded the celebration of its bicentennial.

In the recent observance of the nation's two hundredth birthday, Americans, black and white, reflected on the spectrum of ideals presented in the Declaration of Independence, encompassing freedom, liberty, and equality while at the same time reviewing the stigma of slavery which in 1776 fettered most blacks in the thirteen colonies. The system had been used as a way of providing free labor for the development of a country. More than a hundred years later futile efforts were being made in the Deep South to loose the chains that bound men of color. This system of slavery was based on the thought held by whites that blacks were inherently inferior.

This belief in the "inherent" inferiority of blacks was widespread in the United States before and after the Civil War. The number of blacks who were legally freed by the Thirteenth Amendment to the Constitution was 4 million. Added to this number were a quarter of a million quasi-free blacks. The vast majority of them had never had an opportunity to go to school, to learn to read and write. The task of educating so many illiterates was indeed difficult. The question of who was to take full responsibility for the education of blacks was posed by many.

Among the first to ask this question were black ministers who had observed the social and political situation of the ex-slaves in Mississippi. Legal emancipation had opened the way for the former slaves to enjoy the rights and privileges of freedom in these United States. Yet some ex-slaves in Mississippi would have to wait twelve more years before they could use this privilege of obtaining an education beyond the grade school level.

How they succeeded is, in essence, the story of Jackson State University. Its history constitutes one of the major developments in the education of Blacks in the State of Mississippi for the arts and sciences, for education, for business and industry, for the performing arts, for mass communication, for politics and government. Its memorabilia, gathered at Natchez Seminary, which moved from one site to another, emerging as Jackson State College and finally as Jackson State University, show that through education, Mississippi blacks effected upward mobility of the seemingly unshaken Southern pyramid.

What forces contributed to the founding of this institution? In the following pages this writer makes an effort to interpret the records that tell the story of the establishment, development, and unparalleled growth of Jackson State University.

Jackson State University:
The First Hundred Years—1877–1977

CHAPTER I

THE DECISION FOR GREATNESS

Prologue to the Founding of Jackson State University

THE DEVELOPMENT OF JACKSON STATE UNIVERSITY parallels the growth of a people freed from physical bondage and struggling for survival and quality in a racist environment. Throughout the years, the challenges of society and the desire for self-development have elicited responses that were suitable and pertinent to the advancement of the school and the people it served.

The results of the Civil War freed 4 million black people who then needed an education to fit them into the cultural pattern of American society. For this reason, on March 3, 1865, the newly created Freedmen's Bureau in Washington was authorized to cooperate with benevolent religious organizations in their attempts to educate blacks. The American Baptist Home Mission Society of New York entered this field in many Southern states including Mississippi. Cynical white southerners were hostile to this religious body, since members of the society were considered outsiders, intruders, and iconoclasts who were resolved to destroy the Southern way of life. The Mississippi of the 1860s still presented a social structural pyramid. The sparse apex was composed of wealthy landowners while the overcrowded base included the poverty-stricken who were denied the social, political, and economic advantages of that era.

When the Home Mission Society stated its intention to work in Mississippi for *both* races, white leaders demanded that the group promise to refrain from integrating the blacks socially while educating them to fit into the emerging new South economically. The society's engagement in the education of black preachers and teachers and subsequently of a vast population of black men and women represents the greatest of contributions of free men to the freedmen of the South.

At this time, education of the blacks in the United States involved much more than the instruction of a people twelve years removed from slavery. Educators provided experiences which helped freedmen in efforts to adjust to their economic, civic, and spiritual responsibilities in the larger society.

Reconstruction legally ended in April 1877 with the final withdrawal of federal troops from Louisiana and South Carolina. However, its consequences endured far into the twentieth century. The sheer dimension of the Civil War and Reconstruction left the nation a legacy of suspicion, fear, and hatred, especially in the South. There existed also the inescapable fact that southern whites had been compelled, despite bitter resistance, to return to a nation they had sought to dissolve.

The education of blacks was not a new social concept in the post-Civil War period. Long before Mississippi emerged as a state in 1817, French and Spanish-European Catholics who occupied the territory that is now part of the state provided the rudiments of some education to black children both on their plantations and on the convent compounds. Later, adherents of other religious denominations came from the North to engage in missionary activities within the framework of the law which forbade whites to teach blacks to read. The Methodists at Vicksburg and Congregationalists and Baptists at Natchez were among the proselytizers from the North.[1]

Also in the early years of Reconstruction, the work of benevolent societies among blacks was widespread. There were 1,130 white children enrolled in private schools in Vicksburg in 1867. Natchez was reported as having the "best system of schools but none for blacks." The Jackson private school employed eight black teachers in 1869. Toward the end of the Reconstruction period, the diversion of educational funds to other expenses of the state left the public school with almost no resources.[2]

The Black and Tan Convention which drafted the Constitution of 1868 was dominated by sympathetic Northerners and black delegates. Former slave-holders were a helpless minority in the meeting.[3] Article VIII, Sections 1-10 of that constitution authorized the legislature to establish an informal school system. Section I stated explicitly that the duty of the legislature was "to encourage, by all suitable means, the promotion of intellectual, scientific, moral and agricultural improvement, by establishing a uniform system of free public schools." One of the criticisms of the so-called Democratic press was that there was no provision for the separation of races in the school system.[4]

Mississippi's first public school system for both races was established in 1870. Under this new plan, each county and city in the state with a population of more than 3,000 was organized as a school district. Each young person between the ages of five and twenty-one was to be given free schooling for a period of not less than four months a year. State funds were to be used for school support, and supervisors were required to levy taxes on county residents for the operation of the schools.[5]

Much opposition to public schools existed. Buildings were expensive to erect, equip, and maintain, especially in the black counties. Sometimes black schools were burned and the teachers driven away. At first, white Southerners feared that Northerners might attempt to set up integrated schools. But by the end of Reconstruction, Southern whites began to realize the necessity of educating the freedmen to fit them into their new social life. On the other hand, some whites continued to oppose any kind of education for freedmen. The numerous fears expressed included the thought of government interference, destruction of the Southern caste system, and, more subtly, fear of miscegenation.

Northern whites, like prominent black ministers, on the other hand, believed that education was a prerequisite for equality. They believed that public school instruction would cure all the ills of society—physical, mental, cultural, economic, and moral. In his campaign for the post of lieutenant governor of Mississippi in 1869, Ridgely C. Powers stated that "the Negro is a dangerous element in society because he is ignorant. Move the ignorance and there is no cause for fear."[6]

Insuring for man a competency to contribute his share in life's productive processes, education is not only a privilege but a necessity for all classes of society. Many of the Northern whites who tried to help the cause of the freedmen were ostracized and sympathetic native whites were repeatedly attacked because of their concern.[7]

Mississippi Democrats charged Northern teachers working in the state with spreading the propaganda of the Republican party's doctrine of equality. Northern teachers were also criticized and dubbed as emissaries in disguise who inculcated the political creeds of their party. Political criticism of the school law of 1870 not only proclaimed the measure as "the damn Yankee's import of evil" but also articulated many fears that education for the blacks would destroy the Southern way of life. This is perhaps most clearly stated by T. S. Gaithright, the first Democratic superintendent of education in 1876. Gaithright denounced the school law as "an unmitigated outrage upon the rights and liberties of the white people of the state ... enacted to demoralize our (white) people to proselyte [sic] our children in the interest of a political party hostile to the dignity, interest and sensibilities of the white people of Mississippi."[8]

It is against this political and social background that the concept for Jackson State was perceived. Jackson State University owes its genesis more to the black Baptist ministers of Mississippi than to the Freedmen's Bureau or the American Baptist Home Mission Society. The idea came from men who attended the first Saint's Baptist Missionary Association, which held its initial assembly on March 4, 1869, at King Solomon Baptist Church at Vicksburg, Mississippi. Among the delegates were the Reverends H. P. Jacobs, Randle Pollard, William Gray, and Moses B. Black, all destined to be prominent in the founding of the Natchez Seminary. In reading the proceedings of this and subsequent meetings, one is struck by the recurrence of the ideas of self-help, black awareness, pride, and the necessity for an education if liberty were to be a reality. At this first meeting in Vicksburg, the group members resolved that they would work "for the maintenance of liberty and elevation of our race."[9]

The first annual session of the Baptist Missionary Convention was scheduled for July 12, 1869, at Port Gibson. Reverend Jacobs was elected president and Reverend Pollard, vice president. Most of the meeting was spent in organization, but the idea of establishing a college was again discussed. A resolution was passed authorizing the purchase of land "for the purpose of building a theological school."[10]

From this first meeting in 1869 until the Northern Baptists gave financial assistance in 1877, Reverend Jacobs was the guiding light of this group. There is a dearth of information concerning him, and therefore the historian has to construct a sketchy characterization mainly from his speeches. According to Patrick Thompson, "the life of Reverend Jacobs would be as exciting as that of a novel."[11] Because he was considered too small during his youth to be a field slave, Jacobs was assigned the task of caring for an insane but literate man who was in his master's charge. Jacobs exploited the knowledge of the man and learned to read and write. Finally, in 1856, he formulated plans for his escape to the North, wrote his own "pass," and was able to obtain a wagon, horses, and money from his master. Although Thompson does not mention how Jacobs was able to accomplish this escape, his story points to the keenness and cleverness of the minister's mind. Not only did Jacobs flee, he also took along with him his wife, three children, and a brother-in-law. The flight is particularly remarkable because he went all the way to Canada without any assistance from the underground railroad. Jacobs was successful despite the fact that Southerners, after 1850, were more insistent than ever that Northern authorities obey the Fugitive Slave Law and return runaway slaves. Moreover, Jacobs became bolder after remaining in Canada for ten years. From Canada, he went to Michigan, then to Natchez in 1866, where he become pastor of the Pine Street Baptist Church.

Several ideals of Jacobs, the man, stand out in his speeches. He had a clear sense of mission, a burning dream, and a sense of a place in history. In charging his peers for the task at the first meeting, he admonished them by saying: "So you see, my brethren, how necessary it is for us to stand together, so when time shall have ended with us upon the earth, we will be reckoned in history as the men of the period."[12] From this point on, his overriding concern was the establishment of a seminary for Baptist ministers to work among blacks.

But Jacobs was more than a visionary. He was a realist possessing a certain business acumen. At one meeting, he instructed the ministers to explain to their congregations the importance of keeping accurate accounts so that no one could take advantage of them. In two other sessions, Jacobs discussed the feasibility of organizing farmers' clubs to discuss ways of saving money. In his view, education was important and was the way to economic independence.

It is interesting to note also the growth of Jacobs' ideas. From his obsession with the idea of developing preachers, he expanded his goals to that of preparing teachers. As Natchez Seminary evolved into Jackson State University, there was always specific continuity in the emphasis placed on the education of teachers.

Another side of the realist is seen in the fact that Jacobs participated in the Black and Tan Convention and served in the Mississippi legislature in the early 1870s. One can easily see that Jacobs manifested his perception of the economic, social, and political situation in which blacks found themselves a decade after emancipation. It is significant that a man of the stature of Jacobs was destined to be "the founding father" of the educational institution now known as Jackson State University. As early as August 5, 1869, the Executive Board of the convention had agreed to buy land somewhere in the state for the erection of a theological school.

The second session of the Baptist Convention was held July 12, 1870, at King Solomon Baptist Church at Vicksburg, Mississippi. By his display of charismatic leadership, Reverend Jacobs proved that the Baptists' choice of him as president was indeed a wise one. While he discussed the theme of Christian brotherhood which he believed all Baptists should practice, he also emphasized the need for a self-supporting black church.

Education was essential to realize this dream, and Jacobs urged the members not to adjourn until a decision had been made relative to the education of ministers:

> ... I now come to the subject of education, and what I believe to be the destination of the colored race. To elevate that race, and to save it from

idolatry and corruption, we must educate. Corruption follows hand in hand in the path of ignorance, and to prove this, had the Southern people been educated up to that high and moral standard that should characterize the civilized world, all this war and devastation, and carnage, would not have happened in our midst. But instead of that, they were educated to believe that they were the peculiar and favored work of God's hand, and that the poor African race was born to be their slaves. That made them believe that a Negro had no rights that a white man was bound to respect. But we praise God from whom all blessings flow, we find in the face of all that heathenish teaching, that slavery is dead; and as such we all ought to be engaged in building up the old waste places.

My brethren, when intelligence was brought to light in Rome, the Roman world fell, because a new light had risen upon mankind, and all the aspirations were to inspire man that the past must be blotted out.[13]

In reading this exhortation, one can easily imagine Jacobs telling the group, "You shall know the truth and the truth shall make you free." According to Jacobs, white Southerners had not known the truth, had been miseducated to accept their own superiority and the slaves' inferiority, and corruption, war, and devastation had been the result. Jacobs had a sense of history. He knew the motives of Southern whites who opposed freedom. Jacobs felt that because of the experience of slavery, special care had to be taken in educating ministers so they could rebuild and restore the self-esteem which some blacks had lost.[14]

Committee reports followed the president's message. The Committee on Education and Publication reiterated and expanded the ideas on education. Their report carefully concluded that the school, the press, and the pulpit "are the three agencies by which races, nations, and parties, whether political or religious, are strengthened, vitalized, perpetuated and made influential and efficient." They were convinced that contributions from the churches would make this feasible. Therefore, they recommended the establishment of a Baptist paper and the location of a site for a seminary. The convention followed through on these recommendations and resolved that President Jacobs and the Honorable William Gray be empowered to appoint other members to assist them in establishing the paper and to find a favorable site "for founding a theological seminary, or a Baptist college."[15]

A third but ineffective convention was scheduled for March 13,

1871, in New Orleans, Louisiana. Because the Reverend Jacobs was a member of the Mississippi legislature and an important election was scheduled, the convention was postponed two days.

A fourth session was called and convened at Greenville, Mississippi, on December 12, 1871. In his annual message, President Jacobs reported that in accordance with the previous recommendations, the Executive Board had invited individuals representing towns to submit sealed proposals for land for the theological school. He reported that two proposals representing Natchez and Greenville had been submitted.[16] The two towns were represented by President Jacobs and Reverend Gray respectively. Discussion of this business followed the president's speech.

Natchez offered a lot 94' deep by 50' front on Pine Street valued at $600. In addition, the Natchez community would pay for construction of the first floor which would be used as a church, while the convention would be responsible for construction of the remainder of the building. Upon its completion, the deed would be given to the convention. The Natchez community would offer room and board if the convention would hire a teacher. Greenville offered to give a half-acre of ground and pledged to donate $1,000 for the building of the school. The Greenville proposal was accepted.

The concept of truth, stated in the second meeting, was reiterated in even stronger words at this meeting. According to Jacobs, it was essential that properly educated black preachers re-educate the masses to the truth of the gospel. He pointed out that slave masters had twisted doctrine to their own ends and told Africans that "God has made them to be slaves for the whites." Unfortunately, these writings still comprised a large part of Southern libraries and the only useful purpose was to "burn them in the presence of the people they preached to, and scatter the ashes to the four winds."[17] Jacobs somehow envisioned the role the black church was to play in the lives of his people. Hence, he desired to help develop an educated ministry for the leadership.

On December 6, 1872, Reverend Stevenson Archer of Greenville sent a letter to the Baptist Convention promising to assume the responsibility of providing $140 for the building of the school provided that it be located in Greenville. This offer was made as a result of Elder Gray's knowledge that Archer had failed to raise the promised $1,000. The Executive Board immediately appointed a building committee and a location committee.

The Baptist Convention had survived many disappointments and setbacks in its attempts to found a school. Believing that they were about to achieve their goal, convention leaders appointed a Reverend M. B. Black as special agent to collect money for establishing the school. At the next session of the convention held at Shiloah Baptist Church of Columbus, Mississippi, on December 12, 1872, the Reverend Black shocked his friends by reporting that illness in his family and personal circumstances had forced him to use the money he had collected to found the school. Despite his expressed willingness to repay the money within ninety days, the convention board charged Black with malfeasance in office and discontinued his services. Moreover, in order to protect their future interest, the board then placed a notice of Black's dismissal in the *Greenville Times*, *Vicksburg Times*, and *The Missionary Baptist* of Memphis, Tennessee.

Although highly disappointed, the convention refused to allow one man's mismanagement to hinder their goal of building a school for the freedmen in Mississippi. At the fifth annual meeting, held in 1872, more time was spent discussing the financial situation. Convention president Jacobs made clear the need for monetary support from the Baptist churches in Mississippi. He admonished the convention delegates to support the school with more than three dollars per church as originally decided.

During the sixth annual convention held at the Rose Hill Baptist Church in Natchez, July 24-29, 1873, President Jacobs in his address to the members stated that "the eyes of the world were opened upon the Blacks more than any other human beings in the world." He pleaded with his brethren to spare no pains in educating themselves.

> ... The eyes of the world are opened upon the colored now more than upon any human beings in the world.... We, as ministers, that constitute this convention, have a great work before us; and in order to accomplish it, we must spare no pains in trying to educate ourselves and stand firm and survive....
> ... As for our Baptist Academy, we are hard at work raising money to

start as soon as possible.... You must remember, that this school, if established, has to be sustained by contributions taken from the various churches and three dollars collected from each church that composes this convention will not build a school that will cost $10,000.00 and pay teachers.... There has not been one dollar sent to the board for the erection of the school as yet. What money we have is in the Freedmen's Bank, and the Board will not start to build until they get money to finish.

... The eyes of the country are open upon this convention, to see how long colored men can maintain an organization of such great importance.... We can make this convention of Baptist ministers foremost in the history of the world for its intelligence, and as a source from which the future policy of the Baptists may be shaped.[18]

With respect to building a school, Jacobs declared that the ministers were hard at work raising money to start construction as soon as possible. He chided them for failing to realize that an assessment of three dollars per church was not only insufficient to build a school but also inadequate to pay teachers. He scolded them for their failure to contribute funds and said the board would not authorize erection of a structure until the money was in hand. What funds the convention did have were in the Freedmen's Bank. Such funds were a part of the general educational funds that the convention had been able to save.

Several important decisions were made by the board at the sixth annual session. The name of the original deed was changed from Theological School to Missionary Baptist Education Academy. The board also decided to erect a two-story brick building. However, inadequate funds prevented this decision from becoming a reality.

A special call meeting of the Executive Board on July 22, 1875, changed the course of events. President Jacobs announced a decision of the board to merge the Baptist Missionary Convention with the Northern Baptist churches to establish a theological school in Mississippi. This was the first record of an attempt of the Northern Baptist churches to offer support to the Mississippi Baptist Convention its its effort to found the school which became Natchez Seminary. Jacobs offered this alternative to the convention for two important reasons—the alliance with the Baptist Missionary Convention paved the way for negotiations for support of the school from the American Baptist Home Missionary Society, and the convention had lost all but $287.62 of its savings of $1,547.08 in the Freedmen's Bank, which defaulted.[19] During the eighth session of the Baptist Convention on July 27, 1876, held at King Solomon Baptist Church in Vicksburg, the convention learned of this loss. Pollard, president of the Executive Board, made the announcement.

Benjamin Thompson, treasurer, urged the convention to present a resolution to show appreciation to the Northern Baptists who had come South to help build the school. Reverend Jacobs terminated his tenure as president of the convention at the end of the eighth session. Upon assuming office, the newly elected president, G. W. Gayles, presented a new idea to the convention membership. He urged that the goals of the black Mississippi Baptists be expanded to include the education of teachers. Speaking of their work of evangelization and education, President Gayles suggested that to realize this two-fold purpose, each church member should be assessed ten cents yearly for the education of "young ministers and school teachers."[20]

At the ninth session of the conference on July 24, 1877, Reverend H. P. Jacobs was elected corresponding secretary. It was also during this period that the Reverend F. J. Jones, a former member of the Executive Board of the Baptist Missionary Convention, accused the current Executive Board of having squandered $1,547.08 then in the hands of the convention treasurer for the purpose of building a school. Jones succeeded in "taking the advantage of the ignorance of some, the prejudice of others, and the ambitions of still others." Because of the controversy, a committee was appointed to investigate the charges, to check the bank book of the treasurer, and to report its findings to the convention. The treasurer and the board were exonerated when the committee ascertained that the treasurer, Benjamin Thompson, had, in fact, deposited the money and that it was lost in the Freedmen's Bank.[21]

President Gayles' ideas, outlined in his presidential address, were similar to ex-president Jacobs'. He discussed the intention of the convention to build a college in Mississippi in spite of the loss of over $1,500 in the Freedmen's Bank. He announced that the Northern Baptists had come to the rescue of the convention and had purchased the U.S. Marine Hospital in Natchez as the site for the Baptist Seminary.[22] This business deal was fraught with problems and obstacles which included racial considerations. It had not been customary for whites to relinquish government property to be used for a school for blacks.

The dream of Jacobs and his colleagues was going to become a reality. From 1869 to 1877 they had worked against almost insurmountable odds to realize their vision. Despite internal conflict, the loss of savings, opposition from white Southerners, and an attempt to work within the framework of a "redeemed" state, the convention members achieved their goal. When the American Baptist Home Mission Society came South to buy land and build schools, this small group of dedicated Baptist ministers was ready. In a letter dated July 22, 1875, the society had written to the Baptist Missionary Convention: "Your work and our work is one.... We stand ready to cooperate with you in every good work."[23] With courage and commitment, the black leaders cooperated with the American Baptist Home Mission Society and founded Jackson College. Jacobs and his peers had worked diligently to keep their efforts alive. Even after ending his presidency, Jacobs was the spearhead of the idea and must be regarded, more than any other individual, as the founder of Jackson State.

Reverend H. P. Jacobs, Founder. First President, Mississippi Baptist Convention, 1869-1872

The Memorial

of the American Baptist Home Mission Society to the Senate and House of Representatives of the United States in Congress assembled, respectfully represents

That the American Baptist Home Mission Society is a corporation under the laws of the State of New York, maintained for forty-four years by the Baptist Denomination for missionary purposes;— that in order to raise up competent teachers of both sexes, and competent preachers, among and for the colored population, it has established and is maintaining efficiently, schools for the instruction of such persons, at Washington, Richmond, Raleigh, Columbia, Augusta, Nashville and New Orleans, and that of such teachers of both sexes and of such preachers, it has 918 in these schools under the instruction of 30 persons appointed by this Society;— that it has buildings and grounds for these schools, of the value of more than $300,000, without encumbrance, and is supporting these schools at an annual expense of near $40,000; that an additional school is required in the State of Mississippi;— that believing that the Marine Hospital Building at Natchez could be profitably reconstructed for that purpose, this Society did at public auction purchase the same at regular sale on the 15th day of February 1876;— that the Secretary of the Treasury declines to confirm the sale without further authorization by Congress;— and that such further authorization is hereby respectfully sought by the passage of the annexed Joint Resolution.

Your memorialists further represent that the said Marine Hospital Building has long suffered from dilapidation and decay, and that since the last previous sale in 1870, a part of the roof has been blown off, subjecting to great exposure and diminishing its value. The building is believed to be useless to the United States, but with proper reconstruction can be made serviceable for the purpose desired. Referring to the Supervising Surgeon General for information as to the uselessness of the property for the purposes of the United States, and to the Secretary of the Treasury for any confirmatory information in respect to the objects of this Memorial, this Society asks the early passage of the Resolution in order that work upon reconstruction can be immediately commenced, and the school be opened in October next.

By order of the Executive Board of the American Baptist Home Mission Society.

N.Y. April 5" 1876.

A. B. Caswell
Chn. Execu'tn. Bd.

Attested
Joseph F. Shoards
Re. Sec'y Ex. Bd.

Treasury Department,
OFFICE OF THE SECRETARY,
Washington, D. C., July 26", 1876.

Hon. Frank Hereford,
 Chairman of the Committee of Commerce,
  House of Representatives.

Sir:

In reply to your note of the 24th inst., transmitting Senate Bill No. 699, "To confirm the sale of the Marine Hospital Building and Grounds at Natchez, in the State of Mississippi", I beg to say that said building is not required for the use of the Marine Hospital Service, and that having been severely injured by a hurricane in 1873, a portion of the roof being blown off, it has not since been repaired.

I have the honor to be, sir,

Very respectfully

Lot W. Merrill
Secretary of the Treasury

316

Correspondence from Lott W. Merrill, Secretary of the Treasury, to Frank Hereford, Chairman of the Committee of Commerce, regarding Senate Bill 699—sale of Marine Hospital.

Opposite page shows petition presented by the American Baptist Home Mission Society to the Senate and House of Representatives of the United States Congress to confirm sale of the United States Marine Hospital at Natchez, April 3, 1876.

Natchez Seminary (Natchez, Mississippi) United States Marine Hospital, first home of Jackson State University, constructed in May 1852 at a cost of $66,750.00. It was open for patients August 1852, purchased by the American Baptist Home Missionary Society in 1877.

Architectural rendering of Founders' Hall located on Millsaps College campus, completed in 1885. The building was razed in 1973.

E. B. Topp—1883 Graduate of
Natchez Seminary

P. H. Thompson—1884 Graduate
Jackson College

Inman E. Page—1877 First Black
Faculty Member Natchez Seminary

President Charles Ayer
1877-1894

Presidents' residence located on North State Street, on the site where MIllsaps College now stands.

Mount Helm Baptist Church, located near North Lamar and Grayson Streets. When Jackson State College moved from Natchez to Jackson in 1883, classes were held in this historic church until 1885. Insert: Rev. James A. Mitchell, D. D., Pastor.

Class of 1894/Founders' Hall Jackson College (Now Millsaps College campus)

Scenes from Southern Bank Offices
Jackson, Mississippi

Interior of Southern Bank, Hon. L. K. Atwood, President

The Southern Bank and Officers, Jackson, Mississippi

Office of Progress Printing House, W. A. Scott, Owner

UNIVERSITY PRESIDENTS

DR. CHARLES AYER 1877-1894
Appointed first president of
Natchez Seminary by the
American Baptist Home Mission
Society.

DR. LUTHER G. BARRETT
1894-1911,
Became the second president of
the university, following
Dr. Charles Ayer's resignation
after 17 years of service.

DR. ZACHARY T. HUBERT 1911-1927
Became the third and first black president of the university

DR. B. BALDWIN DANBY 1927-1940
Fourth president of Jackson College. Retiring from the presidency in 1940, he continued to serve the University as registrar until 1949.

DR. JACOB L. REDDIX   1940-1967
Fifth president of the university. The first native Mississippian to become president of Jackson State University. First president under state control.

DR. JOHN A. PEOPLES JR. 1967-
Sixth president of Jackson State University. First alumnus to become president of the institution. B. S. 1950, Jackson State College; M. A. 1951, Ph. D., 1961, University of Chicago, Post Doctoral ACE Fellow 1965-66.

Miss Florence O. Alexander (1940-1959) Professor of Education, Teacher Trainer, Dean (Retired).

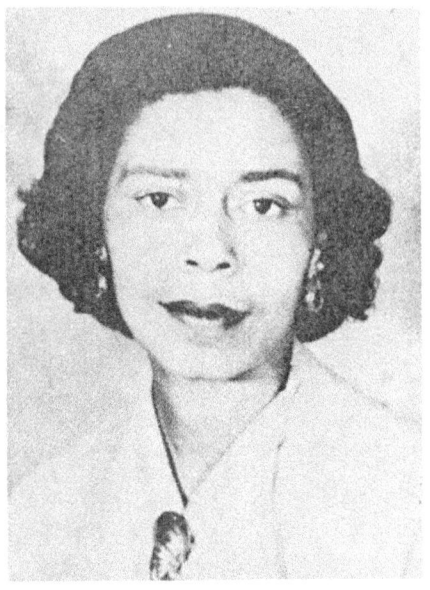

Mrs. Willie Dobbs Blackburn (1934-37; 1940-1974) Associate Professor of Literature; Chairman, Division of Language Arts; Professor Emeritus of English

Dr. Margaret Walker Alexander (1949-) Professor of English; Director, Institute for the Study of Life, History and Culture of Black People.

Dr. Rose Embly McCoy (1944-53; 1957-) Professor of Psychology; Head, Department of Psychology

Mrs. Aurelia Norris Young (1947-1977) Assistant Professor of Music (Retired).

Mr. William W. Davis (1948-) Assistant Professor of Music

Mr. Tellis B. Ellis, Jr. (1940-1977) Associate Professor of Physical Education, Director of Athletics; Head, Department of Physical Education (Retired).

Mrs. Mayne Pendleton Higgins (1944-1974) Associate Professor of Education, Supervisor of Student Teaching, Professor Emeritus of Education (Retired).

Dr. Jane Ellen McAllister (1950-1969) Professor Emeritus of Education

Dr. Gloria Buchanan Evans (1942; 1955-56; 1959-) Professor of English, Speech and Mass Communications

Mrs. Ernestine Anthony Lipscomb (1947-1976) Director of the Library (Retired).

Dr. Dollye M. E. Robinson (1952-) Professor of Music; Head, Department of Music; Chairman, Division of Fine Arts

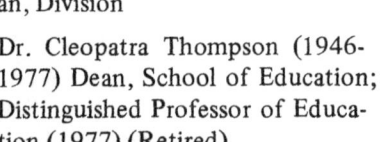

Dr. Cleopatra Thompson (1946-1977) Dean, School of Education; Distinguished Professor of Education (1977) (Retired).

Mrs. Luther G. Barrett
1894-1911

Mrs. Zachary T. Hubert
1911-1927

Mrs. B. B. Dansby
1927-1940

OFFICIAL CAMPUS HOSTESSES

Mrs. Jacob L. Reddix
1940-1967

Mrs. John A. Peoples, Jr.
1967-

Jackson State University National Alumni Association Conference (1976)
Official delegates

MISSISSIPPI BLACK LEGISLATORS

Mississippi Black Legislators
Left to right, Honorable Douglas Anderson, 1975; Honorable Robert G. Clark, 1967; Honorable Fred Banks, 1975; and Honorable Horace Buckley, 1975.

Dr. Joseph Jackson, A. B. 1927, President, National Baptist Convention, U.S.A. (6,300,000 membership). He attended Colgate-Rochester Divinity School and received his Master's degree from Creighton University.

Walter Payton (Chicago Bears), B. S. 1975, National Football League's Most Valuable Player in 1977, star running back for the Chicago Bears.

Robert Brazile (Houston Oilers), B. S. 1975, led Jackson State in total tackles with 208 including 129 individual tackles and led the Southwestern Athletic Conference in interceptions.

UNIVERSITY BUILDINGS

Founders' Hall located on the Millsaps College campus until it was razed in 1973. Originally occupied by Jackson College in 1885 (soon after the college moved from Natchez to Jackson).

New Science Building (1977) 101,986 square feet houses the Biology Department on the second and third floors and the Chemistry Department on the fourth and fifth floors and includes general classrooms, two lecture rooms, two green houses and chemistry and biology laboratories.

Willie Dobbs Blackburn Hall of Language Arts (1961) Named in honor of Mrs. Willie Dobbs Blackburn, professor of English for more than 30 years; provides classrooms, offices & laboratory facilities for the departments of English & Mass Communications, & the Institute for the Study of History, Life & Culture of Black People.

H. T. Sampson Library (1959) The second phase was constructed in 1973. Named in honor of the late Henry Thomas Sampson, who for 25 years served as Executive Dean of the University. Space is provided for the Educational Media Center and television studio.

The New Dining Hall (1977) Located on the North Campus is a modern facility which contains 47,021 square feet of space.

Frederick D. Hall Music Center (1976) Named after Frederick D. Hall, (1921-1927) Director of Music, who set to music the alma mater, "Jackson Fair." It contains 58,638 square feet of space. The main floor level accommodates administrative office areas, a recital hall with a seating capacity of 348, an art gallery, gallery storage, instrumental classrooms, choir rehearsal room, choir office, training and listening laboratories, a secretarial workroom and the library.

Jackson State University Plaza (1974) is located at the east entrance of Jackson State University on J. R. Lynch Street which crosses the campus. It is a concrete and exposed aggregate plaza with brick walls and designed with planting beds for trees, shrubs, and flowers.

Administration Tower and Classroom Complex Building (1974)
Contains administrative offices, classroom facilities, a computer center, and a lecture room.

Jackson State University Administrative Council, February 1976

CHAPTER II

THE CHALLENGE & THE RESPONSE

The Administration of President Charles Ayer, 1877–1894

THE AMERICAN BAPTIST HOME MISSION SOCIETY had encountered considerable bureaucratic red tape in its attempt to purchase a suitable building for the education of preachers and teachers. The old Marine Hospital in Natchez had appeared suitable and was available. The hospital had been completed in May, 1852 at a cost of $66,750. It had opened for patients on August 18, 1852. Following the Civil War, the hospital had been leased to Mississippi officials who had agreed to provide care for the marine patients in exchange for free use of hospital facilities.[1] However, the patients were never numerous enough to require the services of a fully operating marine hospital. During the fiscal year 1873, only three servicemen applied and received an aggregate of twenty-eight days relief at Natchez. No applications were filed during the fiscal year 1874–75.[2]

On October 9, 1875, William Howe, a Jersey City architect, visited Natchez to examine the U.S. Marine Hospital to negotiate a sale for the American Baptist Home Mission Society. He sought assistance from two competent and responsible local builders to help assess the condition of the hospital. They reported that, since the structure had been badly damaged by a tornado, it was in very bad need of repair and remodeling. About one-third of the roof had been blown off leaving the building exposed to the elements. Large portions of the floors were rotted, floor joints were partially decayed, ceilings had fallen, and walls, doors, and windows were badly damaged. Repeated vandalism had wrecked what the tornado had missed. Sinks had been torn out and there were no facilities for heating. The purchase cost would be approximately $20,500, and the hospital stood on a site valued at $22,000. At this total price of $42,500, a new building could be erected.[3]

After the appraisal of the dilapidated hospital, the society felt that it could pay no more than $5,000, and began communications with the United States Treasury Department in an effort to make a purchase at that price. Meanwhile, advertisements for the sale of the property had appeared in all the local papers. The society offered its bid of $5,000. With only this one bid made, the Treasury Department refused to confirm the sale because of the vast difference between the original price and the then current market value of the property.[4]

A memorial of the American Baptist Home Mission Society to the United States Senate and House of Representatives, dated April 3, 1876, requested that the secretary of the treasury, Lott W. Merrill, confirm the sale of the Marine Hospital building at Natchez, Mississippi. This document also gave a brief history of the organization and work of the society, emphasizing its efforts at education among the black population. Eight schools already were operating successfully in the South, an additional one was needed in Mississippi, and the old Marine Hospital at Natchez could be used. Again the society submitted the only bid at public auction on February 15, 1876, but the Treasury Department still refused to confirm the sale without further bids. Since the building had long suffered from dilapidation and decay, it was useless to the government. However, with proper renovation, it could be made serviceable for educational purposes. Therefore, the society asked the early passage of the resolution before Congress, so that repair and renovation could be completed for the opening of school, October 1, 1877.[5]

Justin S. Morrill, Chairman of the Committee on Public Building and Grounds, agreed with the American Baptist Home Mission Society that the property was of no use to the government, and he doubted that there would be a larger bid.[6] Although he was reluc-

The Challenge & the Response 17

tant to conclude the deal because of the low bid, he did suggest that the bill be passed as Senate Bill 699.

> ... In view of the small amount of the highest bid received when the property was offered for sale which was less than the original cost of the grounds, I have not felt at liberty to conclude the sale. On inquiring, however, it does not seem probable that any larger bids can be obtained, and inasmuch as the property in its present condition is of no use to the government, I cannot say that it would not be well to pass the bill.[7]

The memorial was referred to Committee on Public Buildings and Grounds on April 13, 1876.

Finally, on August 15, 1876, an act to confirm the sale of the Marine Hospital building and all of the grounds at Natchez was approved.[8] On August 15, 1876, during the Forty-fourth Congress, the minutes of Session I, register the following resolution:

> WHEREAS, the Marine Hospital building and grounds at Natchez, Mississippi are not required for the service of the United States; and
> WHEREAS, the said building   .n for many years in a process of dilapidation and decay; and
> WHEREAS, the said building a   grounds have been offered for sale at different times by auction under ; .d in pursuance of law: Therefore,
> Be it enacted by the Senate and House of Representatives of the United States of America in Congress assembled that the Secretary of the Treasury is hereby authorized and directed to confirm to the highest bidder the sale made under his direction and in pursuance of law, August fifteenth eighteen hundred and seventy-six; it being satisfactorily shown to him that the said building is to be reconstructed and devoted under responsible auspices, to purpose of instruction for the benefit of the colored people of the United States.[9]

The bill confirmed that the Marine Hospital building and grounds at Natchez, Mississippi would be sold to the highest bidder.[10] Because only one bid was sent in, the property was sold to the American Baptist Home Mission Society.

Unfortunately, their problems were not yet over. After the Senate and House approved the sale, the society discovered that it could not afford even the $5,000. Making an appeal to individuals of its constituencies, the society accepted the charity of Calvin T.

Sampson, a shoe industrialist and deacon of the First Baptist Church of North Adams, Massachusetts, who furnished the entire amount of $5,000 for purchase of the hospital.

The philosophy of the American Baptist Home Mission Society was predicated on the conviction that the success of the black population in the South depended upon capable self-government, moderated and guided by sound Christian ethics. It was to Christian leadership that the bulk of the black people looked for guidance. The society had as its objectives the promotion and encouragement of moral life through the medium of religious education and the instruction and training of minority teachers who, in turn, would elevate their newly freed people to a useful and productive life.[11]

Since this philosophy was similar to that of the Baptist Missionary Convention, it was easy for the two groups to combine forces. The convention made use of its $287.62 which had been recovered from the Freedmen's Bank fund.[12] In deciding on strategies to raise much needed funds for financing the newly founded school, convention leaders insisted that each church member be assessed ten cents annually instead of the $3.00 levy per church. From this time until Natchez Seminary was moved to Jackson, the convention provided guidance and financial support for the educational work of the institution.

Aside from the problem of raising funds to support the newly founded school, the society was often forced to clarify its objectives and goals for unsympathetic whites. A public announcement assured everyone concerned that the Baptists had established a seminary. The title suggested that the Natchez Seminary would train candidates for the ministry and this finally allayed the fears of the white citizenry antagonistic to a black school.[13]

President Charles Ayer of New York assumed the duties of the first head of the seminary. Born at Charlestown, Massachusetts, March 16, 1826, Ayer had entered Amherst College and later transferred to Madison (now Colgate University) where he graduated in 1849. He also attended Newton Theological Institution from 1849–50, where he completed his work for the ministry. He was later sent to Turner, Maine, in 1851, and subsequently held pastorates in various churches in Maine, Massachusetts, Vermont, and

New York.[14] With astute vision and tenacious determination, President Ayer accepted the challenge from the American Baptist Home Mission Society to undertake the task of educating black youths following the period of Reconstruction when the deep wounds of a people were not yet healed. The leadership post at the seminary provided Ayer an opportunity to develop the school under the most challenging circumstances. Appointed by the society to head the school on September 1, 1877, Ayer was given a salary of $1,000 per year.[15] On October 23, 1877, Ayer opened the school with twenty students.

INMAN EDWARD PAGE

The first assistant to President Ayer was Inman Edward Page, a keen educator who had been born on a plantation in Warrentown (Fauquar County) Virginia, December 29, 1853, the son of slave parents. His father, Horace Page, escaped from slavery during the Civil War with his wife Elizabeth and two children. In Washington, young Page was enrolled at a private school (George F. T. Cook) for blacks. To earn money for expenses, he worked as a common laborer in clearing the grounds of Howard University. He also attended a night school taught by Professor George B. Vashon. Page entered Howard University in 1872 and served with General O. O. Howard as a clerk in closing out the affairs of the Freedmen's Bureau. Leaving Howard University in 1873, Inman Edward Page became one of the first black students to enter Brown University.[16]

Undaunted by the prejudices shown by faculty and students, Page made excellent progress. At the end of his sophomore year, he took top honors in an oratorical contest. He moreover received the endorsement of his peers to write a history of the class in his junior year. He was also selected by the faculty to deliver a speech at a junior exhibition and was hailed "the ablest orator of the day" by the *Providence Journal*, a leading Rhode Island newspaper. From that point on, Page was recognized as a brilliant and imaginative scholar of deep insight. His efforts earned for him the position of class orator at the 1877 commencement exercises. He was the first black chosen for this position, and his subject, "Intellectual Prospects of America," was indeed timely.[17]

D. W. Phillips, who was engaged in the eduction of the Negro at that time at Roger Williams University of Nashville, Tennessee, was in the audience when this oration was delivered and was so impressed with it that he offered Page the position in the Natchez Seminary in Mississippi.[18] Page accepted the offer, but remained at the post for only a year. It is alleged by many that the short duration of Page's stay at Natchez Seminary was partially due to President Ayer's wife, who was herself determined to be the first assistant.[19] At the close of the school year, Page, the only black member of the faculty, resigned his post and accepted a position as a teacher at Lincoln Institute, Jefferson City, Missouri. Lincoln Institute, before the arrival of Page, had an all-white faculty. After he had served one year at Lincoln, the Board of Trustees chose Page to head the school and elected black teachers to serve on his faculty. His title soon changed to president and he served well in his post at Jefferson City, Missouri. He subsequently served as president of such other schools as the Agricultural and Normal University, Langston, Oklahoma; Western Baptist College, Mason, Missouri; Roger Williams University, Nashville, Tennessee; and Lincoln University, Jefferson City, Missouri. In 1880, Page received the A.M. degree from Brown University. In 1913, Howard University, Washington, D.C., awarded him the LL.D degree.[20]

Page's resignation from Natchez Seminary in 1878 had been abrupt and unexpected. His position was then assigned to his friend and classmate Edson Gaius Wooster. Unfortunately, Wooster became seriously ill during the academic year and died before the session was over. Records do not show who succeeded Wooster as assistant to the president.

The community in Natchez showed willingness to cooperate with President Ayer and his faculty. Even students who attended the school made great sacrifices to endure difficulty. Nearly all students who came to attend this school reached Natchez by the steam packets. Some came on mule trains across the country, camping out two or three nights on the way. For the students going to Natchez from the central and northern portions of the state, transportation was less than desirable.

Initially, tuition fees were minimal. In his first announcement of costs for attendance, Ayer stated that expenses would be reasonable and would be far below costs at other institutions.[21] Male students were given an opportunity to work to help defray the cost of monthly expenses. Such costs included tuition fees at $1.00 per month; room rent at $1.00 per month; washing at $1.00 per month; and board at $5.00 per month. Day students paid $.25 per day for incidentals and $1.00 additional for the first month. By the end of the 1878 school year, sixty students—both male and female—were enrolled.[22]

Since student fees were low, appropriations from the Home Mission Society and small gifts from donors kept the school going. Rose Hill Church was among the contributors consistently sending annual gifts to the president of Natchez Seminary. Donations received at the seminary during the 1879-80 school term were recorded in the school catalog: Rose Hill Sunday School, $3; Missionary Baptist General Association, $60; Second New Hope Association, $30; Reverend T. L. Jordan, Columbus, $10; Missionary Baptist Convention of Mississippi and Louisiana, $100; and Baptist Sunday School of Canton, $8.[23]

The continued role of the Baptist Missionary Convention should be noted. After members of the convention had visited the seminary, they resolved that "the Missionary Baptist Convention appropriate $100.00 to the Natchez Seminary to aid the intelligent students that are preparing for the ministry." It was stipulated that the money be used for students of the Baptist faith from Mississippi, Louisiana, and Arkansas.[24]

Prevailing pedagogy included conduct and discipline, and Dr. Ayer believed that the institution should be a boarding school where the training of the students could be properly supervised. Explicit regulations regarding student conduct were printed in the catalog. These regulations included policies governing study hours and work habits; care of the building; visiting hours, especially for members of the opposite sex; attendance at religious functions; absences from the premises; and the possession and use of tobacco, firearms, and playing cards. The penalty for any misconduct or infraction of the rules meant suspension or expulsion.[25] The rigidity of the regulations is noteworthy:

> Rooms are to be neat and in order, ready for inspection at any time. All damage of furniture, etc., must be paid by the student before leaving

the Seminary. No one to mark on the blackboard except in recitation. No marking on the building or furniture.

No loud study or loud reading during study hours, no talking during study hours. Study hours from 8:30 a.m. to 3:00 p.m. after 6:00 p.m. All lights out at 9:30 p.m. Everyone must abstain from talking and whispering in chapel and recitation rooms during school exercises. Every student must make the most of his time by close application to the work in hand. Students are to remain in their rooms during the hours of study. Every student must remember that all other students are here for quiet and earnest study, and may not be disturbed.

No visitors allowed in the students' rooms, students and family relatives are the exceptions. The reception rooms will always be open for company. Young ladies will receive no company of the other sex without the permission of their parents given in writing.

No visitors allowed at the tables, and no one allowed to lodge in the Seminary without permission of the teachers. Boarding students must be present at the hours of meals. No meals furnished except at the regular times.

All students are required to attend chapel exercises, devotional meetings, and such Sunday Schools and churches as the teachers may appoint.

No meeting of the students to be held, and no societies to be formed without permission of the teachers.

Young ladies and gentlemen to keep in their own division of the building and grounds, and not to associate at any time.

Students are not to leave the Seminary premises without permission. No strolling in the city allowed. Absences from the Seminary after dark not permitted.

Wastefullness of fuel and food must be avoided in order that the expenses may be kept low. All should care for the Seminary property. All should remember that the student's school expenses are put far below costs, the balance being provided by the generosity of others.

Students not allowed in the kitchen except by the direction of a teacher.

A small number of library books for reading can be loaned to the students, to be kept no more than one week at a time.

Observe neatness in person, politeness to every one, good manners at the table, faithfulness to study, attention to every recitation by the class, punctuality to every call.[26]

The school admitted students to both the Normal and the Theology Departments. Natchez Seminary also had a grammar school which consisted of grades four through eight. One of the requirements for admission to the regular departments was that all students must have attained at least a fourth grade reading level.

The Bible was the daily textbook and teaching was non-sectarian.[27]

Despite the dangers of receiving students with varying intellectual abilities, it was the decision of the administration not to include the primary grades. Academic requirements included the purchase of Hovey's *Manual of Theology* and Anesti's *Hints on Interpretation* which were used in the upper level courses.

To matriculate, students had to possess good moral character and present a positive reference from some outstanding person of their communities. They had to be of an age capable of self-government and had to be able to read the Bible.[28]

A description of the specific instruction and the courses of study as outlined in the Seminary Catalog for 1879–80 were addressed to those who had the ministry in view. Candidates were told that, like teachers, they needed a set of common studies in order that they might become not only preachers but also thorough educators of the people. Teachers were to be given positions of usefulness and honor in the free schools of the state. Because some students were prepared for more strenuous studies, they received instruction in advanced English, Latin, and Greek. Emphasis was placed on the study of core subjects. Everything was made to contribute to thorough preparation for work in the church, schoolroom, and the common business of life. Other elements of the curriculum included lessons on the duties of a citizen and a free government, the ways of business in public meetings and organized societies, the proper methods of keeping accounts, and the law of life and health. The aim of the school was to provide experiences which would prepare an individual for effective living in the larger society.

Humanistic studies were achieved through programs of rhetoric and public speaking. Knowledge of ethics was acquired through the study of moral law. Further instruction was provided through planned discussions on the doctrines of Christianity and the duties of Christ's disciples, the rights and duties of church members, and the obligations of church and pastor. Science was also an integral part of the program.[29]

The organization of the curriculum proceeded from the first through the fourth year. First and second year courses from 1878 to 1890 included arithmetic, geography, reading, grammar, spelling, history, and physiology. Third year subjects were algebra, rhetoric, Latin, physics, parliamentary practice, and the science of government. The fourth year included algebra, physics, Latin, mental philosophy, and moral philosophy. The fifth year focused on biblical interpretation, preaching, sermon-making, and church polity. In systematic theology, the daily lessons included a Bible lesson, vocal music, and penmanship. Declamation and essays were scheduled monthly.

The courses of study in the Normal and Theological Departments "reflected a curriculum that had been established in accordance with the curricula of other institutions located in the South and founded by the Society." The textbooks that were used included the Bible; the *Paragraph Bible;* the *Harmony of the Gospels; The Parliamentary Guide;* Alden's *Science of Government;* Lossing's *History of the United States;* Patterson's *Speller;* Colton's *Common School Geography;* Olney's *Mathematics;* Harkness' *Latin Books;* Steele's *Physiology; English Grammar;* and the *Fifth Reader.*[30]

The classical educational background of New Englanders was reflected in the structure of the curriculum. The Normal Department was designed primarily to prepare teachers. The founders held that it was more important to know what to teach than how to teach. They were of the opinion that no education could be complete without some knowledge of Latin or Greek. President Ayer and his staff were from the classical era, and the curriculum they established was in keeping with tradition and with the educational modes of the day.

By the end of the 1878 school year, there were sixty pupils enrolled: W. Adams; B. Alexander; S. J. Bates; A. Blake; H. Booze; L. Bright; E. Brown; P. K. Bush; C. Calhoun; S. Carter; S. Clark; C. Collins; E. Comer; J. Comer; F. C. Corey; C. Cotton; J. J. Diggs; F. Dickerson; F. Dixon; S. Darries; M. Dorsey; A. Dorsey; J. D. Dunbar; F. L. Fisher; P. L. Fisher; C. L. Fitzhugh; L. A. E. Granderson; C. N. Hampton; M. A. Henderson; W. J. Henderson; E. Jacobs; E. Johnson; R. Jones; J. J. Miderhoff; E. Middleton; M. Miller; A. Morgan; A. Morris; A. E. Morris; P. O'Connel; S. Ouslen; A. C. Parker; E. Parker; M. E. Phenix; L. W. Ramsey; W. C. Rone; E. J. Sanders; M. Sanders; J. Shields; A. Singleton; R. Smith; A. Stevens; M. Stevenson; M. Swan; M. J. Taylor; A. S. West; M. A. White; C. Whitlock; E. Winston; and H. Wood.[31]

The Challenge & the Response 25

Like every developing institution, Natchez Seminary had its problems. From its beginning, students were plagued by fear of dangerous obstacles which were discovered in close proximity to the seminary.[32] Chief among these were a powder house and a pest house which posed a dangerous threat. The Educational Committee of the American Baptist Home Mission Society was successful in getting both houses removed. Other threats included the outbreak of a yellow fever epidemic which gripped the South. Government health authorities enforced the quarantine regulations at the seminary, delaying the opening of the 1878-79 session until December. Edson Gaius Wooster, a former classmate of Inman Page at Brown University and a faculty member of the seminary, became seriously ill and died during the school session.[33] Despite these problems, the school continued its growth in student population.

Additional faculty members were added for the influx of students who came from Mississippi, Arkansas, and Louisiana. The continuous growth of the seminary soon resulted in a shortage of space. The Marine Hospital building served both as a classroom facility and as a dormitory and housed both students and faculty. Overcrowded conditions forced male students to seek lodgings off campus. The Baptist Missionary Convention recommended in July 1880 that an effort should be made to raise money to build a dormitory. Another group of interested Baptists also indicated to the society that the educational needs of the populace were far from being met at Natchez.

The question of relocating the school was seriously considered at a conference held in Jackson November 1882, with Dr. John M. Gregory, Dr. Sylvester Witt Marston, and Dr. Ayer in attendance. These men represented the Baptist Home Mission Society. Representatives of the black Baptists of Mississippi were also present. They recommended to the society that the seminary be moved from Natchez to Jackson, a more central location.[34] The Executive Board of the society voted in favor of the move.

On December 11, 1882, upon the recommendation of Marston and Ayer, the board of the society decided to purchase the 52-acre J. A. P. Campbell estate for $5,000. This property was located north of Jackson just outside the city limits, the present site of Millsaps College.

The terms of the payments were referred to the Finance Committee with the understanding that the friends of the school in Mississippi would contribute at least one-half of the amount within one year from the date of purchase. The cooperation of "the colored brethren in Mississippi" was also sought as a means for the purchase of the property and for the necessary improvements.[35]

The board gave evidence of its desire to open the school in Jackson as quickly as possible. However, in view of the fact that no money was available for a new building until the Natchez property was sold, the Natchez building continued to be used until the sale of the property was complete.[36] Finally, at the October 8, 1883, meeting of the society, Dr. Ayer was instructed to sell the Natchez property at the best possible price and to procure plans for the erection of a building in Jackson at a cost of $10,000.

The municipal authorities, who had expressed an interest in buying the Natchez property, were informed that $15,000 was the lowest sum the board could accept for it—$7,500 to be paid in cash and $7,500 to be secured by bond and mortgage, payable in two years with interest at 7 percent.[37]

In accordance with the provisions of the act of Congress regarding the sale of the property by the government to the American Baptist Home Mission Society, the Baptist board voted that the corresponding secretary was empowered to execute, under the seal of the society, an undertaking with proper covenant of assurance to the secretary of the treasury of the United States that the proceeds of the sale of the society's property at Natchez be devoted to school purposes at Jackson, Mississippi.[38]

In May 1883, the first graduation was held in Natchez. The following received diplomas: Pennie L. Fisher; Lillie A. Granderson-Diggs; Charles N. Hampton; Henderson McKinney; Pezvia O'Connell; Emma M. Phenix-Dunbar, and Agnes S. West-Peyton.[39]

In the fall of 1883, the Natchez Seminary was moved to Jackson. By common consent, the institution's name was changed to Jackson College in honor of Andrew Jackson, for whom Jackson, Mississippi, is named. Immediately, new problems beset the school. The only habitable building on the grounds was the mansion which was to house President and Mrs. Ayer and members of the faculty.⁴⁰ The other building was not worth renovating for a dormitory or a classroom. It had been used as a barn and was constructed as a two-story building before the Civil War. During the Battle of Jackson, General Grant had used the building to position his guns which shelled the city. The gun pits were located at the back of the mansion.⁴¹

Lacking shelter on the campus, students had to find living accommodations in the community. Most of the women were housed in homes of relatives or friends in close proximity to the site, while some male students lived in shanties put together on the grounds. The beginning of the 1883-84 school session was delayed because there was no place to hold classes. The officials of the black Mt. Helm Baptist Church, then located on Grayson Street, heard of the difficulties of Jackson College and offered the use of their facilities to conduct classes for a period of two years, 1883-85. Classes were immediately organized and held in the sanctuary. Dr. Ayer and the administration knew that classroom space was inadequate. Thus, temporary quarters were erected adjacent to the south side of the church to accommodate the growing enrollment.⁴² Mount Helm had had its beginnings in the basement of the white First Baptist Church in 1835. Most of the members at the time were slaves. They had met at that church from 1835 until 1867 when, as free men following the Civil War, they erected their first building at the corner of Church and Lamar (formerly Grayson Street). Mt. Helm was one of the oldest black churches in Mississippi. The Helm family, which was white, had given the land for the structure.⁴³

Meanwhile, under the society's authorization, construction at the cost of $12,500 was begun on the new three-story brick multifacility on the present Millsaps College site. The structure was built under the supervision of Robert McAllister, who engaged male students to help erect it. Upon completion of the building, students were housed on the second and third floors; the first floor held the classrooms; and a large basement housed the assembly hall.

OCCUPANCY

The formal dedication of the school was held in 1885. The faculty that began the school term in 1884 were: Charles Ayer for twelve months at a salary of $1,500; Mrs. Charles Ayer and Miss E. A.

Ayer for a period of eight months at salaries of $400 each; Eli Sanderson for a period of eight months at a salary of $700.[44] Other faculty listed in the 1884 Catalog were the Reverend A. V. Tilton and Miss Rose A. Smith. No salary and terms of contracts were included.

The optimistic outlook for the school's existence had begun to give life to its constituency when, after a few years, Dr. Ayer encountered a new challenge. On February 21, 1890, on the North State Street site just behind the mansion in which Dr. Ayer and the faculty lived, a new institution for white male students (now known as Millsaps College) was built. With the rise of black enrollment at Jackson College, a fairly large number of the white students converged upon the adjoining site. Dr. Ayer received many letters protesting the presence of Jackson College in that part of the city. He was approached by whites who asked him to sell the Jackson College property to Major Reuben Webster Millsaps. Moreover, there were many forces at work to remove from the North State Street site "niggers" who went to and from school on mules carrying their little greasy lunch bags. Black students were thought to give an unsightly appearance to that section of town. Outraged at the audacity of Major Millsaps' offer to buy Jackson College, Dr. Ayer valiantly declared, "I am not interested in selling a college, but rather in building a college for underprivileged groups and giving them an opportunity for self-improvement."[45] To this cause he held on unswervingly in his determination to develop the school which was envisioned by the Baptist Missionary Convention leaders and the American Baptist Home Mission Society.

During Dr. Ayer's seventeen years as president of Jackson College, a combined total of more than 1,000 students had come to be educated under his leadership. The largest enrollment was registered during the 1890–91 term. The record lists 124 male and 153 female students.[46]

Jackson College enrolled its first student from Africa as a result of the influence of some of its graduates of the class of 1883 who had gone to that continent as missionaries. James J. Diggs had persuaded Henderson McKinney and E. B. Topp to join him in Africa. An African chief had entrusted to McKinney a young man known only as Jeer to be sent to the United States for an education.

Before final arrangements were completed, McKinney died and Topp brought the young man to Jackson College.[47]

CURRICULUM

The first seventeen years of the institution's existence were full of challenges for Dr. Ayer. However, his faith in his efforts and in the school coupled with his determination to improve the academic programs kept him from failing. Hence, he accepted the challenges of his arduous task. The mission of the school—to train men for the Christian ministry and to develop teachers for the public schools—was clear to Dr. Ayer. Students who completed the Normal Course were qualified for grade A certificates in the public schools of the state. This program required five years.[48]

A list of courses pursued during the five years is worthy of mention. The first year included: reading and orthography; grammar; arithmetic; geography; history; mental arithmetic; composition and penmanship. The second year included: arithmetic, analysis; geography; grammar; history; algebra; reading; mental arithmetic; and penmanship. The third year included: arithmetic; algebra to quadratics; history; geography; grammar; rhetoric; reading; lessons in business; penmanship and drawing. The fourth year included: Thompson's *Arithmetic;* physical geography; civil government; anatomy; lessons in business; bookkeeping; science of teaching and drawing. The fifth year included: arithmetic; philosophy; botany; Latin; general history; parliamentary practice and essays. The Academic Course comprised all the studies of the Normal Course and two additional years of study. The course included: geometry; algebra; trigonometry; surveying; astronomy; Latin and Greek; chemistry and elocution. For the final year, courses included: mental philosophy; moral philosophy; Latin and Greek; chemistry; zoology; and geology. An academic diploma was conferred at the end of the additional two years.

The Elementary English Course extended for a three-year period. The Advanced English Course Curriculum demanded a four-year period of study. Each year was subdivided into three terms with required courses set for each term. The first year included studies in grammar, arithmetic, geography, history, and Bible. The second year included studies in rhetoric, physiology, algebra, and Bible. The third year included studies in philosophy, bookkeeping, chemistry, physical geography, and Bible. The fourth year included Latin, geometry, general history, pedagogics, and Bible. Throughout the program of study, courses of reading in English and American Literature were required.[49]

Students who completed the studies of the the first year of Advanced English were admitted, if they so desired, into the College Preparatory Course. This program required three years and each year was divided into three terms. The first year included studies in rhetoric; Bible study; Greek; geometry; algebra; etc. The second year included: Latin; Greek, German or French; geometry; Bible; reading; history; etc. The third year included: Latin, Greek, German or French Literature; Greek, German or French Composition; philosophy; economics; logic; state and national constitutions. A special program in 1886 called the Minister's Course was established to help church leaders improve themselves while carrying on their work.[50] With this special effort and program, Jackson College began its work in adult education.

Jackson College had offered to its students certain library resources which were noted in the *Natchez Seminary Catalogue* for 1879 with the statement: "A small number of library books can be loaned to the students to be out no more than a week at a time." When Jackson College was established on the site of the present Millsaps College, a catalog reference was made again to the library: "A beginning has been made in a library: maps and charts are in use as needed. For reference, *The Century Dictionary* and unabridged dictionaries are freely in use, and encyclopedias. A typewriter is provided."[51]

Students of average ability were given an opportunity to choose special instruction in six departments—the Normal Department, the Academic Department, the Theological Department, the Bible Study Department, the Industrial Department, and the Music Department.[52] Students whose academic performance was below average remained in a given class until they "mastered" the subject to the satisfaction of the instructors.

Young men in the Theological Department were provided with instruction in the interpretation of the Scriptures, sermonizing, church history, systematic theology, church polity, Christian ethics, missions, and pulpit oratory. Those candidates who mastered the studies of the Normal Course joined the theology students. Those who completed systematic theology received a certificate.

PATRICK THOMPSON

In 1887, as a Natchez Seminary alumnus, Patrick Thompson returned to teach at his alma mater. He was born in Okolona (Chickasaw County), Mississippi, March 5, 1866. His parents were Milton and Ellen Thompson, slaves of Dr. J. Young Thompson. At the age of eighteen, Thompson had completed the course in the school at Okolona under the instruction of J. H. Henderson, and at nineteen, had been elected to serve as principal of a school with 150 pupils and 3 assistants. However, he held this post only during the 1884-85 school term when he sought employment at an asphalt company in St. Louis, Missouri, as a common laborer at the rate of $.75 per day, then as time keeper at the daily wage of $3.00.[53]

In 1884, the Mt. Olivet Association and Sunday School Convention had offered a free scholarship to Jackson College to the student "standing the best examination."[54] Patrick Thompson was the successful competitor and, in October 1885, he received a letter informing him of the award. He entered Jackson College in the fall of 1885, and in 1887 he graduated with highest honors.[55] In the fall of 1887, he was appointed by the American Baptist Home Mission Society as one of the teachers at the seminary. During the academic year 1887-88, Patrick H. Thompson was teacher of English "Branches" and was also a student of systematic theology in the Theology Department.[56]

In the fall of 1888, Thompson left for Richmond, Virginia, to enter the Theological Seminary where he received the Bachelor of Divinity Degree in 1892. In the same year, upon the invitation of President Ayer, Patrick H. Thompson returned to Jackson College to teach "English Studies."[57] During his tenure, he had great influence on both his colleagues and the community. He was ordained as a pastor in 1893, and shortly thereafter, following the resignation of the pastor of Mt. Helm Church, Reverend C. L. Fisher, he was elected to the post. Unable to carry on both jobs, Reverend Thompson decided to give up the pastorate of the Mt. Helm

Church. Thompson was always proud of his work with Jackson College. Hence, he was happy to remain on the faculty of the college until 1898, throughout the remainder of President Ayer's administration and through four years of Dr. Luther Barrett's tenure.[58] In 1903, Thompson was appointed to the presidency of Kosciusko Industrial College.[59] He had witnessed dozens of graduates who had moved into positions of service and leadership in the society. The list included such persons as George Bell; W. L. Hardy; Phillips Brumfield; N. R. Forril; J. M. Gandy; Z. D. Ratliff; J. H. Robinson; L. V. Rouser Moore; M. E. Stewart Johnson; L. S. Taylor Jones; and Sallie Walker Pickett.[60]

During the academic year 1893-94, some important changes had been made at Jackson College in various courses of study. Students who passed the studies of the Normal Course received the Normal Course diploma. Changes also included new curricula in the Elementary English Course, in the Advanced English Course, and in the College Preparatory Course.

President Ayer's efforts prompted the changes in the curriculum because it was felt that "no young person who can command the means of obtaining a full school training should fail to give all the time and labor required to obtain this training. The best Christian scholars and the best trained minds will be in great demand within a few years. The time is now to get the best preparation."[61]

During the academic year 1889-90, the John F. Slater Fund had made available money to establish an Industrial Department where both sexes were taught useful and practical skills for earning a living by sewing, cooking, carpentry, bricklaying, typewriting, and tin work.[62] As an additional part of the curriculum, students were provided lessons in organ and piano music. Young men were also given the opportunity to observe the Mississippi Senate and House of Representatives and to attend other public assemblies in order to understand the art of government.[63]

As a part of the religious training which was provided by the administration, all students of the college were expected to spend one hour daily in the classroom in careful study of the Holy Writ.

Moreover, morning and evening worship was observed daily, and prayer meetings were held three times a week. There were two sermons on each Sunday. The McKinney Missionary Society held meetings each month. These meetings consisted of readings, essays, and addresses on missions and mission work which were interspersed with songs and prayer.[64] The college paper, *The Baptist Messenger*, published monthly at a cost to the students of $.50 per year, served as a medium of communication among the students, churches, and associations.[65]

As one of the "campus regulations," all letters, telegrams, and packages were sent to the student addressed to the college in care of the president. All students were required to sign the following pledge: "Desiring to be a student in Jackson College, I do hereby pledge myself to obey all regulations; to abstain from all use of tobacco and intoxicating liquors; to apply to my studies and cheerfully submit myself to the College discipline."[66]

During the academic year 1894, Ayer's final year as president, there were no candidates for graduation. Ayer had made a rigid effort to improve Jackson College. He sought to expand, update, and modify the curriculum, provide new physical facilities, and renovate the living quarters. These labors and seventeen years of hard work were taking their tolls on the president. By 1884 his salary had been increased to $1,500. He had earned the raise for he gave diligent service in developing Jackson College.

With astute vision, determination, and deep faith, Dr. Charles Ayer was ready to pass the torch to committed successors. Under his leadership, Jackson College had begun its struggle for survival. Students were building and developing strong self-images and these were reflected in their work and attitudes.

The growth in enrollment from 20 students to a total of more than 1,000 students during President Ayer's administration was indicative of the growing confidence of parents at the time. At the end of the 1893-94 school term, because of failing health and the strenuous work of the presidency, Ayer resigned and entrusted the future of Jackson College to Dr. Luther G. Barrett.

CHAPTER III

THE EXODUS & THE RENAISSANCE

The Administration of President Luther G. Barrett, 1894–1911

Upon the resignation of Dr. Ayer, the American Baptist Mission Society Board of Education appointed Dr. Luther G. Barrett to the presidency. In spite of the social, economic, and political environment inimical to its progress, Jackson College continued its expansion under Barrett's leadership. His appointment to the post came at a time when the black populace of Jackson was growing and demanding more education. Barrett's seventeen-year administration continued the forward thrust of academic progress, as had that of his predecessor. He also brought about many changes resulting from the initiative of a strong faculty.

Luther Barrett was born in Watertown, Massachusetts on December 5, 1838. Young Luther suffered from poor health and therefore was kept in the open air and sunshine on the family farm as much as possible in hopes that his physical condition would improve. Following the practice of many Eastern families, his parents later sent him to an academy where he completed courses for graduation at the age of sixteen. Barrett entered Harvard in 1858 and later drilled for the Civil War. When he graduated from Harvard in 1862, he joined the U. S. Christian Commission, the "Fighting Parsons" organized to administer spiritual aid on the battlefield. In 1865, Dr. Barrett graduated from Newton Theological Seminary with a Master of Science degree in religious education. He subsequently held pastorates in the Baptist churches of

Winchester, Winston, Milford, and Lowell, Massachusetts. He also taught school in Brookline. During the summer months, he was an ardent participant in the religious Chautauquas at Oak Bluffs and College City in Massachusetts.[1]

Like Dr. Ayer, Dr. Barrett had met on many occasions with representatives of the American Baptist Home Mission Society, and frequently the discussion was geared to the problems of the South. It was through such a conference that Barrett had first been offered the presidency of Jackson College in Mississippi. When he assumed the presidency in the fall of 1894, Barrett knew what to expect. He had been told about the attitudes of whites toward Jackson College. Moreover, he soon learned that the permanent home of Jackson College was in question because of its close proximity to the Millsaps campus. What originally had been outside the city limits was now a part of the city whose borders over a period of a decade had expanded both northward and westward. Families representing the higher economic groups were moving in this direction. Needless to say, there were no blacks in this migration because of the strict segregation laws.

Transportation for students living beyond the city limits became a problem. Some of the male students used mules to go to and from school and the unsightly appearance of mules in the wealthy residential sections was frowned upon.[2] The erection of a white institution on property adjoining Jackson College and a decrease in enrollment compounded Barrett's difficulties. He had little choice except to seek another alternative for the continued existence of the school.

When threats began to be made on his life, Dr. Barrett—after consultation with his faculty—appealed to the Board of Trustees of the American Baptist Home Mission Society to consider relocating the school. He believed that the closer an institution was to the people it served, the more effective it would become in fulfilling its mission.[3]

Dr. Barrett also consulted with the white leaders of the city. He visited two secondary schools and brought about an affiliation by which they became feeders for Jackson College.

Barrett found it almost impossible to convince some blacks of the wisdom of his action. His thinking was that, sooner or later, a change was bound to come. He also felt that the earlier the change, the easier and less costly would be the adjustment later on. To many, it seemed a betrayal. White leaders argued that if the school remained at its present site, it would become a cultural island with no possible outlet. Some even said Jackson College would deteriorate in a very short time and thus fail in its stated objectives.[4] After considerable consultation among all concerned parties, the society was convinced by the judgment of Dr. Barrett and supported his contention.

The Board of Trustees of the American Baptist Home Mission Society by a resolution on July 15, 1901, did authorize and instruct Frank R. Hathaway, treasurer of the society, to sell the property for $40,000. The resolution instructed Hathaway to execute a deed in consideration of $10,000 cash paid by Major Reuben Webster Millsaps, for whom Millsaps College was named, transferring the property of Jackson College. The bill of sale stipulated that subsequent payments of $10,000 would be paid on the first of the months of February, May, and July in the year 1902. Also in the bill of sale there was a stipulation to vacate the premises by July 1, 1902.

A representative of the Education Committee of the American Baptist Home Mission Society was sent to confer with Dr. Barrett, and at the meeting of the board on July 15, 1901, the committee submitted its resolution to move Jackson College.

WHEREAS, Since the establishment of Jackson College, at Jackson, Mississippi, a college for white youth has been established contiguous thereto; and,

WHEREAS, There are serious apprehensions that trouble may result between the students of the two schools in the future; and

WHEREAS, The authorities of the white school, known as Millsaps College have offered $40,000.00 for the Society's property at Jackson, Mississippi; therefore, Voted: That the entire property except school furniture and fixtures be sold to Millsaps College for the sum of not less than $40,000.00, the Society to occupy the premises until July 1, 1902, when possession shall be given to the purchaser upon full payment of the said amount, the terms of payment to be determined by the Finance Committee.

VOTED: That upon a first payment of $10,000.00, the treasurer of the Society be and is hereby authorized and directed to execute on behalf of the Society a deed of said property to the authorities of Millsaps College with vendor's lieu for the balance of the purchase money.

VOTED: That the amount derived from the sale of the property be applied to the purchase of a new site and the erection of buildings at Jackson, Mississippi, for the use of the school in the fall of 1902, under the direction of the Board.[5]

On August 12, 1902, the board authorized President Barrett to arrange for temporary quarters to carry on school for the 1902-1903 session. Barrett was also told to make necessary changes in whatever building was found.[6] When the time came to vacate the Millsaps site, Jackson College had no place to relocate. After a temporary location was finally secured, it is alleged that the president collapsed from anxiety and frustration. When the sale of the school was announced, the black population became alarmed. To dispel the obvious fear that Jackson College would fail, Dr. Barrett, along with some of the black ministers of the city, made arrangements to hold the 1902-1903 school session in the large two-story Benevolent Hall located on the southwest corner of Farish and Griffith streets.

These were difficult times for Jackson College. The enrollment dropped from 160 students during the 1901-1902 academic year to 107 students during the following year, when the college finally occupied Benevolent Hall.[7] But Dr. Barrett was not to be discouraged. His critical mind quickly addressed itself to making the best possible use of the new quarters by converting them into temporary accommodations for classroom space and for housing.[8] Dr. and Mrs. Barrett occupied the two-story frame building on Lynch Street, while male faculty members lived in the temporary quarters adjacent to the Benevolent Hall which was converted into a dormitory. Faculty also served as counselors to the young men who lived on the second floor of the hall.

The dictum that "Negroes were outsiders" prevailed among whites. Blacks felt that racial prejudice had forced them to be removed from a prime living area of the city in North Jackson. To many black people, the removal spelled Exodus. Dr. Barrett was fortunate, however, for his search for another site uncovered 150 acres of available land belonging to Anetta Drake in West Jackson. The owner refused to sell anything less than the whole. After lengthy deliberations with the concerned party, Barrett contracted for the Drake property and made a deposit on the land with his personal check for $100.[9] The tract of land conveyed by this deed encompassed 95-97 acres purchased at a cost of $7,800 from Anetta Drake filed and recorded February 27, 1903.[10]

There had been much speculation about the number of acres owned by the college. Mary C. Reynolds cited that there were 150 acres involved in the transaction but "the Society decided to take one fifty-acre lot for the College; one fifty-acre lot for the Society which they sold later for three times the cost. President Barrett purchased the other fifty acres which he sold to individuals who in turn divided their 'parcels' into house lots and sold them to Negroes only."[11] Records indicate that the section of the property located just south of the Yazoo and Mississippi Valley Railroad (YMV) west of Dalton Street did belong to Jackson College. This property constituted:

> All of the west half of the northwest quarter of the section nine which lies north of the Yazoo and Mississippi Valley Railroad; all of the east half of the northeast quarter of section eight which lies north of the said railroad; also...
> Beginning on the south side of said railroad where the east boundary of said west half of the northwest quarter of section nine crosses it, thence south twelve chains and eighty-seven links, thrice west four chains and thirty-nine links to the west boundary of the east half of the northeast quarter of Section Eight, thrice north on said boundary to the south side of the right of way of said railroad twelve chains and eighty-seven links, eastwardly along the south boundary of said right of way to the east boundary of the said west half of the northwest quarter of section nine, the place of beginning except the two areas in the northeast corner of said last described tract, which two acres is a parallelogram being four chains north and south and five chains east and west, being the same land conveyed by Anetta Drake....[12]

This property was referred to as Gowdy in College Addition and Washington Addition. Much of the community is still identified as Washington Addition. The first four streets immediately south of the YMV Railroad are named for individuals who were connected with the society and the college: Henry L. Morehouse (Morehouse Street), corresponding secretary of the American Baptist Home Mission Society; Frances Everett (Everett Street), a member of the faculty; Florence E. Johnson (Florence Street), a teacher in the grammar school; and Barrett Street named for President Barrett.[13]

President Barrett was of the opinion that if the parents of the students lived in close proximity to the school they would send their children to Jackson College. Working under this assumption, Barrett sent out letters to all the patrons informing them of the sale of property near the college.[14] Living in the rural areas of Mississippi many of the parents were skeptical about buying property in town.

Gradually, blacks began to migrate to the newly acquired land surrounding the college. Some were sharecroppers who acquired funds and bought land to relocate. World War I homesteaders began to settle in the area. Just northeast of the campus was a section of town called "Sugar Hill" where the few professional blacks and "blue vein" families with some money acquired land. A similar "society" was also in North Jackson. Gowdy or College Hill–Washington Addition claimed but a few professional blacks as residents. Most of the families were large, with five or more children. Many of the women took in washing and ironing. The men were day laborers who sought employment at the "Mill" which was subsequently demolished. The site is presently occupied by the Jackson State University Health and Physical Education Complex. Other unskilled laborers worked for the city or at such other jobs as in the cotton oil mills, in local hotels, as section hands, pullman porters, and mail room personnel of the Illinois Central Railroad Company.

In February 1903, Henry L. Morehouse, corresponding secretary of the American Baptist Home Mission Society, was authorized to go to Jackson and pre-plan buildings for Jackson College. He was also asked to make arrangements with architects and report to the Finance Committee and Board in March.[15] Dr. Barrett had occupied the one building on the grounds as the president's residence.

A month later, the Finance Committee voted that Morehouse as corresponding secretary authorize the architect to design two dormitories at 3 1/2 percent for the first plans and specifications and

1/2 percent for the plans for the second building. Both buildings were to cost no more than $30,000.[16]

Construction was begun immediately in the fall of 1903. Ayer Hall, located on the west side of the campus, was ready for occupancy by male students in 1904. The hall, named for Dr. Charles Ayer, housed a chapel, the president's office, the library, and several recitation rooms on the first floor; on the two floors above were the reading rooms and 44 sleeping rooms. In the basement were trunk storage and bathrooms.[17]

Barrett Hall, a residence hall for women, was constructed on the east side of the campus. The two commodious brick buildings with equipment, at an outlay of $41,075.55, were erected mainly from the proceeds from the sale of the former site and buildings. The dedication ceremonies were held November 22, 1904. H. L. Whitfield, the state superintendent of education, William Tyndal Lowery, president of Mississippi College in Clinton, and the pastors of the white Baptist churches of the city were present and participated in the ceremonies.[18]

At the board meeting of March 11, 1907, the members voted to sell about 52 acres of land which had been purchased for Jackson College. The proceeds from the sale of a portion of the property amounting to $11,250 were set apart for the erection of an administration building which was to cost $26,000.[19] The net earnings of the college for the 1907–1908 and 1908–1909 school years were applied towards the erection and equipment of the new edifice, named Chivers Hall in honor of the Reverend E. E. Chivers who served as field secretary of the American Baptist Home Mission Society.

From 1903–1908, Dr. Barrett had expended more than $60,000 in the construction of buildings. The temporary and inadequate quarters in prior years had resulted in student displeasure which led to a reduced enrollment. The new location of the school brought new interest and generated an increased enrollment—from 107 to 442 students over a four-year period. A numerical breakdown by levels and interest shows that the grammar school had 245 students; the high school had 67; music had 97; and commerce had 33. By this time, the staff had also undergone changes. Members of the faculty included: President Luther Barrett; Hubert D. Casey, instructor in natural sciences, literature and Latin; Patrick H. Thompson, instructor of arithmetic and history; Ella L. Jacobs, teaching language, grammar, and physical culture; Patrick H. Thompson, geography and writing; Mary E. McIntosh, music and sewing; Alvan A. Kempton, instructor in Latin; R. Roy Perkins, instructor in literature; and Ella M. Barrett, pedagogy, higher mathematics and preceptress.[20]

With the approval of the board, Dr. Barrett set aside a church site as a gift to the community for worship. Known as College Hill Baptist Church, it was used also for training students in the ministry outside the classroom.[21]

Twenty years after the founding of Jackson College, the society began to think about the possibility of black control of the school. At the eighth annual session of the General Baptist Missionary Convention held at Water Valley, Mississippi, July 20–25, 1897, Reverend Malcolm MacVicar, superintendent of education of the American Baptist Home Mission Society of New York, proposed more cooperation in education between the society and the General Missionary Baptist Convention of Mississippi.[22]

Reverend MacVicar circulated a letter to the convention from the Reverend T. T. Morgan, corresponding secretary of the society. His letter set forth the conditions of cooperation between the two parties. The letter included three proposals. The first proposal stated:

> That if the Baptists of Mississippi are prepared to assume the entire responsibility of maintaining Jackson College, he would recommend to the American Baptist Home Mission Society that there shall be created a Negro Board of Trustees acceptable to them to whom the grounds and buildings of the College shall be leased for a period of not less than five years at the nominal rent of $1.00 per year with the privilege of renewal at the end of that time for same or for longer period.[23]

This proposition was made with provisions that the standard of instruction and discipline in the college be fully maintained; that the trustees be held responsible for the entire support of the college including salaries, boarding department, insurance, buildings, and all other expenses; that no debt be allowed to accumulate, and that the college be subject to visitations by the superintendent of education or other officials of the Home Mission Society, and render to the society an annual financial report and such other reports as it may require.

The second proposition stated that if the convention were not in a position to assume the full responsibility, that the society would pay the salaries of the president and of the associate teachers as recommended by the society. And if this were done, the regulations and all amendments that were adopted by the board regarding the internal management of the institution were subject to approval by the American Baptist Home Mission Society.

The third proposition suggested the inauguration of a board of trustees composed of black and white men. Jackson College would be placed under the governance of this board whose powers would be to appoint the president and associate teachers nominated and paid for by the American Baptist Home Mission Society. After discussion of the three propositions, the convention appointed a special committee to study the proposals and to submit its recommendations. The special committee studied carefully the suggestions, and accepted the third plan which called for a biracial board of trustees for the control and management of Jackson College. The president and associate teachers were nominated by and their salaries paid by the American Baptist Home Mission Society.[24]

In opposition to a recommendation of Reverend T. T. Morgan, who stated that an Education Society be initiated, the convention held that education could be more effectively accomplished if instead of an Education Society, a Board of Education be assembled to which the convention would report annually. Hence a Board of Education was established at once. Appointed by the convention, the members of the Board of Education were ministers: Reverend W. H. Hightower, chairman; C. A. Buchanan, secretary; A. A. Hamilton; A. M. Johnson; C. R. Custard; W. H. Higgins; H. W. Scott; R. J. Temple; professors: S. W. Brown; J. Anderson, Jr.; B. P. Gayles; A. D. Snodgrass; J. J. Peyton; E. B. Topp; C. A. Buchanan; E. B. Jones; H. W. Scott, professors C. H. Owens and A. M. Johnson were the Auditing Committee; and professor P. H. Thompson, treasurer.[25]

The convention issued a statement to friends of the college recommending that Jackson College be adopted as the great school for higher education. The convention further announced, "This summer, the College will be incorporated and a Board of Trustees appointed."[26] Thus, in 1899, after twenty-two years of existence, Jackson College had a biracial board of eleven trustees, four of whom were blacks.[27] Their names appeared in the 1899–1900 college catalog: Stephen Green, Esq., and John H. Chapman, New York City; Nathan B. Barton, Providence, R.I.; John T. Blodgett, Esq. and Reverend Henry F. Sproles, D.D., Vicksburg; John T. Buck and Reverend Thomas H. Bailey, Jackson; Samuel W. Brown, Winona; Reverend J. J. Peyton, Faisonia; Reverend W. H. Higgins, Bolton; and Reverend Amos M. Johnson. The Advisory Committee included: Reverend A. V. Rowe, D.D., chairman; Reverend H. F. Sproles, D.D., Vicksburg; F. L. Fulgham, M.D.; and J. T. Buck, Jackson; and J. B. Chrisman, Esq., Canton.[28]

The trustees continued to express their desire to improve the quality of the college. Because they were men who had distinguished themselves as leaders, they provided the institution with wise leadership and stability. They appealed to the black citizenry to rally behind them in supporting Jackson College with prayers, money, and books for the library.[29]

A new step for the development of the school was in the direction of the reorganization of the course of studies to meet the needs of the more advanced students in the state. The original curriculum that was drawn up under the administration of Dr. Ayer was founded on the pattern of the old English Normal courses. There were few variations during the first seventeen years of the school's existence because it was considered unwise to alter a plan before adequate time was allowed to determine the success of the program. However, by 1895, it became clear that the interests of the pupils were quite varied and something had to be done to satisfy the many needs that were in evidence. Dr. Barrett had noticed these lacks and set about to reorganize the then existing English Normal course which was comparable to four years of modern high school training. In order to reach his objective, and at the same time to satisfy varying publics, Barrett set about planning a curriculum that was divided into three parallel courses. Instead of the old five years of schooling, the new work would be completed in four years. Each of the parallel courses was intended to stress some phase of the students' particular interests and wishes. The differences in the courses lay in the amount of emphasis placed upon the real vocational objectives of the student. It will be seen in Table I that Course "A" was almost similar to the old Normal Course, with the study of the Bible becoming a necessary qualification for gradua-

TABLE I Innovative Programs

PROGRAM A

FIRST YEAR	SECOND YEAR	THIRD YEAR	FOURTH YEAR
Algebra	Agriculture	Geometry	Chemistry
Arithmetic	Bookkeeping	Physics	English
Grammar	Algebra	Political	Literature
Physiology & Health	History of Mississippi	Economy	American History
Bible	Government	General History	General History
	Physical Geography	Bible	Psychology
	Bible		Ethics
			Bible

PROGRAM B

Algebra	Agriculture	Geometry	Chemistry
Arithmetic	Bookkeeping	Physics	English
Grammar	Algebra	Rhetoric	Literature
Physiology & Health	History of Mississippi	Latin	American History
Bible	Government	Bible	General History
	Latin		Latin
	Bible		Bible

PROGRAM C

Algebra	Agriculture	Geometry	English
Arithmetic	Bookkeeping	Greek	Literature
Grammar	Algebra	Rhetoric	American History
Physiology & Health	History of Mississippi	Latin	General History
Bible	Government	Bible	Latin
	Latin		Greek
	Bible		Bible

tion from a church-related school. Students who took Course "A" more than likely would proceed to the profession of teaching, and that was why such courses as History of the State of Mississippi, General History, and Geography had a prominent part in the curriculum. The students who took courses "B" and "C" were those whose interests centered around the church and religion. On that account, the classical languages of Latin and Greek were introduced to give students the ability to read the Latin Vulgate Bible and the Greek New Testament.

This new choice of courses enabled the students to conserve a great deal of their time, in that they would not study what they would not use in the further pursuance of their profession. It was also in conformity with the original plan of the society which sought to train teachers and ministers who would minister to the needs of the blacks of the state.

It was in 1904 that the administration decided to put the innovative plan into operation. This effort to modify the program was not without problems. There would have to be created another division in the school if the new college courses leading to the degree of Bachelor of Arts were to be given to graduates. In order that the work would be effective, there was established a model practice school, supervised by an expertly trained critic teacher. In 1905, the Grammar School Division of Jackson College became the practice school and the laboratory for the training of advanced students preparing to teach.[30]

The Industrial Department continued to operate for the benefit of both sexes, since it was designed to provide useful and practical knowledge for students. Female students could attend classes one hour a day in beginning sewing, dressmaking, and embroidery in the hope that they would not only master the art of dressmaking but also develop a good taste in clothes and learn to make them with a minimum of expense. Their handiwork was exhibited on Commencement Day. It was always the tradition of Jackson College to use male labor in helping to build new edifices and landscape the campus. Graduates of the Industrial Department joined the ranks of skilled labor, a prime need of Mississippi. As early as 1883, industrial training of students was supervised by Robert McAllister, an older student. The skills of Industrial Department students were utilized in making the bricks to build the first brick structure on the Millsaps site.

The 1906–1907 catalog listed typewriting for the first time. "It should be offered only to a limited number of students." Requirements included "a fair academic knowledge in grammar and languages."[31]

Music, which held a primary place in church services, continued to be part of the curriculum at Jackson College. Classes in both choral and instrumental music were organized. The 1896–97 catalog lists instruction in piano, cabinet organ, cornet, and vocal music. The organ fee for four lessons a month was $2, piano instruction, $3. Public recitals were given each month and two public concerts were staged each year. Music at the commencement exercise played a significant role.

The McKinney Missionary Society, named in honor of alumnus Reverend Henderson McKinney, a missionary to Africa, was among the many organizations in which students actively participated. Among its members was Dr. Harry H. Jones, class of 1898, who entered Jackson College for the study of the ministry in 1893, graduating in a class of ten. He studied for the ministry in Chicago and then went to Monrovia, Liberia, West Coast, Africa as a missionary. After ministering to the physical and spiritual needs of the African people for several years, Jones returned to the United States to study medicine in Chicago. In 1912, he received the Doctor of Medicine degree. Without delay, he returned to Africa and founded the Klay Industrial Mission at Klay, Liberia. After serving in Africa for more than fifty years, he returned to Mississippi to his alma mater and spoke to a large audience of faculty and students. Less than six years later, he died in his sleep.

Organizations played a major role in the life of students at Jackson College. Under the administration of President Ayer, an organization concerned with work in the foreign missions field was organized. Other groups included the Young Men's Lyceum, the College Debating Team, the Young Men's and Young Women's Christian Association. Under faculty supervision, a Young Men's and Young Women's Temperance League was organized and held meetings once a month in the campus chapel. The Ministers' Institute, begun in 1886, continued to function under Dr. Barrett.

All students of Jackson College had to take an entrance exam-

THE ADMINISTRATION OF LUTHER G. BARRETT

Jackson College moved to its new location on John R. Lynch Street. Shown in this photograph taken in the early 1900s are Ayer Hall at left and right is Chivers Hall. The Bell Tower stands in front of Chivers Hall.

Scene near Founders' Hall taken in early 1890s shows faculty of Jackson College on North State Street on what is now Millsaps College campus.

Mrs. Luther G. Barrett

Faculty 1894-1895

President Barrett

Mrs. Patrick Thompson

Hubert D. Casey

Faculty Members

FACULTY 1894-1895

Miss Eva Hill

P. H. Thompson

Faculty of 1904-1905

Class of 1895
Front Row—Edgar P. Cheek, Octavia Nixon, Andrew G. Ranson
Back Row—G. M. Reese and Virgil Shipp

Class of 1903
Left to right—Cordelia Carter Williams, Dr. Robert W. Henry, and Lula A. Hicks

Presidents' Residence— J. R. Lynch Street. President and Mrs. Luther Barrett and Faculty member in forefront

Ayer Hall 1904

JACKSON COLLEGE CAMPUS SCENE

Chivers Hall—1908

Barrett Hall

Early Buildings

THE ADMINISTRATION OF ZACHARY T. HUBERT

In 1925 the first college seal was designed. The seal of the institution bore the motto, "Line Upon Line—Precept Upon Precept", and the name of the institution was written in Latin.

Mrs. Zachary T. Hubert

Ministers' Institute

Campus View 1911

Class of 1912—First class to graduate under all-Negro faculty. Bottom row: (left to right) Nicholas Hopkins, Pearl Tillman, Ralph Franklin, Middle row: W. B. Griffin, F. O. Alexander, Jesse Heslip, Beatrice Adams, George McLaurin, Top row: Alonzo Myers, Chauncy Haynes, Cammie B. Cox, DeWitt T. Ford, Joseph C. Wright.

First College Graduate—Mrs. Annie Mae Brown McGhee, A. B. Degree conferred in 1924.

Members of the Class of 1924, 1925, 1926. Top: Zee Alfin Anderson Barron, Mary G. Whiteside, Maude T. Alexander, Richie Hudson, Annie M. Brown McGhee, and Ada M. Olive Moon.

Class of 1925. R. A. Hudson, M. G. Whiteside with President Z. T. Hubert

Class of 1926. Left to right: Maude Thelma Alexander, President Z. T. Hubert, Walter Aaron Reed, Jr. and Commodore Dewey Higgins

Student Sewing Class

Football Team 1911. Coach John R. Pinkett (left)

Football Team 1912

Coach B. V. Lawson, Jr.—Director of Athletics

Basketball Squad 1924. Left to right: William H. Walton, Manager. Front row: Clara Charleston, Lula M. Hopkins, Rosa Lee Covington. Back row: Inez Gray, Florida Barr, Alberta Marshall

Baseball Team 1924. Left to right: Coach Furr, Louis Richards, Joe Leonard, C. D. Higgins, Eugene Wilcher, Forest Cavette, Girtie Cannon, Benjamin Blackburn, Allen Hayes, Dewey Grace, Newnan Cornelius, G. V. Johnson, Charles Westbrook, Luther Marshall, A. A. Alexander (Manager).

Iron 13

Football Team 1923-24

YWCA's Cabinet. 1st row l-r:
Velena W. Betts, Isabella Ambrose,
Ada Lee Olive, Marie Glover, 2nd row:
Jo Anna McAllister, Zee A. Anderson Barron
Maude Alexander, 3rd row: Estella Gipson,
Clara Charleston, Clara Henry

Jackson College Choir with Miriam Dansby Johnson at the organ.

The Debating Team. Top—Almanus Crosby, Coach, left to right—Henry Young, Luther Marshall, J. H. Jackson and Marion Reed

Jackson College Choir—Frederick D. Hall (front right) Director

ination and a written monthly examination until graduation. Two days per month were scheduled for these tests. Students averaging less than 70 percent per session were prohibited from advancing into the next class unless they reached this average by a makeup examination.

February 1911, President Barrett submitted his resignation to the board. He strongly recommended that, in an effort to establish rapport, to effect improved relationships between the races and to dispel doubts among the black brethren of the community who had begun to voice their dissatisfaction with the white administrators (many viewing the latters' services as paternalistic). They felt that Jackson College should be run by a black administration and faculty.[32]

In attempts to strengthen and conserve the feeling of racial consciousness and self-development, the society began a movement for more involvement in leadership roles among the black faculty and staff. The racial makeup of the faculty changed and immediately the enrollment began to increase. Some people attributed increased enrollments to the new location of the college and the new curriculum. Others believed the increase reflected the satisfaction with new leadership.

The conditions of Jackson College were ripe to transfer the office of the presidency from white Northerners to black Southerners. On a number of occasions, President Barrett apprised the society of the "estranged" relationships that manifested themselves between the school and the community. Representatives from the society did on frequent occasions visit the campus to observe the school in operation.

At its regular meeting of February 13, 1911, the Education Committee of the American Baptist Home Mission Society voted to present a commendation:

WHEREAS, Rev. L. G. Barrett, President of Jackson College, Jackson, Mississippi, has placed in the hands of the corresponding secretary, his resignation as President of the College, and
WHEREAS, President Barrett has occupied this position for more than sixteen years, during which time he has conducted the affairs of the College with rare business skill including the sale of the old Jackson College property and of the new, with the erection of new buildings thereon,
RESOLVED: 1. That the resignation of President Barrett be accepted to take effect September 30, 1911.

2. That in accepting this resignation the Board desires to put on record its appreciation of the devoted services of President Barrett and his wife during the long course of years, its recognition of his efficient and economical management of the affairs of the College both in the transfer to the new site and the conduct of the institution from year to year, and its gratification at the marked improvement in the College during President Barrett's administration and its excellent condition and large enrollment at the present time.

The resolution records the sentiments of the Education Committee of the American Baptist Home Mission Society towards a man who served it well by heading one of its schools and implementing the ideals of the society with honor and dignity. M. J. Latham, Esq., president of the Alumni Association of Jackson College, focused on President Barrett's contributions in his seventeen-year administration, during which more than 4,200 students had enrolled at the school.

President Barrett moved the college from North to West Jackson. He also encouraged blacks to migrate from the rural areas into the city. His dynamic leadership placed black men on the Education Board of the college. Table II shows a profile of student enrollment and Table III shows a profile of graduates 1883–1911.

At the Sunday commencement exercises of 1911, Dr. James Buchanan Hutton, pastor of the First Presbyterian Church of Jackson, extolled the religious fervor of the departing president. Barrett's final act was the distribution of diplomas to eleven

TABLE II Profile of Student Enrollment, 1877–1911

YEAR	TOTAL NUMBER	ACADEMIC	GRAMMAR & PREPARATORY
1904	291	—	—
1905	329	23	306
1906	299	32	267
1907	316	28	288
1908	356	41	315
1909	384	64	320
1910	366	80	286
1911	442	67	375

TABLE III   Profile of Graduates, 1883–1911

YEAR	NORMAL CERTIFICATES	MEN	WOMEN
1883	7	2	5
1884	3	2	1
1885	5	4	1
1886	9	5	4
1887	9	7	2
1888	5	2	3
1889	7	6	1
1890	3	2	1
1891	18	12	6
1892	20	16	4
1893	8	—	—
1894	No graduating class—Expanded curricula		
1895	4	3	1
1896	No graduating class—Expanded curricula		
1897	4	3	1
1898	10	9	1
1899	4	3	1
1900	No graduating class		—
1901	4	4	0
1902	6	3	3
1903	3	1	2
1904	5	4	1
1905	2	2	0
1906	2	2	0
1907	3	2	1
1908	6	2	4
1909	8	4	4
1910	13	7	6
1911	11	7	4

graduates: Taylor S. Adams, Blanche Creathe, Arthur A. Gipson, Arthur F. Hoyle, Tatsy Huddleston, Emma J. Irby, Anna M. Johnson, J. Wyatt Kelley, Annie M. Loach, Henry W. McNamee, and Oscar D. Robinson. He also awarded seventeen prizes, first among which went to Florence O. Alexander for the highest average—97.64.[33] Thus, did President Barrett also move students to their highest potential of attainment.

CHAPTER IV

THE ACADEMIC REVOLUTION

The Administration of President Zachary T. Hubert, 1911–1927

THROUGHOUT THE FIRST THIRTY-FOUR YEARS of the existence of Jackson College, two presidents—both of whom were white Northern missionaries—came to Mississippi to help establish an institution for black ministers and teachers. Ayer bought an old building and converted it into a school. Forced by racial circumstances to relocate, Barrett sold school buildings on the Millsaps campus and built new ones on another. Both created their boards of trustees. Both engaged faculties because of increases in student enrollment. Both developed academic communities conducive to effective learning. They were both diligent in carrying out the goals and objectives of Natchez Seminary and Jackson College.

Having educated a cadre of Mississippi black ministers and teachers, Barrett realized that black students needed positive images of their own race to help boost their self-concepts and carry out the special mission of educating the disadvantaged youth. The time had come to place this task into the hands of a new leadership.

On the horizon were changes in the American scene—the revolt of black intellectuals in the tradition of the social, educational, and political ideology of Booker T. Washington and William Edward Burghart Du Bois. Du Bois through his writings was pleading for the "talented ténth" of the black race to give leadership to black people's struggle for survival and progress.

The American Baptist Home Mission Society also recognized

that the "patient interest" as it related to the organizational structure of Jackson College was viewed by some of the black and white constituency with a great deal of skepticism. The leadership exhibited by the former white administrators had made some efforts toward racial harmony. The relocation of the college with the available property enhanced by a black president proved to be a wise move for the society and black people. On May 8, 1911, the board elected Professor Zachary T. Hubert to serve as the first black chief administrator of Jackson College, beginning June 1, 1911.[1]

President Hubert had the professional qualifications for the position, and they were impressive. Having been born near White Plains, Georgia, on March 27, 1877, a few months prior to the founding of Natchez Seminary, Hubert graduated in May, 1901, from Atlanta Baptist College (now Morehouse College) with a Bachelor of Arts degree. He was invited immediately to become a member of the faculty at his alma mater. After serving a period of one year, he resigned his position to continue his academic pursuits at Massachusetts Agriculture College. In 1904 that institution conferred upon him the Master of Arts degree. President Hubert's reputation as an authority in matters of application of scientific techniques in the field of agriculture began to extend throughout the Southland where his services were in great demand.[2] Following his graduation from Massachusetts Agriculture College, Florida A&M College, a black college (now Florida A&M University) located in Tallahassee, appointed him to serve on its faculty. He resigned after one year to become superintendent of buildings and grounds at Spelman College in Atlanta.

Spelman College was one of the thirteen schools which the American Baptist Home Mission Society sponsored. During Hubert's five-year employment at Spelman, the society had an opportunity to observe him closely and evaluate his performance. Representatives from the society were so impressed with his competence that they strongly endorsed Hubert to become President Barrett's successor at Jackson College. In support of this belief, the society voted:

> That the Superintendent of Education be authorized to confer with Prof. Hubert in reference to the presidency of Jackson College, to offer

him the position and to present as early as possible completed plans for the reorganization of the institution on its new basis. Mr. Hubert is a colored man, a graduate of Atlanta Baptist College and of Massachusetts Agriculture College; a Christian man of education and culture, with considerable experience in teaching and in administrative work.[3]

The conditions of Jackson College were ripe to transfer the office of the presidency from white Northerners to black Southerners. On several occasions President Barrett had informed the Home Mission Society of the "estranged" relationships that manifested themselves between the school and the community. The society had given its earlier attention to the potentially explosive racial situation on the Millsaps campus and had allowed President Barrett to begin procedures for relocating Jackson College. In his resignation letter to the board in February 1911, President Barrett strongly recommended that, to establish better rapport between the races and to dispel doubts among the black parents who had begun to voice their dissatisfaction with the white administrators, Jackson College should be run by both a black administrator and an all-black faculty.[4]

Concomitantly with the designation of Hubert on May 8, 1911, the board also appointed Budey Baldwin Dansby, A.B., as dean of men and instructor of Greek and mathematics for a period of eight months at a salary of $700. Other appointments included Jubie B. Bragg, A.B., natural science and mechanics; Miss Emma O. Bryant, A.B., domestic science, philosophy and hygiene; Miss Bessie Clark, instrumental and vocal music; Miss Mamie E. Granderson, A.B., German and mathematics; John R. Pinkett, A.B., instructor of Latin and history, first athletic director; Miss Rhoda L. Simms, assistant in music; and Miss Mamie F. Strong, A.B., instructor of English. Teachers in the grammar school division included: Miss Alice M. Paxton, superintendent of grammar school and director of practice school; Miss Marietta E. Hubert, instructor; Miss Etta L. Latham, instructor; and Miss Sarah O. Stanley, instructor.[5]

Other faculty and staff included in the catalog for 1911–12 were Bessie C. Cobb, stenography and bookkeeping; Helen G. Crompton, plain sewing and dressmaking; Edna M. Hutchins and

Florence S. Lovett, matrons of the dining hall, each serving a half-year.

From the beginning of the school year in 1911-12, President Hubert began an assessment of his faculty. In selecting it, he said, the management endeavored to give the school the very highest grade of workers in order that present high standards should not only be maintained, but that the challenge might go forth to higher attainments. In addition to their academic preparation, all the teachers had some years of experience in professional work.

This extra insight into the professional world brought to Jackson College a keen and alert leadership which served to create a special atmosphere for black students who came to learn. President Hubert felt that with this kind of faculty the school had a brighter outlook than ever before.[6]

The credentials of the faculty suggested that they were competent in their areas of teaching. The assembly of the black faculty represented various alumni of such well-known higher educational institutions as Amherst College, Atlanta Baptist College, Chicago University, Jackson College (Rhoda L. Simms), Massachusetts Agriculture College, Oberlin Conservatory of Music, Spelman Seminary, Talladega College, Tuskegee Institute, and Yale University.[7]

Not long after President Hubert had begun the work of the presidency, black supporters and students began to demand that the administration upgrade the curriculum and expand its programs to make them comparable with those of other institutions in the South. This placed pressure on the all-black faculty to prove that they were competent enough to teach on an advanced level. Instead of doubting their work, the faculty pointed to their graduates as living testimonials of the quality of the work the Jackson College faculty had engaged in.

President Hubert had begun in 1911 to draw up a list of the school's graduates. He had compiled an impressive list: Reverend Henderson McKinney (1883), who died as a missionary in Africa; Reverend Egbert B. Topp (1886), pastor and editor of the *Baptist Reporter*, Jackson; Reverend Preston J. Jackson (1887), pastor, Greenwood; Reverend Patrick H. Thompson (1887), president, Kosciusko Industrial Institute; Reverend Daniel H. Butler, D.D. (1889), presiding elder, Jackson; D. J. Randolph (1889), school principal of Ellisville; John Walker (1889), druggist, Demopolis, Alabama; J. M. Candy (1891) A.M., professor, Virginia Normal Institute, Petersburg; Va; W. P. Ross, L.L.B. (1892), Walden University; Jackson; William L. Latham Lawyer (J.L.B.) (1893), Walden University, Jackson; G. M. Reese (1893), principal of Baptist Seminary, Meridian; Reverend Edgar P. Cheek (1895), pastor, Columbia, S. C.; Harry H. Jones (1898), missionary, Monrovia, Africa; Robert W. Henry, M.D. (1903), Philadelphia, Pa.; William K. Flowers (1908), Meharry Medical School, Nashville; James E. Ramsey, D.D.S. (1909), Meharry Medical School, Nashville; Fred K. Ross (1909), Leonard Medical School, New Orleans, La.; Florence O. Alexander (1912), Hunter College, New York; Jesse S. Heslip (1912), Howard University, 1st Lieut., U.S.A. Camp Meade, Md.; Leon E. Proctor (1914), Lincoln University, Pa.; Eva. V. Jordan (1915), Selma University, Jackson; Andrew J. Howard (1916), Howard University; Hattie V. Jones (1916), music student.

 The new faculty members who joined the staff as circumstances warranted and some of whom served Dr. Hubert to the end of his administration were: Adolph L. Rice, A.B. and B.D., college chaplain, psychology, ethics; Annie Mae Brown McGhee, A.B., Jackson College, 1924, assistant in science; William E. Griffin, A.B., Morehouse College, 1916, graduate student, University of Minnesota, professor of economics and history; Florence Octavia Alexander, A.B., Hampton Institute, 1912, Hunter College, 1918, education, director, practice school; W. Clyde Allen, B.S., Morehouse College, 1926, professor of chemistry and biology; Green C. Maxwell, A.B., Howard University, 1924, mathematics; Harvey A. Clemons, B.S., Lincoln University, A.B., University of Indiana, English; Oswell A. Combs, A.B., Atlanta University, 1882, Latin and English, acting president of Campbell College; Clarence L. Porter, certificate in music, Oberlin Conservatory of Music, music instructor; Necie E. Edwards, Indiana State Normal, 1926, home economics; Musetta V. Scott, Indiana State Normal, 1926, practice school; Beulah Courtney, Mississippi Industrial College, music; Ruth W. Anderson, A.B., Wilberforce University, Latin; Irene B. Maxwell, preceptress; Marietta Hubert, buyer and girls' industries; Kathleen H. Simons, bookkeeper; W. P. Thomas, matron, men's dormitory and laundry. Other staff personnel included James Kirksey, shopwork; C. C. Williams, farmer and custodian; A. J. Thomas, M.D., college physician; and William J. Thompson, college chef. Indeed, President Hubert had an excellent team.

The central preoccupation of President Hubert was the upgrading of the program of studies at Jackson College. He firmly evaluated current offerings. He found that the programs offered were: (1) Primary and Practice School Course aiming (a) to prepare for the grammar school and (b) to offer the opportunity to interested and in-service teachers to learn how to teach; (2) Grammar School Courses, fourth through eighth grades; (3) Academic Courses (a) Classical, (b) English and Latin and Commercial, each covering four years. Music, manual training, rhetoricals, sewing, cooking, and physical activities were extracurricular offerings.

President Hubert significantly modified program offerings in his first year. He soon published the new program in the Jackson College annual of 1912: (1) Four Years' College Course leading to the Bachelors' degrees, (2) College Preparatory (four years); (3) Normal Course (three years); (4) Teacher's Course (one year beyond the normal course); and (5) the Minister's Course (six weeks). Special courses were listed in instrumental and vocal music, domestic art (including plain sewing), dressmaking, cooking, agriculture, manual training, stenography, and business methods. The number of students enrolled by specific departments follows: the College Preparation program had 78 students; the Grammar School, grades from four to eight, enrolled 193 students; the Primary School, grades primer to three, listed 90 students; the students in special classes numbered 139; and the Ministers' Course had 17 enrollees. The true total of students enrolled included some duplications since some students were listed in more than one program.

During the academic year of 1912-13, the night school was introduced for young men. In 1913-14, the two-year program under the rubric of "Courses Offered" was listed for the first time. The student register lists four sophomores and five freshmen in this department.[8] Dr. Hubert extended the agricultural program to three years. Professor Dansby, who was close to the scene, observed that many harsh critics of the time felt that Hubert would eventually turn the school into an agriculture institution.[9] Hubert often made moves to prove his critics wrong. The extending of the agricultural program paralleled the expansion of music. The Music Department boasted six pianos, six organs, and a large suite of practice, chorus, and teachers' rooms in the main College Hall.

All modifications and expansions of existing curricula in teacher education were approved by the society. Even those new programs in music and agriculture were welcomed by the Home Mission Society. It was only when Hubert asked for permission to develop a degree program in liberal arts that the society voted non-approval. The administration, faculty, student body, and interested supporters registered dissatisfaction with this decision of the society. Several groups petitioned the society to allow Jackson College to offer liberal arts baccalaureate degree programs. Some argued that Jackson College would be in a better position to compete with neighboring schools in attracting high caliber students. The administration pointed out that the faculty was capable of handling advanced subjects and assured the society that professors were willing to offer content programs without added compensation. They reviewed the period from 1911 to 1921, showing how the graduates had vigorously represented Jackson College in the ministry, in teaching, and in many other professions.

The task of convincing the Home Mission Society of the viability of the liberal arts baccalaureate program continued with eloquence and persuasion until the society finally permitted the college, in 1921, to expand its curriculum. Jackson College was then regarded with greater respect than ever before.

Dr. Dansby, who taught mathematics and Greek in the college during this period, recalls the reaction of the faculty to the event:

> This request, which was granted, met with a most enthusiastic reception; and the staff knew what would be expected of them. They had asked for additional responsibilities, and they were given much for which they sought. This had to be accounted for in terms of how they would use them for the advantage of the students under their care and the community in which they worked. They knew that their obligations to the State of Mississippi were greater since they would be expected to turn out better materials which would assist in integrating the separate and weak sections

of the State into a cohesive whole. Needless to say, in 1924 when, for the first time in the history of the College, the degree of Bachelor of Arts was conferred on Mrs. Annie Mae Brown McGhee, the College felt justly proud of itself; and once again another landmark in the historical achievements of the Institution was established.[10]

The first specialized academic baccalaureate degree program was outlined in the 1927 Jackson College catalog:

FIRST YEAR

FIRST SEMESTER	SECOND SEMESTER
English (a) 3	English (a) 3
Mathematics—Greek—Latin (a) 3	Mathematics—Greek—Latin (a) 4
Chemistry (a) 5	Chemistry (a) 5
Modern Language (b) 3	Modern Language (b) 5
History (b) 3	History (b) 3
Education (b) 3	Education (b) 3
Music (b)	Music (b)

SECOND YEAR

English (a) 3	English (a) 3
Political Science (a) 3	Political Science (a) 3
Mathematics—Greek—Latin (b) 4	Mathematics—Greek—Latin (b) 4
Chemistry (b) 3	Chemistry (b) 4
Biology—Zoology (a) 4	History (b) 3
Education (b) 3	Biology—Zoology (a) 4
Music	Education (b) 3
	Music

THIRD YEAR

English (b) 3	English (b) 3
Economics (a) 4	Economics (a) 4
Physiology (b) 3	Geology (b) 3
Physics (b) 4	Physics (b) 4
History (b) 3	History (b) 3
Logic (a) 3	Psychology (a) 4
Education (b) 3	Education (b) 3

FOURTH YEAR

English (b) 3	English (b) 3
Economics (b) 3	Economics (b) 3

FOURTH YEAR (CONTINUED)

FIRST SEMESTER	SECOND SEMESTER
Ethics (a) 3	Ethics (a) 3
Sociology (a) 3	Sociology (a) 3
History (b) 3	History (b) 3
Education (a) 3	Education (b) 3

(a) Required   (b) Elective[11]

The first graduate of the program was Annie Mae Brown McGhee on whom the Bachelor of Arts degree was conferred in 1924. Interviewed on the subject, she recounted her reminiscences of personal struggles and successes in an intimate revelation:

> When I was in high school, the students made demands for a college's curriculum. The Society was slow to concede to the demands. In the meantime, we began to collect and study catalogs from colleges that were already accredited by the Association of Colleges. The people in the community were really interested. The problem was being duly discussed. In the meantime, I was quietly working to be ready if ever the Society conceded. I attended school winter and summer. I took every course I could get. By 1924, I had accumulated more than enough hours required for graduation. I was then called into the Office of the President and asked what University would I like to attend? I was speechless because I had never anticipated such an honor. I chose the University of Chicago—made preparations and left for Chicago. I was shocked because my transcript never arrived and I had to attend as a special student. I was told later that it was miraculously destroyed.[12]

The nature of the new programs and the old dictated the need for more complete facilities. Jackson College had been established on 50 acres of good, elevated, arable land. President Hubert had shown practicality in his decision to designate some of the land to develop a school farm. Ayer and Barrett halls continued to serve as dormitories. The original frame structure on the campus was remodeled to provide a home for the president and his family. A small frame cottage was used as a farmer's home and a barn housed the stock, farming implements, and the gathered crop.

Chivers Hall provided the chapel-auditorium with a capacity to seat 800 students. Classrooms in this hall were used by all divisions of the institution. Chivers Hall also contained two suites of rooms for the Music Department and a well-lighted sewing room. The chemical laboratory provided working space for only 12 students at a time. The college library and reading rooms were also housed in Chivers Hall.

The quality and quantity of the library's holdings are recorded in the 1913-14 catalog which noted that there was a library and reading room in Chivers Hall for the use of students and teachers. In addition to the daily and weekly papers and magazines, the library contained about 1,200 books suitable for student use. Efforts were made to add to these from year to year, and students were encouraged to make the greatest use of the facility.[13]

The first sizable amount of money for the purchase of materials for the library was allotted in 1919 when the General Education Board appropriated $500 toward $1,123.88 for the purchase of library books. Up to that time, very small allocations had been made. One alumnus who contributed a set of *Americana Encyclopedia* bemoaned the fact that the library—so vital to an academic program—was woefully inadequate. Numerous volumes were given as gifts by the faculty, alumni, and friends of the college. By 1926 the number of volumes had grown to more than 2,500. President Hubert set out to appoint a full-time professional librarian.[14]

Other buildings were also being added to the physical plant. A blacksmith and woodwork shop was erected in the summer of 1919. This building, a one-story brick structure, was to form a single unit of what was planned for an industrial arts building. While President Hubert was working to advance the quality of the college, he was also interested in job opportunities in areas other than teaching.

On June 19, 1919, Hubert sent a letter to Dr. Wallace Buttrick, then president of the General Education Board, asking him to increase appropriations for a manual training building on a scale more extensive than that being offered in any other section of the state. Hubert pointed out that Jackson College had justified its existence in such a way as to qualify for the grant. He specifically noted that courses were offered in dressmaking, sewing, and domestic sciences, in manual training and in agriculture. He stated that such a building would cost $60,000. Considering the location of the then 2.5 million blacks in Mississippi, Hubert stated that his request was in keeping with the needs of the people of new times and new conditions demanding more than in the past years. He wrote, "You will find enclosed also a copy of the sketch I have made showing the relation of Jackson College to this vast Negro population. I am asking that you make up a budget for Jackson College and that in this budget may be included also an item of $10,000.00 to cover the cost of a heating system to be installed to provide for the present equipment and the new buildings to come."[15]

Undaunted by the delayed responses regarding the needs of Jackson College as submitted to the General Education Board and to the American Baptist Home Mission Society, President Hubert, in his report to the Board of Trustees March 8, 1923, again cited the needs of the institution. Dr. George Hovey was authorized to further present the needs of Jackson College to the General Education Board and ask that the present allowance of $5,000 for salaries be increased 50 percent on condition the college raise locally an additional $1,000.

President Hubert went on to request an appropriation of $160,000 from the General Education Board to be distributed as follows: science building, $80,000; dining hall, $20,000; heating plant, $20,000; teachers' cottages, one single and one double, $10,000; dairy barn, $5,000; repairs of Ayer Hall (basement and first floor) $10,000; other repairs, $7,000; old barn remodeling, $3,000; athletic field, $5,000.[16]

On April 9, 1926, the board approved the erection of a practice school. According to board records, this building was to be erected according to the specifications approved by the Department of Architecture of the society and by the secretary of education at a cost of $7,000. Of this amount, $2,000 was voted by the Home Mission Society, $2,000 was to be secured by President Hubert, and $3,000 was promised conditionally by the General Education Board and as indicated in the revised plan of the Julius Rosenwald Fund. It was explicitly understood that the work would not be undertaken until the full assessment of the building was completed. President Hubert was successful in securing $2,000 from the white citizens of Jackson. The new structure consisted of four classrooms with lavatories. The walls were thirteen-inch common brick throughout; the partitions were made of lath and plaster, and the ceiling of pine. The roof was covered with slate; the floors were cement, covered with linoleum.

Although a teacher's cottage was built and occupied during the 1924–25 school term, the new structure was a far cry from what had been requested. Hence, Hubert sent a letter to the secretary of education bemoaning the fact that "There is not one of the schools owned by the Society, except Jackson College, for which the Society has not in a material way done something every year in the last thirty years."[17] Hubert drew attention to the fact that the society had not shown adequate attention to Jackson College in the realm of financial support and physical maintenance.

At their meeting of March 30, 1926, the Board of Trustees voted unanimously to petition the General Education Board of New York for the sum of $90,000 in order to build and equip a science building for Jackson College. This petition was signed by H. M. King, R. R. Gunther, C. L. Barnes, and J. M. Hartfield. On April 3, 1926, President Hubert sent a letter to Dr. E. C. Sage of the General Education Board apprising him of the board's action in its March 30 meeting. He enclosed a copy of the vote taken by the trustees and the document signed by the executive committee.

It is hardly necessary for me to recount for you our needs here or to mention the serious handicaps even under which we work this year. You and Mr. Davis have studied the school and its situation too recently for that. I want very much, however, that you will back our petition to the General Education Board for this Science building for college use... an outright grant of $90,000.00 for building and equipment as the Board so generously did in the instances of Benedict College and Shaw University.

This college building, you will remember is the central unit of the budget I presented for the Board's consideration last year for Jackson College. For the information of your committee, let me mention the following facts which we think have bearing:

1. Jackson is in the midst of the South's most densely populated Negro sections, with New Orleans 200 miles south, Memphis 200 miles north, Shreveport 175 miles west and Birmingham, 250 miles east. Jackson is immediately accessible to more rural Negroes than any other city. Jackson College, then is near to the population it seeks to serve.

2. Jackson College heads up the educational work of a large constituency. Sixty seven out of every hundred persons in the state (colored) belong to this denomination. It has therefore a very large and growing demand made on it.

3. It is centrally and well located. Has been operating continuously 49 years and is permanent in all aspects.

4. The growth of the school now is distinctly college work and it is the natural head of a series of lower schools over the state.[18]

The following table shows appropriations to Jackson College from the American Baptist Home Mission Society during President Hubert's administration:

YEAR	SALARIES	PROPERTY	OTHER EXPENSES
1912	$ 8,525.00	—	$ 733.95
1913	8,322.50	—	630.00
1914	8,337.90	—	1,214.85
1915	8,740.00	—	254.80
1916	8,616.00	—	384.00
1917	8,503.50	—	1,192.88
1918	8,433.75	—	100.00
1919	11,752.50	—	803.03
1920	13,594.23	—	41.25
1921	14,654.11	—	1,450.00
1922	13,670.19	—	500.00
1923	15,455.71	$ 1,636.75	560.80
1924	13,999.96	2,071.94	—
1925	12,166.25	2,000.00	625.61
1926	9,625.00	5,014.60	1,182.66
1927	9,033.08	1,115.35	2,066.92
TOTAL	$173,429.68	$11,838.64	$11,740.75

From 1912-27 the American Baptist Home Mission Society had contributed $197,009.07 to Jackson College. Of this amount, $173,429.68 had been expended for salaries, $11,838.64 for property, and $11,740.75 for other expenses.[19]

CONSERVATORY OF MUSIC

Beginning with the 1923-24 academic year, as previously noted, the Music Department had been organized. This had taken the form of a conservatory. The board had approved the President's recommendation to this effect beginning in 1923-24.

The 1925-26 college catalog gives prominence to the Conservatory of Music under the directorship of Frederick D. Hall. The records show that, beginning with the 1923-24 school session, the Jackson College Department of Music was called a conservatory. In an effort to give a broad approach to music, the college offered the subjects of piano, organ, violin, voice, band and orchestra instruments, public school music, harmony, and theory; these were well organized and the methods of instruction were thorough. Jackson College had sufficient musical instruments to carry on effective instruction for the learner. The instruments available included a new pipe organ, a grand piano, several upright pianos, and complete sets of band and orchestra instruments.

Every opportunity was offered the students for personal development. Adequate emphasis was given to various performance groups in each phase of music. The large orchestra, the band, the chorus, the glee clubs, and quartets were available for music students who desired these experiences. The conservatory presented several concerts each year in Jackson and around the state. Such efforts rendered music students more proficient in the applied aspect of their instruments and voices.

The Conservatory Extension Department was quite unlike anything else in that section of the country. Music classes were organized in cities and towns anywhere within a radius of 200 miles of the college. The same instruction was given the students of these classes as that received by those who attended the college. Bands, orchestras, choirs, and choruses were organized and all grades were taught. Certificates and diplomas were awarded upon completion of the courses. Besides piano, violin, pipe organ, and voice, the curriculum included church music, music history, language, community music, music theory, and elocution. A group of instructors was maintained for this work. They made visits to each town or city once or twice each week and the courses taught were continuously evaluated and upgraded.

The Conservatory was also regarded as a service agency. Various groups performed in schools, churches, and communities. Faculty members were also called on to serve as consultants from time to time. The conservatory director often invited and recruited students who were especially interested in studying music in any phase.[20]

All had been a part of the curriculum organized by Frederick D. Hall and assisted by Mrs. Gustave Mason Gooden, an accomplished musician specializing in piano and voice and a graduate of Jackson College, class of 1926. Mrs. Gooden went on to give many more years of rich service to her alma mater.

The society had authorized President Hubert to purchase a pipe organ costing $3,800 on condition that he raise the money through the Music Department and from private contributions. Because of the vital role that music played in the religious services, there was little objection on the part of the society. Both President Hubert and Frederick Hall accepted the challenge to raise the money. Far and near was Jackson College known for its superior Music Department.

In 1916 Thomas D. Pawley wrote the official school song, "Jackson Fair." Frederick Hall edited and revised it in 1921. Copyrighted in 1926, the Music Department dedicated it to President Zachary T. Hubert.

With such a strong music department, it was natural for the college orchestra and band to be organized. Many of the community church choirs were made up of voice students from Jackson College. Male and female quartets and the Lyre Club were components of the Music Department. One of the functions of the Lyre Club was to promote the musical interests of students in the institutions where extension courses were offered. The president of the Lyre Club for the 1927-28 session was M. M. Reid. In 1926, C. D. Higgins served as president with W. H. Walton as assistant director. Pawley and Wright served as faculty and student director, respectively.[22]

As in other departments, the staff of the Music Department was made up of teachers who were specialists, having been awarded certificates and/or degrees from such various schools as the Oberlin Conservatory of Music and the University of Chicago School of Music. The financial returns from the Department of Music were so sizable that the college could equip the music studios with small organs, pianos, and even a grand piano that was used for concerts and recitals. Each music program was designed to make students proficient in their chosen field along with building up a career which enabled them to earn a living. The band served the dual purpose of attracting many citizens to the campus for performances and as a recruiting tool for students to the college from all over the

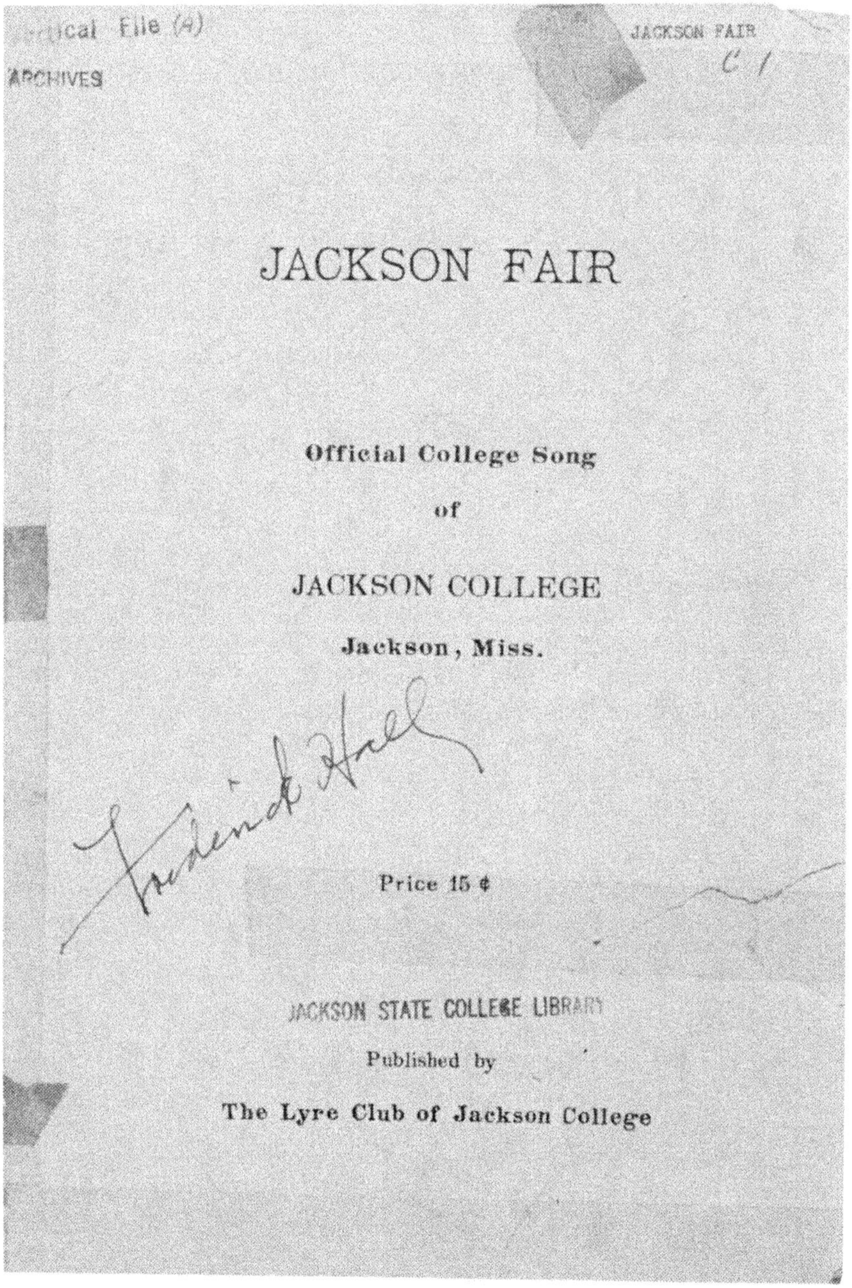

The Academic Revolution 65

JACKSON FAIR

Official College Song

of

JACKSON COLLEGE

Jackson, Miss.

Frederick Hall

Price 15 ¢

JACKSON STATE COLLEGE LIBRARY

Published by

The Lyre Club of Jackson College

The Academic Revolution 67

state. A young men's glee club was under the directorship of Thomas D. Pawley and Arthur D. Wright.

ATHLETICS

As a part of the college program, athletics was first described in the 1911-12 catalog. An athletic group composed of students and a faculty advisory committee promoted physical education on the campus. Emphasis was placed first on football and later on baseball. In 1919 and 1920, a winning state champion intercollegiate football team was established. President Hubert backed the organization wholeheartedly. He appointed John R. Pinkett, an Amherst graduate who was employed at Jackson College in 1911 to teach Latin and history, to serve as director of athletics.

The college began the football season of 1920 with only 13 men who were known as the "Iron Thirteen." It was the nucleus of the full-scale athletic program. The team went undefeated for three years. Upon the resignation of Coach Bragg the previous term, Jackson College was without a football coach during the 1920 academic year. For at least two weeks there were but five or six players present. In view of Hubert's fondness for the game, it must have been with some reluctance that he suggested the players forget about football for that year. The students, however, continued to practice daily until their number reached thirteen. The team selected Ernest Richards, a teacher of French and a man who had never played football, to serve as "coach." These thirteen men, possessing such unity of purpose and strong dedication to the game, needed only a supervisor as they made their own plays and directed their practice. Acting on the calls made by teammates Edgar Stewart and Percy Greene, the 1920 team was victorious in their first game defeating Tougaloo 13 to 0. Jackson State went on to win every game that was scheduled that year, including victories of 63-0 over Utica and a 21-14 triumph over Mississippi Industrial College on Thanksgiving Day.

The famous "Iron Thirteen" included Henry Johnson, right end; Earl Banks, right tackle; Horace Johnson, right guard; Edgar "Tripp" Stewart, center; Luther Marshall, left guard; Theodore Ambrose, left tackle; Joe Boothe, left end; Roy Bolton, fullback;

Percy Greene, left halfback; W. A. Scott, quarterback; and Horace Bolton, right halfback. Substitutes were Howard Courtney and Aureleus Scott.

Jackson State has had a history of honoring its deserving athletes. John R. Pinkett gave a gold medal both in the 1911-12 and 1912-13 school years to the best all-around athletes in the college. In order to be eligible for this award, the student was required to be free of any "conditions" at commencement and never subjected to suspension during his college career. Succeeding coaches also continued the practice.

In 1925, Coach B. V. Lawson, who came to Jackson College from the University of Michigan, was appointed director of athletics. He was also professor of social sciences and director of the Teachers' Professional Department. His work proved significant for the further development of athletics. His policies were unchanged for many years.[23]

STUDENT ACTIVITIES

One can gain reasonable insight into student life of the twenties by reviewing *The Jacksonian* of 1925, published by the Lyre Club. The editor wrote in the foreword that "through the medium of its editorial staff and generosity of several classes, the College has attempted herewith to set forth in this, *The Jacksonian*, a succinct review of several phases of campus life at Jackson College."[24] Indeed students were anxious participants in racial activities and academic experiences offered in this day. Members who composed the yearbook were organized similarly to staff groups of the 1970s. The gleeful faces included H. H. Young, editor-in-chief; Mary G. Whiteside, assistant editor; W. H. Walton, business manager; M. G. Glover, secretary; W. A. Reed, humorist; Z. T. Hubert, Jr., cartoonist; A. L. Olive, music editor; W. A. Reed, Jr., organization editor; R. A. Hudson, literary editor; J. B. Wilcher, treasurer, and C. D. Westbrooke, Jr., athletic editor.

The Jacksonian of 1925 featured the college administration, students by classes, athletics, academic departments, student organizations, and campus humor. The first volume covered activities of the school year and it is particularly valuable for its photographs of the ceremony during the second commencement when two students were graduated with the A. B. degree—Mary G. Whiteside and Richie A. Hudson.

The Jacksonian of 1925 made an impressive appearance with the Jackson College seal and logo on its cover. The date indicating that the college was founded in 1877 is an official part of the logo.

The first college paper, *The Baptist Messenger,* was published monthly at the subscription rate of $.50 per year during the administration of President Ayer. Not a student publication, it served as a medium of communication among the churches and associations, delivering news about the affairs of the college with emphasis on religion, education, and temperance.

Religious services were a daily part of the students' activities. In addition to the teaching of the Bible during all courses, there was daily devotion at 8:15 A.M. and regular preaching services on Sunday at 3:00 P.M. On Wednesday evening the Young Women's Christian Association and Young Men's Christian Association conducted prayer meetings. During Sunday evenings there was a joint meeting of the entire school. The Young Men's Christian Association and the Young Women's Christian Association were annually represented in regional and national meetings. Each had a faculty advisor. There was the campus Sunday school as well. For a period of time Miss F. O. Alexander served as superintendent of the Sunday school. For many years the YWCA and the YMCA were organizations that effected wide participation by the student body along with the Sunday chapel service. The McKinney Missionary Society, named in honor of one of Jackson College's graduates who died on the foreign mission field in Africa, also flourished.

Literary societies, one for the young men and one for the young women, met separately three times a week for individual programs, then jointly, at which time an outside speaker was invited. In 1915 a college debating team was organized in connection with the young men's Letter Society. Cash prizes were awarded to the winning team.

In an effort to encourage and promote high standards of excellence, both in scholarship and character among the students of the college, scholarships and prizes had been awarded as early as 1895. President Barrett gave $12 to six students ($2 each) in recognition of their "rhetorical" performances. The recipients were Harry H. Jones and Melissa A. Brown, first prize; William T. Blackman and Mary E. Todd, second prize; and James Holloway and Emma J. Coleman, third prize.[25] President Hubert continued this tradition.

The 1912-13 catalog indicated that for the highest general average in class work, a student of the academy would be awarded a $25 first prize. The second prize of $15 would be awarded to the student reaching the second highest average.[26] Cash awards were also made for students who exhibited unusual performance in music and in oratory.

Medals awarded during the academic exercises were donated by the president of the college and the president of the Alumni Association.

The president's awards of a silver loving cup and a college pennant were given annually to those classes demonstrating outstanding performance in singing. Each class competed by singing two selections, one of which was the college song.

For many years, William J. Latham, first president of the Alumni Association, offered a cash prize of $3-$5 to the Sewing Department and $2 to the Cooking Department for the student in each department making the greatest progress for that year. John R. Pinkett, who taught Latin, history and mathematics and also served as the registrar and coach, awarded a medal to the student beyond the second year of the academic program who had proven he was the best all-round athlete in the college.

During the years of President Hubert's administration, rules for behavior and decorum remained the same as in previous times. (Some of the observations pointed up in the 1926-27 catalog affecting the deportment of students held that good moral character and good work alone would keep a student at Jackson College.) Intoxicating liquors, tobacco in any form, and firearms were strictly forbidden. In a case of suspension or voluntary withdrawal, no refunds of tuition or board would be made. A student might be dismissed at any time, if in the opinion of the faculty his general demeanor was considered unsatisfactory. The college uniform for young ladies was the navy blue skirt and white middy-blouse, with white or black stockings and white or black shoes. High-heeled shoes were not permitted in the school. On Sundays and public occasions the white waist was exchanged for the blouse. Parents were advised to communicate with the college authorities before sending or spending money for student clothing.

Students were advised to read carefully and be cognizant of rules governing conduct. For violations of these, students would accumulate demerits. When seven demerits had been earned, students were warned by the president. When fourteen were earned, the parents were notified. An accumulation of twenty demerits was cause for complete dismissal.

In developing his multifaceted programs, President Hubert utilized the help of many persons. He had the support of the Jackson College Board of Trustees. The charter of March 9, 1899, signed by Governor A. J. McLaurin and recorded by J. L. Power, secretary of state, stated that there would be eleven members of the board, four of whom should be black. As recorded in the 1918 Jackson College catalog, President Hubert saw fit to include the names of general officers and the trustees of the college on its pages.

The first group representing the American Baptist Home Mission Society of New York were: Charles L. White, D.D., corresponding secretary; Lemuel C. Barnes, D.D., field secretary; Frank T. Moulton, treasurer; and Gilbert N. Brink, D.D., superintendent of education of New York City.

The second group included four trustees that came from New York and eight from Mississippi. From New York were Dr. Charles S. White, chairman; Dr. E. T. Tomlinson; Dr. Gilbert N. Brink, superintendent, and W. B. Hale. Eight members were from Mississippi: Reverend H. M. King (Jackson); Reverend A. A. Cosey (Mound Bayou); J. M. Hartfield (Jackson); Reverend R. T. Sims (Canton); Dr. J. B. Lawrence (Jackson); Reverend J. D. Zuber (West Point); Dr. D. W. Turner (Jackson); and Dr. Z. T. Hubert, secretary (Jackson).[27]

The 1927 commencement marked the golden anniversary of the institution. Through the years the highlight of the school activities was commencement. Festivities increased year by year. The 1927 year was special: literary societies gave programs; the industrial arts, manual training, and sewing and cooking students prepared exhibitions. A series of orations and essays interspersed with vocal and instrumental numbers brought parents and friends of the college from far and near to celebrate fifty years of achievement for a black school in the heart of the state of Mississippi.

While accepting at this occasion the praises for his leadership in the development of Jackson College from 1911-27, President Hubert also had to bear his share of criticism. Some people perceived him as an educational statesman; others in the black community felt that he lacked time for less educated people, and that he could have effected change more rapidly. E. W. Banks, alumnus of Jackson State and former board member (and pioneer businessman in the city of Jackson for more that fifty years), stated that President Hubert exhibited a "rare sense of independence; was a clear thinker, played no favorites and was very outspoken. He ignored the whites who found his personality a little rash. There were some blacks who resented his attitudes but respected his program."[28]

The pressures had become greater over the years and Hubert's critics would not let go. The demands for Jackson College to "deliver" increased annually. The lack of sufficient operating funds augmented by the demands of faculty to be compensated for what they had given up elsewhere, the low economic status of the parents who barely survived financially in a state whose one economic product was cotton, the increased enrollment which took its toll on the buildings pointed to progressive physical deterioration and all began to weigh heavily on President Hubert.

From 1924, when the first degree was conferred, to 1927 thirteen students had earned the A.B. degree. In 1924 Annie Mae Brown McGhee; 1925, Richie A. Hudson and Mary G. Whiteside (deceased November, 1977). The graduates of the class of 1926 were Zee Alfin Anderson Barron, Commodore D. Higgins, Maude T. Alexander Jackson, and Walter A. Reed, Jr. The graduating class of 1927 listed six students: Joseph Jackson, Vera I. King, Luther J. Marshall, Hazel B. McDonald, William A. Shirley, and Charles D. Westbrooks.

President Hubert raised the standards of Jackson College and expanded the curriculum to a new level. The Theology Department, granting the degrees of both Bachelor of Arts and Bachelor of Science, was not phased out. Instead, the department was strengthened by the addition of competetent faculty who extended their services to the Ministers' and Bible Institutes.

Concomitantly with the students' engagment in academic and performance activities was the enjoyment of athletics and other recreational pursuits.

On September 19, 1927, Hubert resigned and accepted the presidency of Langston University in Oklahoma. The trustees accepted his resignation effective October 1, 1927. The board sent a resolution to the president expressing appreciation for his long and faithful administration in effecting a program that "developed from a high school to an established college that won a high place among Negro colleges of the State."[29]

Looking back at his presidency of Jackson College ten years later, Hubert could say with satisfaction:

> ... from this distance certain things come to prominence which at that time were not so evident; it was really a transition period in Negro education in Mississippi. My going to Jackson College marked a change in the general policy of the Home Mission Society of New York in the placing of Negroes at the heads of its institutions in the South. This was the first instance in which a Negro was actively placed in authority as president.
>
> Prior to my going to Jackson, the institution was really doing high school work. The faculty was recognized, placing capable Negro men and women on the staff from the best institutions; the courses of study lengthened and strengthened others added and the college formed and authorized. During the period there was a tremendous lift in the ideals and the aspirations of the youth of the state. The bringing into the state of cultural, well educated men and women as teachers inspired local teachers as well as students in large numbers.[30]

Having worked closely with President Hubert, Professor Dansby was saddened at the president's resignation: "Not only was the personality of the man a means of commanding admiration, but also his many achievements were vital links in the building of that powerful chain of developments in the college during its fifty years of existence."[31]

CHAPTER V

A CHARGE TO KEEP
WE MOVE FORWARD FROM HERE

The Administration of President Budey Baldwin Dansby, 1927–1940

THE 1927–28 ACADEMIC YEAR ushered in a new administration but not a new face. The presidency of Budey Baldwin Dansby, a member of the first black faculty under the previous administration, was far different from his service as dean of men and teacher of mathematics and Greek. President Dansby took up the torch and labored to improve Jackson College programs and physical plant.

The grandson of a slave, Dansby knew the value and necessity of education for his people. From 1911–23, he worked with President Hubert. For a short while, he left Jackson College and accepted a position in the Mississippi Department of Education as assistant state supervisor of Negro schools. Three years later, he became the recipient of a General Education Board Fellowship grant of $1,500 to enter the University of Chicago where he pursued graduate study. When he completed the academic year, a representative of the American Baptist Home Mission Society approached Dr. Dansby offering him the presidency of Jackson College. Dansby accepted the invitation because he felt that he could be of service to the people of Mississippi, declining at the same time the presidency of Virginia Union University.

The Committee on Education of the American Baptist Home Mission Society voted on September 19, 1927, to enter into contract with Dansby as acting president.[1] However, the Board of Trustees of Jackson College reconsidered and on October 10, 1927, appointed Dansby president effective October 1, 1927.[2] The board held that Dansby had already proved himself to be capable. As a vital link in this historical continuity, Dansby's creative genius was what the institution needed. The invaluable experience he had gained as state Rosenwald school building agent under the Department of Education prepared Dansby, with his colleagues, to formulate the kind of programs that Mississippians needed.

Cognizant of Dr. Dansby's familiarity with the internal aspects of Jackson College, the academic community accepted his presidency with feelings of joy.

Dansby was born April 17, 1879 in Hogansville, Georgia, near Atlanta, a farming district with limited educational opportunities. To secure better educational advantages, his parents, William and Eliza Dansby, enrolled him in Atlanta Baptist Seminary (now Morehouse College). Completing his education from elementary school to college, he was awarded the Bachelor of Arts degree with a major in mathematics. Immediately after graduation (at which he was valedictorian), Dansby began to teach mathematics at Morehouse. A year later he was appointed as head teacher of mathematics and language in the Florida (St. Augustine) Normal College, an institution formerly known as Jacksonville Baptist Academy.

During Dr. Dansby's movement to the presidency, philanthropic agencies from the North continued to come to the aid of many black colleges in the South. These efforts to provide charity ceased with the advent of the 1929 depression. As a result, many black schools discontinued some of their programs. Others merged and still others ceased to exist. Under these conditions, President Dansby was bracing himself to become the helmsman who would pilot Jackson College out of deeply troubled waters of the Great Depression.

As an officer of the Department of Education, Dansby had had an opportunity to assess firsthand the needs of the blacks in the state, their low economic status, and their relationship with Jackson College in terms of how the school could help them get ahead in every facet of personal and social life. His first act of service to local teachers was to initiate extension programs for them. Black teachers were in desperate need of upgrading themselves and reorienting their experiences to fit the times. Following the lead of neighboring Alcorn College, he initiated for them a program that hopefully would ground them in their professions.

During the first few months of Dansby's administration, more than $4,000 in debts gave rise to serious questions. Inefficient bookkeeping compounded the plight: "The financial predicament of the college . . . became a sound force that impelled the college to take a specific direction, and in this institutional movement every individual associated with it was influenced one way or the other. This sound force of financial problems was the medium that tested the capabilities of all personnel."[3]

The Committee on Education reviewed a letter dated February 4, 1928, from President Dansby regarding the $4,000 inherited debt, a large sum of money at the time. The debt was traced to an unauthorized purchase of an organ which the committee later validated with the understanding that the needed money would be raised by the faculty of the Music Department of the college. In an effort to surmount some of the institution's financial hurdles, President Dansby initiated the College Budget Drive. A "get acquainted with the college" program became an all-out campaign to strengthen the fiscal office and assure supporters of the soundness of the school.[4] The blacks responded and contributed more than $1,700. These contributions represented not only financial help but the assurance that the community stood behind Dansby. This financial crisis at the beginning of President Dansby's administration often made him have second thoughts about accepting employment at Jackson College over other more lucrative offers. His guiding motto in troubled times was "A charge to keep: we move forward from here."

Since Dr. Dansby had been elevated to the presidency, the post of dean of the college had become vacant. Henry T. Sampson, teacher of mathematics, remained in that position until 1930 when he was appointed head teacher of the faculty. In 1932 Sampson was awarded a fellowship by the General Education Board to study one year at the University of Chicago. In August 1933, the degree of Master of Science in Mathematics was conferred upon him. Upon his return to Jackson College, Sampson was appointed dean of the college.

Sustained by Dean Henry T. Sampson and many other faculty members, President Dansby pushed on toward his goals of improving programs at Jackson College. His perseverance toward his goals was not always accepted by everyone on his team. Several voices began to speak out against Dansby's leadership. One example can be seen in a letter written by faculty member Oswell A. Combs. Having been refused promotion, this Latin and English professor wrote Dr. George Hovey on August 24, 1928, stating that President Dansby had "ill will against him."[5] Upon investigation, Dr. Hovey responded that Combs' teaching methods had also been criticized by President Hubert and others who visited his classes. Under the circumstances, Combs was forced to vacate his teaching duties at Jackson College. Such treatment was quite a shock to Combs, because he had served as acting president of nearby Campbell College during 1920-21. Hence, with deep feeling generating against Dr. Dansby, several persons called on Dr. Hovey to chastise the president.

In 1928, Dr. Hovey called Dr. Dansby to task, requesting that he review both his and Dr. Hubert's records with respect to the handling of society funds and outside contributions. The matter was soon clarified by proper documentation and explanations from Dansby.

To help combat the impact of the Depression, President Dansby in 1929 proposed a possible Jackson-Natchez College merger. He informed Hovey that on May 18, 1929, a committee of six men headed by Dr. Joseph T. Patton, executive secretary of the American Church Institute for Negroes, headquartered in New York City, had presented to him plans to merge several institutions in Mississippi. Chief among them were three Methodist and Episcopalian black schools. Campbell College in Jackson was to relocate to Okolona. The respective church bishops with Bishop Bratton (white) of the Episcopal Church taking active part were present and urged the Utica Normal School, the Okolona School, and the presidents of Jackson and Campbell colleges to examine the idea of organizing these schools into combined units of services and costs.

President Dansby advised Dr. Hovey that his primary concern was that the plan proposing the withdrawal of Campbell College from its present site, diagonally across from Jackson College, made

THE ADMINISTRATION OF B. B. DANSBY

Mrs. B. B. Dansby

Class Picture 1931

Senior College Class for Bachelor of Arts Degree 1931
Front row—left-right—R. P. Williams, Beatrice Rice, Alice Thomas, Mayne Pendleton, Marcus Williams. Top row—left-right—O. W. Ford, Harry Ward, Julia Clark, C. N. Buchanan, Jack Young.

Class of 1933

Class of 1935

College & High School Graduates

French Club

Lyre Club—1925

Jackson College Orchestra—Frederick Hall, Director

Jackson College Orchestra—Kermit Holly, Sr., Director
Miriam Dansby Johnson at the Organ

The Jackson College Choir

Quartet: Left-right—unidentified, C. Stewart, Beatrice Hope Peters, and Helen Washington.

it necessary and imperative that Jackson College take over the property. As the reader will discover later in this volume, the purchase of the property did not become a reality until more than thirty years later. Dansby recommended an appraisal of the Campbell College property. The committee had almost been sworn to secrecy—that no publicity be given the ideas before definite steps had been taken by authorities for the transfer of the property. Hovey received the idea of purchasing the Campbell property with enthusiasm.

During a 1929 summer turmoil, Dr. Hovey, still secretary of education of the American Baptist Home Mission Society, made new complaints regarding the bookkeeping errors in the accounts of Jackson College. Miss Kathreen H. Simons, bookkeeper, wrote Hovey disclaiming and discounting her errors. The full impact of the bookkeeper's response can be gathered from her total missive:

Upon returning from my vacation—Mr. Dansby handed me your letter of September 5, asking me to locate and correct a seeming mistake. I am answering your letter because it contains a very personal reference to me, the bookkeeper.

Mistakes, of course, are made—no one is infallible—but to say the least, Dr. Hovey, your letter is very inconsistent and insinuative, especially in the last paragraph.

I have no apologies to make whatever, but I want to say this: during my three years here, I believe I have been scrupulously careful in attending to the business of Jackson College, and trying to have accounts and reports as accurate as possible. It is a part of me to be methodical and careful and painstaking, and I believe I am at least, honorable. When my reports were not according to form, and you offered a correction or a suggestion, I welcomed them and made the next one better; but recently, it seems that you are given to finding mistakes when there are none. I do not object to explaining things and I want to correct my mistakes—but it does seem that your secretary might have been able to recall and refer you to a correspondence that would have obviated your writing as in this letter of September 5th. You are a hard task-master.

Why, I would be stupid indeed to make a deduction in the Society's check, knowing that it must come back to you in the report, and that I must make a receipt for it before it is deposited. You give me credit for having little sense or intelligence. I have nothing to cover up, Dr. Hovey, but if I wished to play with accounts of Jackson College, certainly I would not tamper with the Society's check. And again, if I were making such mistakes as you say—'many other mistakes of which we *cannot* know', there would of necessity be shortages somewhere and someone would be complaining. Is it not so? And as technical and detailed as this system is—it would be pretty difficult for one to get away with anything. I lay no claim to such cleverness.

And has it ever occurred to you that I am actually doing twelve month's work and receiving pay for ten? When I return here September 1st, I am required to take up the work beginning July 1st, write up the books for July and August and make reports for the work across the summer. I have done this for three years and said nothing. The business phase of this school makes great demands upon one; it is exacting, technical, detailed, and my work day is considerably longer than the others—yet comparatively, I am paid less than any one else. It is very unfair—then add to this your letter of recent date—certainly, it does not tend towards one's peace of mind and happiness.[6]

The summer of 1929 was a trying one because President Dansby found it difficult to meet the payroll. Meanwhile, the report on Jackson College from the United States Bureau on Education by William Tyler to Dr. Hovey stated that Jackson College was one of the best educational institutions in the state for Negroes. If its plight were as bad as it was stated, Tyler noted, the Negroes were bound to suffer.[7] In this same letter, Tyler referred to the college physician, Dr. A. J. Thomas, as a "bad check artist" who had allegedly misrepresented himself and the institution in false reports. Allegedly, Dr. Thomas reported to the Century Life Insurance Company that a woman was not pregnant at a time when she actually was. His alleged carelessness resulted in the death of the lady. On another occasion Dr. Thomas reported to Universal Life Insurance Company that he examined a person who was not even present in the state. Still again, Dr. Thomas reported to Universal Life that a woman whom he was treating for cancer was in good physical condition. Tyler stated that President Dansby had been apprised of Dr. Thomas' actions and had promised a thorough investigation. Thus Jackson College remained under close scrutiny in every department, and attention was focused sharply upon the inadequacies of the institution.

The library was also woefully out of date and needed the expenditure of at least $10,000 to make it an up-to-date facility which could adequately serve the college. The president had failed repeatedly to employ a trained librarian who would give full time to this service. The facilities of the college for the teaching of science likewise were very limited and needed the expenditure of a considerable sum of money. There was a great need for faculty members to acquire the higher degrees if Jackson College were to become a standardized college that could render the highest services.[8]

In no uncertain terms, Hovey stated that the society had no thoughts of Jackson College as a standard college. He stated that it took time to develop a real college and Jackson College would under the administration of President Dansby make far more progress, given a chance to do so. Hovey also stated explicitly that the American Baptist Home Mission Society was in no position to increase appropriations to any considerable extent to Jackson College. Moreover, he expressed his disappointment in the failure of Jackson College to merge or at least to affiliate with the Natchez school.

He stated that President Dansby had the welfare of the college at heart and the goodwill and friendship of educators in general. Further, Hovey said: "I have great hopes that within a very few years, Jackson College will have an enrollment and equipment and faculty which will justify its recognition as a standard college; but to be frank, I do not see any likelihood of our Society contributing the money to bring about the results at the present."[9]

Dr. Hovey's communication to Dr. Dansby in response to a review of the college's programs addressed itself to some specific suggestions that Hovey felt would alleviate some of the college's inadequacies. Hovey felt the entrance requirements at Jackson College should be more in line with those of other colleges and require "conditions" to be removed by the end of the freshman year, or at least the end of the sophomore year. He also thought that not more than 45 semester hours should be allowed except under specific conditions. For departments, Hovey focused the importance of securing heads who had post-graduate degrees; in case a professor did not have such a degree, he should attend summer school and work until he secured it.

No annual appropriation for the purchase of new books was regarded as an unsatisfactory condition for the rating of a college department if the school were to move up in its rating.

In an effort to assist the state school authorities in Mississippi and Louisiana in developing a well-organized statewide program for the training of black teachers, N. C. Newbold, state superintendent of public instruction, Raleigh, North Carolina, was appointed chairman of the Committee on Teacher Training for Negro Schools in Mississippi and Louisiana. In appraising the situation of Jackson College, his report of January 4, 1930, stated that President Dansby was making a serious effort to run a good college, but the financial difficulties under which he was working were grave. In fact, they were of such magnitude that Newbold requested Dr. Hovey's permission to appeal to a group of Baptist leaders in Mississippi for financial support. Newbold strongly felt that the Education Department officials of Mississippi and the society could meet such a group and point out to them the needs of Jackson College. The facts were that unless some group put up the money, the institution was going to fall further behind the other colleges of the state. Yet, the college had tremendous opportunities to serve not only the Negro groups of the state but Mississippi as a whole.[10]

To help counteract the financial strain, Jackson College, in cooperation with ten other colleges located in neighboring states, promoted the annual continuation school for ministers which resulted in the National Ministers Institute, organized October 10, 1929, by Dr. Hovey, who was still secretary of education of the American Baptist Home Mission Society. Seeking to improve the quality of ministers within the state, the National Ministers Institute set out to find support. Mississippi headquarters of the official branch office was at Jackson, with other centers in Forest, Laurel, New Hebron, Newton, and Waynesboro.

The schools were opened on a three-day basis under the directorship of the dean of theology at Jackson College. President Dansby served as state director. The faculty was composed of the best trained ministers in each area: C. W. Frisby, area director; J. J. Overstreet, club leader and director of club leaders; W. J. Barlow, Shubuta; George Berry, Crystal Springs; A. H. Hardaway, Enterprise; W. M. Mallory, Richton; A. D. Purnell, Canton; and W. L. Varnado, Jackson.[11]

The program was designed for three years and upon completion the ministerial students received a diploma. The membership of the Institute was 91. These additional students represented an increase of $650 toward the budget of the school. However, this amount made only a small difference in the growing debts incurred by Jackson College. A series of projects was begun in an effort to find revenue to offset some of its debts.

During 1928, the State Department created and partially sponsored a College Grade Grammar School designed to train teachers for elementary and high schools. This in itself was a separate entity from the school's extension course which spanned the entire year. Upon the recommendation of the administration, a two-year teacher program was instituted in an effort to help students with limited funds to earn credits and secure a certificate.

Dean H. T. Sampson proposed and implemented a two-year curriculum. To complete the requirements for the certificate, there were nine courses in education, three courses in biology, one course in music, three courses in English, two courses in sociology, and one course in nature study.[12] Other programs were also implemented.

Organized in 1926 under the directorship of Miss F. O. Alexander, the Practice School fitted into a program covering a period of two years. Its stated function was to provide competent teachers for the elementary and high schools of the state and to offer the necessary professional training for supervising positions. Graduates of the program were to receive, upon recommendation, a state teacher's certificate which would exempt them from examination for two years. If the certificate were renewed, it would become a permanent license at the end of five years.

April 11, 1929, Dr. Dansby presented to the board a proposal to introduce the quarter system. The purpose of this academic calendar was to divide the nine-month school year into three equal parts of twelve weeks each. In September 1929, the board approved the new academic schedule which was to remain in operation for the next four decades. The rationale for such a change was to allow farming students three opportunities per year to enroll in college. The economic survival of the students' parents depended on the success of the cotton yield. Since more emphasis was placed on crop yield for the family's survival than on academic pursuits, many students interrupted their studies to pick cotton during the fall months. With the quarter system, a three-month period away from college would offer students the option to withdraw during certain months and then return to school the rest of the year.

This arrangement necessitated a change in the calendar of paying fees. The fall quarter registration fee of $10 was unchanged. High school tuition was $12 per semester. Board assessment of $16 per month was unchanged. For the college students, registration was set at $10 per year, tuition (12 weeks) at $16.67 per quarter. Books, studio and laboratory fees were extra.

The general admission requirements were not altered; however, the descriptions of course work and the number of quarter hours needed in accordance with specific requirements were changed. The original 120 semester hours were converted to 180 quarter hours for graduation.

The 1928-29 catalog stated that the degree of Bachelor of Arts was conferred upon students who had earned 120 hours credit, 15 of which had to come from each of three groups: (1) rhetoric and composition; ancient language and literature; modern language and literature; (2) mathematics; astronomy; physics; chemistry; geology; botany; (3) history; philosophy; political science; sociology; political economy; education. With the introduction of the quarter system, the 1929-30 catalog modified the statement holding that credits must include 15 hours from either of two groups: (1) arts and natural sciences; (2) social sciences.[13] Electives included Introduction to the New Testament, offered during the freshman year, and Teachings of Jesus, during the junior year.

This addition to the requirements heightened the faculty's cry for library resources to supplement classroom teaching. Throughout the tenure of each preceding president, references were made in the college catalogues regarding the establishment and maintenance of a "good library." Records indicate that during the 1929-30 academic year, Barbara Zenobia Benton, who earned the B.S. Degree from Bishop College, was instructor in high school sciences- and mathematics, and keeper of the library.[14] During the 1930-31 school term, Frank L. Stanley, who earned an A.B. Degree from Atlanta University, was instructor of English, and also served in the library.[15]

During the year 1931-32, the library was organized and books were catalogued for the first time using the Dewey Decimal

Classification System. The absence of a trained librarian forced the administration to seek the services of a professional librarian from Mississippi College in Clinton to catalogue the collection. During the academic year 1931-32, S. R. Tillinghast, head of the Social Science Department, and Velena Willie Betts together were responsible for making accessible to the students the library collection. Despite sharp concern for full-time service in the library, it was not until the academic year 1932-33 that the board of the American Baptist Home Mission Society named a librarian. Velena Willie Betts accepted the job at a salary of $729 per year. Former assistant to Tillinghast, Miss Betts had earned an A.B. Degree from Jackson College in 1930, and had taught English in the high school. She had also attended Hampton's Library School under the direction of Florence Curtis. Even after fifty years, the library was still inadequate. The administration sought finally to augment the holdings and the Rosenwald Foundation agreed in 1929 to underwrite 50 percent of the cost in the construction of a library. Because of the desperate need for a library, the faculty organized themselves and, with their classes, raised $3,000. Fifty percent of the $3,000 was used to purchase books for the library and 50 percent went for the erection of a small grandstand for the college.[16]

In the spring of 1932, the Board of Managers of the American Baptist Home Mission Society engaged in a serious study of the program of work carried on by the society for the purpose of determining its future direction. As a result of the study, they approached the officers of the Board of Education to ascertain if they would be willing to take over supervision of the Negro colleges then under the direction of the society. The Board of Managers was convinced that these schools had ceased to be primarily missionary institutions, and had become educational institutions which were outside the "territory" of missionary activity.

Jackson College, in the midst of its financial crisis, experienced many episodes that would seemingly close the doors of the institution forever; but somehow, there was always the little ray of hope. Dr. Dansby recalled to the writer his daily prayers, "Give us this day our daily bread." This period in the college's history was indeed filled with many doubts about the continuation of the school. On April 5, 1933, W. F. Bond called a meeting of the local Trustee

Board and had Dr. Frank Smith announce that, because of financial difficulties, the society could no longer grant funds to support Jackson College and voted not to reopen the school September, 1934. Nevertheless, President Dansby was given the option to continue operating the college until the committee formally closed the school. This decision shocked the president, the faculty, and the entire constituency of the college.

Reviewing Dr. Dansby's petition for appropriations for the academic year 1932-33, the Committee on Education approved $27,512.80 with the distinct understanding that the total liability of the society would not exceed $12,000.00. Income and expenditures examined during the meeting played a leading part in the decision. The record of the 1933 college budget is revealing:

	INCOME	EXPENDITURES
Education	$20,056.50	$18,247.50
Board and Rooms	5,325.00	6,967.00
Laundry	125.00	105.00
Bookstore	675.00	670.00
Farm	450.00	320.00
Athletics	500.00	435.00
Permanent Improvements	250.00	250.00
Miscellaneous and Designated	131.00	131.00
	$27,512.50	$27,125.50

ADMINISTRATION

B. B. Dansby	$ 2,600.00	
Roy B. Ware, Bookkeeper	1,130.00	
Miss Velena W. Betts, Office Asst. & Librarian	729.00	

PRACTICE SCHOOL

Miss Josie M. Turner		$ 720.00
Miss Latie Wilson		729.00

INSTRUCTOR—COLLEGE

Miss Doretha W. Jones		$ 1,242.00
Charles A. Proctor		1,170.00
Augustus A. Latting		1,035.00
Miss Mary G. Whiteside		1,170.00
Timothy R. Wells		1,050.00

	INCOME	EXPENDITURES
THEOLOGY		
Rev. Clarence W. Frisby		$ 1,050.00
HIGH SCHOOL		
Rev. Clarence W. Frisby		$ 1,050.00
Kermit W. Holly		787.00
Miss Marie A. Young		900.00
Mrs. Mamie E. Dansby		720.00

In its decision not to reopen the school in the fall of 1934, the society was closing a record of courage and service to its missionary activities in the South.

The American Baptist Home Mission Society had entered the field of founding schools for the freedmen soon after the close of the war in 1865. At one time or another, it had been active in at least thirteen schools and colleges. It gradually withdrew from one school after another for various reasons until, in 1934, its supervision was limited to five colleges, though it held trust funds for several others. The colleges that were under the aegis of the society in 1934 were Morehouse College at Atlanta, Georgia, rated by the Southern Association of Colleges and Secondary Schools as ClasssA; Bishop College at Marshall, Texas; Virginia Union University at Richmond, Virginia, rated as Class B; Benedict College at Columbia, South Carolina; and Jackson College at Jackson, Mississippi.

Jackson College had suffered from severe competition with rival schools. Though there had been a slight increase in enrollment the previous year, the students were able to pay very little. Marked decreases in the number of students living in the dormitory, due in large measure to the need of extensive repairs, further decreased the college income. As an emergency measure, the dining room had to be closed and a few of the boarding students took their meals at the president's home. The treasurer's report pointed up the fact that since "a very high grade institution only six miles away is meeting the educational needs of Mississippi, the Society felt justified in view of all the circumstances in withdrawing its annual appropriations." The institution referred to was Tougaloo College north of Jackson.

Jackson College had been offered to the Negro Baptists of Mississippi, but they had declined to accept it on the grounds that they could not meet the requirements set by the American Baptist Home Mission Society. In an effort to save the college, the major educational activities were directed toward teacher training for in-service teachers and in-service ministers.

At a board meeting January 16, 1933, the Committee on Education voted to request the secretary of the Department of Education of the United States to correspond with the Department of Education of the State of Mississippi with a view toward transferring the property of Jackson College to the state of Mississippi "as a teacher training college for Negro teachers."[17]

Four years before, Dr. P. H. Easom, officer of the Mississippi Department of Education, had advocated a normal school for the training of black teachers holding that, in spite of the fact that about 54 percent of the total educable population of the state was Negro, there was only one state-supported institution for teacher training—which did not meet the needs of the state. It seems that Mississippi should have taken more steps in this direction.

A letter sent to the State Board of Education on May 17, 1933, expressed the attitude of the American Baptist Home Mission Society Finance Committee regarding the proposed transfer of the school to this board. Responding in a sympathetic vein, the Board of Education approved in general the idea and awaited a definite proposal from the Home Mission Society authorizing the school for the exclusive purpose of training rural and elementary teachers for the small black schools of the state.

In spite of the fact that the state had little interest in assuming control and support of the college, Dansby tried hard to force the issue. According to Dr. Dansby, Mississippi Negroes, for whom the school was established, failed to put back into the school the money and the support they should have; therefore, the society was going to sell the property. The society intended to sell the school, take the proceeds, and set up a school for blacks in some other state that would support it. In a folksy manner, Dansby related how he tried to secure state support:

Well, I tried, and I tell you the man who supported me... W. F. Bonds. He said he went to Bilbo and Bilbo said "no." He didn't want any Negro College up here in town. He said Negroes would be ready to take his job if you put them up here in town.

You just lay low, Bilbo is not in favor unless the school is somewhere way down upon the river like Alcorn. Then he might get behind it.... The Society gave me a letter and said if I could get the State or some strong corporation to support the school for Negroes, the Society would give it to them. I got that over to Bilbo, he said, "No, we don't need a school, but we'd like to have the grounds and building out there."[18]

Reacting to the allusion to Alcorn College, Dansby pointed up that Alcorn's job was to train teachers in agriculture, home economics, and trades, county home demonstration agents, county farm agents, and high school teachers. There remained that task of training thousands of teachers for the then one-, two-, and three-room schools found all over Mississippi. He saw a direct need for training teachers in the rural areas in Mississippi. Dansby insisted that this proposal would in no way conflict with or duplicate the efforts of Alcorn College.

On June 10, 1934, Dr. Dansby wrote a letter to Dr. Frank Smith, secretary for the American Baptist Home Mission Society Education and Missions, announcing that he was working to enlist interested citizens who would help financially to keep Jackson College open for another year. He said citizens of Jackson regarded the educational work of Jackson College in the past, present, and future of so great importance that they expressed themselves as favoring a citywide financial campaign for Jackson College. He reinforced his statements by enclosures from the two Jackson dailies which reflected the interest of the citizenry in saving the college.

Dansby's letter further focused upon the fact that he had held conferences with the Jackson city fathers, the mayor and two commissioners, the city Board of Education, the regular Board of Trustees of Jackson College, and the editors of the two daily papers of Jackson; in every case a very favorable attitude was expressed towards joining hands in sponsoring a drive for the college. Further hope was expressed that in two years, Jackson College would be presented to the Mississippi legislature for a state teacher's college for negroes.

The forcefulness of President Dansby's appeal persuaded the society to delay its withdrawal from the college and make new arrangements to stop the inevitable foreclosure. An advisory board of trustees, fourteen men and women who would pledge themselves to operate and support the college, was organized. The members were to be educated Christian leaders—men and women, white and black, in and around Jackson who would pledge themselves to operate and support Jackson College as a corporation under the laws of the state of Mississippi, and submit the incorporation to the society for approval. The name of the American Baptist Home Mission Society was to be deleted from the original charter and the new or amended charter was to be submitted for approval so as to free the society of future responsibilities. All current financial obligations of the college were to be settled and cancelled.

As soon as President Dansby was given the signal that he could, with a corporate board, keep the school open, he immediately began to search for funds in an effort to meet the expenditures of the college. The Jackson Chamber of Commerce played a vital role in formulating a citizens' committee whose primary function was to assist in raising funds for the college. Hence, Dansby presented the case of Jackson College to the Jackson Chamber of Commerce Board of Directors on June 22, 1934. To them, he explained the plans and attitude of the American Baptist Home Mission Society towards the future operation of Jackson College. Before the meeting, he had begged the society to advise him fully what he should say to the Chamber of Commerce as to the society's plans for Jackson College and the attitude of the society toward a citywide drive for the school. He had also asked what the hope might be to request money from some philanthropic board outside the state.

The reply from the society, dated June 19, 1934, was both negative and discouraging. While a million-dollar institution was in jeopardy of being phased out, the society saw fit to chide Dr. Dansby over such trivialities as the installation of gas service and the sale of a truck. The sale of the vehicle was given as much consideration as the closing of the school: "With the closing of the school, there will be no need for the truck and you are authorized to sell the truck at the best possible price and send the money to our organization here in New York."

The chairman of the board, W. F. Bond, immediately informed the local Board of Trustees of the decision of the society to discontinue the institution. Dr. Dansby reflected most candidly on his immediate reaction to the communication. The decision was a severe disappointment, so definite, so final. He was cognizant of the waning support, but not of the unqualified decision to close the college. He was even angered by the society's resolution.

Having accustomed himself to setbacks and disappointments, and yet determined to accept each new challenge in an effort to preserve an institution that had "weathered the storm for more than a half century," Dr. Dansby appealed to the society once more begging it not to close the doors of the institution, pleading for another opportunity to carry on.

While Dr. Dansby was away in Chicago raising funds for the college, a colleague, Augustus A. Latting, head of the Social Science Department and acting dean in the absence of H. T. Sampson who was on study leave, granted the seniors the "unthinkable" permission to hold a bridge party on campus. Latting told Mrs. Dansby, dean of women, of his intent. Dean Latting had also abandoned the requirements for girls' uniforms, which consisted of blue skirts, white middy blouses, and cotton stockings. With such a display of liberality the juniors approached him for permission to hold a dance. Heretofore, students were prohibited from participating in such "worldly" pursuits as bridge-playing and dancing, since it was felt by many that these activities distracted from the effort to build a Christian character. Dean Latting described his reaction to the event many years later:

> I didn't see anything wrong with it. They were dancing at Alcorn and Tougaloo. So, I sent an order to the Dean of Women and gave them permission to have a dance. They had no hall or any place to do it; so, I let them have it in the women's dormitory right in the hall... you see I played the saxophone when I was in college, so I joined the little combo. We stopped at midnight.

When Dr. Dansby returned to the campus, he called a faculty meeting and said he heard that the campus had shifted since he left and this was going against the tradition of the school. He did not call any names, but he said that certain members of the faculty were instigating.... Well, I immediately told Dr. Dansby in the presence of the faculty that in my opinion, Jackson College was behind the times and it had to move forward and that unless it moved forward, kept pace with things that were happening in the collegiate world not only in Jackson but throughout the country that the school would disintegrate and die.... President Dansby said he decided to abolish everything and he wanted a motion.

A motion was made and seconded by Mrs. Dansby but the faculty failed to back it. Learning of what had happened in the faculty meeting, the students decided to stage a walk-out of classes and to strike at commencement. At Dansby's request, Latting prevailed upon the students to return to class and appear at the commencement.

Despite his efforts during the summer following commencement exercises, Latting received a letter from Dr. Dansby stating that, in the interest of economy, the Social Science Department had been abolished. Latting then resigned his post at Jackson College to take a position as instructor at LeMoyne College in political science and economics. He subsequently went into law practice where he served until his death in 1975.[19]

Having settled the internal troubles caused by students, Dr. Dansby turned his attention to financial problems and the issue of closing the college. One of his most trusted friends in the society was W. F. Bond, state superintendent of education. In an address to the faculty on September 17, 1934, he held that: "Jackson College has the best possibilities of becoming the most ideal place for the training of Negro school teachers in the State of Mississippi. The possibilities being in the college's unique location in the State, its faculties, and its distinguished reputation of having trained many of the best teachers in the State." Bond worked tirelessly with Dansby in carrying out the requirements of the society; however, it was the latter who had to identify the persons who were willing to serve on the board. Those who were finally chosen represented some of the leading citizens in Jackson and in Mississippi.

Dr. Dansby characterized the new board members as "stalwarts, as giants in their respective professions." Their names were sent to the society for approval: Dr. C. L. Barnes, dentist; E. W.

Banks, director and owner of Peoples Funeral Home, Inc.; Miss F. O. Alexander, Jackson College and State Department of Education; W. F. Bond, state superintendent of education; J. H. Coates, president, Universal Life Insurance Company; W. W. Blackburn, executive secretary, Mississippi Teachers Association; John W. Dixon, former treasurer of the Jackson College National Alumni Association; Reverend C. A. Greer, pastor of Farish Street Baptist Church; P. K. Lutkin, president, Lamar Life Insurance Company; W. B. McCarty, president, McCarty-Holman Wholesale Grocery; Dr. J. W. Provine, educator and Baptist leader; Dr. S. D. Redmond, lawyer and real estate dealer; Judge J. Morgan Stevens, lawyer; Miss Fannie Traylor, executive secretary, Women's Missionary Union. Among this board were eight blacks and six whites. The racial cooperation was so visible in its efforts to effect a viable program for the existence of the college that many other community leaders caught its spirit and rallied to the cause of the survival of Jackson College.

At the suggestion of some of the citizenry of Jackson and on the recommendations of the new board, a Bill was drafted in 1936 and presented to the Mississippi legislature during the administration of Governor Hugh L. White. The Bill recommended that the state assume the support of the institution. When the Bill failed, local and regional cohesiveness generated even a greater effort to keep the college in operation. In a characteristic mood, the alumni shifted into gear to move behind the president and pledged their support.

The first favorable sign that Jackson College would survive grew out of the correspondence dated January 6, 1936, from Dr. Dansby to Dr. Frank W. Padelford, executive secretary, Board of Education, Northern Baptist Convention, in which he stated that W. F. Bond, state superintendent of education and chairman of the Jackson College Board of Trustees, was going out of office January 20, 1936, but would remain as chairman of the board. During the then current session of the state Legislature, he would present the case of Jackson College.[20] Dr. Bond advised Dr. Padelford of his plans to try to get the state to take over the college as a training institution for Negro teachers.

At the close of the regular biennial session of the Mississippi legislature, Dr. Dansby reported to Dr. Padelford the very strong and determined efforts made in presenting the plight of Jackson College to the legislators. He added that the governor had said it was unwise at the time for the state to accept the offer as presented by the American Baptist Home Mission Society.[21]

Following the close of the legislature and its rejection of Dr. Dansby's proposal, a committee of prominent citizens approached the governor for a conference regarding the state's ownership of the college. Dr. Bond, who was present, believed that Governor White seemed amenable to the state's assuming control. The chairman of the College Committee of the Mississippi Senate further informed Bond that he could get the bill passed two years later at the next regular session of the legislature.[22] The immediate disposition of the school property was nebulous. Dr. Bond suggested to Dr. Padelford that the best solution would be to close the school down immediately unless the faculty was willing to operate it for whatever pay was available from student fees. Subsequent to Bond's report, Dansby had sent a special appeal to the society "begging" for monies to be expended for the desperately needed repairs and a sub-minimum budget for teacher salaries for the term 1936–37. In this itemized application of budget estimates, he listed the expenditures of $8,135; income from tuition, $3,500; registration fees, $250; library fees, $100; concerts, $100; graduation fees, $75; transcripts, $10; and alumni campaign, $500. President Dansby requested $3,600 of the total expenditures. The Board of Education approved $2,100. President Dansby applied for financial assistance to two foundations, the Slater Fund and the General Education Fund, but to no avail.[23] Despite the absence of any promise of support, Dansby vowed to continue to operate the college on the assumption that he could gain state support during the next legislative session.

During the summer session, on July 8, 1937, Governor Hugh White, Bishop Bratton of the Episcopal Church, Dr. P. H. Easom of the Mississippi Department of Education, and Dr. Bond visited Jackson College. After the visit, Governor White felt that it would be a good thing for the state to accept the property and operate it as a teacher training school for blacks. Dr. Easom, state agent for Negro education, was known to be in favor of transferring the college to state ownership. Easom would later write in an article,

"The Greatest Educational Needs in Mississippi," that according to the 1930 census, Mississippi had a population of 996,856 whites and 1,009,718 blacks. Easom estimated that to teach these children, the state had a staff of approximately 10,000 white teachers and 6,000 black teachers. His survey on the training of the black teachers showed that there were only 600 college graduates, approximately 2,400 who took college courses, and 3,000 below the college level. His story proved the unquestionable need to train black teachers. Easom proposed that the state take over Jackson College and operate it as a two-year teacher-training school, and further stated:

> ... Still more fortunately, one of the foundations of our country has offered to help bear the burden of this undertaking for a number of years by offering to give $30,000 per year on a fifty-fifty basis (that is $1.00 from the foundation for every dollar from the state) to help run this school. An additional offer by the same foundation is made to provide $40,000 to $60,000 for repairing and putting in usable condition the buildings of Jackson College. This amount could be used to match WPA funds and the plant could be put in first-class condition with no expenditure by the state. This same foundation offers to continue to appropriate funds from year to year to help run this school over a period of years.
> Here is Mississippi's greatest educational need today. Here is, also, a golden opportunity for meeting this need.
> "They that are well need not a physician, but they that are sick."[24]

However, when the Mississippi legislature convened in January 1938, it found itself once more unable to accept the proposal of the society to "take over" Jackson College. The legislature held that: (a) the authorities of the state land grant college (Alcorn A&M) claimed that they could do the same work which Jackson College proposed in a "new set-up"; (b) that Jackson College occupied too much territory in the city of Jackson; and (c) that Jackson College's buildings needed too much financial outlay on repairs to make them suitable for a modern plant. The issue became a country versus town problem; since more than two-thirds of the representatives and senators resided in the smaller towns and rural sections of the state.[25] The claims of Alcorn College carried the day in the legislature. The case for Alcorn College as the sole black public college was shortlived, however.

On May 30, 1938, Jackson College passed from the jurisdiction of the American Baptist Home Mission Society to that of the Board of Trustees of the college who amended the March 9, 1899, charter.[26] W. F. Bond, president, Dr. C. L. Barnes, secretary, and B. B. Dansby served as a committee of three to obtain the approval for the amendments to the charter of Jackson College. Attorney Greek L. Rice and W. W. Pierce, assistant attorney general, examined the document and stated that it was not in violation of the constitution and laws of the state or of the United States. On May 30, 1938, the Honorable Hugh White, governor of Mississippi, signed and affixed the seal of the state of Mississippi to the document.

On June 2, 1938, pursuant to the call of W. F. Bond, president of the Board of Trustees of Jackson College, the board, under the original charter of 1899, met for the purpose of reorganizing itself under the amended charter granted Jackson College on May 30. The new board, on a motion by Dr. J. W. Provine, seconded by Dr. C. L. Barnes, elected the following persons: Dr. S. D. Redmond, W. B. McCarty, W. W. Blackburn, P. K. Lutken, Fannie Traylor, J. W. Dixon, and J. H. Coates. Named trustees under the new charter were: W. F. Bond, Dr. C. L. Barnes, Reverend C. A. Greer, and Dr. R. B. Gunther. The following persons constituted the Executive Committee: W. F. Bond, W. B. McCarty, Dr. S. D. Redmond, Reverend C. A. Greer, and Dr. C. L. Barnes. This new Board of Trustees on June 13, 1938, signalled its willingness to accept the offer of the American Baptist Home Mission Society to transfer the property known as Jackson College to the Board of Trustees subject to the following conditions:

> That the American Baptist Home Mission Society will deed to the Trustees of Jackson College the property now known as Jackson College without any financial consideration;
> That the Board of Trustees of Jackson College will accept a deed containing a reversionary clause to the effect that if the property ceases to be used for Negro education, it shall revert to the American Baptist Home Mission Society;
> That the Board of Trustees of Jackson College shall assume responsibility for all obligations outstanding against Jackson College at the time of the execution of the deed and that the American Baptist Home Mission Society shall have no further responsibility for the college.

On June 20, 1938, the Finance Committee, Board of Managers, American Baptist Home Mission Society reviewed succinctly the events that spelled the agonies of President Dansby from the moment he assumed office.

The Society has held title since 1903 to a piece of property in the city of Jackson, Mississippi, comprising about 50 acres of land with six brick buildings and several farm buildings upon which has been conducted a school and college for the Negro people, known as Jackson College. In 1937, the Society offered to convey Jackson College to the State of Mississippi, provided the State Government would agree to conduct under its auspices a normal training school for training of Negro teachers. The Legislature of Mississippi refused to accept title to the property and to continue a school there, so the proposed transfer was dropped. Since the Board of Education assumed responsibility for the Negro colleges, an annual appropriation of $2,000.00 has been made to Jackson. The buildings are in such poor repair that several thousand dollars would be required to put them in safe condition.

The College was incorporated under the laws of the State of Mississippi on March 9, 1899, and the Articles of Incorporation were amended as of April 30, 1938.[27]

The Finance Committee voted that the personnel of the Board of Trustees was of a character that gave assurance that the college would be continued as a Christian educational institution for Negroes. The new board assumed full responsibility for the continued development of Jackson College. In addition, the board would be liable for any obligations the college had at the time of the execution of the deed and that the society or the Board of Education would have no further responsibility for the college. The committee voted that the assistant treasurer of the American Baptist Home Mission Society be authorized in the name of the society to convey to the Board of Trustees of Jackson College by bargain and sale a deed without consideration of the following described property situated in Hinds County, State of Mississippi, lying in Sections 8 and 9, Township 5, Range 1 East, with all of the furniture and appurtenances pertaining thereto: "All of the West half of the Northwest quarter of Section 9, which lies North of the Yazoo and Mississippi Valley Railroad; also all the East half of the Northeast quarter of the Section 8, which lies North of the said Railroad."[28]

The committee made it clear that from the time of receiving its "conveyance," the Board of Trustees of Jackson College had the obligation to forge ahead in its efforts to assure blacks of Mississippi opportunities to acquire education suitable for roles in the larger society.[29]

As soon as President Dansby was assured that he could, with the corporate Board keep the school open, he began seeking funds to meet the expenditures of the college. Several forces from both white and black camps combined to defeat the negative politics which had previously rejected the college. The feeling was that the college was a community—symbolic of its mission—education and development of a disadvantaged people. Leaders of the community urged everyone to respond regardless of their race, their color or their religious affiliation. The building up of the state could be done only by the members of both races being developed mentally, physically, and spiritually.[30] A great deal of assistance came from the Jackson Chamber of Commerce as they had the machinery to arouse additional sentiment and a positive attitude towards the salvaging of the college. The Alumni were a major catalytic agent that pledged their loyalty through some financial support and appreciation through resolutions to President Dansby for carrying through these years of hopelessness.

Jackson College and the Negro community also praised two very influential persons for their efforts in securing support for the college: Governor Paul B. Johnson, for his farsightedness, sympathy and his loyalty to the cause of freedom; and Mr. Tom Hederman, Sr., who in his own inimitable and silent way played a prominent part in the historical transition.[31]

Due to these combined efforts, in April 1940, the Mississippi legislature under the provisions of House Bill No. 722, 1940 regular session accepted Jackson College as a training school for black teachers and voted to provide a biennial appropriation of $20,000. Very specific stipulations narrowly set the mission for the sixty-three year old school: "TO HAVE AND TO HOLD the same unto the party of the second part, its successors and assigns forever *subject however, to the condition that said premises shall forever be used for and in connection with the education for Negroes, the party of the first part hereby reserving the right to re-enter said premises at any time hereafter upon breach of said condition."* "IN WITNESS WHEREOF, the party of the first part has caused its corporate seal to be hereunto affixed and these presents to be signed by its duly authorized officer the day and year first above mentioned. (signed) THE AMERICAN BAPTIST HOME MISSION SOCIETY by /s/ H. Estelle Hendry, ASSISTANT TREASURER"

The Board rejected the deed outright, holding that the society questioned the integrity of its willingness to fulfill the original mission of the college. In the final analysis, when the state informed the society on July 23, 1940, that the school would be named and function as the Mississippi Negro Training School, the society issued a quitclaim deed without reservations to the Board of Trustees of Institutions of Higher Learning. The mission of Dr. B. B. Dansby was complete. He had had a charge to keep and he had kept it by saving the school he had served as dean and instructor of mathematics before becoming president, registrar, and author of the college history.

On July 26, 1951, at the meeting of the Board of Trustees, a resolution was passed unanimously recognizing the retirement of Dr. Dansby, who had served Jackson State for forty years. Without doubt, Dansby had given the longest continuous period of service in the history of the college. In 1952, the B. Baldwin Dansby Hall of Expressive Arts was dedicated in his honor and it still stands as a signal of his unforgotten leadership.

Upon the recommendation of President John A. Peoples, Jr., the Board of Trustees of Institutions of Higher Learning, State of Mississippi, conferred upon Dr. Dansby the title of president emeritus of Jackson State College, 1967.

When asked in 1973 what he thought to have been his greatest achievement as president of Jackson College, Dr. Dansby responded simply: "I think the biggest thing that I did was to transfer the school from private hands to state hands whereas it could be tax supported."

The resolution of the Board of Trustees of State Institutions of Higher Learning, State of Mississippi, on Dr. Dansby's death echoed the same conviction:

WHEREAS, Dr. B. Baldwin Dansby, President Emeritus of Jackson State University, departed this life, at the age of ninety-six, on November 20, 1975, and

WHEREAS, Dr. Dansby served as president of Jackson College from 1927 to 1940, and during his tenure of office was responsible for the continued existence of this educational institution which was suffering from inadequate financial support during the depression years, and

WHEREAS, Dr. Dansby climaxed his administration in 1940 by arranging for the transfer of Jackson College from private control to the State system of education, and

WHEREAS, prior to becoming associated with Jackson College, Dr. Dansby had long been in the field of education, teaching at Morehouse College and Florida Memorial College and serving as Assistant State Supervisor of Negro Schools for the State Department of Education, and

WHEREAS, His devotion to his family, friends, and his participation in community affairs, as well as his loyal support of Jackson State University, will long be remembered.

NOW, THEREFORE BE IT RESOLVED That the Board of Trustees of State Institutions of Higher Learning does mourn the death of this body to his daughter, Mrs. Mariam Dansby Johnson, and his stepdaughter, Mrs. Ida Mahoon Olive.

BE IT FURTHER RESOLVED, That a copy of this resolution be spread upon the minutes of the Board of Trustees of State Institutions of Higher Learning and the appropriate copies be sent to his daughter, Mrs. Mariam Dansby Johnson, and his stepdaughter, Mrs. Ida Mahoon Olive.

Adopted this 20th day of November, 1975.[32]

In delivering the memorial address at the funeral services of President Emeritus Dansby, paying tribute to both the man and his dedication to Jackson State University, President John A. Peoples said:

In the Fall of 1911, God sent to this community his servant, B. Baldwin Dansby. This servant was a man whose attributes fulfilled all of the askings of that prayer: "God Send Us Men." For Dr. Dansby, as he became affectionately—yet respectfully known, was indeed a man with clear vision and a mind well equipped, both with formal training and profound wisdom. He was indeed a lover of truth and a hater of wrong. His record of service shows him to have been strong, and courageous yet patient and steadfast in his determination to carry out his mission as a worker in a vineyard where God has chosen to send him.[33]

Dr. Peoples assessed his predecessor's service to Mississippi by holding that, for sixty-four years, Dr. B. Baldwin Dansby served as a leader in many capacities.

Best known for his great and unequalified work as a teacher, administrator, president, and president emeritus of Jackson State University, there has never been, there is not now and, I think, there never will be another person whose life can be more indelibly identified with Jackson State University than Dr. B. Baldwin Dansby. *Who* can equal his wise, scholarly leadership? *Who* can equal his long, dedicated, fruitful service? And, *Who* can begin to equal the deep love he manifested for Jackson State University by his deeds as well as his words?[34]

In Dr. Peoples' words, Dr. Dansby was an inspiration to all those who had the good fortune to associate with him as students, colleagues, or friends. Moreover, Dr. Peoples confided that he "always admired and even sought to emulate his eloquence and his courageousness. He always encouraged me when I was a student as he continued to do when I became entrusted with the position he had so well filled." Dr. Peoples went on to ask the Jackson State University family to join the Dansby family and the community in mourning the passing of President B. Baldwin Dansby. He prayed that all should *"rejoice* that his influence, his works, and his love will be with us forever."

At the age of 96 Dr. Dansby passed November 20, 1975. Miriam Dansby Johnson his only daughter survived him. His first wife Mammie E. Grandson Dansby passed in 1956.

CHAPTER VI

THE SYMPHONY OF THE WHOLE INDIVIDUAL

The Administration of President Jacob L. Reddix, 1940–1967

EACH JACKSON STATE UNIVERSITY PRESIDENT has had a recurring theme which vivified his thoughts, words, actions, hopes, and aspirations for the institution he headed. For President Jacob L. Reddix, this theme was "the symphony of the whole individual" training in all areas of human living—intellectual, cultural, social, economic, and spiritual. For himself and for others he built strong programs. His travels to Africa, Europe, and to the Holy Land indicated his interest in international affairs. He served as an inspiration to black education in Mississippi.

Jacob L. Reddix assumed the presidency of the Mississippi Negro Training School (formerly Jackson College) on August 15, 1940. Born March 2, 1897, he was the youngest of nine sons and the grandson of North Carolina slave parents. His early years were spent in Vancleave, Jackson County, Mississippi. Young Reddix attended Miller's Ferry Normal and Industrial Institute at Miller's Ferry, Alabama from 1909–1914. After serving in the U.S. Army from 1917 to 1919 as a noncommissioned officer, Reddix taught school in Birmingham, Alabama for two years, 1921–23. He studied engineering at the Lewis Institute of Chicago from 1923 to 1927. Although deeply interested in a professional career, he turned to teaching again and joined the faculty of Roosevelt High School in Gary, Indiana, from 1927 to 1939. Refusing to give up his desire to study, Reddix accepted the Rosenwald Fellowship for graduate study at the University of Chicago in 1939, where he remained until beginning a new job. Reddix was soon appointed to the post of advisor to cooperatives with the United States Department of Agriculture, Washington, D.C., in 1939.

While becoming acquainted with his new position, Reddix was making many new friends everywhere. He was pleasantly surprised when he was offered the presidency of Jackson College during a luncheon meeting of the Board of Trustees of the Julius Rosenwald Fund in Chicago. He was further flattered when he was introduced to each of the members of the board, including Mrs. Eleanor Roosevelt and Dr. Will W. Alexander, vice president of the Julius Rosenwald Fund and administrator of the Farm Security Administration (FSA) of the United States Department of Agriculture.

Two months earlier—May 6, 1940—House Bill No. 722 had been introduced in the state legislature by Milton H. Grisham, Elmer E. McCoy, Mildred Alexander, Mrs. Horace S. Stansel, Halvert O. Laevell, and Zack Hilt. The bill was approved and signed by Governor Paul B. Johnson, Sr., making the college officially a state-supported institution. The name was changed from Jackson College to Mississippi Negro Training School. The events surrounding the passage of House Bill No. 722 are indeed interesting and revealing. When the measure to transfer Jackson College to the state was being discussed on the floor of the Mississippi House of Representatives, one member objected to it. He stated frankly that he was not interested in a college for Negroes: "what a 'Nigra' needed to learn was how to work—how to run a middle buster. I am against calling this school a college; I move that we name this institution the Mississippi Negro Training School."[1] Without fanfare, the motion was passed.

School began a month late on October 2, 1940. There were only 96 students. The delay was necessary to give the new administration and faculty enough time to effect a viable program. Clearly definite goals and objectives of the state-controlled school had to be clarified since the school was now established as a teacher training institution for the exclusive purpose of training elementary teachers for the rural schools of the state. The opportunity for growth and limited expansion was provided for in the law which stated that

Jackson College could enter into any other such studies as the Board of Trustees of State Institutions of Higher Learning in cooperation with the Mississippi Department of Education might from time to time deem necessary.

On August 8, 1940, the chairman of the old board of Jackson College presented the keys of the institution to the new chairman, W. F. Bond, and he in turn gave them to the new president.

Four days later President Reddix attended his second meeting with the Board of Trustees of Institutions of Higher Learning, and he presented his first recommendations. Reddix's proposals were sensible and urgent:

> Because the basic objectives of the College were being changed from those of a liberal arts college to those of a teachers college, and also because the budget available for operations was totally inadequate to support a four-year college, I recommend that the curriculum be temporarily reduced to two years. The curriculum of the two-year program would consist of approximately one hundred quarter hours of credit, distributed roughly with seventy-five credit hours for basic subjects in the arts and sciences and twenty-five credit hours in subjects known as professional teacher education. Two years of college training are, of course, inadequate to produce satisfactory teachers. Better training is especially important in states where the system of elementary schools has been poor. Indeed, it is tragic for prospective teachers to be studying the methods of instruction when they themselves are not well grounded in the basic subject matters which they will teach.
>
> As soon as sufficient funds are available, I believe that the curriculum should be restored to a four-year program with strong emphasis in the arts and sciences and with solid courses in psychology, child growth and development, and practice teaching. Public school teachers should be the best educated persons in our society. I wanted the board to commit itself to a four-year college in the very beginning rather than a junior college.
>
> The third recommendation dealt with the budget of the college. The Rosenwald Fund had pledged $30,000 per year to support the college, provided the State would match this amount. The 1940 session of the legislature refused to appropriate more than $10,000 per year. The Rosenwald Fund seriously considered withdrawing its commitment to the State, but Governor Paul B. Johnson urged the Fund not to withdraw, since he believed that he could get the State to meet its commitment as agreed. Thus, the annual income budget for the first two years was somewhat as follows:

Grant from the Rosenwald Fund	$ 30,000.00
Appropriation from the State	10,000.00
Tuition from 100 students at $30 per quarter	9,000.00
Miscellaneous Income	2,000.00
	$51,000.00

I suggested that the opening of classes be delayed until October 2, in order to give the new administration and faculty more time to organize the program of the College.

I recommended that for the present the College should not engage in intercollegiate sports because the facilities and budget were insufficient to support such a program.[2]

Under the auspices of the state, the school should have depended upon it for financial support. This was not the case, however. For many years President Reddix had to depend upon the Julius Rosenwald Fund and the General Education Board for financial support for the institution.

PERSONNEL

At the outset of the Reddix administration, the school was intended to function as a two-year training school for teachers. President Reddix, having insisted that this short span of time was insufficient to prepare teachers to enter the field of education, joined with the faculty in appealing to the Board of Trustees to add two more years to the program on a gradual basis. He suggested that the third year should be added in 1942-43 and the fourth year in 1943-44.

The college personnel for the 1940-41 session, the first year of the state's administration included: E. M. Barron, instructor of physical science; Zee Anderson Barron, instructor of English; Willie D. Blackburn, instructor of English; B. B. Dansby, registrar; Tellis B. Ellis, biology and physical education; J. D. Hardy, agriculture; Arelia W. Harris, nurse and health education; Juanita G. Jackson, home arts and craft; Leonard James, social sciences; Ariel M. Lovelace, music; Addison L. Perkins, social sciences; Gladys D. Shirley, demonstration teacher; Pearl R. Tate, demonstration teacher; Marie Y. Ware, music; Mary G. Whiteside, education; Lee E. Williams, demonstration teacher; J. Y. Woodard, shop; Etta Augusta Zuber, home improvement; Vernon C. Cade, custodian; Mary E. Jackson, clerk; Lelia C. Davis, matron; Harold Jacobs, business manager; Miriam D. Johnson, clerk-bookkeeper; J. E. Porter, cook; Benjamin F. Roberts, steward; Sara Jane Watts, librarian; and Melita A. Weatherall, secretary to the president. Two of the most effective and interesting consultants were also assigned by the State Department of Education to work with Jackson College. Dr. Jane Ellen McAllister, secondary education, and Miss Florence Octavia Alexander, supervisor of Jeanes teachers, who have figured significantly in the history of Jackson College. Both have interesting backgrounds and should be mentioned here.

Florence Octavia Alexander was born near Summit, Mississippi, and graduated from Jackson College in 1912. She studied at Normal University (Illinois), the University of Cincinnati, and Hunter College, from which she received an A.B. degree in 1918; she obtained a B.S. degree in education from Hampton Institute and a M.A. degree from Columbia University in 1931. Her employment included positions at Jackson College, Langston University, Southern University, Louisiana Normal (Grambling, Louisiana), Alcorn A&M, and Rust. She first became associate consultant to Jackson College in 1940 and continued her work for more than two decades. "Beyond any doubt," President Reddix held, "Miss Alexander knew more about the Negro schools of that time than did any other person in the State."[3]

Florence Alexander was involved in various educational activities in Alcorn A&M College, Rust College, Tuskegee Institute, Chicago University, and Fisk University. Her greatest contributions to education were summarized by Charles H. Wilson, *Education for Negroes in Mississippi Since 1940:*

(1) Her work with rural teachers in the State; (2) the organization of the 58 Jeanes teachers of the State and the work in the small rural schools they have done; (3) the encouragement as well as the work she has given the 6,000 rural teachers (most of whom she knows by name); and (4) the organization and coordination of the work and program of the colleges in teacher education. Her work has been chiefly with the teacher-training programs.[4]

The F. O. Alexander Residence Hall for Women on the campus is a monument to the rich life of devotion and services Miss Alexander gave to Jackson State College.

A native Mississippian, Dr. Jane Ellen McAllister was born to Flora McAllister and Richard Nelson McAllister in Vicksburg, October 24, 1899. Her mother had been a protégée of President and Mrs. Ayer, with whom she used to spend her summers at Martha's Vineyard, Cape Cod. She kept in touch with the Ayers all through her life. Both parents attended Jackson College from which Flora graduated in 1891.

Jane McAllister received her B.A. degree from Talladega College in 1919 and her M.A. degree from the University of Michigan in 1921. She was the first Negro woman to obtain her doctorate from Teachers College, Columbia University in 1929. Writing about Dr. McAllister in the *Advanced School Digest*, Mabel Carney claimed: "The real history of the study of American Negro education on the advanced level in Teachers College began with the pioneer achievement of Dr. Jane Ellen McAllister, with the completion of her doctoral thesis on 'The Training of Negro Teachers in Louisiana.' She became not only the first black candidate ever to receive the doctor's degree from this institution, but also the first black woman holding a doctoral degree in education throughout the world."[6]

Before coming to Jackson College, Dr. McAllister served with distinction on faculties of Fisk University, Virginia State, Petersburg, Morgan State, Baltimore, Hampton Institute, Straight, Grambling, and Miners Teachers College in Washington, D.C.

She began her service at Jackson State College as a curriculum consultant and later as professor of education. During her later tenure she served as director of the College Readiness Program and held that position for seven years with a grant from the Southern Education and Marshall Field Foundations. Always with striving vigor, Dr. McAllister became director of numerous other programs, workshops, and institutes on and off campus. She was the originator and patroness of several student activities which added to the vitality of Jackson College as a developing institution.

Her service on various national committees included: Evaluation Committee of the Eastern States (Association of Colleges and

Secondary Schools); Executive Committee of the National Association of Supervision of Student Teachers; Accrediting Committee of the Southern Association and others. An observer at the White House Conference in 1955 as an appointee of the U.S. Department of State from the United States to UNESCO in Prague, Czechoslovakia, Dr. McAllister gained deep insight into national and international affairs.

APPROPRIATIONS

When President Reddix came to Jackson State College, the buildings were in a state of disrepair, most were poorly built and over forty years old. So, he became the president who was called the "builder" and developer of Jackson College. Table IV illustrates the record of physical growth of Jackson College from 1940 to 1967.

In the process of buying land adjacent to the campus, President Reddix seized the opportunity of purchasing the holdings of the J. P. Campbell College, which was in a state of financial crisis. He directed the Negro Education Committee to petition the Board of Trustees to request the governor and legislature to acquire the site and buildings. The committee did so on June 29, 1961, with the result that on February 14, 1963, the Board of Trustees of the J. P. Campbell College, in accordance with its by-laws and the requirements of its incorporation, resolved that the J. P. Campbell property, including all real estate and buildings on Lynch Street, was sold to the Mississippi State Building Commission for the sum of $375,000.[6] It was on this site that the Reddix Campus Union building was erected in 1966–67.

The sum of $11,310,354.64 covering the erection and equipment of the building program between 1940–67 came from the state (Table V); the sum of $1,280,182.05 was received from the foundations listed in Table VI.

More important than the revision of the building program was the plan for an expanded, improved academic program. A chronology of the development of the academic program of the college during the decade 1940–50 showed that, in 1940–42, one-year and two-year elementary education curricula were established. In 1942, a four-year elementary education program leading to a bachelor's degree in teacher education was approved. During its first year

TABLE IV   First Phase of Physical Growth
            Buildings, Equipment, Completion, &
            Cost, 1940–1967

BUILDING	DATE COMPLETED	COST
Old President's Home	1941	$ 5,562.79
Security Building	1943	21,919.12
Johnson Hall of Social Science	1944	111,516.00
Zachary T. Hubert Health Center	1944	40,586.56
Johnson Hall Annex	1945	24,386.96
Garage & Maintenance	1947	23,456.92
Student Affairs (Green Hall)	1947	213,750.00
Barrack 1A	1947–48	44,609.00
Barrack 2A	1947–48	44,609.00
Barrack 3A	1947–48	25,000.00
Barrack 4A	1947–48	25,000.00
Barrack 5A	1947–48	25,000.00
Barrack 6A	1947–48	25,000.00
Dean of Students' Home	1947–48	10,000.00
Old Education Building	1947–48	90,711.00
Industrial Arts Annex	1948	69,306.49
Harry H. Jones Hall	1948	95,133.99
Calvin T. Sampson Hall	1948	134,490.76
Alumni Field	1949	51,248.46
Old Band Building	1949	20,000.00
Old College Gymnasium (Band Building)	1949	87,570.93
Security Building (Old)	1949	1,005.00
B. B. Dansby Hall of Expressive Arts	1951	201,518.89
B. F. Roberts Dining Hall	1953	210,303.17
Just Hall of Science	1954	356,053.36
Warehouse & Physical Plant Office Building	1957	31,968.17
H. T. Sampson Library	1959	391,901.42
Old Early Childhood Building (Campbell Hall)	1959	56,000.00
Chapel	1960	7,000.00
Willie Dobbs Blackburn Hall of Language Arts	1961	394,814.38

TABLE IV (CONTINUED)

BUILDING	DATE COMPLETED	COST
Faculty Apartment Complex	1961	370,213.15
Storage House	1964	1,500.00
Just Hall of Science (Extension)	1964	494,850.43
Stewart Hall	1964	707,525.50
F. O. Alexander Residence Center for Women	1964	2,628,609.36
Jacob L. Reddix Campus Union	1967	1,111,000.00
J. Y. Woodard School of Industrial and Technical Studies	1967	602,376.00
Plant Science Greenhouse	1967	130,000.00

under state support, the college had an enrollment of 96 students. There were only two dormitories and one academic building on the campus at that time.

The first graduation class under state control saw 29 young women receive the Bachelor of Science Degree, May, 1944. Johnnie Cotton, a native of Indiana was class valedictorian. Lottie Williams Thornton was salutatorian. It was March, 1944 that the Mississippi legislature approved the change of the institution's name from the Mississippi Negro Training School to Jackson College for Negro teachers.

During the decades 1940 and 1950, the college helped to fulfill one of the greatest needs of the state: that of all teachers holding at least a bachelor's degree. This was important because in 1954, of a total of 6,450 black teachers in the state, only 25 percent held the bachelor's degree or above.

During 1947, a four-year secondary education major in selected fields leading to a bachelor's degree in teacher education was added. By 1953-55, the expanded curriculum leading to a degree in liberal education and an organized program of graduate studies leading to a master's degree in administration and supervision had been established.

The methodology proposed for equipping new teachers who would be able to meet the demands of the community was mainly through work experiences and self-directed experiences as provided in the operation and maintenance of the college. Other experiences were provided in several one-year centers located in Greenwood,

In 1940, when the institution came under state control, the Coat-of-Arms of the State of Mississippi was used on official bulletins. The name of the institution at that time was Mississippi Negro Training School. The Coat-of-Arms of the State of Mississippi was also used from 1944 to 1951 when the institution was officially named Jackson College for Negro Teachers.

In 1951, a new seal was affixed to official bulletins of Jackson College for Negro Teachers and it bore the motto "The Whole Individual—Learning—Teaching." The same seal design was used from 1956 to 1968 during which time the name was changed to Jackson State College.

THE WHITE HOUSE
WASHINGTON

April 22, 1952

Dear Dr. Reddix:

Please accept my congratulations and best wishes on the occasion of the seventy-fifth anniversary of the founding of Jackson College.

Americans can well be proud of the fact that we have understood the importance of providing educational opportunity for all of our citizens. In this time of crisis the Nation looks to its colleges and universities with particular concern, for we know that they must provide our young people with the skills and understanding that will give the fullest support to our democratic way of life.

That the State of Mississippi is giving important support to Jackson College is a tribute to the long history of your institution and testifies to the contribution you have made to the life and work of a great State.

In the years to come we shall need the wisest leadership and the deepest understanding. As we rise to the challenge of our time we look above all to our country's educational institutions.

It is my sincere hope that the seventy-fifth anniversary of your institution will be marked by satisfaction for the years that have passed and hope for the years that lie ahead.

Very sincerely yours,

Harry Truman

Dr. Jacob L. Reddix,
President,
Jackson College,
Jackson, Mississippi.

Congratulatory message from President Harry Truman on the occasion of the celebration of the seventy-fifth anniversary of the founding of Jackson College.

President Jacob L. Reddix receiving citation from Governor Paul B. Johnson, Jr., Governor Paul B. Johnson, Sr. is pictured in the background.

President Jacob L. Reddix visiting with the governor

First graduating class after state assumed the control of Jackson State College—Class of 1944

Class of 1947—Ten returning World War II Veterans participate in graduating exercise. *Top Row*, Z. Turner, G. Swan, L. V. Randolph; *Second Row*, E. Stewart; *Third Row*, J. Rhodes, H. Gamblin, I. Manning; *Fourth Row*, L. Miles (deceased), O. Barnes, W. Moore (deceased)

President & Mrs. Jacob L. Reddix and daughter, Shirley Ann (Mrs. Vanderpool) return visit from Liberia April, 1949.

Conference on Higher Education—President Reddix poses with Miss F. O. Alexander and Dean H. T. Sampson following chapel assembly

Governor Hugh White in conference with President Jacob L. Reddix, Jackson State College, President Oatis, Alcorn College and President J. H. White, Mississippi Valley State College

H. T. Sampson Library constructed in 1957-58—occupancy January 1, 1959—28,029 square feet, 75,000 volume capacity, and 544 seating capacity

Stewart Hall—Residence Hall for Men
Named in honor of Edgar "Tripp" Stewart—Dedicated 1964

B. F. Roberts Dining Hall—Erected 1953

President Jacob L. Reddix poses with his predecessor and his successor at his retirement program. *Left*, President John A. Peoples, Jr., 1967- ; *Center*, President Jacob L. Reddix, 1940-1967; *Right*, President B. B. Dansby, 1927-1940.

Jacob L. Reddix Campus Union

Mound Bayou, Clarksdale, Brookhaven, and Meridian. The purpose of the centers was primarily to satisfy a specific need of the state for teachers with some professional training beyond high school. Some viewed the centers as an extension of high school, a fifth year. Additionally, they served to keep Jackson College in touch with other sections of the state as an in-service agency that worked cooperatively with the Jeanes teachers.

A student enrolled in the one-year centers was admitted to college on an individual basis upon recommendation of the teacher. However, the amount of credit given by the college was provisional and was withdrawn if the student's performance did not prove satisfactory. The areas of instructions carried a two-year cur-

TABLE V   State Appropriations for Jackson State College, 1940–1967

YEAR	AMOUNT
September 1, 1940–June 30, 1941	$ 10,000.00
July 1, 1941–June 30, 1942	10,000.00
July 1, 1942–June 30, 1943	29,999.28
July 1, 1943–June 30, 1944	30,000.72
July 1, 1944–June 30, 1945	66,000.00
July 1, 1945–June 30, 1946	66,000.00
July 1, 1946–June 30, 1947	103,737.36
July 1, 1947–June 30, 1948	103,737.36
July 1, 1948–June 30, 1949	132,300.00
July 1, 1949–June 30, 1950	134,391.36
July 1, 1950–June 30, 1951	182,280.00
July 1, 1951–June 30, 1952	213,509.56
July 1, 1952–June 30, 1953	311,280.00
July 1, 1953–June 30, 1954	247,947.19
July 1, 1954–June 30, 1955	336,003.61
July 1, 1956–June 30, 1957	404,012.73
July 1, 1957–June 30, 1958	415,851.40
July 1, 1958–June 30, 1959	571,270.07
July 1, 1959–June 30, 1960	581,224.71
July 1, 1960–June 30, 1961	777,814.25
July 1, 1961–June 30, 1962	796,949.84
July 1, 1962–June 30, 1963	938,591.40
July 1, 1963–June 30, 1964	923,456.14
July 1, 1964–June 30, 1965	1,139,166.33
July 1, 1965–June 30, 1966	1,148,461.33
July 1, 1966–June 30, 1967	1,636,370.00

TABLE VI   Jackson State College, Foundation Support

FOUNDATION	AMOUNT OF GRANT	PURPOSE	DATE
Rosenwald Fund	$75,000.00	General Operating Expenses and Building Repairs	1940–42
Southern Education Foundation	35,000.00	Library Science Summer	1957–60
Southern Education Foundation	3,839.00	Administrative Problems in the Supervision of Student Teaching	1964
Southern Education Foundation	4,043.66	Administrative Problems in the Supervision of Student Teaching	1965
Southern Education Foundation	2,250.00	Workshop—Improving Pupil Achievment in Elementary Schools	1966
Mississippi Power and Light Company	17,500.00	Scholarships	1965–67
National Science Foundation	650,000.00	Summer Institutes in Biology & Mathematics for Secondary Teachers	1962–67
Fund for the Advancement of Education	2,921.25	Collection of Paperback Books—Science, Art, Music, etc.	1966
Fund for the Advancement of Education	9,600.00	Improvement Placement Services	1967
General Education Board	150,000.00	Construction of Library Building	1955
General Education Board	195,880.48	Construction, Library Books & General Operating Expenses	1919–47
Field Foundation	10,000.00	Young at Heart Program for 9th, 10th, and 11th Graders	1966
Ford Foundation	120,000.00	College Readiness Program & Continuing Education Program	1965
Southern Education Foundation	4,147.66	Workshop—Administrative Problems in the Supervision of Student Teaching	1966

riculum initially and later a four-year curriculum (1942-44). The two-year curriculum encompassed the areas of Creative Arts and Recreations Arts, the area of Language Arts, Rural Living, the area of Science and Mathematics, and the area of Teaching and Related Service courses. A total of 100 quarter hours earned was necessary for completion of the two-year curriculum.

CURRICULUM

President Reddix's most challenging task of the 1940s was to redirect the college curriculum toward teacher education with emphasis on specialization. In the first place, he encouraged the recognition of teaching, especially for blacks, as a profession. Helped by his consultants, he modified the teaching goals to include "education for the needs of the people," "functional education," "child growth and development," "practice teaching," and other facets of education that were the needs of the moment.

Reddix tried to help solve the special problems facing Jackson College's entering students during the 1940s by initiating four projects—remedial or compensatory education, special high school services for veterans, the college readiness program, and the college reading program.

By 1947, the Bachelor of Science in secondary education was offered with concentration in six academic areas: Science and Mathematics, Social Sciences, Language Arts, Music, Industrial Arts, and Home Economics. President Reddix led his academic administrators forward in establishing undergraduate and graduate programs of quality. As better prepared faculty were added in specialized fields, undergraduate programs were expanded.

Such specialized programs were based on well-developed general education courses which exposed students to a variety of experiences leading to self-development through physical and mental activities.

As more attention was focused on the performance of the students who attended Jackson, more criticism was directed toward the quality of the programs. Racial prejudices and inequalities of appropriations multiplied many of Jackson College's problems. In an article by P. H. Easom and J. A. Travis, State Agents, State Department of Education, entitled "Status of Negro Schools in Mississippi, 1939", statistics show that the total expenditures for white public schools was $12,035,969.87, while the amount spent on black public schools was only $1,491,932.89. This ratio meant that for every white child, $9.88 was spent in comparison to the $1.00 that was used to educate a black child. The article also reveals that 92 percent of the eligible high school black students were not enrolled. Furthermore, 25 of the 82 counties in Mississippi did not have high schools for black youths.[7]

The *Shreveport Sun* on June 20, 1942, as well as many other local and regional papers, judged the governor of Mississippi as being fair, with a favorable attitude toward Negroes. This medium quoted from the remarks of Governor Paul B. Johnson, Sr., as he spoke to the Mississippi State Building Commission following Reddix's request for new buildings. Said Governor Johnson:

> Gentlemen, I personally request that you grant Jackson College this request. We must do something for the Negro in Mississippi. We have stalled long enough. We have promised them something ever since Reconstruction days and we have never given them what they deserve.
>
> The Negro is our best friend. He has cultivated our fields, has done our work, and we have not given him his just share in the income of the State. At this time, there is fine feeling between the races in the State of Mississippi. Let us cultivate this feeling by refraining from stalling and take this opportunity to do something tangible for the higher education of the race.

Efforts were slowly made to improve some of the inadequacies of the institution. Hence, funds were soon appropriated for new buildings.

Jackson State University had devoted three quarters of a century (1877-1952) to the education of teachers; yet, "fewer than a hundred black teachers in Mississippi taught only senior high school." Furthermore, no black high school in the state was a member of the Southern Association of Colleges and Secondary Schools. Rural schools for black children were conducted in abandoned homes, churches, lodge halls, and almost every conceivable kind of shack.

The 1968 report of the Carnegie Commission stated that one-third of all black principals and one-half of all black teachers in Mississippi were graduates of Jackson State College. Just as Reddix had accepted the challenge of educating veterans, he had unqualifiedly accepted the mandate of the 1940 legislature to train rural and elementary teachers.

From the satellite teacher-training extension centers established by the preceding administration at Carthage, Greenwood, Louisville, Mound Bayou, Magee, Clarksdale, Brookhaven, Yazoo City, and Meridian came persons who enrolled in Jackson College for further study.

The curriculum of Jackson State College was a functional program of teacher education and made no attempt to give degrees in any specific phase of teacher training. Sufficient work was given in Social Sciences, Music, Language Arts, Science and Mathematics, and Home Economics. All four-year graduates received the degree of Bachelor of Science in Education.[8]

The program or curriculum was organized into seven areas, comparable to what is designated as a division in most colleges and universities. Within each area were two or more departments. The seven areas were: Education; Fine Arts; Health and Physical Education; Language Arts; Practical Arts; Science and Mathematics; Social Sciences. The area chairman was responsible for the administration and coordination of the services rendered by the division.

The educational area offered programs and services designed to facilitate the preparation of teachers and to assist all areas of the college in their efforts to utilize available institutional resources in the interest of the learning process.

In 1940 when Jackson State College became a state-supported institution, the college had the single purpose of training elementary teachers. This permitted a simple, very closely knit organization and channel of responsibility.

A great demand for teachers in all fields on the secondary level was an important factor in the expansion of the program offering curricula leading to degrees in secondary education. As the college grew, changes in organization and in levels of communication became necessary.

The divisions of the Education Area included the Psycho-Educational Center, Audio-Visual Department, Department of Graduate Studies, Department of Special Education, and the Department of Directed Teaching and Field Experiences. W. Bruce Welch, Lee E. Williams, and F. O. Alexander served as chairmen of the area during the decade of the 1940s.

The Language Arts Area was comprised of four distinct departments, each with a department head responsible to the area chairman, which included: Department of Modern Foreign Languages; the Department of Literature and Humanities; the Department of Speech and Theater; the Department of English and Composition. Mrs. Willie Dobbs Blackburn served as chairman of the area for more than thirty years. The Practical Arts Area was designed to prepare teachers of Industrial Arts for secondary schools and to provide courses in homemaking. Joseph D. Hardy served as chairman of this area. The Science and Mathematics Area embraced three distinct departments: Biology; Chemistry; Mathematics and Physics. Bolton C. Price served as chairman of the area for more than a quarter of a century. The Social Science Area, as one of the major divisions of the college, emphasized two undergraduate programs, Teacher Education and Liberal Education. The Teacher Education program, offering a major in the social sciences covering courses in Economics, Sociology, Government, History, and Geography, was designed to prepare teachers of social sciences in the secondary schools. Additionally, it offered professionalized subject matter courses for prospective elementary teachers and a major in business education for prospective teachers of business in the high schools. The Liberal Arts Program offered several curricula with emphasis on Economics, Sociology, Geography, and Political Science. A. V. Battle served as chairman of the area through 1950. In 1952, Dr. Elbert L. Tatum was appointed chairman of the Area of Social Sciences. Dr. Tatum served in this post until his death on June 4, 1956.

On January 18, 1951, the Board of Trustees received a report from Dr. Ivy, who chaired a committee on Negro Education, regarding plans for an overall program of development for the three Negro colleges. Tentative proposals were directed to each school which defined the role and scope without duplication of programs. Also there was a proposal indicating that facilities and personnel of all the institutions could be combined in the development of a graduate program.

It was at the January 18, 1951 meeting that Dr. P. H. Eason, then supervisor of Negro education for the State Department, was charged with the responsibility of preparing a plan for higher education for Negroes which covered a period of ten years. He was further requested to recommend a committee of not less than twelve Negro citizens who would cooperate with the Board of Trustees in planning for the development of higher education for Negroes.

For more than a decade, beginning in 1944, Jackson College had cooperated with rural schools in Hinds County. At one time, seven cooperating rural communities—the schools of McRaven, Mare Grove, Pleasant Grove, Mt. Sinai, Bracey, St. Thomas, and New Hope—had served as laboratories for students to gain meaningful experiences in handling children. All of these schools were led by principals who were willing to cooperate despite the absence of necessary supplies and equipment.

The curriculum was divided into six broad areas: the Area of Education; the Area of Language Arts; the Area of Science and Mathematics; the Area of Social Science; the Area of Practical Arts; and the Area of Creative and Recreational Arts. The purpose of the Area of Education was to develop in students a desirable educational philosophy and a sensitiveness to socioeconomic problems, particularly to those of rural life. All students who were planning to teach were required to take at least 36 quarter hours of credit in this area.[9]

Twenty-seven hours of credit were required for students in the Area of Language Arts. These hours were distributed in (1) Oral and Written Expression, (2) Literature, and (3) Speech. Students who planned to teach on the elementary school level were required to take courses related to Language Arts for Children. If a student planned to major in the Area of Language Arts, preparatory to teaching on the secondary school level, he was required to earn at least 45 quarter hours in this field.[10] Special remedial courses in English were offered to students who had deficiencies in oral and written expression.

All students were required to take six quarter hours of general mathematics and eighteen hours of science (biological and physical). Students who majored in science earned 55 quarter hours of science; students who majored in mathematics were required to take 30 quarter hours in mathematics.[11]

In the Area of Social Sciences, various courses were integrated either directly or indirectly as vehicles to aid students in acquiring knowledge about and gaining experience in several related fields of human relationships; to enable the students to use the information gained as a basis for understanding and solving socioeconomic problems; and to help them to perceive better the global relationship. Students were required to take 28 hours, which included Human Geography, World Civilization, Community Leadership, Study of Socioeconomic Problems, and American History. The college offered a major in social science designed primarily to train students to teach on the secondary level.

In the Area of Practical Arts, the main thrust was to teach students how to use the resources of his environment to promote a program of better living.[12] A student majoring in the Department of Home Economics earned the degree of Bachelor of Science in Home Economics Education. Students were trained to become teachers of home economics for the public schools. The program was designed to offer a sequence of industrial art courses to equip one to become a teacher of the various vocational trades on the high school level. The Area of Creative and Recreational arts included general courses in music, art, physical education, and recreation. A student specializing in this area could major in Music, with a voice or instrumental emphasis, Public School Music and Art, and Physical Education and Health.[13]

The years 1953-55 were the beginning of a four-year program leading to a bachelor's degree in liberal education in the arts, humanities, and sciences. While the college was primarily a teachers' college, the changing demands for educational services for Negro youth in the state of Mississippi caused the Board of Trustees to add a Division of Liberal Arts Education to the primary purpose of the college. This move changed the aim of Jackson College not only to sponsor a program in teacher education but also in Liberal Arts. The main difference between the two curricula was that the Division of Teacher Education emphasized teaching and professional courses in education, while the emphasis was on subject matter and general education in the Division of Liberal Arts Education.

The Division of Teacher Education was committed to a functional program which was tailored to the "needs of the people."

The program was designed to develop teachers to guide the youths and to coordinate and organize community agencies and promote a program of better living. All graduates in the Division of Teacher Education were required to do practice teaching in a community school and share in the experiences offered by a rural community.

Students with the interests and abilities could major in one of the following fields: Art; Health and Physical Education; Home Economics; Industrial Arts; Language Arts; Music Education; Science and Mathematics; Social Science. All four-year graduates of this curriculum received the degree of Bachelor of Science in Education, except majors in home economics who received the degree of Bachelor of Science in Home Economics Education.

Unlike the Division of Teacher Education, the aim of the Division of Liberal Arts Education was to provide for nonteaching majors in the arts, sciences, humanities, and the pre-professional fields. In the fall of 1954, the Division of Liberal Arts Education offered majors in the following fields: Art; English; Music; Science and Mathematics; Social Science. The following pre-professional courses were offered: Pre-Dentistry; Pre-Law; Pre-Medicine; Pre-Ministerial. The Division of Liberal Arts Education offered the degree of Bachelor of Arts and the degree of Bachelor of Science. Formal degrees were first awarded in 1954.[14]

In the 1950s, President Reddix emphasized the importance of expanding the graduate program in order to increase the number of teachers with master's degrees. He found that the Board of Trustees was moderately sympathetic with his desires for a better quality institution.

Because Jackson State's primary mission was that of training of teachers, it was in an excellent position to focus its attention on advanced work in the area of supervision and administration already being offered.

Reddix focused on 35 in-service principals who were in attendance at a workshop in supervision and administration being held at Jackson College. This was significant because at no time in the history of the institution had there been any work beyond the undergraduate offerings.

In an effort to expand the curriculum and to advance the levels of curricular offerings to serve better the needs of students in Mississippi, proposals were submitted to the board by President Reddix requesting graduate work leading to the Master of Science in Education. Reddix' request was referred to the Committee on Negro Education. On March 18, 1954, on a motion by H. G. Carpenter and seconded by R. D. McLendon, the committee recommended the approval of the graduate program as proposed by President Reddix at a cost of $15,000, together with a supplement of $15,000 from other sources for the 1954 session.

Concurrently Reddix recommended that the study of Negro secondary education with reference to high school students be authorized at Jackson College and that the amount of $1,000 be allocated from the 1954 study fund to finance the work. In order that official recognition for the master's degree be achieved, he requested a director of the graduate program.

Because of the lack of classroom facilities, an appeal was made for authorization to use facilities from the Jackson public schools for some night classes and to rent homes in close proximity for purposes of additional classroom space. Houses across the street on Lynch Street were used. The graduate program was begun with great enthusiasm and interest.

Proposals for the establishment of the Department of Foreign Languages and the Department of Secretarial Science were postponed until the allocations were made for the 1956-58 biennium. It was agreed at this time that the planning for a Foreign Languages Department should be limited to Modern Foreign Languages.

By 1947, secondary education programs leading to the Bachelor of Science in Education were offered in Science, Mathematics, Social Science, Language Arts, and Home Economics. By 1955, additional curricula leading to degrees in liberal education and a limited program of graduate studies leading to a Master's in Administration and Supervision were offered. The years since 1960 have emphasized the development of departmental majors in liberal education and the improvement and enrichment of the course sequence in teacher education.

With the increased enrollment and increase in support funds, the curriculum expansion and growth of the college were accelerated and were accompanied by a parallel but not equally adequate expansion of physical facilities.[15]

In 1956, the Mississippi legislature, in recognition of the expanded function of the college, in Senate Bill No. 1524 changed the institution's name from Jackson College for Negro Teachers to Jackson State College. The bill was finally approved February 21, 1956. Soon after the name change, President Reddix and Dean H. T. Sampson appeared before the board to present the need for a director of the Graduate Program in order that official recognition of work for the master's degree could be obtained.[16] The graduate program for principals and supervisors had already been initiated because of an increased need for trained administrative personnel to manage the larger school units anticipated as a result of the reorganization and consolidation of existing school units under the state's plan of equalization of educational opportunities. Without adequate leadership from a qualified director, the program would have been seriously limited. Reddix and Sampson were successful.

Initially, there were 26 principals or students aspiring to become principals who enrolled. By the 1960–61 school year, four courses were taught in the Graduate Division of the college. A total of 104 students were enrolled in these courses. During the summer session, the graduate program had a total of 99 students. The graduate faculty consisted of seven.

H. T. Sampson, the academic dean of Jackson State College, recommended in his *Annual Report* that, in view of the fact that less than one-fifth of the 99 students enrolled in the Graduate Program were administrators or supervisors, the graduate program should be expanded in the fields of elementary education until adequate facilities, finances, and faculty could be obtained.[17]

The policies governing the administration and supervision of the graduate program were formulated by a Graduate Council. The composition of the council included: the director of graduate studies; chairman of the Education Area; the academic dean; the assistant dean of instruction; the director of elementary education; the director of secondary education; the director of student teaching; a professor of education; and other persons appointed by the president of the college. The Graduate Council functioned by formulating policies for the Graduate Program. For instance, the council stipulated that each candidate for the master's degree at Jackson State be required to pass the American College Entrance

Psychological Examination and Cooperative English Test (Higher Level); the GRE Advanced Testing Education; a written comprehensive examination, and a final oral.[18] The mission of the Graduate Program had been clear from the beginning:

> The Board of Trustees, State Institutions of Higher Learning, State of Mississippi, has recently authorized Jackson College to initiate a complete training program for high school and elementary school principals and supervisors on the graduate level. In cooperation with the Mississippi State Department of Education, the College is beginning a graduate program in which the prescribed sequence of courses and related experiences will lead to the degree of Master of Science in Education. For the present and for an indefinite period of time, this program will be offered only during the summer session.
> All the details of the complete training program have not yet been determined. Only its broad outline has been tentatively conceived. The College plans to develop a functional graduate training program for school administrators and supervisors relative to their ever increasing responsibilities in administering and supervising larger quality of instruction, and in assessing the proper functions of the school in a democratic society. In the development of this program, the College will need the sole counsel of the educational leaders, competent laymen, as well as principals and supervisors themselves.[19]

At President Reddix's request, the first director of the Graduate Program had been Dr. Charles C. Mosley, professor of education. A graduate of Eureka College (Illinois), Dr. Mosley had received his M.A. from Illinois University and his Ed.D. from Indiana University. A former coach at Jarvis Christian College (Hawkins, Texas), high school principal at Humble High School (Humble, Texas), French and Latin teacher, dean of Jarvis Christian College, and a scholar who had published numerous articles in the field of education, Dr. Mosley was well qualified to take over the task of directing graduate studies in administration and supervision.

One of the first assignments given Dr. Mosley by President Reddix and the Board of Trustees of State Institutions of Higher Learning was to make a study of Negro high schools in Mississippi and their relationship to the Negro colleges of the state, especially the state-supported colleges.

In an effort to move the Graduate Program forward, President

Reddix requested permission to implement plans for a doctoral program at the December 17, 1959 Board of Trustees meeting. This request was referred to the Finance Committee on a motion by Tally D. Riddell which was seconded by T. J. Tubb.[20] However, nothing positive ever developed from Reddix's request.

Nevertheless, under President Reddix's administration, the curriculum was expanded in teacher education and liberal education. In keeping with this forward thrust Jackson State College could now offer three major emphases: (1) teacher education, (2) liberal education, and (3) graduate studies.

The Division of Liberal Education was to provide for more teaching majors in the arts, sciences, humanities, and the pre-professional fields which included biology, chemistry, English, literature, foreign languages, history, and political science, mathematics, and sociology. Programs in the Division of Liberal Education also served as pre-professional preparation for such fields as: Dentistry, medicine, law, ministry, and social work.[21]

The college administration often studied the state of affairs and assessed the future. Several formal investigations were made. *Predicting College Enrollment for State Colleges from 1954-70*, undertaken with H. T. Sampson, L. B. Fraser, Dr. Jane Ellen McAllister, Lee E. Williams, B. J. McCullough, D. W. Wilburn, DeLars Funches, and Inez Gray listed twenty conclusions which were transmitted to the board. Among the study's findings were too heavy loads for administration, poor libraries, inadequate curricula, no laboratory equipment, inadequate buildings, and the poverty of native Mississippians (the state average outlay of $600 per individual per year contrasted with $1,200 average per year per individual for the nation as a whole). In another investigation, Dr. Charles C. Mosley, director of the Graduate Program, served as a member of a Task Force on Graduate-Professional Education to determine the status of graduate and professional education in Mississippi and to make recommendations for the development of graduate and professional education and research. Together with his colleagues on the task force, who produced their findings in the *Role and Scope Study* (1966), Mosley recommended that immediate steps be taken to strengthen its long-range planning, that information be exchanged among institutions on proposed new developments, and that negotiations and mutual agreements be carried out among institutions on new programs.

Such studies reflected not only the findings of the researchers but also the fact that the faculty of Jackson State College had officially entered the mainstream of educational scholarship in Mississippi and that it could be counted upon to help in the future development of state-supported education.

During 1954, the Study Commitee on Higher Education in Mississippi reported to the Board of Trustees of Institutions of Higher Learning that staff and additional facilities for the education and training of librarians in Mississippi were urgently needed to meet an emergency need for qualified librarians and that "an undergraduate major in library science should be established at Jackson State which has the potential resources for developing an acceptable program." The study further stated that in addition to an undergraduate program in library science at the five white institutions, that a graduate program leading to the master's degree in library science should be established at the University of Mississippi. (An unaccredited master's degree program in library science has for some time been inaugurated in Mississippi.)

In 1972, Lester Asheim, at the request of the Board of Trustees of Institutions of Higher Learning, made a feasibility study of the state institutions in library holdings and facilities to ascertain which of the institutions was most qualified to offer a master's degree program in library science that could meet the American Library Association standards for an accredited library school. During the 1950s, because of the state's system of segregation in education, blacks who pursued degrees beyond the bachelor's and master's programs applied for and received out-of-state scholarship aid.

Many of the black librarians serving in state institutions had received their undergraduate degrees from Jackson State and were recipients of financial aid from the state to obtain a degree in library science from an out-of-state A. L. A. accredited library school. The committee thus recommended that, in the area of libraries and library science, future plans should include new library buildings at three of the institutions of higher learning—Jackson College, Alcorn, and Mississippi Southern; provisions for an undergraduate minor or major in library science should be made in the five institutions for white students and at Jackson College.[22] Yet, Mississippi at this writing (1976) does not have an American Library Association accredited library school.

In 1965 Jackson State began taking advantage of such federal programs as National Defense Education Act (NDEA) and Elementary and Secondary Education Act (ESEA) to aid teachers in Mississippi. Dr. McAllister was responsible for getting support for teachers under Title XI of the National Defense Education Act Foundation. This program provided opportunities for approximately 1,200 teachers.

In the summer of 1966, more than a dozen institutes and workshops were initiated on Jackson State College's campus: four programs funded by NDEA (English, history, disadvantaged youth, and reading); three by Higher Education Act (leadership, elementary mathematics, and secondary mathematics); two by Southern Education Foundation (administering student teaching and improving pupil achievement); one by National Science Foundation (biology); one by Office of Economic Opportunity (a theory-action institute for all elementary school personnel); and a Self-Help Opportunity Center (SHOC) which aided 100 disadvantaged children. A sister program to the latter, Self-Help Elementary Program (SHEP), dealt with the younger children. Both these programs were "adopted" by the NDEA institute participants. Teachers were recruited under the slogan "Tough Job—Help Wanted," and many were severely disadvantaged themselves.

Dr. McAllister was extremely concerned about "broadening the outlook of students by bringing them into contact with people outside their limited environments." She called it "A Window on the World" and invited scholars and visitors who came with pleasure. She began a program of telephone interviews using telelecture equipment to further her goals. The Ford Foundation became aware of Dr. McAllister's project and provided funds for television-telephone lectures on Greek drama with Moses Hadas of Columbia University. Also members of the Southern University, Tougaloo, and Stephens College faculty telephoned courses in the humanities.

These breakthroughs inspired new outlooks at Jackson State. Supported by Dr. Reddix and his growing faculty and inspired by Dr. McAllister's dynamism and know-how, the College staff banded together and invited support from every possible source to finance innovative projects.

In the South, the granting of approval to an institution of learning by an official review board after the school had met specific requirements was in the hands of two agencies: the Association of Colleges and Secondary Schools and the Southern Association of Colleges and Secondary Schools. The first was made up of the accredited senior and junior colleges and high schools for blacks in an area served by the second.

President Reddix brought Jackson State College from initial approval in 1946 to full membership in the Southern Association of Colleges and Secondary Schools in 1961 when the separate listing of black colleges and universities was discontinued. Thereafter, all black institutions could seek membership in the Southern Association of Colleges and Schools, a step that was taken in the next administration.

THE LIBRARY

Concomitantly with the expansion of the academic program, President Reddix tried to enlarge the library both in terms of the book collection and in physical facilities. During the first year of President Reddix' administration, the one-room library in Chivers Hall had been enlarged by removing a partition in an adjoining classroom. The collection had consisted of 525 usable volumes. Also during Reddix's first year, Mrs. Sara Jane Watts-Lovelace, with degrees both in history and library science, had assumed the duties of head librarian. Five years later, the head librarian resigned to take a maternity leave and Mrs. Rubye E. Stutts Lyells, the first black Mississippian to receive a Master's degree in Library Science, was appointed to the post which she held for two years.

In 1944, the library was moved from Chivers Hall to the basement floor of the newly built Johnson Hall, which also housed an auditorium above the library. The library consisted of a reading room with a seating capacity of 125, and an adjoining book stack room which would accommodate approximately 5,000 volumes. [23]

The *Mississippi Study of Higher Education*, 1954, made under the auspices of the Board of Trustees of Higher Learning, stated that "lighting and service arrangements are poor at Jackson College for Negro Teachers and that the stack space was entirely inadequate." However, a positive observation was made for the future of the library, "The Library at Jackson State College, though then handicapped by lack of books, space, and money, bids fair to make rapid progress. The collection is small, but growing. Leadership is progressive and active." At that time, the college was operating off-campus a three-teacher rural training school in Rankin County, another in Jackson with four teachers, and four other cooperating schools—all of which used materials from the college library.[24]

During the early years under state control, the institution received conditional matching offers of funds for library books from the Rosenwald Fund and the General Education Board. The largest offer—$12,000—came from the General Education Board in 1944, which was dependent upon a matching appropriation of $6,000 from the state of Mississippi. Approximately 914 used gift books were received from Works Progress Administration (WPA) through the Mississippi Library Commission.

In October 1947, Mrs. Ernestine Anthony Lipscomb became head librarian. By then the collection had grown to approximately 5,570 volumes, including a small number of bound periodicals but excluding multiple copies of elementary textbooks, manuals, and other obsolete duplicate gift books, discovered through a careful examination of accession records several years later. The library staff consisted of Mrs. Lipscomb, a professional librarian, and two nonprofessional workers who were both college graduates.

Overcrowding in the library became acute during the 1950–51 school year. Books, back files of magazines, and newspapers were stored outside the library in the basement of Ayer Hall in an attempt to relieve the situation. The school enrollment peaked, and seats in the library were at a premium. The library staff had been increased to five professional workers with no added work space. The crowded catalog department still occupied a corner of the stacks with no privacy for the concentration needed for cataloging. The only work space available to other staff members was a desk provided either in the reading room or in a section of the stacks.

The situation was somewhat eased later in the year by President Reddix's offer to turn over his former office in Johnson Hall and the old Public Relations Office to the library. Immediately, shelves were built in both offices and the catalog department was moved to the old Public Relations Office, comprised of two small rooms. New and uncataloged books were transferred there as well as all books in process. The president's vacated office was used as a library storeroom housing overflow gift books, backfiles of newspapers and magazines. Most of these were transferred from the Ayer Hall basement; many had to be discarded because of mildew and dampness.

Plans were made in the spring of 1951 for expanding the library. The new auditorium had been officially opened in the new Dansby Hall, and the old auditorium in Johnson Hall was to be used as a new library reading room. In June, the entire book stock had to be moved and shifted so that a stairway could be cut in the stack room and space for a book lift could be cut leading to the old auditorium. During this period, the services of the library were carried on in spite of the constant bits of falling plaster, noise from drilling, nailing and knocking, and general confusion. When this was completed, all of the book stacks had to be dismantled and rearranged, and all of the books had to be returned to the shelves, shifted, arranged, and rearranged several times in order to accommodate the new plan.

Early in the spring of 1952, remodeling was completed and the Johnson Hall Auditorium was at last converted into a spacious room with fluorescent lights. New furniture was purchased, including 29 blond maple tables and 133 matching chairs and a new modern section for the card catalog. Some of the furnishings were placed in the new browsing area, which was located in a corner of the reading room. Fixed wooden wall shelving accommodated the reference collection, bound periodicals, elementary textbook collection, and fiction, all on open shelves. Books by and about the Negro, and new state-adopted textbooks were shelved in glass-enclosed bookcases in the auditorium reading room near the loan desk. Reserve books were shelved behind the loan desk near the entrance to the room. All other books, representing the main collection that could be taken for two-week home use, remained in the old section of the library which now had two reading rooms—one upstairs and one downstairs with a seating capacity of 220. The plan for a book lift did not materialize, and this was an inconvenience to the library staff as well as to the users of the library. Books had to be transported from one floor to another by hand rather than by book truck on a book lift.

As the college enrollment increased and new books were added, the library soon outgrew the reading rooms and work area in Johnson Hall. During 1954-55, preliminary steps in planning a new library building were begun as a result of a conditional offer of $150,000 from the General Education Board. The major activity for the year was the "Faculty-Library Study of Library Requirements for Courses Offered at Jackson College." From this study, based on a questionnaire prepared by the library staff and the Faculty-Library Committee, the librarians made a report of "Requirements for a New Library at Jackson College" to meet curricular needs for teacher education, liberal arts, and graduate work in education.

Ground-breaking and the beginning of construction of the proposed new library occurred during the academic year 1957-58. The "Report of the Library" for that year stated that "all thoughts were focused on moving into the new building." Everyone envisioned relief from "crowded book shelves, cramped working quarters, lack of adequate storage, noisy floors, overcrowded reading room, the poor lighting in the downstairs reading rooms, the intense heat, and transportation by hand of books from one floor to another."

The new air-conditioned library was completed by the end of 1958, and the long-awaited moving day came in January 1959. The three-story white brick (blue aluminum trim) building, modern and functional in design, covering 28,029 square feet, included six reading rooms with a seating capacity of 544, and book stack capacity of 75,000 volumes. Separate reading rooms were provided for reference and reserve books. Pamphlets, and periodicals, bound and unbound, were housed in the reference reading room. Other features were open book stacks for easy access to books; 76 individual study carrels; browsing areas in every reading room; 7 faculty studies for research purposes; 4 student conference rooms for group study; exhibit areas; seminar room; Founders' and Archives rooms;

catalog department and staff work room; receiving room; library classroom; newspaper alcove; typing area; and staff lounge. From the entrance lobby surrounded by glass, a full view of the center campus could be seen. The library building was reflected in the pool outside the building. The display area with exhibit cases and public telephone was located in the entrance lobby from which could be seen the main loan desk, library directory, a comfortable browsing area for viewing new books added to the collection, card catalog, kardex file for periodicals, and books by and about the Negro.

The beauty of the building, including the many facilities for improved services, was a tribute to the dreams and years of planning of President Reddix, under whose administration the library became a reality. The college was fortunate to have had the expert guidance of Dr. A. F. Kuhlman, director of Joint University Libraries, Nashville, Tennessee.

HENRY T. SAMPSON

The library was dedicated to Henry Thomas Sampson, administrator and scholar. The name was recommended by the National Alumni Association of Jackson State College. Recogition of the library as the true center of learning on a college campus was reflected in Sampson's educational philosophy, in precept and by example in his persistence and guidance in expanding library holdings and acquiring the role of a true scholar. He so disciplined his busy work schedule that he spent some time each day in the library reading, browsing, and discovering new books, articles, and ideas that kept him informed and fresh in his approaches to the broad spectrum of all the academic disciplines, and to life itself. Sampson's tenure as executive dean coincided with the period of greatest expansion and growth of the Jackson State College Library.

For more than half his life, Sampson was a vital part of the growth and development of Jackson State College. Born in Quitman, Georgia, he was educated in the public schools there, in the high school division of Savannah State College, and at Morehouse College in Atlanta where he received the B.S. degree in Science and

Mathematics in 1928. That fall, he came to Jackson College as a teacher of mathematics—and a teacher, in the true sense of the word, he remained. Even though his responsibilities increased and his talents for leadership and academic organization led him into college administration, he always found time to teach a class in mathematics and to discuss with students and faculty their personal and professional problems.

Sampson had the longest tenure as dean at Jackson State University (1933–38; 1942–67). He assumed this post when the institution was forty-four years old. The president saw fit to record in his history of the college the dean's standing in the academic community: "For his keen scholarship in mathematics and leadership ability among both faculty and students, he was granted a fellowship awarded by the General Education Board to study one year at the University of Chicago; he received the degree of Master of Science in mathematics in August, 1933, and thereupon, immediately returned as Dean of the College."[25]

Sampson served in this capacity till 1938, when he accepted the position as Junior Division dean at Savannah State College. Returning to Jackson State College in 1942 upon invitation of President Reddix, he served as executive dean until his death in January 1967. Two years of post-graduate study at Chicago University, in education and in administration, added professional insight and depth to the natural capabilities and creative mind of this educator.[26]

SEVENTY-FIFTH ANNIVERSARY CELEBRATION

In commemoration of the seventy-fifth anniversary (October 1952), of the institution, the Jackson State campus sparkled with Diamond Jubilee events sponsored by students, faculty, and alumni. The anniversary celebration focused on four components: (1) Literary Arts Festival, (2) Arts Festival, (3) Conference on Education, and (4) workshops. The artists who appeared on the first program included: Sterling A. Brown, author of *American Dilemma, Negro in American Fiction*, Negro poetry and drama, books of poems, *Southern Road*, and other writings, who addressed the audience on the topic "Backgrounds of Folklore in Negro Literature"; and Mrs. Willie Dobbs Blackburn, chairman of the Language Arts Division, who served as chairman of a panel on "The Role of the Writer in a Changing Culture." Participants on the panel included: Arna Bontemps, librarian-poet and novelist; Era Bell Thompson, author; Owen Dodson, poet, novelist, and playwright; and Langston Hughes, "Poet Laureate of the Negro People."

A pageant, "The Spirit of Jackson College," Depicting 75 Years of Educational Progress, was written by Margaret Walker Alexander in collaboration with President Jacob L. Reddix, Dr. Gloria B. Evans, and Rollin P. Greene, with music by William W. Davis. There were seven episodes, each treating a significant era in the history of the institution. The A Capella Choir presented a concert with Rowena Savage as guest soloist in an original work, "Psalmus Negroicus," a choral arrangement by E. Roger Clark, who was director of the Music Department.

The Education Conference drew to the campus nationally and internationally known speakers: Francis Russell, U.S. Department of State; James C. Evans, Department of Defense; William H. Hastie, governor of the Virgin Islands; David Goitein, minister plenipotentiary of Israel; and Joseph M. McDaniel and Clarence Faust of the Ford Foundation.

Luana Franklin Clayton conducted a workshop on "The Craft of Writing." Included in it were: Dr. Margaret Walker Alexander, novelist and poet, Langston Hughes, Arna Bontemps, and Robert Hayden. "The Negro in Drama" was the topic of a workshop conducted by Mrs. Ola Tatum Ford. Melvin Tolson was the featured speaker; Owen Dodson and Carolyn Hill Stewart were co-participants. A workshop, "Breath to the Life," a speech program, was under the directorship of Dr. Gloria B. Evans. Also staged was a play, "Divine Comedy," and "An Evening of Poetry," initiated by Dr. Margaret Walker Alexander, distinguished member of the faculty and writer.

It was during the Diamond Jubilee celebration (1951-52) that a new seal was designed. The first college seal had appeared on the *Jacksonian* in 1925. In 1940, when the institution was taken over by the state, and for a period of ten years, 1940-50, the Coat-of-Arms of the state of Mississippi was affixed on official documents. A special feature of the celebration was the publication of the *Brief History of Jackson College* by B. B. Dansby.

RESEARCH STUDIES OF GRADUATES

In 1951, Dr. Lee E. Williams' thesis presented to the Graduate School of the Ohio State University concerned itself with a study of the recent Jackson State graduates engaged in teaching. Included in his findings he stated that the study, "has helped the personnel at Jackson College to ascertain the extent to which its products have been prepared for the work they are doing."

In 1960, Dr. Cleopatra Thompson's dissertation, presented to the Graduate School of Cornell University, concerned itself with a follow-up study of 306 graduates of Jackson State for the period 1944-53. Dr. Thompson's study was concerned with how the graduates perceived their college training in preparing them to meet the problems of the world of work and of continued professional and general growth; the assessment of their effectiveness in contributing to the solution of community problems; and an assessment of the strengths and weaknesses of the program of education as it affected their preparations for employment and advanced academic pursuits.[27]

Appropriately, Dr. Thompson recommended that the institution no longer limit itself to the present structure as its major thrust in the training of teaching personnel to meet the needs of higher education for Negroes in Mississippi. Dr. Thompson felt that Jackson State must evaluate the curriculum offerings in light of a more meaningful program. She held that a major part of the program under state administration was geared to serving the rural area of Mississippi. Moreover, the college should face the problem of expanding its program to include more course offerings for pre-professional and professional students. She predicted that the impact of technological and scientific changes would add to the problems of job appointments for the Mississippi Negro if his educational opportunities failed to keep pace with these changes.[28]

By 1965, Dr. Elaine Paige Witty's dissertation, *A Proposed Master's Degree Program in Elementary Education at Jackson (Mississippi) State College*, took up where Dr. Thompson's thesis stopped. Dr. Witty saw that the objective of the program should be designed to (1) meet the needs of the teachers, (2) broaden their cultural horizons, and (3) help them learn how to broaden the cultural horizons of the pupils they teach. Dr. Witty felt that the program should focus on what teachers do as individuals and as members of the profession who work with disadvantaged children in relatively unfavorable school situations.[29]

The investigation focused mainly on problems of college evaluation and professional growth, community participation, occupational opportunity, and economic status with implications for improving the program of teacher education at Jackson State. One of the major findings included in the study revealed that 50 percent of the Jackson State graduates asked whether emphasis on courses in rural living was not too great and not very useful. The academic program should be, they said, strengthened notably by adding foreign languages and other courses in liberal education and specialized education.[30]

NAME CHANGES

Since the school had undergone four changes of name during his administration alone, President Reddix saw fit to mention all six such changes in his *Memoirs* stating the probable and real reasons for the various titles:

Natchez Seminary, October 23, 1877. According to a statement at the opening of the first session: "This Seminary is designed for the moral, religious, and intellectual improvement of Christian leaders of the colored people of Mississippi and the neighboring states."

Jackson College, March 1899. The College was moved to Jackson in order to be more centrally located for the black population of the state. The curriculum of the school was modified to emphasize the arts and sciences, as well as religious subjects, in order to better prepare ministers and teachers.

Jackson College, Incorporated, 1940. The legislature of 1940 was seriously discussing a bill to make the College a state institution. The lawyers for the state found that the corporate name Jackson College, as chartered in 1899, had a reversionary clause in the deed of the property written in such a way that should the property of the College cease to be used for the education of Negroes it would revert to the American Baptist Home Mission Society. Therefore, the state would not have a clear title to the property. A new charter was granted changing the name from Jackson College to Mississippi Negro Training School.

The Mississippi Negro Training School, 1940. When the bill to transfer Jackson College to the state was being discussed on the floor of the

House of Representatives, a member of the House objected to the bill. He stated frankly that he was not interested in a college for Negroes, what a 'Nigra' needed to learn was how to work—how to run a middle buster. He was reported to have said, "I am against calling this school a college; I move that we name this institution The Mississippi Negro Training School." The motion was carried.

Jackson College for Negro Teachers, March, 1944. The alumni went into action again. They were happy to eliminate the 'training' school stigma, but they were not pleased with the phrase 'for Negro Teachers.' This part of the new name not only limited the College as a race but also limited the curriculum to the training of teachers.

Jackson State College, 1956. When the Bill to change the name to Jackson State College came before the legislature in 1956, there was little or no opposition. Governor J. P. Coleman signed the bill without hesitation. Jackson State College is ready to serve the people of Mississippi in whatever field the Board of Trustees of Institutions of Higher Learning shall assign to it. The evolution of the name of the College throughout the years is an indication of the great progress that has been made in the area of human relations.[31]

ATHLETICS

The 1939-40 school year saw intercollegiate sports' demise—it was the fourth down, fourth quarter, and long yardage—for Jackson College, it was "time out." The academic year 1940 opened with the suspension of intercollegiate athletics. T. B. Ellis, who had joined President Dansby's staff as football coach, saw one year of action, 1939-40, in the private institution. Ellis' coaching career at Jackson State began with the 1939-40 school term.

From 1940-45, athletic competition was limited to intramural sports—basketball, softball, and track. Coach Ellis served as instructor of physical education and was in charge of the intramural activities. Those were the war years and there were few male students on the campus. Across the nation after the Second World War, returning football players found their services generated an enthusiam igniting the spark to put the team in motion again. The first play was called in the 1946-47 school year.

The Board of Trustees of State Institutions of Higher Learning approved the recommendation of the president of the college to sponsor a program of intercollegiate athletics. The approval of the recommendation by the governing board initiated the first competitive sports program for the college under state control. The program was inaugurated with the following objectives: to establish wholesome athletic relationships with comparable colleges; to acquire personnel, equipment, and facilities needed to support the program; to establish an athletic scholarship program for talented athletes; to seek membership in regional and national athletic associations. (Another section of this volume has been devoted to more definitive treatment of athletics.)

Based on his personal conviction that if an institution does not have funds necessary to develop intercollegiate sports it should drop them, President Reddix in 1940 recommended the elimination of sports from Jackson State College. Later on (from 1946-69), athletics was one of the programs conducted within the Department of Physical Education. In 1946, Jackson State was admitted to membership in the South Central Athletic Association.

In 1956, Jackson State College reorganized its athletic program with T. B. Ellis as director; Dr. Harrison B. Wilson, head basketball coach; Joan A. Merritt, head football coach; Alvin C. Coleman, line coach; and Joe Gilliam, backfield coach. Having become a member of the Southwest Athletic Conference, Jackson State College defeated Florida A&M University at the Orange Blossom Classic, and intercollegiate sports at Jackson State College reached the summit of popularity at that time.

The early 1960s served as a high moment of sports at Jackson State College. Since the team was the 1962 champions, recruiters came to the college at the end of every season to enroll professional players. This fact confirmed President Reddix's belief that intercollegiate sports, especially football and basketball, played an important part in breaking down segregation in sports throughout the United States.[32]

STUDENT ACTIVITIES

During World War II, not only sports but all student activities declined, resuming at an accelerated pace after the war. To accompany the transformation of the physical plant in the late 1940s was the augmentation of the student activities and organizations. The students and faculty had been able to develop a unique and effective system of student government which was an integral part of student life. Lottie Lorene Williams Thornton was the first student to serve as president of the Student Government Association under state control. John A. Peoples, Jr., is the only student to have served a two-year term, 1949–1950, as president of the Student Government Association.

In 1947, the institution permitted fraternities and sororities to establish chapters on the campus. Chapters of Alpha Kappa Alpha, Delta Sigma Theta, Sigma Gamma Rho, and Zeta Phi Beta sororities and Alpha Phi Alpha, Kappa Alpha Psi, Omega Psi Phi, and Phi Beta Sigma fraternities were formed at Jackson State. Two years later, in 1949, the establishment of Kappa Epsilon chapter of Alpha Kappa Mu Honorary Society was also initiated.

Other student organizations included the Dunbar Dramatic Guild; the Social Science Forum; the 4-H College Leadership Club; the Concert and Vesper Choirs; the Art Club; the "J" Club; the Mable Carney Chapter of the Future Teachers of America; the Industrial Arts Club; and the Vocational Veterans Club. The *Blue and White Flash* was the official student publication on the campus.

In his *Memoirs*, President Reddix held that peaceful protest is a powerful and dramatic instrument for bringing about social change, especially for the poor and neglected citizens of a democracy. The poor and the young want changes now, not tomorrow. During Reddix's 27-year tenure as president of Jackson State College, the institution granted upwards of 5,000 degrees to its students. He believed that this contribution was as important as participation in organized protests.

However, in the climate of the 1960s, some students acted irresponsibly and even dangerously in asserting their stand against racial injustice, war, and even the school itself.

CAMPUS UNREST

Beginning in 1965, there had been trouble every spring at Jackson State. Each time, it began on Lynch Street, a major four-lane thoroughfare that bisected the campus. According to a report from the President's Commission on Campus Unrest:

> Beginning one block east of the campus, the Commission reported bars and pool halls dot a three-block area along Lynch Street known as

"the corner." At night, black youths referred to locally as "corner boys" loiter in the area, mingling with and sometimes fighting students. There is a long history of friction between Jackson State students and corner boys; Dr. Peoples testified that he had been involved as a student in a gang fight with corner boys in 1950.

Alexander Hall (the largest women's dormitory), Stewart Hall (a men's dormitory), and the Campus Union were all on the north side of Lynch Street. During the day, pedestrian traffic by students was heavy on Lynch Street, and at night the Lynch Street area was a center of student activity.

Lynch Street connects downtown Jackson to the east with white neighborhoods farther west. For years, college authorities had urged the closing to automobile traffic of that portion of Lynch Street passing through the campus. Publicly, the problem of safety to pedestrians has been cited as the reason for the request; privately, members of the college community maintained that closing off Lynch Street would reduce friction by halting the flow of white policemen and white motorists through the campus.

According to the Commission's report, in 1965 rock-throwing began after a Jackson State College coed was struck on Lynch Street by a white male hit-and-run motorist; she received serious injuries. The driver of the car was never apprehended. Another minor rock-throwing incident occured on Lynch Street in the spring of 1966.

The Report chronicles incidents that happened in 1967. Jackson City police were pelted with rocks on the evening of May 10 after chasing a student and stopping him on campus for an alleged traffic violation. A band of angry students and nonstudents later roamed the Lynch Street area and set small fires, broke windows, looted stores, and threw rocks and concrete blocks at passing cars. Lynch Street was sealed off in the disturbance area. The next night rocks were thrown at policemen who manned a barricade near a Lynch Street intersection several blocks from the campus. An officer received a serious cut on the neck after being hit by a thrown bottle. Reinforcements from the Jackson City police and Mississippi Highway Safety Patrol were brought into the area. Some officers fired shotguns when a group of bystanders advanced toward the barricade. One black youth, Benjamin Brown, a Jackson resident, was found dead in the street from buckshot wounds, and two students received birdshot wounds. The protest was incomplete. The worst was yet to come. Another fatal incident would occur in May of 1970, but President Reddix would not then be in office.

THE FINALE

President Jacob L. Reddix will always have a place in the history of Jackson State College not only because of his lengthy tenure (1940–67), but also because he was a man of vision and action. The college really knew three Reddixes—a relatively young man, a middle-aged man, and an older man. He came to Jackson State directly from graduate school at the University of Chicago. He had taught mathematics and served as advisor on cooperatives in the U.S. Department of Agriculture; but he was a novice in college administration.

The youthful Reddix went about the task of "learning to be President" with high determination, a dedicated "old" faculty, and the wisdom of the former president, who served as his registrar; he also had assistance from the State Department of Education and the consultative service of Miss F. O. Alexander and Dr. Jane Ellen McAllister. As the years passed, he formulated and codified a program of instruction that greatly contributed to the educational opportunities of the black people of Mississippi.

In the midst of the crisis of integration, of the need for land acquisition, of expanding curriculum and increasing enrollment, many saw the middle-aged Reddix move the institution to a higher plateau.

Upon the approval of the Board of Trustees, the older Reddix broke loose from the limited concept of a college occupying a restricted area and laid out the metes and bounds of a greatly expanded institution. He pointed out and demonstrated the way by which the development could be financed. He laid a basis for the maintenance of a faculty and staff that could worthily people an institution. The tangible effects of his long and fruitful administration left an indelible seal on Jackson State College: curricula; auxillary programs; faculty; facilities; enrollment; state appropriations;

federal grants, foundation support; physical expansion concomitant with academic vision.

When Jacob L. Reddix took over the presidency of Jackson College, there was little fanfare, no pomp and circumstance, no parade of dignitaries from colleges and universities, no representatives from learned societies for an inauguration. President Reddix was welcomed by the Board of Trustees that controlled the college before state control and by the Board of Trustees of State Institutions of Higher Learning at the commencement exercise in 1940.

On February 26, 1967, a special recognition program for President Reddix was sponsored by the National Alumni Association of Jackson State College. Mrs. Frances D. Robertson, president, Jackson State College National Alumni Association, presided at the program. The theme "The Spirit, Service and Dedication of President Jacob L. Reddix" permeated all the tributes presented in honor of the out-going president.

Dr. W. W. Clark, associate director of programs and planning, representing the Board of Trustees of Institutions of Higher Learning; J. M. Tubb, the Mississippi State Department of Education; Dean Lionel B. Fraser, the faculty and staff; Hermel Johnson, president of the Student Government Association and the student body; B. L. Sykes, second vice president of the Jackson State College Alumni Association; President Reddix's minister, the Reverend Dr. S. Leon Whitney, pastor of Farish Street Baptist Church; and many other civic, educational, and fraternal organizations paid tribute to him. Lee E. Williams and Lelia G. Rhodes served as chairpersons of the program.

On March 3, 1967, in honor of Dr. Jacob L. Reddix, President John A. Peoples, Jr. sponsored an appreciation dinner in the B. F. Roberts Dining Hall. Dr. Lee E. Williams, director of placement, served as master of ceremonies. The invocation was given by the Reverend Leon Bell, the college chaplain; the occasion by Dr. Rose McCoy, professor of education and psychology.

The sonnet "Jacob L. Reddix, the Builder," written by Dr. Margaret Walker Alexander, professor of English, during the seventy-fifth anniversary celebration of the college, was set to music by Mrs. Aurelia Young, assistant professor of music, and presented by the Jackson State College Ensemble.

The Symphony of the Whole Individual   141

Special tributes were given by Dr. B. B. Dansby, President Emeritus; Mrs. Willie D. Blackburn, chairman of the Language Arts Area; Dr. Dollye Robinson, Head of the Music Department, on behalf of the faculty; Mrs. Lottie Thornton, class of 1944, assistant professor of education; Ruben Gentry, class of 1967, senior class president; Hermel Johnson, president of the Student Government Association; and the administration represented by Dr. John A. Peoples, Jr.

President Reddix closed the service with his response—expressing thanks to President Peoples, the faculty and staff for the testimonial dinner. Obviously moved by these tributes to his twenty-seven years as president, Reddix praised the administration, faculty, staff, students, and friends for helping him make the college the great institution it had become.

On May 9, 1973 President Reddix died. Memorial services were held in the Dansby Hall Auditorium May 14, 1973. His immediate survivors are his widow, Mrs. Jacob L. Reddix (Daisy Shirley Reddix), his daughter, Mrs. Shirley A. Vanderpool and a granddaughter, Dwan.

CHAPTER VII

THE ADVANCEMENT OF TRUTH AND FREEDOM

The Administration of Dr. John A. Peoples, Jr., 1967–

IN HIS INAUGURAL ADDRESS OF MARCH 8, 1968, Dr. John A. Peoples, Jr. stated, "The mission of Jackson State to this day is that of providing for education under such conditions that meaningful truth is derived and such that those who are involved in the process will be able to experience freedom, not theoretical freedom, but actual freedom as well. Freedom that is tangible, freedom that is relevant, not only to all ethnic groups, but also to all economic and social groups." Thus did he begin a new era in the development of Jackson State University.[1]

Excited at the opportunity to serve his people, President Peoples saw his task as that of opening doors for more and better students and of giving them the faculty and resources that would assure them a quality education. He wished to train their intellect to see the truth in order that the enlightened intellect would influence the will to choose the good. "Teaching," said Peoples in his inaugural address, "is the process of setting up and conducting situations which will bring about positive changes in behavior of the learners." For college learners, teaching is primarily concerned with intellectual changes of the type which are dynamic and applicable. Teaching is concerned with behavioral changes which will literally transform the mind and spirit of the student, along with adding to his factual knowledge and vocational skills.

Investing Dr. Peoples with the insignia of the presidency, Dr.

THE ADMINISTRATION OF JOHN A. PEOPLES, JR.

THE PRESIDENT'S EMBLEM

At the Inaugural Convocation Mr. S. R. Evans, Chairman of the Board of Trustees, Institutions of Higher Learning, representing the Board of Trustees, invested Dr. Peoples with a new emblem symbolic of The Office of The Presidency. The Medallion, (which became the official school seal) five inches in diameter and executed in bronze, was designed by Lawrence and Marie Jones in 1968. In the new seal the rays of the sun symbolize the trivium and quandrivium while the rising sun symbolizes hope. The scroll is for learning and the raised torch is symbolic of truth. The motto encircling this new seal is, "You Shall Know the Truth and the Truth Shall Set You Free." On March 15, 1974, this seal was also revised to include the official name—Jackson State University.

Board of Trustees of State Institutions of Higher Learning

The Inaugural Address

Mr. S. R. Evans, President of the Board of Trustees, Institutions of Higher Learning, State of Mississippi presents medallion emblematic of the Office of the Presidency.

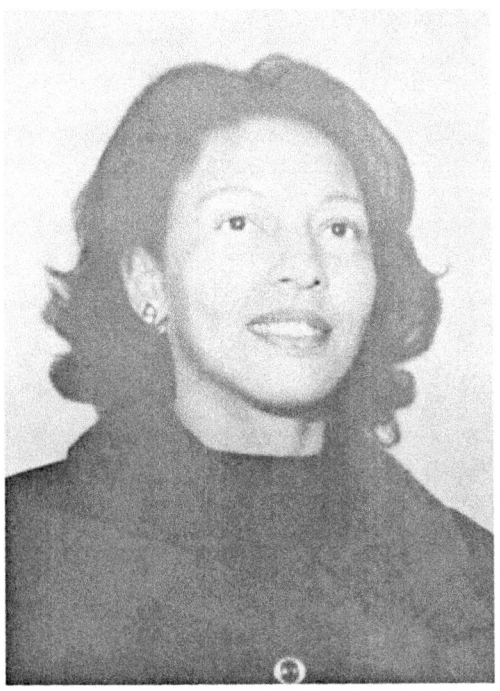

Mrs. John A. Peoples, First Lady—Official Campus Hostess

The Presidents at President Jacob L. Reddix' Retirement Program. (Reading Left-Right) The Scholar-Innovator—President Peoples, The Builder—President Emeritus Reddix, The Preserver—President Emeritus Dansby.

VICE PRESIDENTS/ACADEMIC DEANS

Dr. Lee E. Williams
Vice President for Administration,
1940-

Dr. Estus Smith
Vice President for Academic Affairs,
1962-

Dr. Paul W. Purdy (1967-)
Vice President for Fiscal Affairs

Dr. George A. Johnson (1970-)
Vice President for Student Affairs

Dr. T. J. Robinson (1963-) Associate Vice President for University Relations

Dr. Oscar Allan Rogers, Jr. (1960-) Dean, The Graduate School

Dean Henry Thomas Sampson, Professor of Mathematics and Executive Dean of Jackson State College 1933-1938, 1942-1967.

Dr. Wilbert Greenfield
Dean of Instruction (1968-71)
Dean of Academic Affairs (1971-72)

Dr. Haskell Bingham (1965-) Dean, Admission and Records

Dr. Dennis Holloway (1966-) Associate Dean for Academic Affairs

President Richard Nixon and staff meet with selected presidents of the historically black colleges 1970.

President Peoples, chairman of the Board of American Council on Education along with the Executive Directors of several higher educational associations meet with President Gerald R. Ford to discuss problems regarding federal support for higher education.

Scenes depicting the ceremony with Governor William Waller and President John A. Peoples designating Jackson State College as a University, March 15, 1974.

Governor Waller and President Peoples following signing ceremony.

Governor Waller speaks to assembly before signing document designating Jackson State as a university.

JACKSON STATE UNIVERSITY RIOT
MAY 1970

Phillip L. Gibbs 21, Jackson State University student. Killed in riot May 14, 1970.

James Earl Green 17, a graduating senior of Jim Hill High School in Jackson. Killed in riot May 14, 1970.

West wing of Alexander Hall viewed from the south side of Lynch Street the morning after the riot of May 14, 1970.

SCENES FROM JACKSON STATE UNIVERSITY RIOT
MAY 1970

Shown with President John A. Peoples, (right) touring the campus are Charles Evers, (left) Field Secretary for NAACP with Senator Edward Brooks and Dean Tommie Smith in the background.

Campus scene in front of West Wing of Alexander Hall, students, sympathizers and on-lookers.

Students are advised by Rev. Ralph Abernathy, Leader Southern Christian Leadership Conference "to keep cool."

Civil Rights Congressional Delegation Hearing (left to right) Roy Wilkins, National NAACP Director; Joseph Rauh, Civil Rights Attorney; Congressman Don Edward (D-Calif.), Senator Birch Bayh (D-Ind.), Cliford Alexander, former Chairman Equal Employment Opportunity Commission; not shown are: Senator Walter Mondale (D-Minn.), Congressman William Clay (D-Mo.)

Jackson State University Band—1977

Jackson State University Choir—1977

Governor Jimmy Carter's Presidential Campaign visit to Jackson State University—October 7, 1975. Left to right are Dr. Oscar A. Rogers, Dr. Curtis Baham and Governor Jimmy Carter.

Scenes from Jackson State University's observance of the Nation's Bicentennial.

Scenes from Jackson State University's Opening Centennial Celebration, September 1976

Upper left scene, Dr. Sam Cobbins presents Centennial Mace to President Peoples. Upper right scene, President Peoples addresses opening Centennial Celebration on Lynch Street Plaza.

Scenes from Centennial Convocation Tenth Anniversary of President John A. Peoples, Jr., March 2, 1977.

President Peoples at the lectern introduces Dr. Samuel Proctor.

President Peoples with speaker, Dr. Samuel Proctor, Martin Luther King Professor, Rutgers University

JACKSON STATE UNIVERSITY
NATIONAL ALUMNI ASSOCIATION
PRESIDENTS

Edgar T. Stewart 1938-44 (Deceased) A. B. Jackson College 1932, LL. B. LaSalle Extension University, Chicago, Illinois, 1938. Teacher-Letter Carrier, Mississippi/Tennesse.

Mr. A. A. Alexander '28 1944-48 Principal Alexander High School, Lincoln County, Assistant Supervisor of Public Schools for the State Department of Education, President of the Mississippi Teachers Association; Inducted into the JSU Sports Hall of Fame.

Mrs. Lottie W. Thornton '44 (1948-50) Assistant Professor of Elementary Education and Director of Early Childhood Center.

Mrs. Estelle Young 1950-54 Extension Home Economist—Lauderdale Branch of Mississippi State University.

ALUMNI PRESIDENTS

Dr. Lee E. Williams '40 1954-66
Assistant to President John A. Peoples, Jr. and Vice President for Administration.

Mrs. Frances D. Robertson 1966-72
Assistant Principal, Greenwood High School

Mr. Edward S. Bishop '30 1972-76
Coach at Lanier High School; Principal, Eastview High School, Corinth; Director of Community Child Development Program, Corinth; Guest Professor at Jackson State; Inductee—JSU Sports Hall of Fame

Dr. Estemore A. Wolfe '47, 1976-
Vice President and Secretary for Wright Mutual Insurance Company in Detroit, Michigan. He is organizer and reactivator of eleven alumni chapters for Jackson State University. He is now serving his second term as President

The Bell—Ringing of the bell ushered in the beginning of the Second Century—October 23, 1977

West Entrance to the Campus

S. R. Evans, president of the Board of Trustees, State Institutions of Higher Learning, gave Peoples the following charge:

> The education of our citizens is a tremendous responsibility in our state. However, I am convinced that we in Mississippi can build and support a program of excellence in higher education on which we and our posterity will look with pride. Jackson State College has an important role in this program. Under your leadership, this institution is expected to continue to inspire responsible activity from students, vigorous achievement from faculty, devoted loyalty from the alumni and respectful appreciation from all of us.

In the presence of B. Baldwin Dansby and Jacob L. Reddix, presidents emeriti of Jackson State College, Dr. Peoples accepted the charge, pledging to emulate his five predecessors, each of whom had made a unique contribution to Jackson State University. He vowed to etch his mark of service on the shield of the presidency.

Accepting what he termed "the awesome charge," President Peoples delivered his inaugural address with characteristic straightforwardness, basing it on the motto of Jackson State College—"You Shall Know the Truth and the Truth Shall Make You Free."

> Both concepts, truth and freedom, are too often conceived merely in abstract, having little or no relationship to the real affairs of men. Truth is seen simply as the opposite of falsehood; and freedom merely as the opposite of slavery. Only the naïve will venture to tell the whole truth and only the dreamers will consider themselves absolutely free.
>
> If the simple truth were to be forthrightly advanced in our political system, demagogues in high places—whether to the right or to the left of the ideological center—would precipitously demise for lack of false issues with which to exploit the minds of the ignorant. If the honest truth were to be advanced in our social system, misanthropes, hatemongers as well as paternalistic do-gooders, would be foiled for lack of pseudocauses to champion.[2]

From the moment of his inauguration, President Peoples vowed that the motto of Jackson State would be the guiding light to steer him through Scylla and Charybdis dangers of contemporary Mississippi. He would be free in the service of truth.

Most serious, however, was the constriction of freedom to seek and promote the truth. There was not only reluctance, but a genuine fear to advance the truth even though such truth might provide solutions to the most pressing problems of society.

In his inaugural speech, Peoples recalled that Jackson State College had been established by the American Baptist Home Mission Society in 1877. The explicit and implicit purpose of that institution was to provide for the education, under free conditions, of that group of American citizens which previously had been held in bondage. And though there may have been some variation over the years in this explicit role as stipulated in legal or official documents, there had been no change in its implicit mission, said Peoples, pointing out that not even legal decisions and laws regarding discrimination had altered this original purpose "to free the unfree of mind and spirit."

Peoples' address was a blueprint for the future development of Jackson State College. While accepting its original purpose, "to free the unfree of mind and spirit," President Peoples opened the door for all youth who wished to be educated in a community dedicated to truth and freedom.

In order to involve the whole academic community in implementing the hopes of the inaugural address, a symposium, "Truth and Freedom on the College Campus," was held March 8, 1968, under the chairmanship of Dr. Margaret Walker Alexander. Featured in each of four sessions were addresses by Arna Bontemps, professor of Negro history and Negro literature, University of Illinois; Dr. Charles Hayes, Chief, Developing Institutions Branch, Division of College Support, U. S. Office of Education, Washington, D. C.; Dr. Matthew Walker, head surgeon, Meharry Medical College, Nashville, Tennessee; and Dr. St. Clair Drake, professor of sociology of Roosevelt College, Chicago.

Many alumni were proud of the fact that Jackson State's sixth president was a graduate of the college. The university nearly missed this honor when the ex-marine was searching for an institution at which he could study mathematics. In focusing on Mississippi, Peoples fortunately chose Jackson State and set out to prepare for his mission.

Upon returning to civilian life in 1947, Peoples' options were limited for entering the kind of institution of higher learning he desired. He dreamed of entering Massachusetts Institute of Technology or the California Institute of Technology. With hundreds of other veterans also clamoring to enter these schools on the GI Bill, however, education authorities limited entrance to in-state veterans. Out-of-state veterans would have to wait at least two years to become eligible to register at MIT and CIT.

Peoples realized the utility of choosing a college in Mississippi. Having been born and reared in Starkville around Mississippi State University, he had considered it a worthwhile opportunity to visit and evaluate institutions of higher learning in the Carolinas while visiting friends who were studying there. He had hardly heard of Jackson State before he approached A. C. Henderson, his high school principal, for advice. Henderson himself had gauged the caliber of Dean Henry T. Sampson as a teacher of mathematics. He advised Peoples to matriculate at Jackson State and carry out his studies in mathematics under Dean Sampson. Henderson had signed Peoples' high school transcript, not realizing that some accidental erasure on it prevented the applicant's chances to enter Jackson State.

Since two cousins of his attended Tougaloo College as premedicine students, Peoples was tempted several times to join them. Furthermore, relatives and friends attempted to discourage him from going to Jackson State by claiming it was nothing but a teachers' college. Dean Sampson had several talks with him and finally influenced him to enroll at Jackson State. After securing a completed and correct transcript, Peoples began his career preparation in 1947. Discovering that Jackson State did not offer a major in mathematics, Peoples registered his concern with Sampson who assured him that the administration would add a program in mathematics for secondary school teachers before his junior year. Dean Sampson also assured Peoples that he could enter mathematics classes for college sophomores in the second quarter of the academic year. Peoples agreed to follow Sampson's suggestion. Moreover, Peoples had proved himself convincingly because he had earned A grades in freshman first quarter courses. Hence, Sampson was delighted to instruct him for the remaining undergraduate years. He was greatly influenced in his career choice by his freshman advisors, Gloria Evans and Rose Embly.

Joining other activities on the campus, Peoples failed to make first string of the football team in his freshman year. Peoples achieved this difficult goal of proving his worth to Coach T. B. Ellis by accepting the position of end instead of halfback. Called in when others were losing the game, Peoples proved his mettle and finally excelled. He never ceased to work diligently as an athlete during the remaining football seasons. As the young athlete performed with great enthusiasm and vigor, Ellis, who was always stingy with praise, was heard to say: "Peoples, you're looking a little more like a football player."

Chosen as president of the Student Government Association, Peoples was often called upon to show good judgment and courage in defending the rights of students. The experiences he had lived through in the Marine Corps—segregation, leadership of a platoon—prepared him to handle problems and to deal both with his peers and his superiors at Jackson State. A case in point was his appeal to President Reddix who had summarily dismissed several athletes who were hazing freshmen. One of the athletes dismissed was not involved in the hazing, but just looking on. Peoples sought a conference with President Reddix and Rev. Richard Middleton, dean of men, and requested that the student who was not involved be readmitted. The appeal was successful and Peoples won the respect of the president for his tactfulness.

Peoples had an opportunity to further gain the respect of the president when the athletic scholarships were established at Jackson State University. For budgetary reasons, the scholarships were not at first awarded to athletes who were veterans. Representatives of the veterans asked Peoples, a former military man himself, to make an appeal to President Reddix on their behalf. The president consented to talk with Peoples about this situation and Peoples was able to convince him that veterans should not be denied these scholarships. After considering the matter, President Reddix on the next day issued a memorandum in favor of the veterans.

Not all of Peoples' encounters with administrators were as successful as the veteran affair. On one occasion, Peoples became the victim of opposing instructions from two powerful administrators. Coach Ellis assigned Peoples to the barracks to be occupied by freshman athletes who were veterans and who also needed tutoring.

Odessa Howard Waters, the dean of students, viewed Peoples not as a tutor of veterans, but as a "radical" always asserting himself for student rights. Fearing that Peoples might "radicalize" the freshmen, Dean Waters countermanded Ellis' assignment and demanded that Peoples be sent to another dormitory. Ellis asserted himself and again assigned Peoples to the barracks. Dean Waters still insisted that Peoples, the "persistent radical," the ex-marine, tutor, and defender of students rights, be sent to another dormitory. In answer to her upbraiding, Peoples confirmed the dean's fears by pointing out that administrators ought to make up their minds among themselves on what they wanted students to do instead of kicking them around like footballs. The dean countered that she would get Peoples out of Jackson State if he did not watch his impudent tongue. The dean prevailed in her effort to prevent Peoples from residing in the barracks. But, despite her orders, Peoples did tutor the incoming freshman veterans who were athletes.

During his senior year in 1950 (he completed his college career in three years), Peoples continued his efforts in defense of senior privileges which were often interfered with by Dean Waters. Together with members of the class of 1950, Peoples drew up a resolution which he presented to President Reddix March 27, 1950, which read in part:

Whereas we believe that every individual admitted into college regardless of academic status should be assumed to be of unquestionable moral character, unless past record shows otherwise or until he exhibits the contrary after entrance, and

Whereas we believe that students of college age are generally sufficiently mature to conduct themselves in a manner becoming to ladies and gentlemen, and

Whereas we consider it unfair that the personnel administration of Jackson College in trying to adjust their policy to preclude immoral conduct by an isolated few, has inadvertently abrogated the opportunity of the vast majority of students to gain the invaluable experience of social adjustment without undue restrictions, and

Whereas we believe that seniors because of their training and experiences, and consequent prudence in social relationships should be categorically considered as persons of high moral character and integrity, and

Whereas since underclassmen usually aspire to attain the status enjoyed by seniors and such aspirations serve as an incentive for them....

After graduation, Peoples, in trying to emulate Dean Sampson, went directly to the University of Chicago in June 1950. He wanted to obtain an M.A. in mathematics from the same school Sampson had attended, but was not allowed to enter into the program because he had not taken the necessary requirements in physics and foreign languages on the undergraduate level. In order to bypass these requirements, he was advised to enter the program of teaching mathematics in secondary schools, a program similar to Jackson State's current M.A.T. in mathematics.

Life at the University of Chicago was a different kind of challenge to Peoples, different from life in the Marine Corps and different from life at Jackson State. The only black student in the dormitory at the time, Peoples did not swerve from the challenge before him. Graduate studies were more exacting than his undergraduate experience. The competition was much keener and Peoples realized the seriousness of the matter. With vigor and diligence, he nevertheless mastered his assignments and proved his ability to compete.

It was the era of President Hutchins. Men in the dormitory voted against the use of television sets in the public halls. Instead, they met and talked incessantly on topics which sharpened Peoples' mind. He had to read voluminously, including at least three newspapers a day, to keep abreast of the topics that were discussed. And such discourses were held at any given time and at any given place, including the cafeteria, where one could join even foreign language groups in discussing current topics in foreign tongues.

Peoples joined the Sunday after-dinner Speaker's Club where he further sharpened his wit. While his logical and rhetorical skills were enhanced by constant practice, his exposure to classical music helped him to appreciate it in the climate in which it was presented.

The Indiana town where Peoples found employment upon receiving his master's degree from the University of Chicago, was one of the twenty-five cities to which he inquired by letter in search of a job. The response from Gary had simply been negative. Refusing to give up, Peoples consulted President Reddix and told him about his plight. Reddix told him he would write a letter to a Bernice Engels, who had been a supervisor of mathematics when he worked in Gary. In response, the public school administrator called Peoples in for an interview and gave him a job which he accepted in March 1951. Meanwhile, he married on July 13, 1951, to the former Mary Galloway of Canton. They are the parents of two children, Kathleen, a doctoral candidate in Clinical Psychology at the University of Michigan; and Mark, a freshman pre-med student at Mississippi State University. The 13 years at Gary, where Peoples served as a mathematics teacher, an assistant principal, and a principal, were filled with experiences that matured him both as a man and an administrator and prepared him for the presidency of Jackson State. During the entire period, he carried on an intimate correspondence with President Reddix, who valued him as a student, an athlete, and a potential leader.

As early as 1948, President Reddix saw in Peoples the potential of becoming an administrator. Meeting Peoples by chance on the campus after a football game in which Jackson State had defeated Dillard University by a score of 46 to 6, Reddix praised the athlete for his two touchdowns during the contest and added, "I had known that you were a good student; but I never knew that you were such a good football player." The administrator later engaged in a conversation with the athlete, asking the latter about his future plans. Peoples had told Reddix he was going to the University of Chicago to get a master's degree in mathematics. Vehemently, Reddix started persuading the young man to major in administration. Peoples took note of the recommendation, but chose to be a teacher instead. Apparently he was much more influenced by the mathematics teacher in Dean Sampson than he was by the administrator in President Reddix. Sampson had been to Peoples an affectionate mentor; Reddix was a symbol of authority. Peoples' dream was to become a great mathematics teacher.

President Reddix had followed the course of Peoples' life. During a visit to Chicago on one occasion, he phoned Peoples at the University of Chicago and invited him out to dinner, during which Reddix assured Peoples that he could become an administrator. This was the first time that Reddix had alluded to the fact that sooner or later he would have to retire. He confessed openly that he wanted someone like Peoples to be his successor.

On frequent visits to Gary, President Reddix visited him, he would communicate with Peoples and remind the Mississippian that he would like to see him return South as president of Jackson State. Upon learning that Peoples had begun his studies for a doctorate at the University of Chicago, Reddix tried to entice him to return to Jackson State as an instructor in order to secure a fellowship to complete his doctoral studies. Peoples refused to take the offer. In fact, the situation became embarrassing, for on visits to Jackson, Peoples avoided encounters with President Reddix. However, friends of Peoples would report to President Reddix that the young man was in Jackson.

As time went on, Peoples became entrenched in Gary. As a principal, he had tenure, and so did his wife, a teacher. They had built a home. Reddix was persistent in his pursuit of Peoples. In 1962, the president of Jackson State invited Peoples as guest speaker on Alumni Day. He was affording the young administrator the exposure he would some day need on home grounds.

Coming to Jackson State in 1962, Peoples began to perceive Jackson State in a new light. The Language Arts Building had just been completed and gave a new view to the growing campus. Jackson State had just gained national attention through a victory in football over Florida A&M in the Orange Bowl Classic. President Reddix was very optimistic about the future of Jackson State and convinced Peoples that Jackson State was going to be the school of the future because of its location.

Meanwhile, having obtained his doctorate from the University of Chicago in 1961, Dr. Peoples seriously began to think of leaving Gary, which was getting stagnant and politicized. He had several attractive offers from the New York Public School System as a principal and another from an Illinois county system that was thinking of getting a black superintendent. He had a third offer from Pasadena, California—this one to assume the post of assistant superintendent. In 1963, Reddix went to Gary on a visit and revealed to Dr. Peoples that he was very close to retirement, pleading with Peoples to come to Jackson "to save the institution." Dr. Peoples made no commitment but promised to think about it together with his wife.

In 1963, Dr. Lee E. Williams, the National Alumni Association president of Jackson State, went to Gary with an alumni resolution naming Dr. Peoples as outstanding man of the year and their choice to succeed Dr. Reddix. Williams was so convincing in persuading Peoples to accept the post of service to higher education that the latter seriously began to consider leaving Gary in spite of his attachment to the city and the comfort of his home.

Subsequently, President Reddix repeatedly telephoned Dr. Peoples requesting him to return to Mississippi. In the spring of 1964, Reddix succeeded in getting Peoples to Jackson State to meet a group of alumni and talk with a committee of the college board. The trip resulted in Dr. Peoples' decision to join the administration of Jackson State as assistant to the president. He was also named associate professor of mathematics.

In 1966, Peoples was chosen as a Fellow in the American Council on Education Program. Placed at the State University of New York at Binghamton, Peoples studied academic administration under President Bruce Dearing. His assignment was to assist President Dearing in the top administrative post at the university. At the end of the experience, Peoples returned to Jackson State as vice president to President Reddix. Of his class of ACE Fellows, Peoples was the first to become president of a college, on March 3, 1967.

Four priorities were the immediate concern of the new president: reorganization of the academic program; reorganization of the administration; strengthening of the faculty; and improvement of the administration–faculty–student relations.

ACADEMIC PROGRAMS

Functioning in the college when Dr. Peoples began his presidency were six academic areas: Fine Arts: art education and music education; Health and Physical Education; Language Arts: English literature, modern foreign languages, speech and theater, and professional education programs; Practical Arts: industrial arts and homemaking; Science and Mathematics: biology, chemistry, mathematics, pre-dental, pre-medical, and pre-engineering; Social Sciences: history, sociology, business administration, economics, geography, social science, and business education.

President Peoples initially reorganized the six areas into two divisions: Liberal Studies with four areas: fine arts, language arts, natural sciences, and social sciences; and Education and Technical

Studies with two areas: education and technical studies. The two divisions encompassed sixteen departments and a single graduate studies program functioning within the divisions and departments. Peoples worked closely with the Board of Trustees, Institutions of Higher Learning, who on April 20, 1967, approved the instructional reorganization of Jackson State to become effective July 1, 1967.

In 1970, Peoples upgraded the two divisions into the School of Liberal Studies and the School of Education and Technical Studies. The first had five divisions: fine arts, language arts, natural sciences, social sciences and military science. The second had six departments: educational psychology, health and physical education, industrial arts, librarianship, reading, teacher education and field services. The Division of Business became a separate unit with three programs: accounting, business administration, and business education.

By 1973, the schools were expanded in number to include the School of Liberal Studies (1968), the School of Education (1969), the School of Business and Economics (1972), the Graduate School (1972), and the School of Industrial and Technical Studies (1973).

The school reorganization facilitated a more efficient administration of the rapidly expanding enrollments and programs with continuing qualitative improvements. The evolution of the organizational structure was indicative of the forward thrust of the college.

Major developments since 1968 in the School of Liberal Studies included developing a Master of Science in Teaching Program in Natural Sciences, an Army ROTC program, and a B.S. degree program in Computer Science, all in 1969. In 1970-71, master's degree programs in English education and social studies and a bachelor's degree program in industrial chemistry were organized. Appropriation of funds for the fine arts building and Administration Tower and classroom complex, commissioning of the first ROTC graduates, and faculty publications through the University and College Press of Mississippi were among the major developments of the 1968-76 academic years. Twenty-three degree programs in seventeen departments were developed at the bachelor's level. Master's degrees were granted in five teaching specializations, and the specialist in education degree program was developed in three fields of study.

In addition to its varied curricula, the instructional departments in the School of Liberal Studies make vigorous efforts to contribute to the intellectual and cultural life of the college and the community through numerous curricula and special activities, such as performing groups, lecture series, and lyceum presentations. In 1971, the USO European Tour by student representatives of the Jackson State College Music Department carried the music talent of the college to foreign countries. Participation and leadership of the Music and Art departments in Opera/South have added a new dimension to the cultural life of the South. A more definitive account of the company and their productions is indicated elsewhere in this volume.

Curricular changes, evaluation, innovation, experimentation, and research typified the continuing search for better means of achieving the aims of the School of Liberal Studies. Construction of a music center and a classroom complex housing social sciences, computer science, and business augmented the physical facilities supporting the academic programs in the school. The growth of the School of Education is equally revealing.

In 1976, the eleven departments in the School of Education offered academic programs and services leading to the bachelor's and master's degrees. Eight degree programs were offered at the bachelor's level. Master's degrees were granted in five teaching specializations.

In addition to its regular curricular offerings, the school employed a wide variety of programs and activities in pursuit of its goals. These programs and activities included the regular academic year, summer terms, evening and weekend classes, conferences, institutes, workshops, seminars. Other innovative projects and research have included the Teacher Corps Program; Education for Handicapped Children; the Adult Education Project; Early Childhood Education Project; and a Career Opportunities Program for the improvement of education for young children and the building of careers for veterans and other adults. A new three-story modern structure built in 1974 is currently housing the School of Education programs.

The School of Business and Economics became a reality in 1972. All disciplines comprising the school evolved rapidly. The Department of Business, begun in the 1965-66 school year, grew to such an extent that in 1969 it was designated the Division of Business. Reflected in the division was the nationwide emphasis on business training for black students.

Growing out of the social science curriculum, the Department of Economics was transferred from the School of Liberal Studies to the School of Business and effected the present name change to School of Business and Economics. In 1966-67, the Department of Business, Economics, and Geography was comprised of six faculty members. The new School of Business and Economics currently has 30 faculty members, six lecturers, and 989 student majors.

Graduate studies at Jackson State were authorized by the Board of Trustees in 1953. Instruction was limited to educational administration and supervision, for which the first Master of Science in Education degrees were awarded in 1957. Dr. Augustus C. Blanks was the first professor to give direction to graduate studies. In 1959, Dr. Charles C. Mosley was named as director and eventually became dean of the graduate program. Dr. Mosley was succeeded by Dr. Oscar Allan Rogers, who became dean of the graduate program in 1969. In 1972, the graduate program was elevated to school status, the result of a comprehensive expansion effort. In that year, the Master of Business Administration, the Master of Arts, and the Specialist in Education degrees were offered for the first time. In 1974, the Master of Science degree was offered.

The Graduate School is composed of those departments which offer graduate instruction leading to master's and educational specialist degrees. Members of the graduate faculty actively engage in scholarly pursuits such as teaching, research, writing, publishing, and participating in professional organizations. The Graduate School dean has supervision of all graduate work at the university.

As noted in the *Jackson State University Graduate Catalog, 1976-78*, the Graduate School offers: Master of Arts programs in economics, English, history, linguistics, political science, sociology; Master of Science in biology, chemistry, community and agency counseling, computer science, environmental science, and mathematics; Master of Arts in Teaching in art, English, modern foreign languages, and social studies; Master of Science in Teaching in biology, chemistry, mathematics, and general science; Master of Science in Education in adult education, elementary education, early childhood education, educational administration and supervision, guidance, health, physical education and recreation, industrial arts, reading, special education, and educational technology; Master of Business Administration; Master of Business Education; Master of Music Education; Specialist in Education Degree in biology, chemistry, early childhood education, educational administration and supervision, elementary education, English, guidance and counseling, mathematics, and physical education.

Another historic milestone in the growth and development during this era occurred March 15, 1974, in a special convocation, the Honorable William Waller, Governor of the state of Mississippi proclaimed a change in the name of Jackson State College to Jackson State University. Copies of this document are on file in the university archives.

ADMINISTRATIVE REORGANIZATION

Concomitantly with the reorganization of the curriculum, President Peoples expanded the administrative structure of the college. Under three deans and the chief fiscal officer he grouped several officers. Reporting to the dean of instruction were the assistant dean of instruction, the assistant dean of graduate studies, the head librarian, the director of admissions, a director of the Audio-Visual Center, the registrar, the dean of education and technical studies in charge of six departments, and the assistant dean for liberal studies in charge of four divisions. Responsible to the dean for administration were the director of public relations, a director of development, an alumni secretary, the director of placement, an athletic director, and the college secretarial personnel.

Working under the chief fiscal officer were the director of plant operations, the coordinator of student aid, a chief accountant and budget and payroll officer, a purchasing agent, a director of food services, and a bookstore manager. Answering to the dean of students were the assistant dean for men and security police, the assistant dean for women, the director of the Campus Union, a coordinator of student activities, a health center officer, and the director of housing.

In 1968, President Peoples appointed chief administrative officers: Wilbert Greenfield, dean of instruction; Lee E. Williams, dean for administration; Cleopatra D. Thompson, associate dean for education and technical studies; Estus Smith, associate dean for liberal studies; Oscar A. Rogers, acting assistant dean for graduate studies.

Titles and positions in 1973 reflected quite a change in the administrative structure. With at least one resignation and several new appointments, the following persons were in place: Estus Smith became vice president for academic affairs; Lee E. Williams, vice president for administration; George A. Johnson, vice president for student affairs; Paul W. Purdy, vice president for fiscal affairs; T. J. Robinson, associate vice president for university relations; Oscar A. Rogers, dean, School of Graduate Studies; Cleopatra D. Thompson, dean, School of Education; Robert H. Smith; dean, School of Liberal Studies; George F. Currie, dean, School of Business and Economics; Jay T. Smith, dean, School of Industrial and Technical Studies. Parallel to efforts to strengthen the administration, President Peoples also began developing and assembling a strong faculty.

When Peoples was appointed to the presidency in 1967, the faculty consisted of 124 members with only 24 holding earned terminal degrees. Peoples used three basic approaches to strengthen the faculty: he provided financial support for dozens of young instructors to pursue advanced degrees; he increased his faculty with new members, most of whom held the terminal degree; he began appointing as heads of departments only persons holding the terminal degree. Peoples requested and received higher salaries from the Board of Trustees and used these funds to attract well-prepared specialists who could carry out effective teaching, significant research, and varied services. Table VII illustrates the progressive increase of terminal degrees from 1967 to the present.

In the academic year 1975–76, 360 faculty members served Jackson State University, with 51 percent holding earned doctoral degrees. A breakdown in racial composition showed that in 1975, the faculty was 68.4 percent American black; 2.9 percent foreign black; 20.5 percent American white; 8.2 percent foreign non-black. The statistics continue to change as various specialists are added.

The current growth shows that one third of the faculty (28.7

TABLE VII   Faculty Members Holding Terminal Degrees, 1967–77

YEAR	NUMBER	NUMBER OF PH.D'S
1967–68	124	24
1968–69	158	33
1969–70	208	37
1970–71	245	56
1971–72	295	76
1972–73	313	87
1973–74	330	118
1974–75	347	127
1975–76	357	163
1976–77	358	182

percent) is American and Caucasian revealing the broadness of the president in his commitment to affirmative action. Asked by an administrator why he employed the relatively high percentage of whites, Peoples gave several reasons. He explained that in the late sixties, when whites were employed, it was not a question of race but a quest for persons with terminal degrees in the liberal arts fields and a few others. Black professors were in fields other than in liberal arts—history, physics, chemistry, languages. Black professors who held doctorates in these fields in other states were secure in their jobs and could not be attracted at first to Jackson State. As more black professors received highly specialized degrees in greater numbers, Jackson State was successful in recruiting them for all disciplines functioning in the five schools.

In assessing the present faculty (1976), President Peoples admitted that hasty hiring of numerous faculty without close screening can result in some error. For instance, there were some faculty hired who were not committed to the philosophy and objectives of Jackson State. Others had no teaching experience and were unprepared for college teaching. President Peoples has shown patience in correcting this small problem. As funds have become available, the focus has changed, as more of the Jackson State faculty were given leaves of absence for study in fields in which the university needed special development. Between 1967–76, numerous leaves of absence were granted and several persons have returned with terminal degrees to do their part in strengthening Jackson State University.

Calling on the expertise of senior members and the enthusiasm of young members of the faculty, President Peoples has invited both groups to participate in the governance of Jackson State University through elected and assigned membership in committees, councils, and the Faculty Senate. In broad terms, eighteen administrative, seventeen instructional, two faculty and staff, four student, and ten *ad hoc* committees provide the faculty with opportunities to help govern the affairs of the university with competence and diligence. Active participants in these bodies often promote relevant educational programs and policies for the university. These bodies provide channels through which faculty can take positions on university practices and policies and make recommendations to the administration. They can open channels of communication among other faculty members, departments, divisions, schools, students, and the administration.

FACULTY SENATE

The main body, the Committee on Committees, appointed another committee in the fall of the 1967–68 academic year and charged it to develop a rationale for a Faculty Senate which became a reality in 1970 amid the tug-of-war tactics that usually accompany the birth of such a power structure. The first faculty members elected to fill official positions were Dr. Jesse C. Lewis, chairman; Dr. Ivory C. Manning, vice chairman; Dr. Oscar A. Rogers, Jr., secretary-treasurer, and Dr. George F. Currie, parliamentarian. Exofficio members were President Peoples and two other vice presidents, Dr. Paul Purdy and Dr. Estus Smith.

In addition to the Faculty Senate, some faculty members joined the campus chapter of the American Association of University Professors. The November 10, 1976 announcement of their meeting indicates a sampling of the concerns of the chapter.

> The Jackson State University chapter of the American Association of University Professors will hold its first meeting of the year on November 10, 1976, in the faculty lounge on the third floor of the Jacob L. Reddix Campus Union. The purpose of the meeting will be to organize for the current academic year and to decide which issues the organization should

study. Proposed questions include discount athletic tickets for faculty and staff, the problem of student retention, and the concern of the faculty with sex discrimination (Title IX).

From the very outset of his administration, President Peoples proposed to encourage truth, freedom of speech, and responsibility on the part of the faculty with the belief that a mature and well-prepared faculty would never betray its leader.

Peoples focused on other areas of campus life at Jackson State University. From the beginning, he has been strongly student-oriented. One of the vestiges from the time when Jackson State was a church-related institution was compulsory student attendance at Wednesday Morning Assembly services and student participation in Sunday vespers. Non-attendance was punishable by temporary suspension or permanent expulsion. Holding that religion was a life to be lived and not a set of rules forced upon them, students rebelled against the system. In the first year of his administration, the new president eliminated Wednesday Assembly and abolished compulsory Sunday vespers. He did, however, encourage students to attend religious activities. He also provided funds for religious leaders to come to the campus to address students on religious questions. A steering committee for religious activities functions on the campus to accomplish three goals: to coordinate all campus religious activities; to assist individuals and campus clubs in arranging and promoting on-campus religious activities; and to seek to provide for Jackson State University students and faculty a variety of wholesome activities which will contribute to their spiritual and moral well-being.

Peoples then set out to attract more and better students to Jackson State. The Admissions Office has continuously kept him aware of the student profile reflected by ACT scores. Jackson State was failing to attract students with high scores, a fact the administration deduced from applicants' designating their first, second, and third choices of colleges listed on the score sheet. To secure quality students for the quality programs and the quality faculty his administration was developing at Jackson State, Dr. Peoples first initiated giving ACT scholarships and then engaged in an all-out effort to secure large sums of money to develop Jackson State to the level he projected for the next ten years. Through federal and private grants that grew from $741,424.00 in 1967 to $7,016,414.00 in 1976, he has been able to make significant strides toward achieving the goal of a truly excellent university.

Having been exposed to numerous national figures through his own contacts and his ACE Fellows Program experience, Peoples has had ample opportunity to witness all facets of university administration, including that of funding programs which attract both faculty and students into the college atmosphere. He had begun early to orient himself as to how to secure federal, state, and private funds. He took mental notes of names and faces of men with know-how both on the Binghamton and the Washington fronts. With Dr. Charles Wilson from SUNY at Binghamton, he devised a cooperative plan called the SUNY-Jackson Project. Federally funded, the project provided graduate level educational opportunities, experiments in the improvement of teaching, visiting professors program, Institute for the Study of the History, Life and Culture of Black People, and a variety of other cultural experiences.

To implement the plan, Wilson and Peoples came to Jackson State to confer with Dean Sampson and President Reddix, who also invited Dr. Stewart Gordon from SUNY at Binghamton to help in the project. Their cooperative efforts secured a grant valued at $107,000, which was initially turned down by the Board of Trustees, Institutions of Higher Learning, State of Mississippi after the *New York Times* praised SUNY for cooperating with a "poor Negro Mississippi college." Their attitude undoubtedly was affected by the fact that Robert Kennedy, then the attorney general of the United States, went to the University of Mississippi and created quite a stir there.

President Peoples refused to give up. Together with Dean Sampson, he reworked the proposal in line with suggestions offered by Dr. E. R. Jobe, executive secretary, Board of Trustees. From the proposal, he eliminated all references to student and faculty exchanges. The plan was accepted. President Peoples scored a success, the first of special programs that would place Jackson State in the national limelight. Once the proposal was completed and took shape as the SUNY-Binghamton-Jackson Project, it was meticulously described in the 1969-71 *Bulletin* of Jackson College.

The SUNY-Jackson Project, initiated in 1965, was a long-term cooperative arrangement between the State University of New York at Binghamton and Jackson State College. In the cooperative arrangement, each institution drew upon the resources and talent of the other in an effort to strengthen its academic program. A few of the mutual advantages of this program to the institutions were reasoning together about problems in education, engaging in joint research experiments, and sharing cultural groups and activities.

The major activities of the program fell broadly within the scope of the following categories: (a) *Curriculum Development*—the introduction, revision, and development of curricula and curricular materials; programs designed to make consultants and distinguished scholars available to the institution; (b) *Faculty Development*—faculty fellowships for additional preparation for teaching, college administration, librarianship, etc., and institute and workshop participation; (c) *Administrative Improvement*—programs including participation in academic institutes, measures for improving business office procedures, the development and fund-raising functions, physical plant administration, auxiliary enterprises operations, and non-academic personnel administration; (d) *Student Services Improvement*—programs including operations of office of admissions, counseling, testing, guidance, placement, college union, student exchange, and the development of programs of student cooperative education.

As vice president, Peoples had been accorded by President Reddix the privilege of reading the President's non-personal mail. In keeping with this practice, Peoples noted one day on Reddix' desk an invitation from the Institute for Service to Education to come to Washington to work with a group of black college presidents on a proposal for Title III funds. Excitedly, he asked the president to allow him to represent Jackson State in Washington to work on what appeared to be a promising project. Journeying to Washington at first with sixty, then thirty and finally twelve college administrators, Peoples and his colleagues devised the Thirteen College Curriculum Program which was funded under Title III. This program was designed to improve and upgrade developing institutions which had been kept out of the mainstream of higher education.

In September 1967, Jackson State College, as part of the Thirteen College Curriculum Program, began to implement it for the distinct purpose of developing a curriculum based on relevant materials that would effectuate attitudinal, academic, and desired social behavior in students. The overall objective of the program was to modify traditional curricula so that the rate of student attrition would be considerably lowered.

The curricula for five freshmen courses and two sophomore courses were written and constantly upgraded by the Thirteen College Curriculum Program teachers, who attended an eight-week writing conference for this purpose in the summer.

Paperback and hard-cover books on contemporary themes, magazines, newspapers, scientific equipment, and IBM Dictaphone Writing Laboratory were the foundations for the innovative and inductive approaches to learning. Cultural enrichment experience included educational field trips, tours of historical, social, and artistic sites, concerts (symphony, opera, dance, drama), movies, lectures, student debates, plays, and musical programs.

Financial aid was available for students who qualified and the program was annually open to any student, regardless of race, creed, or color who met the admission requirements of Jackson State College. This program was funded by the United States Office of Education, National Science Foundation, Carnegie Foundation, Ford Foundation, and the Institute for Services to Education.

Peoples moved Jackson State to the forefront in many other areas as well. He sought parent bodies and consortia arrangements after Jackson State became a member of the College Placement Services, Incorporated—Title III Consortium on July 1, 1969. The consortium was made up of forty-one developing colleges and was being coordinated by College Placement Services, Incorporated, and the Atlanta University Center. The purpose of the consortium was to deal cooperatively with local placement problems and to strengthen programs at the member colleges. As a result of individual proposals submitted by the forty-one colleges through College Placement Services, Incorporated and the Atlanta University Center, the United States Office of Education made annual grants to the institutions under Title III of the Higher Education Act of 1965 to support their programs.

The forty-one colleges were arranged into eight regional groupings to provide them the opportunity to share each other's strengths and to work cooperatively with common problems. Jackson State College was in Region VI along with five other institutions of the Deep South.

One of the programs at Jackson State College became the Allied Health Professions Program, administered by the Biology Department, in cooperation with the University of Mississippi Medical Center, since 1969. The curriculum for this program was structured for the training of new types of health technologists in order to meet the new needs created by advances in the health sciences. The Allied Health Program provided basic professional and technical training in medical technology and medical record librarianship, offering a Bachelor of Science degree in each field.

Other programs housed at Jackson State included the Moton Development Consortium and the Harvard-Yale-Columbia Intensive Summer Studies Program. The objectives of the Moton Consortium were centered around the implementation of the management team approach to development. Pioneered by a grant from the Sloan Foundation, this consortium of thirty-three colleges was directed by the Robert R. Moton Foundation.

First participation of Jackson State in the Harvard-Yale-Columbia Intensive Summer Studies Program occurred in 1969. The program was initiated with the purpose of identifying and evaluating students from selected colleges for advanced degree programs. Since the beginning of this program, each summer Jackson State students have participated in it.

Each of the interinstitutional programs has afforded new visibility to Jackson State in its curriculum and faculty development and in its improvement of administration and student services. Furthermore, the programs have elicited federal and private grants which have helped Jackson State become first a developing and, then an advancing institution of higher learning.

In the first decade of President Peoples' administration, Jackson State was the recipient of $25 million from federal and private sources. Table VIII illustrates the federal and private dollars awarded to Jackson State from 1966 to 1976.

TABLE VIII   Federal & Private Grants to Jackson State, 1966–76

YEAR		AMOUNT
1966–67		$ 741,424.00
1967–68		1,200,000.00
1968–69		1,600,000.00
1969–70		1,553,513.22
1970–71	(Federal)	1,653,998.32
	(Private)	189,120.00
1971–72		2,205,997.08
1972–73		2,744,074.68
1973–74		3,593,257.18
1974–75		5,123,004.17
1975–76		6,442,776.63
1976–77		7,016,414.00

Faithful to its pledge of March 2, 1967 to support Dr. Peoples, the Board of Trustees has been well aware of its obligation to work with him to provide the means so that the university will continue in its greatness and continue to be a place where research and teaching may be carried on under the best possible conditions. To that end, the board had pledged its support and also the support of a host of others who believed in Jackson State. The board carried out its commitment and appropriated $45 million over a ten-year period to Jackson State University to educate the student population who enrolled at the institution and to help place those who graduated from it in the first decade of Dr. Peoples' administration. Table IX illustrates the progression of appropriations from 1967 through 1976.

President Peoples and his staff were instrumental in vigorously recruiting thousands of students, which raised the enrollment rapidly from 2,359 students in 1966 to 8,000 in 1977. Over that same period, Jackson State graduated more than 1,000 students. Table X illustrates both the enrollment and the graduates by years.

Now in its one hundredth year of educational service to the state of Mississippi and the nation at large, Jackson State University is more financially solvent and academically sound than at any other time in its history. Students enroll in ever greater numbers, attracted by new programs and opportunities for financial aid offered them. In November, 1973, 80 percent of the student body was receiving some kind of financial assistance.

Brought to the campus through personal choice or institutional recruitment, 8,000 students are offered quality programs which are implemented by a quality faculty. One of the major problems of the university, as perceived by Dr. Peoples, is a need for a concerted effort on the part of the administration and faculty to see that the students attain their desired outcome for their personal growth within the general statement of purpose of Jackson State.

The purpose of the university is to provide for the needs of the students in all aspects of education—general education, liberal education, special education, teacher education, and professional education. The programs at the university are designed to guide students in developing the knowledge, skills, appreciations, and attitudes which are essential to an education. They are further intended to provide learning situations and experiences designed to help students choose courses of study, initiate careers, and contribute to the economic development of the state and nation. Jackson State University, the only one of the senior Mississippi universities located in the largest urban center of the state, has a special mission to provide educational opportunities for needy and disadvantaged students from both urban and rural environments.

TABLE IX — State Appropriations for Jackson State University

YEAR	AMOUNT
July 1, 1967–June 30, 1968	$1,637,553.81
July 1, 1968–June 30, 1969	2,302,122.03
July 1, 1969–June 30, 1970	2,430,905.89
July 1, 1970–June 30, 1971	4,052,384.96
July 1, 1971–June 30, 1972	4,825,408.00
July 1, 1972–June 30, 1973	5,778,745.00
July 1, 1973–June 30, 1974	6,373,536.00
July 1, 1974–June 30, 1975	6,992,892.00
July 1, 1975–June 30, 1976	8,519,882.00
July 1, 1976–June 30, 1977	8,219,882.00
July 1, 1977–June 30, 1978	10,172,360.00

TABLE X   Annual Enrollment & Graduates, 1967-77

FALL ENROLLMENT		ANNUAL GRADUATES	
YEAR	TOTAL	YEAR	TOTAL
1966-67	2,359	1966-67	393
1967-68	2,990	1967-68	507
1968-69	3,686	1968-69	410
1969-70	4,541	1969-70	649
1970-71	4,665	1970-71	769
1971-72	5,058	1971-72	1,001
1972-73	5,101	1972-73	1,057
1973-74	5,205	1973-74	1,193
1974-75	5,960	1974-75	1,013
1975-76	7,718	1975-76	1,063
1976-77	7,928		

The following desired outcomes for student growth are implicit in the general statement of purpose: understanding and accepting the maturing self; relating to others with sympathy and understanding; appreciating one's ethnic and national heritage; understanding the nature of one's physical and social environment; developing the ability to think and communicate clearly and effectively, to make sound choices and value judgments, and to analyze, synthesize, and evaluate ideas and data; and developing a social consciousness which will enable one to assume responsibility, to think critically about social problems, and to contribute to the improvement of society.

Belonging to a deprived minority, a few students at Jackson State often reflect the characteristics of deprivation, subdued repressions, and an inability to function properly within the confines of moral freedom which philosophers define as the ability to do what one ought: behave as an accountable learner and a responsible citizen. In his repeated addresses to the faculty and administration, President Peoples has stressed the need to create a climate of this kind of freedom and to take every measure to prevent the student from opting for ignorance just as they would try to prevent him from starvation or suicide. The majority of the student body accept freedom because they accept responsibility for their actions. An exceptional few, as in most colleges, fail to develop with rapidity, nevertheless, the struggle goes on.

BUILDING PROGRAM

Along with his preoccupation with administration, faculty, students, and programs, President Peoples has been concerned with expanding the physical plant of Jackson State and with obtaining state funds to cover the expansion. In 1967 Dr. Peoples with the assistance of Governor Paul B. Johnson, Jr. was successful in getting a seven story men's dormitory for the university. This structure was the first of a gallery of facilities the president managed to get from the state in order to house the programs of the rapidly expanding university. The university also received $1,700,000.00 in 1967 to construct academic buildings with federal matching funds of 33.3 percent. The university was able to construct the Physical Education Building for $1.3 million and an industrial technology building for $600,000.00.

The next new buildings were the administrative tower-classroom complex constructed at the cost of $2,530,000 appropiated to the college over a two-year period. Again, with careful handling of expenditures, some leftover funds were used to build a new president's home. Governor John Bell Williams, who was pushing for the renovation of the governor's mansion, lent his prestige and office to support this venture.

To make sure that the educational program was bolstered by an excellent library, both qualitatively and quantitatively, a six-story addition to Sampson Library (1973) doubled its square footage and volume capacity. The old structure had to be remodeled to harmonize with the new. The cost of the library addition and renovation was $2 million.

The School of Education building (1973) was erected at a cost of $1.5 million; the Frederick Hall Music Center (1976) was built for a cost of $2 million.

Other repairs and renovations were done on practically every other building on the campus. Work included painting, sandblasting, air conditioning, redecorating, partitioning, surfacing and resurfacing the parking lots, sidewalks, streets, and roads inside the campus, constructing an athletic field and track ($154,977), and acquiring land for a plaza on the west entrance of J. R. Lynch Street. The permanent closing of a portion of West Lynch Street in 1970 provided space for the plaza structured to serve the university both functionally and aesthetically.

During the centennial year of the Jackson State University, two new buildings were completed, a dining hall and a science building. A recapitulation of the capital outlay for construction of new facilities at Jackson State University during President Peoples' administration from 1967 to 1977 is as follows: men's dormitory (1969), $1.3 million; health and physical education building (1969), $1,328,972; administration-classroom complex (1972), $2,380,000; J. R. Lynch Street Plaza (1973), $87,457; H. T. Sampson Library extension (1973), $2 million; president's home (1973), $145,000; education building (1973), $1.5 million; athletic track and field (1974), $1 million; Frederick Hall Music Center (1976), $2 million; new dining facility (1976), $2,549,050; new science building (1977), $5,198,070; new assembly building with a seating capacity of 10,000 (1977-78), $5 million; new men's dormitory (1977-78), $3 million.

The growth and expansion of the library was greatly accelerated during the first five years of the administration of President Peoples. In one year alone, 1969-70, the professional library staff was doubled from five to ten librarians holding graduate library science degrees. By the end of 1971-72, the library staff consisted of twelve professional librarians and twenty-one non-professional staff members. Financial support increased from $160,090 in 1967 to $509,151 in 1976. Through special efforts initiated by Dr. Peoples with the Board of Trustees of Institutions of Higher Learning and with members of the state legislature, the regular library book budget was augmented by special allocations and "catch-up funds," earmarked for books alone, amounting to more than $555,000. The total amount allotted for library materials specifically during 1971-72 was $331,996.97, including a special library allocation for books of $254,713. Added to this were three federal grants amounting to $54,809. As a result of additional financial support, the collection grew from 57,942 volumes in 1967 to 380,000 volumes in 1976. The quality of the collection was further enhanced by a substantial variety of non-book materials obtained with the aid of federal library grants under Title II-A, College Library Resources.

Since August 1, 1968, all new books (with the exception of juvenile books) have been catalogued by the Library of Congress System of Classification. Also, since 1968, Jackson State's library has been a depository for United States government publications on a selective basis. These publications make available to students, to faculty, and to the public an authentic source of recent materials on a variety of subjects: education, health, social security, labor, civil rights, housing, agriculture, science, legislation, economic conditions, national and international affairs, statistical and other information. The library is also a depository for certain publications and official documents of the state of Mississippi. The memorial dedication and official naming of the Henry Thomas Sampson Library occurred October 25, 1970.

Perhaps the most far-reaching development of the library for 1967 to 1976 was the $2 million appropriation of early 1970 for remodeling and expanding the Henry Thomas Sampson Library in order to provide additional space for library materials, equipment, readers, and staff. Following nearly a year of planning, groundbreaking and construction began in May 1971. The expanded six-story facility, with a capacity for more than 400,000 volumes has enhanced library services for the rapidly expanding undergraduate and graduate programs for 8,000 students.

Ernestine Anthony Lipcomb, who served as director of the library for 29 years, gave excellent leadership to this position. Mrs. Lipscomb retired June 30, 1976.

MEDIA CENTER

Upon the completion of the addition to the H. T. Sampson Library, the Jackson State University Media Center was removed from the Willie Dobbs Blackburn Building of Language Arts to the ground floor of the library. The facility and its resources have been incorporated into the library services and have rendered the facility a true resource center. Since 1972, the Media Center has expanded its services and has added a wide variety of instructional materials. Moreover, the center has a production studio and a control room for color video taping and has the capability of recording programs broadcast by Mississippi Educational Television and/or other local stations. Locally or commercially produced videocassettes may be viewed by individuals or groups in any of the thirty-two carrels located on the first floor of the library. As many as twelve different programs may be shown simultaneously. However, if an instructor prefers to show a videocassette tape in his classroom, the instructor may check the tape out for class viewing in the department.

The switching room of the center is equipped with a routine switcher connected to the twelve videocassette players. The routine switcher is housed in a 12 x 32 matrix capable of feeding an audio-fellow-video signal from any one of the twelve videocassette players to any one or all of the thirty-two carrels located on the first floor of the library. Communication between the two floors is by means of an intercom system or by telephone.

The center has access to a lecture room with a seating capacity of 80. This room may be used for previewing 16mm films of which the center has a collection of more than 300. Additionally, students and faculty may use the facilities to produce graphics, transparencies, and instructional recordings. Workshops, consultation services, and instruction in the use of resources are available.

Currently, the Media Center has more than 500 hours of video tape covering a wide variety of subjects that may be used to enrich teaching and learning. Also, it has the capability to provide portable monitors and players to any classroom. Sixty classrooms have the capability of closed circuit television.

The Media Center provides the following services: audio taping, audio/visual supplies, cassette duplication, film library, graphic arts, information distribution, live color video taping and audiotaping, media storage, TV carrel playback, videocassette dubbing. The available equipment includes: audio, Mic, Rf, and video cables, color TV production studio, filmloop projectors, filmstrip projectors, public address system (microphone, amplifier, and speaker), record players, 16mm movie projectors, slide projectors, videorecorder.

Through the use of the above named resources, students are exposed to a wide variety of media and methods which will enable them to gain insight into their fields of concentration. They are able to observe good teaching in action, become familiar with many of the instructional materials which are placed on the market each year, and they can learn to evaluate the resources in the light of their present and future usefulness.

STUDY OF HISTORY, LIFE AND CULTURE OF BLACK PEOPLE

A humanistic program adding significantly to the academic atmosphere is the Institute for the Study of History, Life, and Culture of Black People, which had its inception in the SUNY-Jackson Project in 1965. The institute is an interdepartmental, interdisciplinary, and intercultural program within the regular college curriculum of Jackson State University. The inherent philosophy is one of racial inclusion rather that exclusion. The courses are designed to enrich the students' general knowledge with specific information concerning the heritage, culture, and life of all black people. Thus, the regular college offerings are enriched in terms of the broad perspective of the institute and students are able to relate more meaningfully their knowledge and experiences to life and their immediate environment. Problems of identity and alienation within the individual are studied with an eye toward widening the circle of understanding, upgrading student self-concepts, and preparing the student for greater service to the community.

The institute's curriculum includes the following fields: history, politics, literature, music, art, rural and urban sociology, religion and philosophy, and cultural anthropology. A cocurriculum program of cultural enrichment is an integral part of the institute. The director of the institute is the nationally and internationally recognized Dr. Margaret Walker Alexander, poet, novelist, and professor of English.

From February 17 to 20, 1971, the institute sponsored a National Evaluative Conference on Black Studies which drew to the campus as consultants: Chuck Stone, United States News and Information Bureau, Washington, D.C.; John Conyers, Jr., Representative from Detroit, Michigan to the United States Congress; C. Eric Lincoln, professor of religion, Union Theological Seminary, New York City; St. Clair Drake, professor of sociology, Stanford University, Palo Alto, California; Jessie Carney Smith, university librarian, Fisk University; Alex Haley, author of *Autobiography of Malcolm X* and the famous *Roots: the Saga of an American Family*.

Ossie Davis and Ruby Dee appeared in concert during the conference. "A Soul Extravaganza" was held with the Pharoahs of Chicago. Other consultants included: Lawrence D. Reddick, former curator of the Schomburg Collection of Negro Life and History, New York Public Library; Dorothy Burnett Porter, Washington, D.C., and Ernestine Anthony Lipscomb, director of the Henry T. Sampson Library, Jackson State College. The Jackson State University library staff prepared a special bibliography of the Afro-American Collection at Jackson State.

Seminars specifically designed for the institute were: (1) Black American History, with specific research on the life and works of Dr. W. E. B. DuBois; staff members were Dr. E. C. Foster and consultants Dr. Rayford Logan, Dr. Lawrence Reddick, and Ernest Kaiser; (2) Black American Literature, giving specific attention to the life and works of Langston Hughes; Dr. Margaret Walker Alexander and consultants Ann Shockley and Dr. Dorothy B. Porter directed the seminar; (3) The Black Man in Art, focusing specifically on African art of the Caribbean; Lawrence Jones, together with Elizabeth Catlett Mora and Jean Blackwell Hutson, consultants, handled the seminar; (4) Sociology and Anthropology, with special emphasis on family genealogies; directed by Kathryn B. Mosley with consultants Dr. St. Clair Drake and Dan Williams, archivist, Tuskegee Institute, Alabama. More that 200 participants attended the last conference.

A Summer Institute for Directed Research in Black Studies was held June 11–July 27, 1973, for college teachers, librarians, and beginning graduate students. The program was geared to prepare students in the methodology of research and to establish centers of black culture encompassing black history, literature, art, sociology, and anthropology.

To honor the two hundredth birthday of the first book published by a Black living in America, twenty black women poets from all over the country gathered to celebrate the legacy of its author, Phillis Wheatley, a "pretty little slave girl" who managed at seventeen to become a poet.

The four-day festival at Jackson State was the event which featured the unveiling of a bronze sculpture of Miss Wheatley by Elizabeth Catlett. Several panels were held on the significance of

Miss Wheatley's works; there were poetry reading sessions and a drama by Vinie Burrows about aspects of the poet's life. The festival ended with the examination, as a public policy issue, of the exclusion of black women from the textbooks of America.

The poets raised many questions, among them the crucial one of whether they as black poets are as stymied in reaching their full potential as they felt Phillis Wheatley was.

Miss Wheatley, born in Senegal about 1754, was brought to America and sold to John Wheatley, a Boston merchant. She then learned to read and write in eighteen months. In her lifetime, she gained recognition for her poems and broadsides on religion, on America, on death, and on politics and freedom. Her only book, celebrated during the festival, is called *Poems on Various Subjects, Religious and Moral,* published first in England in 1773.

Margaret Walker Alexander graced the Dansby Hall stage with young and not so young giants whose voices rang out with meaningful poetry describing the black experience in Africa and America. The poets, whose themes ranged from celebration of black liberation to the politics of confrontation, included such well-known younger poets as Nikki Giovanni and emerging ones such as Malaika Ayo Wangara (Joyce Whitsitt Lawrence), a pan-Africanist from Detroit.

And there were pioneering ones like Margaret Danner, Margaret G. Burroughs, and Margaret Walker, the festival organizer, whose volume of poetry, *For My People,* published in 1942, broke with tradition and presaged the development of black writing that was unabashedly for and about blacks. They read from their works and discussed their thoughts not only with each other, but also with the students who flocked to see them.

Carolyn Rodgers, a Chicago-based poetess, said she was glad to be in Mississippi because she felt "as if I've touched home." "As a child," said Miss Rodgers, "I grew up terrified and afraid of Mississippi because it was a place where the 'Klan' ran wild and you were brutalized and afraid and if you were from Mississippi, people snickered and sneered. So you didn't tell people. But I really feel as if I have touched home. Some roots. Because I expected to come to a place where if you go home you see blood flowing in the streets."

June Jordan from New York said, however, that she did not

want anyone to forget the sight of bullet holes still on a dormitory from "that twenty-eight second fusillade of unfettered murder" dating back to the disorder in May, 1970.

Mari Evans read from her book of poems, *I Am a Black Woman*, and later talked about controls on black writers. Margaret Walker Alexander told the poets that "all the terrible stuff wasn't just myth. America is like this—the horror is here, the corruption is here, the evil is here. But there is also some love and some beauty as we see in this festive atmosphere." Nikki Giovanni read to a packed audience in the auditorium a poem about hands... "in fact/two brown butterflies fluttering/across the pleasure/they gave my body." Though the students sat as if enthralled as she jubilantly read to the background music of the Tougaloo College Gospel Choir, they never tapped their feet or clapped their hands. And while they gave Miss Giovanni three standing ovations, there was silence in between.

Festivity was present around Dr. Alexander, a figure styled by Miss Giovanni as "the living personification of the spirit of Phillis Wheatley." Having served at Jackson State for twenty-nine years, Dr. Alexander felt the festival was particularly significant because of the many parallels between what happened to Phillis Wheatley and what happens to black women and black men who try to get materials published today.

Charlayne Hunter was on hand to interview the participants and she described the event in the *New York Times*, November 9, 1973. *The Jackson State Review* printed a special issue of the Phillis Wheatley Poetry Festival in the summer of 1974.

A library-oriented project at Jackson State University is the humanities program which experimented with three intermittent phases of development: Interdisciplinary Study of Man and His World (1953-60), and directed by Dr. Margaret Walker Alexander; Project LAMP: (Literature, Art, Music, and Philosophy) (1970-75), funded by the National Endowment for the Humanities and the Council on Library Resources and directed by several Jackson State University librarians; and the Sophomore Humanities Pilot Program (1974-76), also funded by the National Endowment for the Humanities and supervised by Dr. Judith Krabbe.

OPERA SOUTH

Another program which has enriched Jackson State is Opera/South. A production company of the Mississippi Intercollegiate Opera Guild, Opera/South was chartered by Jackson State University, Utica Junior College, and Tougaloo College to give students the opportunity to work in a professional production and to give people in the South the chance to hear young, talented black performers.

The first production, *Aida*, was presented May 7, 1971, in the Jackson Municipal Auditorium. Walter Herbert, one of America's top music directors, conducted the orchestra of professional musicians. Donald Dorr, designer for New Orleans Opera, designed and staged the new production. Young black singers, starting their careers, starred. Sets were built by Jackson State's theatre and industrial technology department. Choruses were drawn from the combined groups of the sponsoring colleges. The first Board of Directors was Dr. Estus Smith, chairman, Dr. Ben Bailey, Dr. Dollye M. E. Robinson, Dr. John A. Peoples, Jr., Dr. George A. Owens, Louis Stokes, Sister M. Elise, S.B.S., and Delores Ardoyno.

Guiseppe Verdi's *Aida* was the first production (1971), followed by Giacomo Puccino's *Turandot* (1972), William Grant Still's *Highway 1, USA* (November 1972), George Bizet's *Carmen* (April 1973), Guiseppe Verdi's *Otello* (April 1974), William Grant Still's *A Bayou Legend* (world premiere performance, April 1974, and repeat performance, 1976), Richard Wagner's *The Flying Dutchman* (April 1975), and Margaret Walker Alexander's *Jubilee* (November 1976) a world premiere performance. Grants to sponsor these productions were awarded by the National Endowment for the Arts, the National Opera Institute in cooperation with Mrs. DeWitt Wallace, Guest Artist Program of the Mississippi Arts Commission, and the William Matthews Sullivan Foundation. Jackson State's students gained rich experiences from participating in Opera/South's production.

From the music department of the University other flourishing performance groups have been developed. The stellar performance of the Jackson State University Marching Band caused it to become known as "The Sonic Boom of the South." The band, 150 pieces strong, made its debut into the world of professional football in October, 1972. True to its new-found title, the "Sonic Boom" presented earth-shaking pre-game and half-time performances at the game between the New Orleans Saints and the Atlanta Falcons, played in New Orleans. The band's crowd-pleasing entertainment opened doors for subsequent offers by professional football organizations. Such performances provided wide exposure for both music majors and non-majors.

In August, 1975, Jackson State was able to install an FM educational radio station on campus. On the air since August, WJSU-FM Radio Station received the statewide award in public affairs programming from the Mississippi Broadcasters Association at its summer 1976 meeting in Biloxi. The public affairs program which earned the award for WJSU was "Global Connection," a production of the Department of Modern Foreign Languages in which foreign students and faculty members on the university campus were interviewed about their native countries. Mass communications majors at Jackson State were solely responsible for the technical production of the award-winning series.

WJSU exists primarily for the purpose of training students in all facets of radio broadcasting, and mass communications majors, especially those concentrating in radio, use the station as a laboratory. Announcers are MC majors and other selected students. The music format is a variety of jazz, rhythm and blues, folk, spiritual, classical, and such other forms as suit the varied tastes of the university's audience. Cultural programming reflects the multifaceted character of Jackson State and the Jackson community. Dr. Johnny Tolliver, associate professor of English and head of the Department of Mass Communications, serves as general manager of WJSU.

RIOTS AT JACKSON STATE UNIVERSITY, 1970

As stated in the *Report of the President's Commission on Campus Unrest*, chaired by William W. Scranton, the disturbances at Jackson State began after dusk on Wednesday, May 13. On the following day, after a barrage of rock throwing, 674 guardsmen of the National Guard were stationed at the armory. Many rumors flew about

The Advancement of Truth & Freedom 177

campus, including a false announcement that Charles Evers, mayor of Fayette, Mississippi, and his wife had been killed. Anonymous telephone calls quickly spread alarm across the campus and the level of tension rose. The commission report related that the National Guard was armed with special riot shotguns that held seven rounds. The first four rounds were number nine birdshots, the smallest pellet used in shotguns, backed up by three rounds of double-o buckshots, the heaviest used in shotguns. In fact most highway patrolmen were armed with shotguns loaded with double-o buckshots; others carried personally owned rifles or carbines, and two were armed with loaded submachine guns. There were conflicting reports of small caliber gunfire from the area of Stewart Hall, one of the men's dormitories. Suddenly, the Mississippi Highway Patrol opened fire on the students assembled on the lawn in front of the women's dormitory.

When the sounds of the shooting had subsided, two students were dead. Twenty-year-old Phillip Gibbs, a junior and father of an eighteen-month-old son, had been gunned down about 50 feet east of the west wing doorway of Alexander Hall. A pellet had entered just beneath the left eye, two through his head and still another under his left arm. James Earl Green, a high school student returning home from work, was felled by a buckshot slug that entered his side and pierced his liver. He was standing across Lynch Street in front of B. F. Roberts Dining Hall. Other students who were wounded included Fonzie Coleman, Redd Wilson, Jr., Leroy Kenter, Vernon Steve Weakley, Gloria Mayhorn, Patricia Ann Sanders, Willie Woodard, Andrea Réese, Stella Spinks, Climmie Johnson, Tuwaine Davis, and Lonzie Thompson.[3]

The Federal Bureau of Investigation report stated that nearly 400 bullets or pieces of buckshot struck Alexander Hall. The area of the south end of the west wing alone contained 301 separate bullet marks. The upper floor levels were hardest hit, with 105 marks or bullet holes in the window panels and walls. There were 83 separate buckshot or bullet marks counted on the fourth floor area. There were 64 marks counted on the third floor, 36 on the second floor, and 13 separate bullet or buckshot marks in the doors, and frames at ground level.[4]

On June 13, 1970, then President Richard Nixon, established

the President's Commission on Campus Unrest. The commission held its first meeting June 25, 1970. Subsequently, it conducted thirteen days of public hearings in Jackson, Mississippi; Kent State, Ohio; Washington, D.C.; and Los Angeles, California. At the Jackson hearings, the administration, faculty, staff, and students testified. There were no convictions and no arrests.

The one tangible result of the hearings was the permanent closing of Lynch Street to through traffic. The *Jackson Daily News* gave an account of the voting of the Jackson City Council relating to the closure of Lynch Street. While Commissioner Ed Cates cast the only negative vote, Mayor Russell C. Davis and Commissioner Tom Kelly voted in favor of the permanent closure of the thoroughfare. Mayor Davis further proposed that a mall be developed inasmuch as monies were available for such. It was during this council meeting that the initials J. R. were added to the existing street signs for one of Mississippi's leading black statesmen.

A few months following the tragedy at Jackson State College, the *Clarion Ledger* carried the text of a proposal by Commissioner Ed Cates recommending the relocation of Jackson State and the conversion of the present facilities on Lynch Street to federally subsidized housing. Commissioner Cates asserted in the description of his plans that, in view of the fact that the Jackson Housing Authority had just received a commitment for $3.5 million in federal subsidized housing, he felt that it would be economically feasible to take some $10,000 of this money to conduct a study to determine the feasibility of converting Jackson State University from a college into housing and to utilize the present classrooms for vocational educational facilities, as there was a dire need for skilled labor within the Jackson market.

As stated in the *Clarion-Ledger,* December 31, 1970 Cates recommended that the city of Jackson, through its housing authority, purchase the college for some $35 million, to be paid for completely out of federal funds with no expense to the city of Jackson since the federal government was going to fund the housing anyway.

"Funds from the sale," he said, "would be used to purchase a new campus and facilities within the city but on the outskirts in order that the college might have an orderly and healthy transition and growth." Lynch Street would be returned to through traffic.

The plans would offer these benefits to the people of both races "at no expenses" to the city or the college.

The following day, President John A. Peoples responded to Commissioner Cates in a televised speech. The *Clarion Ledger* also carried President Peoples' response to Commissioner Cates' suggestion that Jackson State College be moved to the outskirts of the city. Dr. Peoples pointed up the following facts:

> The College employs about 500 people with a payroll of about $4 million, the college's 4,700 students spend more than $3 million a year locally and the College spends approximately $2 million annually on food, laundry, supplies and services.... these expenditures have benefitted both whites and blacks, and whites particularly in purchases of supplies and in construction.... Most importantly, the College represents hope and opportunity for 4,700 young men and women, many of whom would have no chance for a college education if there were no Jackson State College.

Peoples further stated that although Cates had proposed relocating the college and converting its facilities, he had not precisely mentioned a new site for the college.

Dr. Peoples emphasized the fact that Cates' proposal was contrary to his own thinking, making it clear that he had no authority to negotiate a sale of the college since the authority belonged to the Board of Trustees of Mississippi Institutions of Higher Learning. He felt that the proceeds from such a sale would never rebuild the college. He held that Jackson State had a tradition of being an urban college serving low income people at a low cost. Peoples added that "the contiguity to the people is the principal reason for the college's rapid growth in the last few years. If the college is moved from the city, its growth pattern and momentum will be decidedly diminished."

> As regards my concern about the needs of the black community, I think my credentials as an advocate for the rights and progress of black Americans are well established and known by the people. The question is whether the Jackson State College site is the best and only location for such housing. A housing project at the Jackson State College site would immediately become just an extension of the existing ghetto.

Alluding to the planning board nomination, Peoples added that his main aspiration was to serve in his post as an educational leader; any other task for which he might be deemed qualified was peripheral. Appointed to some other task, he would put his best into it. President Peoples' firm stand on his convictions and his fearless defense of the principles of justice and equity saved the college from repeating its exodus of 1902 from North to West Jackson.

The two 1970 incidents—the student killings and the plan to remove the school from its urban location in the capital, which is its greatest asset—strengthened rather than destroyed the institution.

After burying the dead with the love and dignity that befitted them, Jackson State turned again its focus to the business of living and fighting for survival academically and financially. One battle bolstered the other.

INSTITUTIONAL REAFFIRMATION OF ACCREDITATION

High on the list of priorities was securing reaffirmation of accreditation by the Southern Association of Colleges and Schools (SACS) to be obtained through institutional self-study and peer evaluation.

Begun in 1969, this intensive self-examination mobilized the administration, faculty, staff, and students in an extended program of fact-finding according to the tenets of the Southern Association of Colleges and Schools. The heart of the self-study lay in the critical analysis of the purpose, of the organization and administration, of the educational program, financial resources, faculty, library, student personnel, special activities, graduate program, research, and ten-year projections.

Dr. Dollye M. E. Robinson, chairman of the Division of Fine Arts and head of the Music Department, directed and spearheaded the self-study. From July 1 through the fall quarter of 1969, the director of the self-study attended several conferences. Faculty representatives were sent to SACS workshops. College personnel were oriented to the study and committee assignments were made. The groups included the Steering Committee, Editorial Committee, eleven principal and twenty-two departmental committees. A grant from the Southern Education Foundation and the provision for ten consultants from the Southern Association of Colleges and Schools strengthened the implementation of the self-study.

For eighteen months, the Jackson State University family worked diligently to identify strengths and weaknesses of the College. Headed by Dr. Granville Sawyer, President of Texas Southern University, a team appointed by SACS visited the college campus May 16-19, 1971. The team made three recommendations: (1) that the statement of purpose be modified to define participation in economic development of Mississippi; (2) that the subsequent delineations of statement of purpose might include identification of Jackson State in relation to other public colleges and universities in Mississippi; and (3) that the urban emphasis become more identifiable in the refinement of objectives. The group further suggested that a black representative be added to the Board of Trustees, Institutions of Higher Learning, State of Mississippi. Dr. Robert W. Harrison, a black practicing dentist, was subsequently appointed to the post.

The education program elicited several recommendations: more electives in various disciplines; more succinct evaluation of grading procedures; increase of doctorates; designation of department heads or chief departmental officers. Because of the vital role of the library in supporting the total program of the college, several recommendations were made by the committee, one of which was the need to increase funds for library expenditures.

The SACS Commission reaffirmed the accreditation of Jackson State at its seventy-sixth annual meeting December, 1971, at Miami, Florida. With the accomplishment of this long-awaited goal, Jackson State began efforts to acquire specific program accreditation from professional agencies associated with disciplines. Faculty from several departments served long hours to meet deadlines and prepare for site visits. On September 1, 1972, Jackson State obtained accreditation of its teacher education program from the National Council for Accreditation of Teacher Education. On April 29, 1975, the American Chemistry Society accredited the program in chemistry; on July 1, 1975, the Council on Social Work Education approved the programs in social work. Under the chairmanship of Dr. Dollye Robinson, the Department of Music became a member of the National Association of the School of Music, November 20, 1977.

Several departments are currently seeking professional accreditation. During the academic year 1977-78 site visits were scheduled for biology, and social work. The School of Business and Economics and the School of Industrial and Technical Studies are, at this writing, finalizing reports for on-site visitations.

Along with the above accreditations, Jackson State holds membership in the following collegiate and professional organizations: Association of American Colleges, American Council of Education, American Association of Colleges for Teacher Education, Association of State Colleges and Universities, American Association of Collegiate Registrars and Admission Officers, American Association of University Women, Institute of International Education, Mississippi Association of Colleges Cooperative Education Association, Assembly of the American Association of Collegiate School of Business, Midwest Association of Graduate Schools.

ADVANCED INSTITUTIONAL DEVELOPMENT PROGRAM (AIDP)

Sometimes imperceptibly but always steadfastly, Jackson State has been moving from a developing to an advancing institution. As one set of goals was attained, President Peoples discovered a new outreach and focused on new goals for Jackson State. Once the institution expanded physically and strengthened academically, gaining ever more recognition by prestigious association which added luster to the university image, the time arrived for advancing Jackson State University into the dynamics of the social growth and change in the final years of the twentieth century with the Advanced Institutional Development Program. Together with faculty, students, and alumni, Peoples' administration formulated a new and specific set of goals: (1) to develop strong, comprehensive academic programs; (2) to develop career-oriented professional programs relevant to a highly technological society; (3) to develop an administrative system which will facilitate the achievement of goals as well as most humanely utilize the skills of all members of the university; (4) to develop harmonious, reciprocal relations with the contiguous as well as the larger university community; (5) to develop an academic atmosphere in which students, faculty, and administrators can freely interact and solve problems with mutual consideration for their respective roles and responsibilities; and (6) to provide for the attracting of students from all ethnic and economic levels.

The president added five more goals in order to achieve the six preceding ones so as to implement the Advanced Institutional Development Program which became a reality in 1974: (1) to foster institutional growth; (2) to improve administrative capabilities; (3) to establish urban career orientation; (4) to establish a multicultural institution; (5) to enhance quality throughout the university. To achieve these objectives, President Peoples sought and obtained university status for Jackson State. Since 1974, he has truly led the university toward excellence in all its fullness.

The AID Program increased the potential of Jackson State University to prepare students to seek meaningful careers and job opportunities. Improving the career development potential of Jackson State meant greater probability of job security and higher incomes for its students. Through the accomplishment of these goals, a greater sense of personal achievement and self-fulfillment has been gained by large numbers of students from deprived circumstances. Providing for career development for persons from low income and deprived circumstances is consistent with the national effort to alleviate the problem of unemployment and underemployment.

The emphasis on improving career development potential is a significant component of the mission of Jackson State as stated in the original proposal for AIDP funds: "In essence, Jackson State University's mission is to provide increased freedom of choice and opportunity for its target population of low income individuals in Mississippi." The emphasis in the proposal also related to one of the major specific institutional goals designed to achieve the university's general mission, which is: "To develop career-oriented professional programs that are relevant to a highly technological society."

Specifics were outlined to initiate a program in career education: (1) to set forth career development as a basis on which to advance relevant teaching and learning with respect to the educational needs of students in an urban system; (2) to establish a career-oriented academic advisement and remediation system; (3) to integrate appropriately career development in the instructional program of the university; (4) to promulgate functional interrelationships with local and regional industrial and public agencies which are concerned with the career development aspect of higher education; (5) to create knowledge and appreciation on the part of the administrative and instructional staff of the significance of career education and the role it must play in helping students make decisions about learning; and (6) to develop organizational structures which are supportive of the career development efforts of the university.

The AIDP effort resulted in more effective use of counseling and skill development to make students more conscious of the steps needed to improve their career potentials. The necessity for increased career awareness was focused for Jackson State students who, in addition to the typical career uncertainty of young people, had never been aware of possible positions in financial analysis, city management, and project management. These students, and in particular black women, face a number of forces which cause them to enter more traditional careers such as teacher education and clerical work. Role models in fields like medicine, law, business, public administration, and technology are not abundant for blacks. This uncertainty can lead to a lack of self-confidence on the part of black youths and even poor whites. This lack of self-confidence is further amplified by the fear of discrimination facing many black students.

Thus, a major activity of the institution is to provide knowledge and motivation through career development programs, facilitating the movement of students into urban-oriented careers. Corresponding with the increase of motivation is a need for a curriculum which prepares students for new careers. As noted earlier, Mississippi is a rapidly growing industrial society. Thus, new special programs must be developed to meet these career needs and faculty development must be encouraged to prepare instructors to implement these new programs.

New career programs were developed in environmental science, speech pathology and audiology, pre-professional health careers, mass communication, meteorology, geology, legal studies, public administration, and historic preservation. Emphasis was also stressed on activities to promote faculty enrichment in career education: in-service experiences in business, industry, and public agencies, exchanges between faculty and industrial personnel, providing actual managerial and technical experiences for faculty in industrial settings; and on-campus workshops, seminars, and institutes dealing with career education.

Hand in hand with faculty orientation in career education, President Peoples saw fit to increase student personnel services to upgrade career potential by providing more career education for all students and special diagnostic and remediation services for students with learning disabilities. Two specific problems with the counseling and remediation programs needed special attention: (1) the assessment of learning disabilities was inadequate because of lack of a viable diagnostic element; and (2) the academic skills and remediation programs were not being coordinated properly with the Counseling Center and with each other. With the AID Program grant from the federal government, President Peoples did, in fact, establish a program for diagnosing student academic weaknesses and strengths with the subsequent decrease of the attrition rate for students; he also established administrative articulation and coordination of the remediation services operated by several departments of the university. He also provided both career orientation courses, enlarging upon the orientation sessions with special emphasis on information about new and emerging careers and offering computer-assisted instruction activities related to skill development and remediation.

President Peoples included the improvement program as an important component of the AID Program at Jackson State. This program had a number of elements which were coordinated to meet a definite timetable for implementation. But additional hardware, software, and personnel were required to meet the established deadlines. Supplementary AIDP funds helped the university to meet these needs and to administer and monitor its radically increased budget and to upgrade the library circulation system.

The Office of Publications, which was established through the original AIDP grant, augmented the effectiveness of the university relations function, so vital to promoting the community image of Jackson State as possessing the instructional effectiveness both to increase the fiscal and operational stability of the university and improve its academic quality.

For the Office of Institutional Research and Planning, President Peoples requested additional funds for activities vital to the development and use of a planning, management, and evaluation system which depended largely upon personnel having the capability to develop, maintain, and use it. He saw to it that training for the administrative personnel was provided; he also purchased the basic software necessary for its development and implementation. The system is still being developed.

Jackson State entered into a cooperative relationship with the Research and Development Center of Mississippi. A bilateral arrangement was worked out to implement the objectives of the career education thrust of the university. The center has played a major role in bringing industry to Mississippi, and it has provided technical assistance and service to maintain the vitality of those industries. The center, with a budget of $4.1 million in fiscal year 1975, is one of the agencies under the Board of Trustees of Institutions of Higher Learning, along with the eight state universities and the Gulf Coast Research Laboratory.

Other efforts were initiated to create opportunities for students. The University Industry Cluster is an example. The cluster is a National Alliance of Businessmen's program aimed at building a close working relationship between business and predominantly black colleges throughout the country. As its name signifies, the cluster brings together members from industry with the university's faculty and student body. Together they explore ways to identify the university's needs and to use all available resources to meet those needs.

The cluster concept had its beginning in 1967 under the auspices of the Alliance for Progress. During the following year, the National Alliance of Businessmen adopted the cluster program as a part of its annual activity. The late President Lyndon B. Johnson provided the brain trust for the National Alliance of Businessmen and for the University Industry Cluster.

Its purpose is to initiate, develop, and expand a cooperative relationship between developing institutions, the business community, and mainstream institutions. It also aims to aid the developing institution in a variety of ways so that its graduates can better be prepared to compete for jobs in the private sector and move up to higher positions of executive and professional responsibility on an equal basis. Three active task forces have been formed to work in the areas of funds, equipment, and membership.

The Jackson State University Industry Cluster meets bi-annually to investigate problems, seek solutions, and develop and implement programs of corrective action. The key concept is cooperative problem identification and problem solving. Some of the areas include curriculum planning and design, research projects, equipment, cooperative education arrangements, student scholarships, internships and exchange programs, and career counseling and placement. Because the needs are great and the resources limited, the cluster participants, particularly industry, must continually reestablish priorities in order to provide a match between the assets and needs of Jackson State University and resources of the participating corporations.

Cooperative action of cluster members gradually increases the capacity of Jackson State University to provide its students with better and more effective education for positions in business, industry, and government. As a result, Jackson State University's graduates are better prepared to compete for higher level jobs. Hence, business, industry, and government gain a highly skilled manpower pool from which to recruit professional and management talents.

As a part of the AIDP effort, Jackson State has developed an undergraduate program in its Center for Urban Affairs encompassing Urban Affairs, Social Work Program, and Criminal Justice and Correctional Services. Begun on July 1, 1974, this program provided the urban thrust of the university by linking existing courses in various disciplines which tended to have an emphasis on the urban crisis. By definition, the urban crisis is inductively a threat posed by the deterioration of the city's physical plants, the failure of its public services, and the decline of the moral standards among its populace.

Furthermore, employment statistics for Mississippi indicate that the total number of black people employed in the 68 state agencies and departments surveyed was only 761 or 5.8 percent of the total work force of 13,070. White employment for the same 68 agencies and departments amounted to 12,309 or 94.2 percent of the total work force. Of the 68 agencies and departments studied, only 24 listed black employees while 62 listed a white employment rate of 90 percent or better. Of the total work force considered, 93.3 percent of all the state black employees work for departments or agencies operating with federal funds. Of the agencies and departments studied, 12 were major recipients of federal funds. Four of the major state agencies and departments at the time receiving federal funds had no black employees, while 5 had less than 10 percent black employment. Four state departments were currently employing 560 of the total 761 black persons working in state government; the Highway Department and Health, Education, and Welfare had 73.6 percent of the total black work force of these departments.

Under the directorship of Dr. C. A. Baham, the institution has undertaken a number of programs to provide students with opportunities in the urban setting by becoming involved in projects designed to improve the quality of education, to ease the problems of urban youth, and to provide continuing education for the city populace. The program is one of four divisions of the Advanced Institutional Development Program contained in the School of Liberal Studies with three basic components—"Out reach," under the direction of Dr. Kathryn B. Weathersby; "Youth," under the directorship of John Morris; and "Curriculum," under the direction of Dr. Jacqueline Franklin. The program was funded out of a $2.5 million grant under Title III of the Higher Education Act of 1965.

Additionally, a Criminal Justice Program is administered through the Urban Affairs Center. The demand for specialized training in criminal justice at the Law Enforcement and Correctional Services level in the state of Mississippi is rapidly increasing. The program at Jackson State exposes students to a variety of course offerings ultimately aimed at the application of social science principles and methods of understanding and controlling crime and delinquency.

STUDENT ENROLLMENT

In 1877 the enrollment at Natchez Seminary was 20 students, including single teenagers and adults; in 1976 the student body numbered 7,718 teenagers, adults, parents, and even grandparents. In 1877 the enrollment was totally black; in 1976, 13 percent was nonblack.

STUDENT ACTIVITIES

Participation in activities has been the watchword for Jackson State University students whether in chapel, choir, on farms, musical tours, or athletic engagements during the past one hundred years. Through them students display self-determination, leadership, and cooperation.

Major activities of student life at Jackson State University are reflected in fraternities, sororities, honorary organizations, professional and departmental associations, and special interest groups. The following Greek letter organizations have established chapters on campus: Alpha Kappa Alpha Sorority, Alpha Phi Alpha Fraternity, Delta Sigma Theta Sorority, Kappa Alpha Psi Fraternity, Phi Beta Sigma Fraternity, Sigma Gamma Rho Sorority, Zeta Phi Beta Sorority, and Omega Psi Phi Fraternity. Honor societies at Jackson State University are Alpha Chi, Alpha Kappa Mu, Alpha Lambda Delta, and Phi Kappa Phi. Departmental honor societies include: Alpha Mu Gamma (languages), Beta Beta Beta (biology), Delta Mu Delta (business), Gamma Theta Upsilon (geography), Pi Omega Pi (business education), Sigma Mu (mathematics), and Sigma Rho Gamma (social sciences).

Professional and departmental associations on the campus are represented by the following clubs: Alpha Beta Alpha Library Science Fraternity, Athenian Art Club, Business Education Club, Chemical Society, Computer Club, Council for Exceptional Children, Health and Physical Education Majors Club, Industrial Arts Club, Mass Communications Club, Mathematics Club, Music Educators National Conference Club, Pre-Law Club, Pierian Literary Society, Social Science Education Club, Social Worker Club, Spanish Club, and the Student National Education Association.

Special interest groups organized on the campus include: the Afro-American Society, the *Blue and White Flash*, Cheerleaders Club, Career Opportunities Program Club, Dunbar Dramatic Guild, Freshmen Social Service Club, "J" Club, *Jacksonian* (yearbook), Jackson State University Choir, Karate Club, Silhouette Club, Tiger Crusaders Club, Ushers Club, and Veterans Club.

STUDENT GOVERNMENT

Since its founding in 1943, the Student Government Association has been the principal voice of students on campus.

It was conceived as a teaching-learning situation for the purpose of providing for the students' first hand experience in democratic living. The functions of SGA are:

1. To provide a central agency through which students may help to promote the interest and welfare of the University Community.

2. To assist in planning and regulating the activities of constituent student organizations.

3. To administer the student activity fund.

4. To represent the student body in ceremonial and official occasions on invitation of the University President.

5. To represent, through membership on University committees, student opinion on curricular and student personnel matters.

From its very onset, the organization lives up to its twofold purpose—to develop a sense of responsibility for adherence to acceptable standards of group life and to demonstrate, through actual living experience, the social skills necessary for intelligent self-government.

The first president of the organization under state control was Lottie Williams Thornton; the first secretary, Mary C. Oates; the first cabinet; Johnnie Cotton, Henrene Wolfe Swann, Gladys Wilson, Cleophas Bingham Sanders, and Lelia G. Rhodes. As this book goes to press the 1977–78 officers are: Henry Banks, president; Lynard Carter, vice president; Camille Stutts, business manger; Shirley Macon, secretary; Carolyn Turner, assistant secretary; Keith Anderson, chief justice; Antoinette Smith, associate chief justice and Leonard Anderson, Burnadette Fairman and Oliver Smith, justices.

SCHOLARSHIPS

True to its mission of serving the poor and deprived youth of Mississippi, Jackson State University offers outright grants to three-fourths of its students who need financial assistance. The university offers these grants as a part of an integrated program of financial aid for students. Policies concerning scholarships are determined by the Scholarship Committee. The strength of academic and personal records is the primary determinant in selecting scholarship winners from among qualified applicants with demonstrated needs.

Jackson State University awards annually a number of renewable half and full scholarships to high school graduates on the basis of scores on the American College Test (ACT), competitive examinations, high school records, and the recommendations of the high school principal or an instructor in the school from which the students graduate.

Special field scholarships are awarded to high school graduates who show special talent in such fields as dramatics, music, art, etc., and who desire to major in one of these fields at Jackson State University. Applicants for these scholarships must be recommended by the high school principal or a member of the school faculty and must be auditioned by a representative of the university from the department in which they are seeking scholarship assistance.

The university also awards annually a renewable tuition scholarship to the two highest ranking graduates of each accredited junior college in the state of Mississippi.

CLASS SCHOLARSHIPS—GENERAL COLLEGE SCHOLARSHIPS

One year renewal tuition scholarships are awarded to the highest ranking student in the freshman, sophomore, and junior classes. These scholarships are offered on a competitive basis.

An unspecified number of renewable tuition scholarships are awarded to members of the sophomore, junior, and senior classes who have a better than "B" cumulative average, whose citizenship is proved, and who are in need of financial assistance. These scholarships are offered on a competitive basis; applications must be submitted to the Scholarship Committee.

Scholarships offered to the students of Jackson State University by groups and individuals include: Jackson State University, Chicago, and Laurel alumni clubs respectively; Jackson Civitan Club; Mississippi Power and Light Company; Army ROTC; Dupont Foundation; President's Tuition Scholarships for Jackson area students, and the Jacob L. Reddix Scholarship Fund.

Students who need short-term emergency loans may borrow from the Alumni Student Loan and the Robert Branson Student Loan Funds respectively. A number of awards are given students in recognition of scholarship ability, leadership, high moral character, talent, and general ability: Dansby-Bond, V. Horatio Henry, Elbert L. Tatum. John Norris, I. P. Hunt, J. Y. Woodard, Ben McGee, Walter Payton, ROTC, Carnation Teaching Incentive.

In 1969, the Development Foundation of Jackson State University initiated the $1,000 Club whose motto of "one thousand one thousanders by one hundred" refers to the goal to get one thousand alumni to pledge one thousand dollars to the university for student scholarships by the institution's hundredth birthday, October 23, 1977.

Jackson State University students participate not only in campus organizations but they also serve on local, regional, and national boards and committees. Miss Mississippi and Miss America pageants feature Jackson State Univerity students; subsequently Miss Helen Ford was crowned Miss Black America. In addition, male students were elected to the National Student Orientation Conference Steering Board. Also, numerous students are cited in *Who's Who in American Colleges and Universities*.

THE COMMITTEE OF EIGHTY-TWO

The Committee of Eighty-Two, sponsored by Dr. Maria Luisa Alvarez Harvey, is a campus organization of student representatives from the eighty-two counties in Mississippi. Their main concerns are to promote political awareness and to foster voter registration. The members of the group have succeeded in encouraging legislation beneficial to Jackson State University. They were instrumental in the institution's securing university status and in the legislature's approval of pre-planning rights and final approval for a new multipurpose building. Organized in 1973, the Committee of Eighty-two merited the expressed praise of Douglas Anderson, member of the House of Representatives.

ATHLETICS

Achievement in athletics is as much a part of the history of Jackson State as is the achievement in the academic arena. In 1941, President Reddix appointed a committee to study how the philosophy, objectives, and course offering of a physical education program would relate to the overall philosophy and objectives of the college. The recommendations of the committee led to the establishment of athletics as an integral part of the Department of Health and Physical Education.

Following the outbreak of World War II, draftees were found to be in poor physical condition. As a result, the Department of Defense concluded that physical conditioning programs had to be augmented to prepare American youths for military service. The federal government appealed to educators, coaches, and school administrators to establish and maintain physical conditioning programs to help fill the void. Jackson State has responded to this appeal by continuing to administer an athletic program.

During the war years, as mentioned elsewhere in this document, intercollegiate athletics were suspended. From 1940-45, athletic competition was limited to intramural sports. However, in 1946, the Board of Trustees of State Institutions of Higher Learning approved the recommendation of President Reddix to sponsor intercollegiate athletics. This approval initiated the first competitive sports program for the college after coming under the administration of the state of Mississippi.

The program had four objectives: to establish wholesome athletic relationships with comparable colleges; to acquire personnel, equipment, and facilities needed to support the program; to establish an athletic scholarship program for talented athletes; and to seek membership in regional and national athletic associations. In accordance with these objectives, Jackson State has continued to maintain a strong athletic program.

The influx of returning servicemen from World War II posed great challenges to most colleges and universities. The Servicemen's Readjustment Act of 1944 established the G.I. Bill, which provided veterans with tuition, books, supplies, and subsistence. Consequently, veterans flooded college campuses. Each institution was responsible for acclimating these students to the academic program and activities. Many of the veterans enrolling at Jackson State were highly skilled in athletics because they had gained valuable experience and recognition while in the Armed Forces. The contributions to the athletic program and the veterans were both symbiotic and nonpareil.

In the summer of 1949, the construction of a college gymnasium and athletic field was completed. During this same year, intramural activities expanded to include volleyball, softball, basketball, football, tennis, and field and track. In 1957, the university expanded its varsity sports program to include football, basketball, baseball, golf, tennis, and track and field.

Jackson State was admitted to the Southwestern Athletic Conference in 1958. This admission came two years after the college reorganized its program with T. B. Ellis as director of athletics. The coaches during that period were Dr. Harrison B. Wilson, basketball; John A. Merritt, football; Alvin C. Coleman, line; and Joe Gilliam, backfield.

From 1946 to 1969, the intercollegiate athletics program was one of several conducted within the Department of Physical Education. The program was administered by the department head, who had an additional title of director of athletics. The director reported to the president through the dean of administration.

In 1970, intercollegiate athletics became an autonomous department with the director of intercollegiate athletics as the chief administrative officer. An administrative advisory committee assists the director: vice president for administration, vice president for fiscal affairs, associate vice president for public relations, two appointed faculty members, and two representatives from the Alumni Association.

The athletics program is a phase of the total educational program at Jackson State It was founded upon the conviction that sports are vital and beneficial extracurricular activities; sports create a proper balance between mental and physical training; sports provide relaxation and enjoyment for student participants and spectators; sports foster a spirit of unity and high morale in the student body; and sports encourage cooperative group relationships which are essential to the democratic process.

In conducting the athletic program, the university requires athletes to be admitted in accordance with regularly published entrance requirements for all students and to maintain the same academic standards as other students.

In addition to the college's rules and regulations, the athletic program is conducted in accordance with policies and procedures of the National Collegiate Athletic Association (NCAA), the National Association of Intercollegiate Athletics (NAIA), and the Southwestern Athletic Conference (SWAC)—in all of which the university holds memberships.

In the fall of 1971, the Board of Trustees approved a program leading to the Master's degree in Health, Physical Education, and Recreation. The program consisted of five areas of concentration.

The Sports Hall of Fame was established in 1973 to give recognition to former athletes who have continued to support the university's program, demonstrated leadership, and shown an active concern for community service. Each year since 1973, five additional honorees have been inducted into the Hall of Fame. When the first annual Sports Hall of Fame Banquet was held on May 26, 1973 to honor former athletes, the honorees included: A. A. Alexander, '28; Earl Banks, '27; Luther Marshall, '27; Luious Mitchell, '55; and E. T. Stewart, '32 (posthumously). Since that time, the following athletes have been inducted: E. S. Bishop, T. B. Brown, Robert Clark, T. B. Ellis, Raymond "Sunshine" Gillian, Percy Greene, Commodore Dewey Higgins, W. H. Higgins, Giles Hubert, Frank "Bear" McCune, John A. Peoples, Jr., Leroy Ramsey, J. L. Sullivan, Clarence Watson, C. D. Westbrook, Jr., Herbert A. Wilson, and Robert L. Wolfe.

The past ten years (1967-77) are considered the golden age of intercollegiate football at predominantly black colleges and universities. These were the years that Jackson State reigned with Grambling College, Tennessee State University, Southern University, and Alcorn State University as one of the five gridiron powers in the talent-packed Southwest Conference.

To attest to the SWAC'S football power coming of age, the conference ranks second in the nation in the number of athletes signed by professional organizations. At the beginning of the 1976 season, Jackson State tied with the University of Notre Dame in the sixteenth spot for the number of professional gridders (15) in the National Football League (NFL).

As is evidenced by the number of graduates who have joined the ranks of professional football players, Jackson State attracts many professional scouts to the campus to recruit players. Over the last ten years, 55 players have been drafted by professional football teams with 10 of them making All-Pro. In 1975, two players were first round draft picks. Robert Brazille was subsequently named the

National Football League's defensive rookie-of-the-year, and Walter Payton was edged only by O. J. Simpson two years in a row as the leading ground gainer in the American Football Conference. (A list of coaches, professional athletes, championships, awards, and records may be found in the Appendix.)

The years 1967 through 1977 were indeed memorable years for the Jackson State University Tigers: the university captured three SWAC championships in football (1972, 1973, and 1975). Four coaches guided the Tigers during this golden age: W. C. Gorden (1976-present), Robert "Bob" Hill (1970-76), Ulysses McPherson (1969-70), and Roderick Paige (1964-68).

Until November 1976, Bob Hill served as head coach. He joined the staff in 1963 and served as an offensive coordinator and line coach until his appointment as head coach in 1970. Hill, a football player himself at Jackson State, was honored as All-Midwestern Athlete Back for three consecutive years before going to a four-year pro-career with the Baltimore Colts in 1956. Later, he joined Toronto of the Canadian Football League. Hill compiled a remarkable 43-15-1 record while he was head football coach, which includes three SWAC co-championships.

W. C. Gorden, Hill's assistant, succeeded him as head coach. For his first game as head coach, the Tigers gave him a narrow victory over Texas Southern. Gorden, a native of Nashville, Tennessee, came to Jackson State University following a successful coaching career on the high school level in Mississippi.

Basketball has figured as much in Jackson State's national prominence for athletic prowess as has football. Since 1949, the basketball team has won over 78 percent of its games. T. B. Ellis coached the hoopers to a 21-5 record in 1949-50 and the team has been on the move ever since. The following year, Dr. Harrison B. Wilson succeeded T. B. Ellis as head basketball coach. Dr. Wilson was equally as impressive as his predecessor. From 1949 to 1967, Coach Wilson's basketball teams compiled a total win-loss record of 346-87. Wilson was considered one of the great coaches during his era.

In 1967, basketball and Paul Covington became synonymous with the "New Breed" image of Jackson State. Emerging from this image during the latter part of the '60s was the adherence to the basic principle that "the price of victory, not unlike the price of freedom, is never beyond the reach of human effort and sacrifice."

The new coach "Covingtonized" many players and fans with his controlled, friendly, easy-to-please personality. Under his leadership, the Tigers were guided to four SWAC titles, three NAIA district championships, and several other tournament championships. Covington has compiled a 212-66 record, which places him third on the list of NCAA Division II highest percentage leaders in percentage of games won among active basketball coaches.

In 1974-75, Jackson State climbed to the top of the prestigious Associated Press Small College Poll. That same year, four players were first round draft picks in the basketball pro draft. Fifteen players have been drafted by professional basketball teams, and three have signed as free agents. (A list of these players is in the Appendix).

Woman's participation in athletics is on the upswing at Jackson State University with the most significant national recognition going to Brenda Finch who reached the finals of the tryouts for the 1976 Olympics. In 1975, Sadie MaGee became head basketball coach of the Tigerettes. During her first year, the Tigerettes compiled an 18-5 record.

Track and field teams have won numerous meet championships over the years. Since 1970, the teams have produced 52 All-Americans. Significant championships include NAIA National Indoor (1973, 1975, and 1976); SWAC Indoor (1976 and 1977); and SWAC Cross Country (1975).

Three University athletes—all natives of Bermuda—participated in the 1976 Olympics at Montreal, Canada, as members of the Bermuda Amateur Athletic Association; and one Virgin Islands native participated under her country's flag. Four other Jackson State athletes qualified for the 1976 Olympic trials but did not compete.

There have been many noteworthy achievements by team members in other sports offered at Jackson State University. For instance, the baseball team won SWAC championships in 1967,

1971, and 1973; the golf team, in 1975; and the university, the All Sports Trophy in 1973 and 1975—symbolic of the best all-around sports program in SWAC.

Campus facilities can no longer accommodate the sports program. Therefore, the Mississippi Memorial Stadium, with a seating capacity of 46,000, is used for all home football games; and the Mississippi Coliseum, which seats more that 7,000, is used for some home basketball games.

Jackson State maintains an Office of Sports Information which compiles, interprets, and disseminates statistical and personal information regarding the programs and athletes.

State funds pay for half the cost of athletics. Financial statements of the athletic departments of all institutions were revealed to the public for the first time in 1976. This public announcement prompted a controversy regarding the handling of budgets of athletics departments. Records from Jackson State's Department of Intercollegiate Athletics revealed that throughout the thirty-one-year history of athletics under the state's control (1946-77), the university's athletic staff has ranged from two full-time coaches in 1946 (T. B. Ellis and Benjamin Blackburn) to fifteen full-time staff members for 1976-77.

No coach has remained with the institution as long as T. B. Ellis. Ellis and athletics are synonymous at Jackson State. He was inducted into the Jackson State University Sports Hall of Fame in May 1974.

Some of the full-time head coaches who served with Ellis during the period 1946-1977 include B. A. Blackburn, Edward P. Norris, Alvin C. Coleman, Joe Gilliam, Harrison Wilson (basketball), John Merritt (football), Roderick Paige (football), W. C. Gorden (football), Robert Hill (football), Paul Covington (basketball), Robert Braddy (baseball), Martin Epps (track), A. F. Smith (golf), and John Shinall (tennis). The assistant coaches include Sylvester Collins, Melvin Pete, Ben McGee, and Houston Markham.

BICENTENNIAL CAMPUS

On January 23, 1976, Jackson State University was designated a Bicentennial Campus. Ceremonies were held on the university plaza with Dr. Dollye Robinson presiding. Ethel Green, Miss

Jackson State University, gave the occasion. Following a rendition of the "Battle Hymn of the Republic" by the Jackson State University band and choir, Perry A. Snyder, director, American Revolution Bicentennial Commission, Jackson, Mississippi, presented the Bicentennial certificate and flag to President John A. Peoples, who in his acceptance stated: "Jackson State was involved in the growth and development of this country for nearly a century." Proud to accept the certificate and flag on behalf of the Jackson State constituency, Peoples invited the audience to rededicate themselves to the democratic principles America was founded on.

Jackson State University became the fourteenth institution in the state to be designated a Bicentennial Campus. Patriotic songs were presented by the choir and band under directors Raymond I. Johnson and Harold Haughton. The fifty-gun salute and the presentation of the flag were under the command of Captain D. D. De Fee, Mississippi U.S. Marine Corps Reserve, Battery F, 2nd Battalion, 14th Marines.

The university's Bicentennial activities included: the Phillis Wheatley Poetry Festival, sponsored by the Institute for the Study of Life, History, and Culture of Black People, November 4-7, 1973, in Dansby Hall Auditorium, directed by Dr. Margaret Walker Alexander; Historic Site Survey July 1975-June 1976, sponsored by Ruth Shirley; Senior Citizens' Recollections of Good Old Days in Jackson and Vicinity, January 1-December 31, 1976, sponsored by the Department of History and led by Dr. Alferdteen Harrison in cooperation with the University Center for Urban Affairs; Musical America, January 19, 1976, sponsored by the Department of Music, faculty and students, Raymond I. Johnson and Gladys P. Norris, concert coordinators; the United States Yesterday and Today, February-August 1976, sponsored by Departments of History and Mass Communications, Dr. Bennie L. Reeves and Dr. Johnny Tolliver, coordinators; the Community Cemetery Project, January-December 1976, sponsored by Jackson State University Student Government Association and Pan-Hellenic Council in conjunction with city engineers of Jackson, Eugene Jackson, director of student activities, Jack Oldfield, city of Jackson; The Me Nobody Knows (Dunbar Dramatic Guild), April 28-30, 1976, sponsored by Edward J. Fisher, director; The Black

Newspaper in Mississippi, 1887–1975, sponsored by Dr. Julius E. Thompson.

THE CENTENNIAL

The celebration of the first centenary of Jackson State University was begun by a series of proclamations honoring the accomplishments of the institution. Governor Cliff Finch called the university a citadel for teachers and liberal arts education. He focused on the fact that Jackson State University served the community, state, nation, and world by educating members of various professions. In addition to its academic programs, conferences, workshops, and lectures, proclaimed the governor, Jackson State University contributed to the spiritual and cultural life of the citizens of Mississippi and the nation.

In his proclamation, Mayor Russell C. Davis of Jackson spoke of the contributions of Jackson State University to the city intellectually, culturally, economically, and socially since 1883. Speaking also of the 21,000 alumni—16,000 residing in the state and 7,000 in the environs of the city of Jackson—the mayor duly admired the university for its annual acquisition of more than $6 million in private and federal funds through the relentless efforts of faculty and administration, thereby adding to the Jackson economy.

Mayor Tony Byrne of Natchez recalled that Jackson State University, once the Natchez Seminary, is linked indelibly with the city of Natchez and Adams County in its purpose of providing educational opportunities especially for those from disadvantaged circumstances. In harmony with the Centennial motto, the Natchez mayor proclaimed that Jackson State University's thrust was to maintain academic excellence through teaching, research, and service to the community, propelling it to the forefront as a multicultural, multipurpose, urban-oriented institution.

The Board of Trustees of State Institutions of Higher Learning deemed it fitting to commend highly the presidents of Jackson State University. They praised Ayer, Barrett, Hubert, Dansby, Reddix, and Peoples for their leadership in bringing Jackson State University to the exalted point in its history.

The Hinds County Board of Supervisors recognized the contribution to the economy of the county—$40 million through wages, salaries, contractual services, construction, and personal expenditures by faculty, staff, and the student body.

The Faculty Senate of Jackson State University paid homage to the faculty and staff which grew from 3 members in 1877 to 850 in 1976. These dedicated men and women confronted awesome tasks which they carried out triumphantly. Having fulfilled what many thought impossible, in 1977 they stand on a new threshold realizing the challenging potentials of greatness with collective determination to continue to make Jackson State an excellent university.

The Jackson State University Alumni Association resolution, signed by Estemore A. Wolfe, president, recounted with pride the many benefits the association members received from their alma mater: encouraging, nurturing, and promoting creative thought; involving graduate and former students in policy-making; maintaining communication and working relationship with all alumni; and moving forward in devising new programs and building new facilities which boost the pride of alumni.

With clear eloquence, Thad Cochran, U.S. Congressman from the Fifth District of Mississippi, narrated the history of Jackson State University in the House of Representatives for an hour. Addressing George E. Danielson, speaker pro tempore of the House, Cochran drew attention to the fact that Jackson State University's Centennial coincided with the nation's Bicentennial. "As the state's largest predominantly black educational institution, it is a university in which we can, with ample justification, take great pride." Congressman Cochran went on to say that Jackson State University had its origins in the wake of the most turbulent and troubled era in history. The Civil War left Mississippi, like most of its Southern sister states, prostrate and devastated. Thousands of its young men lay dead on the fields of battle, and its economy was shattered. Many obstacles, social, political, and economic, had to be overcome before Jackson State University could become a reality. Congressman Cochran recounted the origin and development of Jackson State from 1877 to the present emphasizing its role in the educational process in Mississippi and the nation.

Cochran noted that Jackson State University is the fourth largest university in the state of Mississippi. Said Cochran, "At a time when educational institutions all over the country are increasingly hard pressed for funds and support, Jackson State has prospered. It enjoys one of the highest rates of growth of any institution in the United States." The Congressman pointed out that in the fall of 1972, Jackson State employed 688 faculty and staff with a student enrollment of 5,100. By the fall of 1975, there were 7,718 students and over 830 faculty and staff.

Cochran, in pointing up the identification of Jackson State University with the city of Jackson, said, "the campus is a beautiful 94-acre tract located in Jackson, Mississippi's capital city. Jackson, with a population of 310,200 people, has been identified as a growth city in the Deep South. This hand in hand growth of Jackson and Jackson State University is not coincidental. Thousands of the graduates of Jackson State are now living and working in our capital city and the surrounding area. They are contributing substantially to the economic development of Jackson and the state of Mississippi."

The Congressman singled out the president of Jackson State University as one of many deserving specific recognition—Dr. John A. Peoples, Jr. Cochran stated that Dr. Peoples had presided over the administration of Jackson State University during one of the most difficult and trying periods in its existence. It was a period in which the institution had been making the transition from college to university and from an all-black enrollment to the acceptance of all races. Cochran noted that, due in large part to the president's leadership, Jackson State had met and survived many crises. Dr. John A. Peoples, Jr., he said, was truly a credit to Jackson State University and to the state of Mississippi.

Cochran identified Jackson State University's Centennial objectives: (1) to chronicle the first century of progress of the university; (2) to give prominence to those events which were pivotal with respect to the significant changes in the directions of the university; (3) to focus on those persons who played salient roles in advancing the institution toward its destiny; (4) to involve the constituency of the university in commemorative activities depicting and dramatizing the university's record of service; (5) to bring community, state, and national attention and support to the current thrust of the university; (6) to analyze past and present achievements as a foundation upon which philosophical and operational directions for the future might be built; (7) to determine new dimensions of teaching and learning on the basis of which the university might better carry out its mission; (8) to take definite and positive steps toward launching the university into its second century of service.

Identifying himself personally with the university, Cochran closed his speech and had it incorporated into the *House Congressional Record*, September 14, 1976: "Mr. Speaker, it is a source of pride to me that I have the honor to represent the district in which Jackson State University is located. I have benefited from its presence in the community in which I grew up, and I am privileged to have the opportunity to work with its officials in insuring its continued growth and development."

To memoralize the one hundredth anniversary of Jackson State University, a series of events was planned and carried out by thirty-five committees headed by Dr. John A. Peoples, Jr., chairman *ex officio*, Dr. Lee E. Williams, chairman, Dr. Estus Smith, vice chairman, Dr. Paul Purdy, secretary, and Hilliard L. Lackey, Centennial coordinator. The scheduled programs were printed in an official *Calendar of Events*. Numerous pictures and illustrations of administrators, faculty, buildings, and activities lent authenticity and publicity to past and current events. The six modifications of the university's official seals were recorded and the original score of the official school song by T. D. Pawley and Frederick Hall was photostated and made part of the production. Twenty-three milestones in the history of Jackson State University were outlined and an excerpt of the 1882 catalog contrasted nineteenth-century rules with current regulations.

Besides the calendar, many momentoes were put on sale as souvenirs of the Centennial: medallions, lapel pins, bracelets, key chains, license plates, cigarette lighters, collectors' plates, ashtrays, buttons, patches, and money clips.

Centennial events were described on the pages of national, regional, and local publications, and such official university organs as *Scope*, *JSU Now*, and *Blue and White Flash*. Colorful programs of each particular activity emphasized the importance of the event in Centennial history. Faculty and Staff Seminar Week, September 12–18, emphasized the Centennial celebration. Other events included the Distinguished Artists Series; the drama "Don't Bother Me, I Can't Cope," September 22; the Centennial Ecumentical Forum, October 10; the Jackson State University Appreciation Week, October 17-22; Publication of a Tabloid—The Making of a University Program, October 17; Service of Worship and Thanksgiving at Mt. Helm Baptist Church, October 17; Campus Visit of Jackson Chamber of Commerce, October 19; monthly meeting of the Board of Trustees, Institutions of Higher Learning, State of Mississippi, October 20; the Founders' Day Convocation and Dedication of the Dr. Frederick D. Hall Music Center, October 24; the Coronation of Miss Jackson State University, November 4; the Centennial Alumni Colloquium and Performer Series, November 5; the Media Blitz, November 14; Centennial Industry Cluster Conference, November 18-19; Opera/South production of *Jubilee*, November 20; and the Centennial Christmas Concert, December 12.

The Centennial activities highlighted the evolution of Natchez Seminary to Jackson State University, showing the diligent efforts, perseverance, courage, and unfaltering faith which leaders and faculty have maintained throughout. Determined to meet future challenges with the exalted vision of the founders, the dogged determination of its great men and women who undauntedly turned potential failure into success, the Centennial family displayed in its commemorative events the same persistance and vigor to meet its academic and social commitments as a dynamic educational force both in Mississippi and the nation.

On March 2, 1977 the ten years of President Peoples' progress was reviewed in two public forums by Lonnie Crosby, Director Institutional Research, Dr. Wendell Gorum, Head, Media Center, Samuel Jones, President, Student Government Association, Dr. Clara Grochowska, Professor of Modern Foreign Languages, and Miss Patricia Coates, attorney. While Dr. Rose McCoy presented the occasion; Dr. Anthony Cavell, the invocation; and Dr. Samuel D. Proctor, Martin Luther King Professor from Rutgers University, the principal addresss, President Peoples himself could claim THE WILL TO EXCELLENCE by proclaiming:

We do not use the past as an excuse for failure in the present or the future. We actually subscribe to the dictum that the past is prologue. For the past, having been good or bad, is but a bridge to the present and a guide to the future. Accordingly, with due respect and consideration of the past, we today consider the modern Jackson State University a manifestation of will, A Will to Excellence.

President John A. Peoples, Jr. delivered the commencement address during the University's 1977 Centennial Spring Commencement exercise held Sunday, May 8 in the Mississippi Coliseum as more than 650 students were awarded degrees.

Dr. Peoples spoke on the topic, "An Essay On Education, History, Time, and Inertia." He began his address by commenting on the educational qualifications that today's graduates must have in order to succeed as he commented, "To become a participating member of this society, you must be able to communicate effectively through verbal and written expression. You must be able to quantify. And this means a lot more than counting your fingers. It means being able to measure, to calculate, to compute, to estimate, to extrapolate, to interpolate, to correlate, and to analyze. You must be able to think profoundly, analytically, and critically... further, you must have a basic understanding and appreciation of the world about you."

As he recounted the story of Jackson State University's history, Dr. Peoples beseeched the members of the centennial class to, "know the story of the salient events, the prominent persons, and the pivotal changes which brought into being this institution whose centennial you represent today."

"As members of the centennial," he continued, "you must become an active part of the fight to maintain Jackson State University's crusade toward excellence. And as such, each of you should be able to exhibit a level of academic competence and historical awareness befitting of your representation of a century of academic endeavor."

As he encouraged the centennial class to make effective use of the principles of time and inertia, Dr. Peoples stressed that teaching and learning are reciprocal processes and that only those students who contribute to the learning situation will get something from it. "You must never wait. Inspire yourself, and ever teach yourself, if necessary," he said.

In closing, Dr. Peoples challenged the graduates "to use your education to carry on the fight against ignorance and its by-products, that you will continue to be involved in the struggle to move Jackson State University toward its great destiny of advancing truth and freedom."

Dr. Lee E. Williams, Vice President for Administration was the feature speaker at the University's Centennial Summer Commencement Exercises held August 13, 1977. He challenged the 1977 class to a life-long love affair with our Alma Mater—Jackson State University. You will find it to be a worthy recipient of your affection. He quoted from Robert Frost, "Love for one's Alma Mater should be next to love for his family."

JACKSON STATE UNIVERSITY ALUMNI

The history of an institution is significant, because it gives its alumni both a sense of pride in the achievements of the past and an inspiration to cherish greater hopes and more determined ambitions towards projecting themselves to higher standards for the future. From the original purpose of the institution to train preachers and teachers have emerged giant humanists who evolved from a nucleus of seven high school graduates of Natchez Seminary in 1883.

The nation has to recognize and to respect the fact that Jackson State University, a small black college in Mississippi, within the last 100 years, has provided the state with untold numbers of preachhers, doctors, lawyers, teachers and other professionals. It has been the teachers who have been trained in this black institution who have been able to motivate the youth of our state to become their best selves in spite of the presence of overwhelming environmental circumstances often encompassing the total socio-psycho-economic experience of the family.

In 100 years, Jackson State has undergone six name changes paralleled with six presidents and six college seals. The University grew from mixed faculty in 1877 to an all black faculty in 1911. Fifty years later, the University faculty is multiethnic, multicultured, and multinational.

Every university must choose for itself what its mission will be to meet the challenges of society. The fulfillment of the University's elected mission has been successful during the administration of the six presidents. Each has made his individual mark in the history of the University. Let the record state that new goals are ever set in order to secure higher levels of excellence by the masses of students. In spite of Jackson State's century of achievement, it must yet project even higher levels of attainment, reassess strengths and realize those goals already set in order to attain optimum potential.

To conclude, a century of service reveals a justifiable sense of pride in what has been accomplished. The next century must be rededication to the conviction that growth and new goals to meet changing conditions are necessary requisites for a great university.

When the American Baptist Home Mission Society approved in 1921 a curriculum for the Bachelor of Arts degree, Annie Mae Brown became its first alumna on whom the degree was conferred in 1924. Two graduates received the A.B. degree in 1925. They were Richie Hudson and Mary G. Whiteside. The four graduates of the class of 1926 were: Zee Alfin Anderson Barron, Commodore Dewey Higgins, Maude T. Alexander Jackson and Walter A. Reed, Jr. The number increased in 1927 by two. The graduates were: Joseph H. Jackson, Vera I. King, Luther J. Marshall, Hazel B. McDonald, William A. Shirley and Charles W. Westbrooks. In 1928 the number of graduates numbered seven; Alphonso Alexander, Lala M. Twine Alexander, Joanna L. McAllister Gordon, Giles A. Hubert, John L. Sullivan, Pearl A. Varnado and James A. White.

The Great Depression affected the number in the class of 1929 with only two degrees awarded. The recipients were: Marion Macco Reid and Clara Charleston Thompkins. Nineteen-thirty showed an increase of fifteen bringing the total to seventeen. The graduates of that year were: Frances M. Mannery Alexander, Edward S. Bishop, Valena Willie Betts Fields, Birdie E. Graves, Sylvester B. Hamilton, Wallace A. Higgins, Robert Lind, Brownlee L. Lindsay, Alberta J. Marshall, Anna R. Meelon, Howard W. Moore, Willie W. Moore, Edna Clara Sims, Laurant Smith, Eunice H. Williams, Roland P. Williams and Sandy W. Wilkerson Williams.

The pattern changed slightly in the number of graduates during part of the New Deal Era 1931, with eleven degrees conferred. They were Charles N. Buchanan, Julia F. Clark, Oliver W. Ford, Beatrice Rice Ginn, Mayne D. Pendleton Higgins, Cordelia J.

McNeal, Alice E. Thomas, William Walton, Harry E. Ward, Marcus B. Williams and Jack H. Young, Sr. The class of 1932, Roland L. Buchanan, Edward W. Lawson, Hope Beatrice Mallard Peters, Elma George Smith, Edgar T. Stewart and Edna B. Taylor, In 1933, when the American Baptist Home Missionary Society withdrew support from the college, eight degrees were awarded. The graduates were: Clarence J. Blackburn, Ester Ellis Sampson Marshall, Alfred L. Fields, Helen L. Washington Griffin, Sara E. Whiteside Moore, Mollie W. Young Sims, Sallye M. Stewart and Henrietta B. Trawick.

Following is a listing of the number of students who received degrees from Jackson State University from 1934 to 1977.

Degrees Awarded, 1934–1956

YEAR	NUMBER	YEAR	NUMBER
1934	15	1946	40
1935	22	1947	40
1936	20	1948	45
1937	13	1949	79
1938	17	1950	91
1939	22	1951	120
1940	34	1952	93
1941	1	1953	158
1942	0	1954	200
1943	0	1955	214
1944	29	1956	223
1945	40		

Degrees Awarded, 1957–60 through 1976–77

YEAR	BACHELOR'S	MASTER'S SPECIALIST	TOTAL
1957	234	2	236
1958	284	4	288
1959	234	6	240
1960	350	4	354
1961	351	5	356
1962	279	3	282
1963	309	4	313
1964	309	4	313
1965	336	4	340
1966	389	4	393

Degrees Awarded (CONTINUED)

YEAR	BACHELOR'S	MASTER'S	SPECIALIST	TOTAL
1967	379	7		386
1967–68	459	14		473
1968–69	434	14		448
1969–70	534	31		565
1970–71	675	50		725
1971–72	796	125		921
1972–73	851	182	2	1035
1973–74	829	224	10	1063
1974–75	738	241	32	1011
1975–76	668	355	40	1063
1976–77	682	439	47	1168

PROFILE OF SOME ALUMNI WHO HAVE ACHIEVED DISTINCTION IN DIVERSIFIED FIELDS.*

The selection of noteworthy alumni becomes more difficult as their number increases and their achievements become more competitive. Many alumni did achieve distinction in their various fields of endeavor in many sections of the country and abroad. The consensus of their colleagues acknowledges the fact; personal testimonies, Alumni newsletters and interviews cite their unique accomplishments.

In the 100 years of institutional history the alumni show that the stated hopes and aspirations of Jackson State University contained in its original mission produced tangible results. The degree of precise accomplishments in the changing conditions of history can hardly be determined. However, the fact is that Jackson State repaid the State of Mississippi its fiscal investment by supplying for it teachers, school administrators, doctors, lawyers, businessmen, musicians, artists, scientists and legislators.

The following is a listing of Jackson State University Alumni with doctorates, with dental and medical doctorates, attorneys and certified public accountants:

Jackson State University Distinguished Alumni

ALUMNI WITH DOCTORATES

Dr. Mildred Allen '54
Dr. Amel Anderson '62
Dr. Mildred W. Barksdale '46

Dr. Robert J. Anthony '54
Dr. Ben Bailey '54
Dr. William Luckey '66

ALUMNI WITH DOCTORATES (CONTINUED)

Dr. James Beck '47
Dr. Haskell Bingham '58
Dr. Harold Bishop '64
Dr. Lucille E. Brown
Dr. Roland Buchanan '57
Dr. Archie Buffkins '56
Dr. Cozetta W. Buckley '48
Dr. Emmett Burns '62
Dr. Ralph Burns
Dr. Joe L. Cain '51
Dr. Roosevelt Calvert '56
Dr. Sam Cobbins '63
Dr. Joe Turner Darden '65
Dr. Pearl N. Draine '49
Dr. Morris Dunbar
Dr. Willie Farmer '56
Dr. E. C. Foster '64
Dr. Velvelyn Foster '63
Dr. Jimmie L. Franklin '61
Dr. Delars Funches '40
Dr. Hance Gambling '47
Dr. Percy E. Gambrell '52
Dr. Roosevelt Gentry '69
Dr. Ruben Gentry '67
Dr. Janace Harvey Goree
Dr. Jo Ann Hammonds '64
Dr. Johnny L. Harris '62
Dr. Joyce Harris
Dr. Charles Hicks
Dr. Dennis Holloway '58
Dr. Kermit Holly
Dr. Charles Holmes '57
Dr. John F. Hurley '67
Dr. Florida Hyde '56
Dr. Anita L. Jackson
Dr. Mildred C. Jackson '56
Dr. Jimmie James '60
Dr. Franklin Jefferson '64
Dr. Gladys January Johnson '65
Dr. Walter Lee Johnson '73
Dr. Arthur Jones, Jr. '65
Dr. Willie D. Kyles '53
Dr. Sarah D. Lane '56

Dr. Robert Lewis '69
Dr. Ivory Manning '47
Dr. M. C. Martin '63
Dr. Walter Mercer '47
Dr. Richard Middleton '59
Dr. Earl Miller '62
Dr. Velma Mitchell '53
Dr. Andrew Newsome '68
Dr. Bessie M. O'Banner
Dr. George A. Owens '37
Dr. Roderick Paige '56
Dr. John A. Peoples, Jr. '50
Dr. Ivory P. Phillips '63
Dr. Paul W. Purdy '62
Dr. Leroy Ramsey '52
Dr. Joe Reddix '54
Dr. Walter Reed '55
Dr. Carolyn B. Reynolds '58
Dr. Lelia G. Rhodes '44
Dr. Dollye M. Robinson '48
Dr. T. J. Robinson '63
Dr. Ralph Rogers '63
Dr. Jean Romain '69
Dr. Alice Russell '57
Dr. Richard A. Savage '66
Dr. John L. Shourts '55
Dr. James O. Simmons '49 (deceased)
Dr. Estus Smith '53
Dr. Marzine Smith '62
Dr. Hugh Stevens '55
Dr. Raymond Stewart '56
Dr. Ida J. Barnes Stockman '62
Dr. Johnny E. Tolliver '67
Dr. Charles Vincent '66
Dr. Katheryn Weathersby '54
Dr. Barnes West '53
Dr. Calvin White '48
Dr. Arthur Williams '64
Dr. Hill Williams, Jr.
Dr. Lucious L. Williams '51
Dr. Herbert Wilson '46
Dr. Elaine P. Witty '57
Dr. Jack Witty '57

*As submitted to the author from the files of the National Alumni Office, 1976.

DENTISTS AND MEDICAL DOCTORS

Dr. Frank Bell DDS	Dr. John Nixon '63, M.D.
Dr. Thurman Beasley '67, DDS	Dr. Ruby Perry, DVM
Dr. Ruby S. Belton '68, M.D.	Dr. Arthur Pippins, M.D.
Dr. Shirley Butler '67, M.D. and JD	Dr. Phillip Pittman, M.D.
Dr. Clinton Cummings '69, M.D.	Dr. Tyrone Powell '66, DVM
Dr. T. B. Ellis III '65, M.D.	Dr. Arnold Savage '72, M.D.
Dr. Willie B. Ewing '70, M.D.	Dr. Rome Sherrod '70, M.D.
Dr. Daniel Gambrell '70, M.D.	Dr. Fred Simmons '63, DDS
Dr. Loretta Gilmore '71, DDS	Dr. Eddie Skipper '69, M.D.
Dr. Elwynn Grimes '64, M.D.	Dr. Longston D Smith, DDS
Dr. Pearl Grimes '70, M.D.	Dr. Timothy Summers '69, M.D.
Dr. Wendell Grimes '70, DDS	Dr. Arthur L. Williams '62, M.D.
Dr. Donald Johnson, M.D.	Dr. Clemmie Williams '70, M.D.
Dr. H. H. Jones 1893, M.D.	Dr. Otha Williams '69, M.D.
Dr. John McAdory '69, M.D.	Dr. Earnest Vaughn '70, V.D.
Dr. Joseph McQuirter '71, DDS	

ATTORNEYS

Atty. Warner Buxton '71	Atty. James Frank Jordon '67, JD
Atty. Lucille E. Brown, '76	Atty. Mose Kincaid '67, JD
Atty. Alvin O. Chambliss '67, LLB, LLM	Atty. Cleve McDowell '63, JD
Atty. Lucious Edwards '72	Atty. Bobby Owens '73, JD
Atty. James O. Ford '67, JD	Atty. Benjamin Pigott '72, JD
Atty. Hilman T. Frazier '71, JD	Atty. Alfred Rhodes
Atty. Marlowe Gambrell '67, JD	Atty. Allix Henry Sanders '66, JD
Atty. Maudine Gatlin '71, JD	Atty. Jackie M. Scott '72, JD
Atty. Carsie Hall '37, JD (equivalent)	Atty. Edgar T. Stewart '32, LLB (deceased)
Atty. Geraldine Harrington '67, JD	Atty. Joseph H. Tate '61
Atty. Charles Holmes '57, JD	Atty. Johnny Walls '68, JD
Atty. Tyree Irving '67, JD	Atty. William Thomas Welch '62, JD
Atty. Lee W. Jackson '72, JD	Atty. Walter Williams '62, JD
Atty. Melvin Jenning '72, MSED, JD	Atty. Jack H. Young, Sr. '31, JD (equivalent)
Atty. Hermel Johnson '67, JD	

CERTIFIED PUBLIC ACCOUNTANTS

Orestes Carmichael '72	Eddie Munson '72
Lynn Evans '75	Dicey Thurman Phillips '76

As a result of the reapportionment in Mississippi three blacks were elected in 1975 to the Mississippi State Legislature: Representative Robert Clark, startled the nation when in 1967 he was elected to the House of Representatives from Holmes County. He became the first black man to hold such a post in the State of Mississippi since the Reconstruction.

The 1908-1909 academic year Dr. Luther Barrett pared and released for the first time a roster of the alumni beginning with the class of 1883. This initial publication listed 154 students covering a period of twentyfour years. Since then the names on the alumni roster increased to approximately 22,000.

Heading the list of alumni who served in foreign countries were: Rev. E. B. Topp, (class of 1886); Rev. Henderson McKinney and Dr. Harry Jones, class of 1898. Some of the foreign alumni include: Ms. Wede Jones (class of '50) currently serving as Dean of Humanities, University of Monrovia, West Africa.

Jackson State has produced two university presidents; Dr. John A. Peoples, Jr., President, Jackson State University; Dr. Archie Buffkin, former Chancellor of the University of Maryland at Eastern Shore; Dr. T. B. Brown, President of the Mississippi Baptist Seminary; and Dr. Joseph Jackson, class of,27 has been president of the National Baptist Convention, U.S.A., Inc. since 1953. The convention membership totals over 6.3 million.

Dr. Lucius Mitchell, class of '51 serves as administrative assistant to Porter Fortune, Chancellor, University of Mississippi. Mrs. Betty Williams, class of '59 was appointed in 1976 to the Mississippi State Board of Trustees, Institutions of Higher Learning, becoming the first black woman on the board. Mrs. Wyla King, Principal, Rankin County Public Schools became the first president of the newly merged Mississippi Association of Educators formerly the Mississippi Teachers Association and Mississippi Education Association. Hundreds of Jackson State University graduates serve as elementary and secondary high school teachers; scores of elementary and secondary school principals in the Mississippi public schools. Administrators at Jackson State University include: Dr. Estus Smith, class of '53, Vice President for Academic Affairs; Dr. Lee E. Williams, class of '40, Vice President for Administration; Dr. Paul W. Purdy, class of '62, Vice President for Fiscal Affairs; Dr. T. J. Robinson, class of '63, Associate Vice President for Public Relations; and Dr. Dennis Holloway, class of '58, Assistant Dean for Academic Affairs.

Mrs. Hattie Vera Jones McInnis organized the first alumni chapter in Laurel, Mississippi in September 1926. Currently there are sixty-five alumni chapters, many of which are located outside of the state of Mississippi: Alabama, Georgia, Illinois, Indiana, Louisiana, Michigan, Minnesota, Nevada, New York, Ohio, Tennessee, Wisconsin and the District of Columbia.

The National Alumni Association began presentation of the Distinguished Service Award in 1961. in 1971, the program expanded to include Chapter Awards in public relations, student recruitment, individual awards in sports, public service, politics, medicine, et cetera, and Distinguished Faculty Awards. These Awards have served to heighten interest in Alumni Affairs. In 1977, the registered number of alumni had reached 15,000.

In general, chapters are active in recruiting students for the university. Each of the chapters contributes to the Jackson State University Development Fund and to organized scholarship agencies set up in honor of past presidents and faculty members of the Jackson State family. During this centennial celebration many alumni and family members have pledged $1,000.00 and a roster of the members who pledged $1,000.00 appears in the appendix.

Edgar T. Stewart served as president of the National Alumni Association until 1944, assisting Dr. Dansby in raising money to support the school after the American Baptist Home Mission Society withdrew support. One of his greatest accomplishments was the fight he led to get the Legislature to rename the institution from "Mississippi Negro Training School" to "Jackson College for Negro Teachers."

A. A. Alexander assumed the presidency in 1944 and served during the final stages and the aftermath of World War II, coordinating extensive alumni recruitment of returning servicemen to attend the institution. He was an ardent supporter in revitalizing intercollegiate athletics on campus. He served until 1948, when Mrs. Lottie Williams Thornton, class of '44 was elected president. She served two years recruiting for active membership with success. Mrs. Estelle Young serving from 1950-54 emphasized active membership and the organization of viable extension centers for teachers in strategic cities in central Mississippi.

Dr. Lee Williams served as national president for twelve years; the longest tenure in the history of the association. He established twenty new alumni chapters that brought the membership total from 300 to more than 2,000. He is credited with directing the alumni to buy the first college bus.

Elected to the presidency in 1966 and serving until 1972, Mrs. Frances Dungy Robertson was one of the co-founders of the Alumni Council of Public Universities of the State of Mississippi.

Edward S. Bishop, principal of Corinth School for more than a quarter of a century, served from 1972-1976. He emphasized legislative and financial support and initiated the vncept of regional alumni involvement.

Elected president in 1976 Dr. Estemore A. Wolfe, class of '47, is the first out-of-state alumnus to be elected to the presidency.

The Office of Alumni Affairs was initiated in 1968 with Hilliard Lackey, class of '65 appointed as its first Director.

Jackson State University "Alumnus of the Year" recipients were: 1960, Dr. Estemore A. Wolfe; 1961, John W. Dixon (deceased); 1962, Dr. Lee E. Williams; 1963, Mrs. Hattie J. McInnis; 1964, Mrs. Lottie W. Thornton; 1965, Mrs. Buelah R. Williams (deceased); 1966, Attorney Jack Young, Sr. (deceased); 1967, Mrs. Frances D. Robertson; 1968, Dr. John A. Peoples, Jr.; 1969, Representative Robert G. Clark; 1970, Mr. & Mrs. John L. Sullivan; 1971, John M. Black; 1972, Mrs. Gladys Durr Smith; 1973, Lelia G. Rhodes; 1974, A. A. Alexander; 1975, Mrs. Gustava M. Gooden; and 1976, Edward S. Bishop, Sr.

FOREIGN STUDENTS

Listed among the students enrolled at Jackson State University during the past thirty-seven years, more than five hundred are known not to be United States citizens. At the recommendation of Dr. Fred McCristion of the General Education Board, the Executive Board of the Phelps-Stokes Fund and with the approval of the Board of Trustees, Dr. E. R. Jobe, Executive Secretary, President Reddix was granted a leave of absence with pay 1948-49 to make an educational study in the Republic of Liberia, Africa. It was at this time that the Phelps-Stokes Fund was considering transferring the ownership and operation of the Booker Washington Institute to the

Liberian government to be used as a government owned technical school. President Reddix's educational tour of Africa and personal contact with many officials of the Liberian government greatly influenced African students to come to Jackson State.

The first graduate under state control from foreign countries included: Mrs. Wede Jones, class of '50, now Dean of the College of Social Sciences and Humanities of the University of Liberia, Monrovia, Liberia West Africa, and Mrs. Maude Fagain Freeman. Additional African students to graduate from JSU included: Mwananono Mbikusita-Lewanika, class of 1963, promoted to Chief Education Officer until his death in 1970; Akashambatwa Mbikusita-Lewanika, class of 1970, serving as Comptroller of Development Program of InDECo; Mbuywana Mbikusita-Lewanika, class of 1976, working with the Ministry of Health, (she is one of only a few Zambians with a degree in Special Education); Wamundila Mbikusita-Lewanika, Jr., class of 1975, working with a mine company in Zambia; Mwananyanda Mbikusita-Lewanika, class of 1975, working in Zambia with the National Council for Scientific Research; Kusiyo Mbikusita-Lewanika, class of 1976 working with the Zambian Railways in the data processing center; and Sekufele Mbikusita-Lewanika, class of 1977, working on his doctorate. Austin Fowles of Jamaica, class of 1968 is employed in Cape Coral, Florida.

During the Academic Year 1976-77 more than 191 students from foreign countries were en-rolled. The twenty-one countries represented include: Bermuda, Cameroon, Ethiopia, Ghana, Haiti, India, Iran, Israel, Jordan, Kenya, Lebanon, Mauritus, Nigeria, Republic of China, Rhodesia, Sierra Leone, Taiwan, Thailand, Trinidad, Venezuela and Zambia. The highest number of majors are reflected in such courses as Biology, Computer Science, Economics, Engineering Technology, General Business and Finance, Industrial Management, Marketing, Mass Communications, Mathematics, English and Political Science.

CONCLUSION

THE MISSION OF JACKSON STATE UNIVERSITY for one hundred years has been to assist black people especially, not exclusively, in developing the knowledge, skills, appreciation, and attitudes which are essential for living productive lives.

As a matter of history and tradition, Jackson State accepts a special responsibility for the education of thousands of black students in Mississippi, victims of the system of racial segregation and discrimination, providing an opportunity for needy disadvantaged students from both urban and rural environments.

While forthrightly accepting its primary mission, Jackson State in recent years has increasingly become a university for the education of all youth. It seeks to provide learning situations and experiences to help students choose courses of study, initiate careers, and contribute to the economic development of the state and nation. Jackson State is the only senior state university located in the largest urban center of the state.

The following desired outcomes for student growth are implicit in the general statement of purpose: understanding and accepting the maturity of self; relating to others with sympathy and understanding; accepting one's ethnic and national heritage; developing the ability to think and communicate clearly and effectively; developing the ability to make choices and value judgments; developing the ability to analyze, synthesize, and evaluate ideas; and developing a social consciousness which will enable one to assume responsibility to think critically about sound problems, and to contribute to the improvement of society.

This writer deliberately refrains from attempting to chart the university's future. In the comprehensive Institutional Self-study directed by Dr. Dollye M. E. Robinson in 1971, each of the eleven divisions concluded with suggestions and recommendations. Unrestrained in its criticism of some aspects of life at the university, the visiting committee suggested and recommended improvements and recorded some of Jackson State's outstanding accomplishments.

For the most part this publication concludes with the celebration of the 100th Founders' Day Convocation Sunday, October 23, 1977.

BURNS ISSUES CHALLENGE AT JSU FOUNDERS' DAY CONVOCATION

"What you have been to me, you must be to others a century from now," was the challenge Dr. Emmett Burns issued to Jackson State University at its 100th Founders' Day Convocation held October 23, in Dansby Hall Auditorium.

Dr. Burns, whose message was entitled "JSU: Confessions of an Alumnus," was featured speaker for the 3 p.m. convocation which officially ended the University's Centennial Celebration.

"From a small educational acorn has grown a strong institutional oak," Dr. Burns stated, adding that Jackson State was never intended to become the University that it is today "by those who paternalistically built an observatory here without a telescope..."

"I confess" Burns stated, "that as a civil rights employee I considered an address on equal opportunity in higher education," but he related that "equal opportunity in education has always been the unique calling of Jackson State."

Holding his audience spellbound with his fiery speech and dynamic delivery, Burns continued to amaze all in his presence. In telling of Jackson State's great mission the speaker remarked, "It has taken poor dirt farmers and sharecroppers from the Mississippi Delta and the Pearl River Swamps of Marion County and laid the foundation for them to become doctors and lawyers...snatching them from the periphery of abject poverty and transforming them into professionals."

Tracing the growth of Jackson State from a "fledgling and feeble seminary uncertain in its mission," Burns told the audience that the University has "gone on anyhow" to become "a mighty University now clear in its call." He continued by adding that "from $10,000 in 1940 to a multimillion dollar urban university in 1977, under the able tutelage of the young, dynamic, strong and ambitious President John A. Peoples, Jr., we have gone on anyhow."

The capacity crowd sat anxious to hear every word as the intellectual Baptist minister made his humble confessions. "I confess that I, along with thousands of other alumni owe a great deal of appreciation to the faculty and administration of this University." Adding even more words of praise about the University, the proud alumnus confessed, "You took us as you found us and helped to make us men and women of learning. Not only did you take us then, but you have done so for one hundred years."

The faculty dressed in their academic regalia, students and friends of Jackson State all sat in astonishment listening to each profound statement, re-living the University's past, reflecting upon the future, and believing in the speaker as he shouted, "the Lord still works in mysterious ways, his wonders to perform."

As the hour neared for the Centennial Bell to sound, ending Jackson State's Centennial Celebration, Dr. Burns began to conclude his illustrious Founders' Day Message. "You have stayed, Jackson state University, for one hundred years. You were here when I came alone and needed you, and you must be here over the next century. What you have been to me and others, you must be to others yet unborn who will come after we all shall have gone."

RECAPITULATION

Before October 23, 1877, there was envisioned a seminary for the training of black ministers. Later, the plan included black teachers. The vision of the black ministers of the Baptist Missionary Convention was to lift the veil of ignorance by providing for these people a school. The loss of the money in the Freedman's Bank ($1,547.08) dispelled this dream momentarily until the American Baptist Home Society of New York "confederated" with them and their dream became a reality.

It began in Natchez, Mississippi, in 1877; in 1883, the seminary

Conclusion 219

was relocated in Jackson and renamed Jackson College. For almost two years, classes were held at Mt. Helm Baptist Church until the completion of the school on North State Street, presently known as Millsaps. It was July 1902, that the bill of sale for the then Jackson College property said vacate the premises July 1902 and in 1904 the institution relocated to the present site.

In 100 years, Jackson State has undergone six name changes parallel with six presidents and six college seals. The university grew from mixed faculty in 1877 to an all-black faculty in 1911. Fifty years later, the university faculty was multiethnic and multicultured.

Every university must choose for itself what its mission will be to meet the challenges of society. The fulfillment of the university's mission has been successful during the administration of Presidents Jacob Reddix and John Peoples. Some of the success can be attributed to recent authorized annual appropriations and support by foundations. Like most other institutions of higher learning, Jackson State's service to the community and the nation may be enhanced by the availability of additional funds.

To conclude, a Centennial reveals a justifiable sense of pride in what has been accomplished but not complacency. Instead, there is a rededication to the conviction that growth and new goals to meet changing conditions are necessary requisites for a great university.

Accompanying the reorganization of the administration was a complete change in both student and faculty freedom. A more sophisticated Student Government Association was developed and there was a complete organization of the Faculty Senate. While the Senate adapted an elaborate constitution to a multitude of functions and activities, which were greatly complicated by the rapidly changing nature of the institution and the increasing number of both students and faculty to be served and satisfied, it many times became bogged down with procedural matters. Despite the expected pains of infancy, it looks forward to a role of significance and responsibility in the future.

While the administrative reorganization was underway, President Peoples launched the faculty into a complete revision of the curriculum aimed at making the university truly a "University of Schools."

Enriching academic programs were inaugurated. Simultaneously with the expansion of the undergraduate curriculum and allied activities, the graduate offerings were being augmented. Instructional innovations were carried out. A Computer Center of considerable effectiveness was located on campus.

Accreditation of Jackson State University and its departments and programs is of special significance. The university is accredited by the Southern Association of Colleges and Schools, the American Chemical Society, the National Council for the Accreditation of Teacher Education, and the Council on Social Work Education. In addition to teaching, the university's community service and research activities are continuing to make progress.

The physical changes which have taken place at Jackson State within the past ten years point to the institution's ability to survive. New construction projects along with major renovations have produced a dramatic change in available facilities. In 1967, three buildings were completed—a 252-room annex to Alexander Residence Hall for Women, a Plant Science Laboratory and Greenhouse, and the Jacob L. Reddix Campus Union. In 1969, a men's dormitory with 210 rooms and a health and physical education building were completed. An industrial arts building was completed in 1970 and four portable units installed. By 1974, a nine-story Administration Tower/Classroom Complex, a three-story education building, a six-story annex to the H. T. Sampson Library, a million dollar athletic track and field, and a quarter of a million dollars for renovations and repairs of a women's dormitory had been obligated and completed.

Three major buildings representing $10.1 million worth of new construction were completed during 1976–77: a five-story science building, a fine arts building, and a dining facility. The science building houses the Chemistry and Biology Departments and contains 111,663 square feet of space. Constructed at a cost of $5.6 million, the building was expected to be completed in August 1977. The fine arts building was completed in the summer of 1976. The two-story structure contains 58,638 square feet of space and cost two million dollars. A new dining facility with two main floors and a ground floor, containing 47,021 square feet of space, was completed July 1976. Construction on a $5 million all purpose campus facility is expected to begin in 1978.

By 1974, the campus was taking on a "new look." Many of the new buildings were completed in 1977. Featured on the campus is a mall running east and west in front of Alexander and Stewart Halls on the north and the south side of the campus. As these developments become functional, others are being projected.

In spite of Jackson State's century of existence, it must yet project other levels of attainment, reassess strengths or maximum potential, and realize those goals already set.

It is an unfortunate historical fact that the traditionally black public colleges have suffered from being under-funded by both state legislatures and the private sector. Despite this climate, Jackson State continues to strive to establish high quality academic programs and to provide quality education for black, white, and foreign students who seek higher education.

During the last decade, the minority enrollment has increased. Caucasian and other minorities accounted for .1 per cent of the total enrollment in 1966–68; .6 per cent in 1969; .7 percent in 1970; .5 percent in 1971; .2 percent in 1972; .1 percent in 1973; 6.3 per cent in 1974; and approximately 14.3 per cent in 1975. This unprecedented growth in student enrollment produced a similar increase in faculty size. In 1967, the faculty consisted of 116 members with 21 holding earned terminal degrees. For the 1975–76 academic year, the faculty consisted of 360 members with 51 percent holding earned doctoral degrees. The faculty is comprised of approximately 68.4 percent American blacks; 20.5 percent American whites; 2.9 percent foreign blacks; and 8.2 percent foreign non-blacks.

The university now has five schools which are composed of 32 departments and 4 divisions, with special programs and institutes offering 40 bachelor's degree programs. Thus has been laid, over one hundred years, an unshakeable foundation upon which the university may grow. Having survived trouble and crises uncounted in the past, the university family, undaunted, surveys the future with all its complexities unafraid, ready under God to launch itself into a new century of study, research and service to the human family in Mississippi and the nation.

APPENDICES

I   Documentary and Legal Records
II   Proclamations of the Centennial
III   Administration, Faculty and Staff
IV   Faculty & Staff under Dr. John A. Peoples, Jr.
V   Jackson State University Alumni
VI   Jackson State University Athletics
VII   Cofounders, Board of Trustees, & Administrators
VIII   Centennial Committee Members
IX   Public Schools in Jackson named for Graduates
X   Jackson State University Publications

APPENDIX I

DOCUMENTARY AND LEGAL RECORDS*

Deeds, Charter of Incorporation, "General Laws," and Significant Minutes

Recorded in Adams County Court House, Natchez, Miss.
In Book of Deeds, V.V., Pages 304–8
Dated 1-4-77

UNITED STATES OF AMERICA TO
AMERICAN BAPTIST HOME MISSION SOCIETY
DEED

Dr. Charles Ayer, Trustee

This indenture made this 4th day of January in the year of our Lord 1877 between the United States of America acting in this behalf by Lot M. Morril, Secretary of Treasury of United States of the first part, and the American Baptist Home Mission Society, a body incorporated on the 12th day of April, A.D., 1843, amended February 9, 1849 by the Legislature of the State of New York, Party of the Second Part, witnesseth that, whereas there was purchased by the Party of the First Part by Alexander T. McMurtry and wife of Natchez in the State of Mississippi, and dated the 9th day of August 1837, recorded in the office of the desk of the Probate Court for Adams County, in the State of Mississippi in Book "Z" of the record of Deeds, pages 206, and 207, a certain piece of parcel of

*Copies of all original legal documents are in the archives of the University Library.

land, situated partly in the city of Natchez, Mississippi and adjoining a lot on which the grantor then resided for the purpose of erecting thereon a Marine Hospital, the said land being more particularly described in the deed aforesaid upon which said land, a Marine Hospital was afterwards on the 8th day of February A.D., 1850, the said U. S., Party of the First Part hereto exchanged a part of said property for other property belonging to Charles Reynolds of said city of Natchez, Mississippi, and received for the part so acquired by exchange from the said Charles Reynolds a deed, dated on the said 8th day of February A.D., 1850 which is recorded in the office of the Clerk of Court of Chancery of said county of Adams in said state of Mississippi in Book J.J., pages 256 and 257 of the record of Deeds of said Adams County in which Deed the land so acquired by exchange is particularly described, which said sale and purchase by Exchange was ratified and confirmed by a joint resolution of the Congress of the United States, passed on the 10th day of June A.D., 1855 (10 Statutes at Large—page 738) and whereas by section 4806 of the revised statutes of U. S., certified from Act of Congress passed on the 20th day of April A.D., 1866, Chapter 63, Section I, Vol. 14, Page 40, and Act of Congress passed on the 27th day of June A.D., 1866, Chapter 142, Vol. 14, Page 76 of the statutes at Large, the Secretary of the Trea. of the U.S. was authorized to sell the said herein before mentioned property acquired by purchase and exchange as aforesaid, being the Marine Hospital buildings and land appertaining thereto at Natchez, Miss. and whereas the said Secretary of Treas. of U. S. in pursuance of said law did authorize and empower the collector of customs of the U. S. at Natchez, Miss. to advertise and sell at public auction said property and the said collector of customs did advertise the land for sale at public auction by advertisement duly published in newspapers called the Democrat and Courier in the City of Natchez aforesaid at the Custom House in said city on Tuesday, first day of February A.D., 1876 at 12 o'clock M. of that day, together with the terms of sale and did afterwards by authority and direction of the Secretary of the Treasury dated January 8 A.D., 1876 adjourn said sale by due motion to the 15th day of February A.D., 1876 and did on the last named day at the time and place aforesaid sell the said property at the public auction and the said American Baptist Home

Mission Society, Party of the Second Part hereto did purchase the land at and for the sum of $5,000 that being the highest and best bid, which sale has been approved; recorded and confirmed by an act of Congress passed at the first session of the 44th Congress Chapter 294 approved August 15th A.D., 1876 wherein the Secretary of Treas. is authorized and directed to confirm to the highest bidder, the land sale upon its being satisfactorily shown to him that the said building is to be reconstructed and devoted under responsible auspices to purposes of instruction for the benefit of Colored people of the United States, and whereas the said American Baptist Home Mission Society, the Party of the Second Part, hereto was the highest bidder at said sale and declares itself ready to pay for said property, and to receive a deed therefor, and has satisfied the Secretary of the Treas. that the building on said property is to be reconstructed and devoted to the instruction of Colored people of the United States under auspices of said Society. Now therefore in consideration of the promises and of $5,000 in hand paid by the Party of the Second Part hereto, the Party of the First Part hereto, the receipt whereof is hereby acknowledged, the said party of the first part hath granted, bargained, sold, aliened and confirmed unto the said party of the second part, their successors and assigns forever, all that certain lot or parts of lot of property situated in the city of Natchez, in the state of Mississippi and adjacent thereto and bounded and described as follows:

Beginning at a post, the Southwest corner of said lot near the road which leads from the city of Natchez to the burying ground of the city, running thence North 50° 30′ East, 925 feet to a post thence South 34° 30′ East 528 feet to a post thence South 55-½ ft, West 200 ft. thence North 34-½ ft. West 264 ft. to a post, the place of beginning: more particularly described in a plot hereto annexed together with all and singular, the buildings, appurtenances, hereditaments, privileges and advantages whatsoever unto the above-described premises belonging or in anywise appertaining and also all the estate, rights, title, interests, property and claims whatsoever either at law or in equity of the said party of the first part of in and the same. And the said party of the first part doth covenant and agree to and with the said party of the first part the above described premises and every part thereof with the appurtenances unto the said party of the second part, its successors and assigns will warrant and defend against the lawful claims and demands of all persons claiming by through or under it, but against none other upon express conditions nevertheless as follows the said party of the second part, the American Baptist Home Mission Society for itself, its successors and assigns hereby convenant and agree to and with the said party of the party of the first part, the United States of America, that the building and the said land hereby conveyed shall be reconstructed and devoted under responsible auspices to purposes of instructions for the benefit of the Colored people of the United States in accordance with the law authorizing and confirming this conveyance.

Said Lot M. Morril, Secretary of Treas. of the United States acting in this behalf for the United States of America, Party of the First Part, has hereunto set his hand and seal the day and year above written.

Signed, sealed and delivered in the presence of
Chas. F. Connant   J.M. St.   Lot M. Morrill,
                   J.C.H   Secretary of the
                   J.W.P   Treasury,
E. J. Babcock   C.F.C.   —United States

Adams County Court House
Office of Chancery Clerk, Natchez, Miss.

THE AMERICAN BAPTIST HOME MISSION SOCIETY
TO THE CITY OF NATCHEZ—DEED

This indenture, made the twenty-third day of August in the year One-thousand Eight hundred and Eighty-four between the American Baptist Home Mission Society, a corporation duly incorporated under and by virtue of the laws of the State of New York Party of the First Part, and the city of Natchez, a Municipal corporation in the State of Mississippi, Party of the Second Part witnesseth, that the said Party of the First Part, for and in consideration of the sum of $15,000 lawful money of the U.S.A. to it in hand paid by the said Party of the Second Part, at or before the ensealing and delivery of these presents, the receipt whereof is hereby acknowledged has granted, bargained, sold, aliened, revised, released, conveyed and confirmed, and by these presents does grant, bargain, sell, alien, revise, release, convey, and confirm unto the said Party of the Second Part and to its successors and assigns, forever, all that certain lot or parts of lot or property situated in and adjacent to the City of Natchez in the State of Mississippi, and bounded and described as follows:

Beginning at a post, the Southwest corner of said lot was the road which leads from the City of Natchez to the burying ground of the city,—thence North 55° 30' E. 925 feet to a post; thence S. 34° 30' E. 528 feet to a post; thence South 55° 30' W. 725 feet to a post; thence N. 34-½° W. 264 feet thence South 55-½° W. 200 feet; thence North 34-½° W. 264 feet to a Post. The place of beginning, being the same property which was sold and conveyed by the U.S.A. to said party of first part by deed dated January 4, 1877 and recorded in book V.V. Page 304 to 308 of the records of deeds of Adams County, Mississippi and by—claims deed dated 7th day of August 1884, executed by the Secretary of the Treasury under and by virtue of an Act of Congress approved May 13, 1884 together with all and singular the tenements, hereditaments and appurtenances herewith belonging or in anywise appertaining and the reversion and reversions, rewarder and rewarders, rents, issues and profits thereof, and also, all the estate, rights, title, interest, property, possession, claim and demand whatsoever, as well in law as in equity of the said party of the first part, of in or to the above described premises and every part and parcel thereof, with the appurtenances, to have and to hold all and singular the above-mentioned and described premises together with the appurtenances unto the said Party of the Second Part its successors, heirs, and assigner forever. And the said American Baptist Home Mission Society its successors the said premises in the quiet and peaceable possession of the said Party of the Second Part its successors and assigns against the said Party of the First Part, its successors and against all and every person or persons whosoever lawfully claiming or to claim the same, shall and will warrant and by these presents forever defend.

In witness whereof the said Party of the First Part has hereunto caused its corporated seal to be affixed and these presents to be signed by the Chairman and recording secretary of its Exe-

cutive Board the day and year above-written, sealed and delivered in the presence of
  Charles Nettleton
  Charles L. Beawan
CITY AND COUNTY OF NEW YORK
STATE OF NEW YORK
SS

(SEAL)

THE AMERICAN BAPTIST HOME SOCIETY
by *E. T. Hiscox*
Chr. of Executive Board
J. G. Suelling
Recording Secretary

Personally appeared before me, Charles Nettleton, a Comm. of the State of Mississippi in and for the State of New York residing in said City of New York, the within named J. G. Suelling, Recording Secretary of the Executive Board of the American Baptist Home Mission Society.

In witness whereof I have hereunto set my hand and affixed my official seal this 23rd. day of August, 1884.
Chas. Nettleton
Comm. for Mississippi in New York
115 and 117 Broadway, N.Y. City
Recorded December 5, 1884
Allison H. Foster, clerk

Hinds County Court House,
Mississippi Office of Chancery Clerk at Jackson
Deed Record 13—First District—Hinds County
CAMPBELL TO AMERICAN BAPTIST HOME MISSION SOCIETY

In consideration of $5,000.00 I convey and warrant to the American Baptist Home Mission Society that land lately conveyed to me by S. Given, and situated in Hinds County, Mississippi; near the city of Jackson, and described as beginning on the line between sections twenty-seven and thirty-four in township *six range one*, East, at a front in the public ward one and 29/100 chains West of the Northeast corner of Section thirty-four; thence West with the section line eighteen and 71/100 chains; thence South forty chains to the middle line of section thirty-four; thence with that line to the public road seven and 60/100 chains; thence with the road about N 14° 30′ East to the beginning, containing about 52 acres more or less.

Witness my signature the 29th day of December, 1882.

J.A.P. Campbell

STATE OF MISSISSIPPI—HINDS COUNTY

Personally appeared before me Tim E. Cooper, one of the judges of the Supreme Court of Mississippi, the above-named J.A.P. Campbell who acknowledged that he signed and delivered the foregoing instrument of conveyance on the day and year therein mentioned.

Given under my hand this 29th Day of December, 1882. Files Jan. 16, 1882, at 12 noon

Tim E. Cooper
Judge, S.C.
Recorded Jan. 16, 1883
W. T. Ratliff, clerk, by *A. G. Moore*, Deeds Clerk

Deed Record 39—First District—Hinds County

AMERICAN BAPTIST HOME MISSION SOCIETY TO
R. W. MILLSAPS

Satisfied and cancelled by authority hereto attached. See next page 9-3-1906. *W. W. Downing*, clerk.

Whereas, the Board of Trustees of the American Baptist Home Mission Society by resolution of the 15th day of July, 1901 did authorize and instruct Frank R. Hathaway, Treasurer of said Society to execute a Deed transferring the title of the property known as Jackson College, near Jackson, Mississippi.

Now, in pursuance thereof, the American Baptist Home Mission Society in consideration of $10,000 cash in hand paid by R. W. Millsaps, the receipt whereof is hereby acknowledged: and the further consideration of a second payment of $10,000 to be made on February 1, 1902; and the further consideration of a 4th and last payment of $10,000 to be made on July, 1902 which said deferred payments are to be covered by the notes of said R. W. Millsaps, according to the above tenor, and a vendor's lien to be retained for the payment of said notes, the American Baptist Home Mission Society hereby bargains, sells, conveys and warrants unto R. W. Millsaps, his heirs and assigns, the following described property called Baptist College Property, situated in Hinds County, Mississippi near Jackson, to wit; Beginning on the line between Sections 27 and 34 in township six, range one, East, at a point in the public road one and 29/100 chains West of the N.E. corner of section 34; thence West with the section 34; thence with that line to the public road seven and 60/100 chains; thence with the road about N 30'E. to the beginning, containing about 52 acres, more or less, and all the buildings improvements thereon and appurtenances, equipments and possessions connected therewith, except (1) one oak desk, one oak arm chair, and 8 single chairs, now on the platform in the college chapel. (2) Three oak tables for teachers in recitation rooms. (3) Pictures on the walls in the chapel and other rooms. (4) A map case and maps of Bible lands, screwed on the walls, and case and maps in Geography room. (5) Chemical and Science apparatus. (6) And the bedroom furniture of the dormitories. It is understood and agreed that the American Baptist Home Mission Society is to retain possession of all the within conveyed property until July 1, 1902; that it is to keep the property until then in good repair, and to keep the buildings insured for a sum of not less than $20,000 for the benefit of R. W. Millsaps so far as his interest may appear.

It is further understood and agreed, that on all payments made prior to the surrender of said premises, there shall be allowed the purchaser, interest at the rate of six percent, from the day of payment to the day of delivery of possession of the property.

In testimony whereof, the American Baptist Home Mission Society sets its hand and seal, this the 20th day of November, 1901.

THE AMERICAN BAPTIST HOME MISSION SOCIETY
by *Frank R. Hathaway*, treasurer

($18.75 I.R. Stamp)
STATE OF NEW YORK

CITY OF NEW YORK

Personally appeared before me, Daniel W. Perkins, a Notary Public, the American Baptist Home Mission Society, through Frank R. Hathaway, Treasurer of said Society, who acknowledged that he signed, sealed and delivered for the foregoing deed for the purposes and considerations therein mentioned.

As witnessed my hand and seal of Office, this 20th Day of November, 1901.

D. W. Perkins, Notary Public
Kings County, New York
Certificate on file in New York County
Clerk's Fee:
Recording... $ .65
Certificate... $ .50
Total..... $1.15

Filed at 10:30 A.M. July 5, 1902
Recorded July 5, 1902
    W. W. Downing, clerk

(*Authority to cancel*)
To the Chancery Clerk of Hinds County, Miss.

You are hereby authorized and requested to enter satisfaction of and cancel a record a certain vendor's lien retained in a deed by American Baptist Home Mission Society to R. W. Millsaps and recorded on page 77 of Book Number 39 of the Records of Deeds in your office.

This the 27th Day of August, 1906.
  The American Baptist Home Mission Society
    by *Frank T. Moulton*, treasurer

DEED RECORD 39—FIRST DISTRICT—HINDS COUNTY—AT JACKSON

ANNETTA DRAKE TO AMERICAN BAPTIST HOME MISSION SOCIETY

In consideration of the sum of $7,800 cash, the receipt of which is hereby acknowledged, I Annetta Drake, hereby convey and warrant to the American Baptist Home Mission Society the following lands, situated in Hinds County, State of Mississippi and in Township 5 of Range one East, described as follows to wit:

All of the West half of the Northwest quarter of Section 9 which lies North of the Yazoo and Mississippi Valley Railroads; also all of the East half of the N.E. quarter of Section eight which lies North of the railroad; also, the following lands in said section 8 and 9 described as follows:

Beginning on the South side of said Railroad where the East boundary of said West half of the N. West quarter of Section 9 crosses it, thence South twelve chains and 87 links, thence West 40 chains and 39 links to the West boundary of the E. half of the N. East quarter of section 8, thence North on said boundary to the south side of the right of way of said Railroad 12 chains and 87 links, thence eastwardly along the South boundary of said right of way to the East boundary of the West half of the N. West quarter of section 9, the place of the beginning; except the two acres in the North east corner of said last described tract, which 2 acres is a parallelogram immediately on said Railroad, said parallelogram being 4 chains North and South, and 5 chains East and West, being the same land conveyed by Annetta Drake to Leantha Pulliam on the 8th of February, 1902, by Deed recorded in Deed book 36 and on page 485 thereof, in the office of the Chancery Clerk of Hinds County, Mississippi at Jackson.

This tract conveyed by this deed is in all 95 and 97/100 acres more or less.

Witness my signature this 27th day of February A.D., 1903.

Annetta Drake

STATE OF MISSISSIPPI HINDS COUNTY   SS

Personally appeared before the undersigned Notary Public in and for said county, the above-named Annetta Drake, who acknowledged that she signed and delivered the foregoing instrument on the day and year therein mentioned.

Given under my hand and seal this the 27th day of February, A.D., 1903.

(SEAL)

Filed for record at
12:15 P.M.
Recorded Feb. 28, 1903
W. W. *Downing*, clerk

Amos R. Johnson, Notary Public
Clerk's Fees:
Record Fee   45¢
Certificate   50¢

WARRANTY DEED—DEED RECORD 364—FIRST DISTRICT, HINDS COUNTY

PP279, 280

American Baptist Home Mission Society to a Corporate Body of 14,

Thence to the State of Mississippi, July 31, 1940

Whereas, the American Baptist Home Mission Society by its deed of June 24, 1938 conveyed unto Jackson College a Corporation under the laws of the State of Mississippi the property known as Jackson College property in or near Jackson, Miss. and whereas the only condition and the only consideration for said conveyance was that said property should be used for and in connection with the education of Negroes, and whereas, the Legislature of the State of Mississippi at its regular 1940 session adopted and passed House Bill No. 722 creating Mississippi Negro Training School, a body politic and corporate, for the purpose of operating a school to qualify Negro Teachers for the Negro Public Schools of this State by giving instruction in the art and practice of teaching in all branches of study which pertain to industrial training, health, and rural and elementary education, and such other studies as the Board of Trustees of State Institutions of Higher Learning, in cooperation with the State Department of Education may, from time to time, prescribe; said training school to be located on the property known as Jackson College all as provided by said Act approved May 6, 1940, and

Whereas, the Board of Trustees of Jackson College, Inc., in both regular and special meetings, have voted to convey said property to the Mississippi Negro Training School by its official Board, the Board of Trustees of State Institutions of Higher Learning, has adopted appropriate resolutions authorizing the acceptance of title to said property, and

Whereas, the Board of Trustees of Jackson College, Inc., has authorized and directed the Chairman, the Secretary, and the Treasurer of Jackson College, Inc., to execute the property warranty deed conveying the properties of Jackson College to the Mississippi Negro Training School. Now, therefore, in consideration of the premises and in order to perpetuate more perfectly and completely the use of said property for and in connection with the education of Negroes, the undersigned Jackson College, Inc. by the undersigned of the Board of Trustees, by the undersigned Secretary and Treasurer, does hereby convey and warrant unto the Mississippi Negro Training School, a body of politic and corporate, composed of the Board of Trustees of State Institutions of Higher Learning and their successors in office, and its successors and assigns forever, the following described real property, located and situated in the city of Jackson, in First Judicial District of Hinds County, Mississippi. More Particularly described as follows, to wit:

All that part of the Northeast quarter (NE ¼) of the (NE ¼) North East quarter of Section 8, and all of that part of the Northwest Section 9, Township 5, Range one East, lying North of the right-a-way of the Yazoo and Mississippi Valley Railroad, and laid out, improved and occupied, and West of Dalton Street as now laid out, improved and occupied, together with all the appurtenances and hereditaments thereunto appertaining, and all of the estate and rights of the grantors in and to said promises. Also all of the furniture, fixtures, equipment, books and libraries belonging to Jackson College, Inc. and located on said property and used in connection with the operation of the School known as Jackson College.

Witness the signature of Jackson College, Inc., by W. F. Bond, Chairman of the Board of Trustees, C. L. Barnes, Secretary, and W. B. McCarty, Treasurer, being thereunto duly authorized by resolution of the directors of said Jackson College,

(SEAL)
     JACKSON COLLEGE., INC.
     by *W. F. Bond*, Chairman
     Board of Trustees
     by *C. L. Barnes*
     C. L. Barnes, secretary;
     by W. B. McCARTHY, treasurer

Approved by Us: TRUSTEES OF JACKSON COLLEGE
 J. Morgan Stevens   *F. O. Alexander*
 B. B. Dansby, Presi-   *C. A. Greer*
  dent of College   *W. D. Blackburn*
          John W. Dixon

STATE OF MISSISSIPPI—COUNTY OF HINDS

Personally appeared before me the undersigned Notary Public in and for said County and State, W. F. Bond, Chairman, Board of Trustees of Jackson College, Inc., a corporation, C. L. Barnes, Secretary of Jackson College, Inc., W. B. McCarty, Treasurer of said Jackson College, Inc., and for and on behalf of said Jackson College, Inc. and as the corporate act and deed of said corporation, they execute and delivered the foregoing instrument of writing on the day and year therein mentioned.

Witness my signature and official seal this the 31 day of July, 1940.

Henry C. Latham
Notary Public

(SEAL)
Filed Sept. 29, 1942 at
3:10 P.M.
Recorded Oct. 9, 1942
W. W. Downing,
   Chancery Clerk
     by *J. S. Robinson*, Deeds Clerk

My Commission expires
Jan. 3, 1945
Recording Fee $1.70

THE ORIGINAL CHARTER OF INCORPORATION OF
JACKSON COLLEGE, MARCH, 1899

ARTICLE 1: That the following persons: Namely,

Stephen Green,	Henry Franklin Sproles,
John H. Chapman,	John Thomas Buck,
Nathan B. Barton,	Thomas Jefferson Bailey,
Charles R. Stark,	J. J. Peyton,
Samuel W. Brown,	W. H. Higgins,

Amos M. Johnson.

and their successors in office, be and are hereby constituted a body politic and corporate by the name and style of Jackson College for the purpose of founding and maintaining a Christian Institution of learning with such Literary, Professional, and Industrial Departments as to them may seem necessary to promote the object for which they are made a body corporate.

ARTICLE 2: The said corporations shall be known as the Board of Trustees of Jackson College and shall possess all of the general powers belonging to bodies corporate under the laws of the State of Mississippi, and shall have power to use a common seal which may be altered at the pleasure of said corporators, to sue and be sued; plead and be impleaded; to acquire property by purchase, give, exchange, devise or bequest, to convey the same, the amount of value of such property not to exceed at any one time Two Hundred and Fifty Thousand Dollars; provided, however, that this limit does not include funds designated by the donors for the endowment of a Library, Professorships, Scholarships, Lectureships in the departments of Literature, Economics, Science, Medicine, Law, Theology, and Arts, or other purposes which may promote the object for which the Institute is founded.

ARTICLE 3: The said Board of Trustees shall have power to receive into affiliation with the said Jackson College such Colleges, Professional Schools, and Schools of Industrial Arts in the State of Mississippi as they may deem wise and upon such conditions as they may from time to time determine; and they shall have power to confirm subject to such regulations as they may enact, such honors and such degrees as are conferred by institutions possessing university power.

ARTICLE 4: The said Board of Trustees shall consist of eleven regular members, four of whom shall be Negroes and of such *exofficio* members as are hereinafter provided, a majority of the regular members shall form a quorum and each member of the Board, regular and *exofficio*, shall be entitled to one vote either in person or by proxy, under such regulations as the Board may Establish.

ARTICLE 5: No religious test shall be made for admission to any department of the college, but all members of said Board of Trustees shall be members of evangelical churches in good standing, and not less than eight of the regular members and the President of the College, shall be members of churches now known as regular Baptist.

ARTICLE 6: The said Board of Trustees at their first meeting, which shall be held not later than one year after the granting of this Charter, shall organize by electing a President and Secretary of their own number and a Treasurer who may or may not be a member of the Board. The term of office of each member of the

Board shall be three years and in order that only a part of the members shall retire from office each year, the Board shall, at its first meeting, divide itself as nearly as possible into three equal classes and shall determine who of its number shall continue in office one year, two years and three years from such date as may be determined by law.

ARTICLE 7: All members of the Board of Trustees shall be appointed by the Board itself, the four Negro members on the nomination of the regular Colored Baptist State Convention of Mississippi, and the seven white members on the nomimation of the American Baptist Home Mission Society. All members of the Board shall continue in office until their successors are appointed and shall be eligible for re-appointment.

ARTICLE 8: The said Board of Trustees shall have power to make and establish from time to time such by-laws, rules, and regulations not contrary to the laws of Mississippi or of the United States as it may deem necessary for the transaction of all its business and for the management of every department of said Jackson College. The Board shall also have power to appoint and remove the President of the College and such Professor Instructors, Teachers and other officers, agents, or servants as it may find necessary to employ in carrying on the work of said College, and to determine the compensation for service of all employees of the college.

ARTICLE 9: The said Board of Trustees shall have power to appoint of its own members, an Executive Committee consisting of not more than five nor less than three members which shall have authority during the intervals between the meetings of the Board to transact all the business of the corporation except the purchasing or conveying of real estate, the investment of funds, the appointment or removal of officers or teachers, and fixing their salaries, provided however, the said Executive Committee shall have power to fill temporarily vacancies in the corps of instructors and provide any additional help that may be necessary in carrying on any department of the work until the Board meets.

ARTICLE 10: The Corresponding Secretary and Superintendent of Education of the American Baptist Home Mission Society and the Chairman or President of the Board of Trustees of the college; and the college in all its departments and its affiliated schools so long as they receive any pecuniary help from the American Baptist Home

Mission Society, shall be subject to visitation by the Superintendent of Education of the Society, and the teachers selected and appointed by the Board shall be subject to approval by the Executive Board of said Society.

ARTICLE 11: The Treasurer of said Board of Trustees before entering upon the discharge of his duties shall give bonds with such security and in such penalty as the Board may require, to be made payable to said Board of Trustees for the time being and their successors and conditioned upon the faithful performance of his duty under such rules and regulations as may be adopted by the Board of Trustees.

ARTICLE 12: The said corporation of Board of Trustees and their successors in office are forbidden by this Charter to encumber by mortgage any part of the said college grounds, building, library, apparatus of furniture and they are also forbidden to use the principal or any endowment funds for any purpose whatsoever except that to which it is designated by the donor.

ARTICLE 13: Inasmuch as the welfare of society and not pecuniary gain, is the object for which this Charter is granted, the members of this corporation shall not be counted stockholders in the legal sense of the term and no dividends or profits shall ever be divided among them and there shall be no individual or personal liability for corporate debts but the entire property of the said corporation shall be held liable: nor shall the means or income on corporate property of whatever kind be used for any business, speculation, or other purpose than that for which this corporation is created; all property therefore, held and used for the benevolent purposes set forth in this Charter be exempt from all state, county or municipal taxation.

ARTICLE 14: This Charter shall continue in force for the period of fifty years.

No debt by or to this corporation shall be made payable in gold only, but all such debts shall be so made as to be payable in any kind of legal tender money of the United States.

The foregoing proposed charter of incorporation is respectfully referred to the Honorable Attorney General for his advice as to the constitutionality and legality of the provisions thereof.

A. J. McLaurin
GOVERNOR

Office of the Attorney General
Jackson, Mississippi
March 8th, 1899

The provisions of the foregoing proposed charter of incorporation are not violative of the constitution or laws of the State.

W. N. Nash
ATTORNEY GENERAL

Executive Office
Jackson, Mississippi
March 9th, 1899

The within and foregoing Charter of Incorporation of the JACKSON COLLEGE, is hereby approved.

In Testimony whereof, I have hereunto set my hand and caused the Great Seal of the State of Mississippi, to be affixed, this 9th day of March, 1899.

A. J. McLaurin
GOVERNOR

Office of
Secretary of State
Jackson, Mississippi
March 11th, 1899

I, J. L. Power, Secretary of State, do certify that the Charter hereto attached, incorporating the JACKSON COLLEGE was pursuant to the provisions of Chapter 25 of the Annotated Code, 1892, recorded in the Book of Incorporations in this office.

Given under my hand, and the Great Seal of the State of Mississippi hereunto affixed, this 11th day of March, 1899.

J. L. Power
SECRETARY OF STATE

"GENERAL LAWS OF MISSISSIPPI 1940", PAGE 352
CHAPTER 185: HOUSE BILL NO. 722

An Act to create and establish the Mississippi Negro Training School to qualify negro teachers for rural and elementary negro schools; to provide for the government thereof, to provide where location shall be made; and for other purposes touching the creation, organization, and maintenance of said training school.

SECTION 1. Be it enacted by the Legislature of the State of Mississippi, That a body politic and corporate is hereby created by the name of the Mississippi Negro Training School to have perpetual succession, with power to contract and be contracted with, to receive by any legal method of transfer or conveyance, property of any description, and to have, hold, and employ the same; also to make and use a corporate seal, with power to break or change the same; to adopt by-laws, rules, and regulations for the government of its members, official agents, and employees.

Object and purposes of the Mississippi Negro Training School.

SECTION 2. The object of the Mississippi Negro Training School shall be to qualify Negro teachers for the negro schools of this state by giving instruction in the art and practice of teaching in all branches of study which pertain to industrial training, health, and rural and elementary education, and such other studies as the board of trustees of state institutions of higher learning, in cooperation with the state department of education, may from time to time, prescribe.

Government of training school vested in board of trustees.

SECTION 3. The power of said corporation shall be vested in and its duties performed by the board of trustees of state institutions of higher learning.

Location of the Mississippi Negro Training School.

SECTION 4. The said training school shall be located on the property situated near the city of Jackson, Hinds county, Mississippi, and containing forty-nine acres more or less north of the Y. & M. V. railroad, west of Dalton Street, section 9, township 6, range 1, east, and otherwise known of Jackson College.

Board of trustees of state institutions of higher learning to elect principal—prescribe course of study—prescribe rules for admission of students, etc.

SECTION 5. It shall be the duty of the board of trustees of state institutions of higher learning to elect the principal, determine the number of teachers and number of other employees, and their compensation, and, in their discretion, approve the appointment of all such teachers and other employees; prescribe the course of study which shall be taught and maintained in such institution; prescribe rules and regulations governing the qualifications and admission of students.

Principal to have direct supervision of training school.

SECTION 6. The principal shall be held as the professional adviser of the board of trustees of state institutions of higher learning of all matters pertaining to the inside arrangements of buildings, selection of faculty, and course of study, and he shall have the immediate supervision and management of said Mississippi Negro Training School in all its departments, subject however, to the general supervision, management, and direction of the board of trustees of state institutions of higher learning.

SECTION 7. That this act take effect and be in force from and after delivery to and acceptance by the board of trustees of state institutions of higher learning of deed to the property herein described.
Approved May 6, 1940.

"GENERAL LAWS OF MISSISSIPPI 1944", Page 283
CHAPTER 159: SENATE BILL NO. 323
An act to change the corporate name of the Mississippi Negro Training School to the Jackson College for Negro Teachers.

SECTION 3. Be it enacted by the Legislature of the state of Mississippi, that the corporate name of the Mississippi Negro Training school as created and established by Chapter 185 of the laws of 1940 be hereby changed to the Jackson College for Negro Teachers.

SECTION 2. That this act take effect and be in force from and after its passage.
Approved March 20, 1944.

THE BOARD OF TRUSTEES

The purpose of the so-named Board of Trustees in the life and development of the Negro college in the South was all-important. The place of such a board of "local-leaders" in the growth of Jackson College varied through the years directly with the influence, increased needs, and the broadening curricula of the college.

At the outset during the period immediately following the Civil War known as the "Reconstruction Period," very little or no general public attention was given to the mission schools then being located in the South by northern missionaries for the colored people. Later these schools became evident as community factors in the home and family life of both colored people and white alike.

At this period it was decided that a local and community advisory board should be set up around the college in an advisory capacity to assist the college in promoting good will and a better understanding of its purposes and program of objectives. Secondly, there was a feeling that a board of trustees composed of local and community leaders would serve as a buffer to positive racial antipathy arising from suspicion created by the existing relationship and interest of northern missionaries who were working among colored people. Thirdly, the shifting of the responsibility from the northern to southern basis of operation was growing more and more imperative. It followed that the financial support to these schools was subsequently given and maintained through regular constituted agencies such as State Departments of Education rather than to the Negro college directly, for the purpose of enlisting the co-operation of southern financial support.

Therefore, further co-operation was sought by the customary proposal of "matching funds" in the support of these schools. During the entire first administration of Jackson College no local Advisory Board of Trustees was instituted. The first local Board of Trustees was used in the Second Administration as follows:

ADVISORY BOARD OF TRUSTEES FOR 1895-96
The following is the first Advisory Board of Trustees carefully chosen with special regard to their sympathic attitude to a co-operative program of rehabilitation through education and evangelism.

Rev. A. V. Rowe, D.D., Chairman, Winona, Miss.
J. B. Chrisman, Esq., Jackson, Miss.
Rev. H. F. Sproles, D.D., Jackson, Miss.
F. L. Fulgham, M.D., Jackson, Miss.

Advisory Co-operative Board of Trustees for 1899-1900
Stephen Green, Esq., New York City
John H. Chapman, New York City
Nathan B. Barton, Providence, R.I.
Rev. Henry F. Sproles, D.D., Vicksburg, Miss.
John T. Buck, Jackson, Miss.
Rev. Thomas J. Bailey, Winona, Miss.
Samuel W. Brown, Winona, Miss.
Rev. J. J. Peyton, Faisonia, Miss.

Rev. W. H. Higgins, Bolton, Miss.
Rev. Amos M. Johnson, Vicksburg, Miss.
Rev. T. L. Jordan, Jackson, Miss.
Rev. A. V. Rowe, D.D., Chairman, Winona, Miss.
J. B. Chrisman, Esq., Canton, Miss.
J. T. Buck, Jackson, Miss.
F. L. Fulgham, M.D., Jackson, Miss.

MINUTES OF THE TRUSTEE BOARD OF JACKSON COLLEGE
APRIL 5TH, 1933, 9:30 A.M.
Administration Building (Chivers Hall)

Members present:

Mr. W. F. Bond, Chairman	Dr. Frederick Lent
Rev. W. L. Varnado	Rev. A. D. Purnell
Prof. T. N. Scott	Dr. Frank A. Smith
Dr. C. L. Barnes, Secretary	Pres. B. B. Dansby

The meeting opened with prayer, by Rev. W. L. Varnado, Mr. Bond, presiding. The minutes of the last session were read and adopted with corrections. President Dansby's annual report of the college was called for and read; many comments and suggestions were made concerning the way in which the college was being kept out of debt, the work of the State summer school for teachers, and the activities of the college in its extension program for both teachers and preachers.

Dr. Lent introduced the question of the probability of offering Jackson College to the State of Mississippi for a "Teachers College" to be operated by the State for the preparation of Negro teachers. Mr. Bond answered the question by saying that he believed it was inopportune, since the State was almost to the point of bankruptcy, and such a move now would be detrimental to future efforts along this line. The recommendations were taken up and approved. The elections were next in order as follows:

Mr. W. F. Bond was elected Chairman
Dr. C. L. Barnes, elected Secretary
The class of Trustees expiring 1933 was
re-elected for another year.

Then Dr. Frank A. Smith, the Secretary and representative of the A. B. H. M. S., made an official announcement, "That the Society would not be able to make any appropriation to Jackson College on salaries or repairs after June 1, 1933 for at least one year" and he further said that the Society would keep alive the fire and storm insurance on the buildings as a necessary protection to the property. That the college would be in the hands of President Dansby to operate with whatever funds could be collected and shared with his helpers. President Dansby rose to the occasion and said that the shock of being denied any appropriation for the next year was to him a "call to duty." After a few comments as to the best way to finance the College the Board adjourned with a prayer.

 Mr. W. F. Bond, Chairman
 Dr. C. L. Barnes, Secretary

Whereas, the American Baptist Home Mission Society of the Northern Baptist Convention finds itself no longer able to finance and operate Jackson College, located at Jackson, Mississippi and

Whereas, the said Home Mission Society of the Northern Baptist Convention has signified its willingness to deed said property to the State of Mississippi for educational purposes for colored people;

Be it, therefore, resolved that we, the Trustees of said Jackson College, in regular session November 26, 1935, do concur in and consent to such disposition and transfer of the property, both real and personal, known as Jackson College, Jackson, Mississippi, as evidenced by our signatures hereunto affixed this the 26th day of November, 1935:

      Trustee Board of Jackson College

W. F. Bond, Chairman	A. D. Purnell
H. M. King	A. A. Cosey
R. B. Gunter	C. A. Greer, for Rev. W. L. Varnado
C. L. Barnes	as substitute
J. A. Hartfield	May 19, 1938

MINUTES OF THE

TRUSTEE BOARD MEETING OF JACKSON COLLEGE

MAY 10, 1940, 7 P.M.

Mississippi Fire Insurance Building

At a regular call meeting of the Board of Trustees of Jackson College, May 10, 1940 at 7 P.M. at the Mississippi Fire Insurance Building the following members were present:

                    Mr. W. F. Bond, Chairman
                    Dr. J. W. Provine
                    Dr. S. D. Redmond
                    Rev. C. A. Greer
                    Prof. W. W. Blackburn
                    Miss F. O. Alexander
        and   President Dansby

After announcing the purpose of the meeting, the Chairman, Mr. W. F. Bond, opened the meeting for business. General discussion ensued relative to the transfer of Jackson College to state control in which the following items were stated and agreed upon by unanimous action of the members present:

1—That President Dansby furnish the board at its next meeting an itemized statement of all indebtedness of the college
2—That President Dansby be authorized to have the Deed to Jackson College recorded in the office of Chancery Clerk, Jackson, Mississippi
3—That Dr. Redmond be appointed as a committee of one to write and present proper and fitting resolutions for the board in transferring the title of Jackson College, both personal property and real estate, to state authorities
4—That the insurance on property of Jackson College be carried for three (3) years
5—That President Dansby be refunded $85 paid out of the College treasury for farm mule on college campus, so that this amount might be pro-rated on salaries
6—That the President be authorized to perform the necessary college functions incident to the 1940 Spring Commencement at Jackson College

Nothing else of importance was presented to the board and the meeting was properly closed.

Mr. W. F. Bond, Chairman
B. B. Dansby, Acting Secretary

APPENDIX II

PROCLAMATIONS OF THE CENTENNIAL

State, Local, and Administrative Proclamations

A PROCLAMATION BY THE GOVERNOR

WHEREAS, Jackson State University, for 100 years, has under the American Baptist and state leadership, served the community, state, nation and world as a citadel for teachers and liberal arts education; and

WHEREAS, the graduates of Jackson State University have served and are serving their communities in many vocational and professional fields; and

WHEREAS, Jackson State University has served the community, state, nation and world by educating members of various professions and endeavors; and

WHEREAS, Jackson State University, in addition to its academic programs, has also, through conferences, workshops, lectures and similar activities contributed to the spiritual and cultural life of the citizens of Mississippi and the Nation:

NOW, THEREFORE, I, Cliff Finch, Governor of the State of Mississippi, do hereby proclaim the period of September 14, 1977, as,

JACKSON STATE UNIVERSITY CENTENNIAL CELEBRATION

in Mississippi, and urge the citizens of our State to bestow honor and praise to the service and purpose of this great university.

IN WITNESS WHEREOF, I have hereunto set my hand and caused the Great Seal of the State of Mississippi to be affixed.

DONE at the Capitol in the City of Jackson, this 13th day of September, in the year of our Lord nineteen hundred and seventy-six, and of the Independence of the United States of America the two hundred and first.

Cliff Finch
GOVERNOR

Heber Ladner
Secretary of State

By The Governor:

OFFICE OF THE MAYOR—PROCLAMATION

WHEREAS, Jackson State University has served the youth of this Nation since 1877, especially the disadvantaged youth of the City of Jackson and the State of Mississippi; and

WHEREAS, Jackson State University has been an integral part of the City of Jackson intellectually, culturally, economically and socially since 1883; and

WHEREAS, The University has incessantly continued to strive for excellence in terms of its academic programs, quality of faculty and physical plant; and

WHEREAS, Jackson State University now has more than 21,000 alumni, 16,000 residing in the State of Mississippi with 7,000 residing in the environs of the City of Jackson; and

WHEREAS, Jackson State University is annually the recipient of more than six million dollars in private and federal funds procured through the efforts of relentle faculty and administrators, thereby adding to Jackson's economy; and

WHEREAS, Jackson State University has been a good neighbor for over 99 years;

NOW, THEREFORE, It is altogether fitting and proper that we proclaim 1976-77 as:

JACKSON STATE UNIVERSITY CENTENNIAL YEAR

Witness my hand and Seal this the 14th day of September, 1976.

Russell C. Davis
Mayor of the City of Jackson

PROCLAMATION

WHEREAS, Jackson State University's History is linked indelibly to the City of Natchez and Adams County, Mississippi, in that the

Proclamations of the Centennial 249

illustrious institution was founded in Natchez in 1877 for the purpose of preparing black ministers; and

WHEREAS, the institution prospered in Natchez from 1877 to 1883, at which time it was moved to a more central location in the state, Jackson; and

WHEREAS, Jackson State University, for 100 years, has assiduously provided educational opportunities for all men and women, especially those from disadvantaged circumstances; and

WHEREAS, Jackson State University has enriched the cultural and educational lives of Mississippians and students across the nation through its distinguished educational and cultural programs; and

WHEREAS, the institution's thrust to maintain academic excellence through teaching and learning, research, and service to the community, has propelled it to the forefront as a multi-cultural, multi-purpose, urban-oriented institution of higher learning which enrolls over 8,000 students:

NOW, THEREFORE, WE, the citizens of Natchez, Mississippi, hereby proclaim the period of September 14, 1976, through October 1977, as the

JACKSON STATE UNIVERSITY CENTENNIAL CELEBRATION

and encourage all citizens of Natchez to observe the occasion of this Centennial Celebration.

WITNESS my signature and the seal of the City of Natchez, Mississippi, this the 14th day of September, 1976.
Tony Byrne,
Mayor of the City of Natchez

PROCLAMATION
HINDS COUNTY BOARD OF SUPERVISORS—

WHEREAS, Jackson State University has provided educational experiences to the youth of Mississippi since 1877; and

WHEREAS, Jackson State University has provided these quality services to the people of Hinds county since 1883; and

WHEREAS, the Jackson State University faculty, staff, and student body contribute more than $40 million to the economy of Hinds County through wages, salaries, contractual services, construction, and personal expenditures; and

WHEREAS, Jackson State University has an abiding concern with the total development of the Hinds County area; and

WHEREAS, the Board of Supervisors of Hinds County commends the administration, faculty, staff, students and alumni of Jackson State University for their outstanding contribution to the citizens of Hinds County; and

WHEREAS, the Board extends best wishes to the University as it concludes its first century of service and embarks upon its second century with a commitment to the Centennial Theme—"To Survive and Thrive: From A Century of Service We Go Forward."

NOW, THEREFORE, the Board of Supervisors of Hinds County do hereby proclaim the period of September 14, 1976 to October 23, 1977, as

JACKSON STATE UNIVERSITY CENTENNIAL CELEBRATION

IN WITNESS WHEREOF, I have hereunto set my hand and caused the Seal of the Board of Supervisors of Hinds County, Mississippi.

Pal R. Jones
PRESIDENT OF HINDS COUNTY BOARD OF SUPERVISORS

RESOLUTION

WHEREAS, Jackson State University was established as Natchez Seminary on October 23, 1877, and has for 100 years played an important role in the education of the citizens of the State of Mississippi; and

WHEREAS, in 1940, the State of Mississippi assumed the control of Jackson State University as an integral part of the State Higher Education System; and

WHEREAS, the institution has achieved national reputation for its dynamic, and progressive program of teaching and learning; and

WHEREAS, the 100th anniversary of Jackson State University will be the occasion for a series of commemorative activities by faculty, staff, students, alumni and friends; and

WHEREAS, the Board of Trustees of State Institutions of Higher Learning takes note of the role Jackson State University has played in the education of persons for useful citizenship roles throughout its history.

NOW, THEREFORE BE IT RESOLVED, that the Board of Trustees of State Institutions of Higher Learning of the State of Mississippi, extends high commendations to the administrations of Ayer, Barrett, Hubert, Dansby, Reddix, and Peoples for the leadership which has brought Jackson State University to this exhalted point in its history.

BE IT FURTHER RESOLVED, that September 14, 1976, through October 23, 1977 be officially designated as the period of Centennial Celebration of Jackson State University to be observed by programs, activities, and events so as to encourage its constituencies to pay tribute to its founders, and its leaders of the past and present.

Adopted this nineteenth day of August, 1976.

I, the undersigned, *E. E. Thrash*, Executive Secretary and Director of the Board of Trustees of State Institutions of Higher Learning of the State of Mississippi, do hereby certify that the above and foregoing is a true and correct copy of the minutes of said Board in meeting on *August 19, 1976,* and the same appears of official record.

Witness my official signature this *14th* day of *September, 1976.*
E. E. Thrash, EXECUTIVE SECRETARY AND DIRECTOR
BOARD OF TRUSTEES OF STATE
INSTITUTIONS OF HIGHER LEARNING
STATE OF MISSISSIPPI
FACULTY RESOLUTION

WHEREAS, Jackson State University was founded in 1877 with a prestigious and dedicated faculty of three; and

WHEREAS, Jackson State University has prided itself over the years with a faculty of learned scholars in the demanding academic environment; and

WHEREAS, the current faculty and supportive staff of 850 is comprised of individuals dedicated and willing to serve humanity and has confronted countless awesome tasks, continuously emerging triumphantly; and

WHEREAS, Jackson State University stands on a new threshold, having fulfilled what many once thought impossible, but now realizing the challenging potentials of greatness; and

WHEREAS, one hundred years of solid achievement recorded as history endears this faculty to the limitless opportunities to enhance the lives of peoples; and

WHEREAS, this faculty is the most expert and cosmopolitan assembly in the region; and

WHEREAS, this faculty is the most expert and cosmopolitan assembly in the region; and

WHEREAS, our delightful pride in what this University has accomplished is exceeded only by our collective determination to make Jackson State University synonymous with excellence;

THEREFORE, we the members of the Faculty Senate hereby resolve to recognize that September 14, 1976 through October 23, 1977 as the time span of the Jackson State University

CENTENNIAL CELEBRATION

IN TESTIMONY WHEREOF, I hereunto set my hand and commit the active support of the Faculty Senate this the 14th day of September, 1976

E. C. Foster, D. A.
CHAIRMAN, FACULTY SENATE, JACKSON STATE UNIVERSITY

ALUMNI RESOLUTION

WHEREAS, Jackson State University has provided its graduates and most former students with the capabilities of being productive citizens; and

WHEREAS, Jackson State University has encouraged and nurtured the development of creative thought within its academic structure; and

WHEREAS, the University has steadily moved forward in terms of academic programs and physical facilities thereby enhancing the credentials of its alumni; and

WHEREAS, Jackson State University has always involved its graduates and former students in policy making; and

WHEREAS, the University has put forth every effort to maintain communication and a working relationship with all alumni; and

WHEREAS, we the alumni, believe in the ideals and precepts fostered by our alma mater; and

WHEREAS, we are unequivocably proud of both its accomplishments and its potentials;

THEREFORE, the members of the Jackson State University National Alumni Association, Incorporated do hereby resolve that the

Proclamations of the Centennial 253

dates inclusive September 14, 1976 through October 23, 1977 be

JACKSON STATE UNIVERSITY CENTENNIAL CELEBRATION

IN TESTIMONY WHEREOF, I have hereunto set my hand and caused the great seal of the Jackson State University National Alumni Association, Incorporated to be affixed this the 14th day of September, 1976
Estemore A. Wolfe, President
Jackson State University
National Alumni Association, Inc.

APPENDIX III

ADMINISTRATION, FACULTY AND STAFF

*Reddix's Final Tenure in Office, 1965–1967 &
The Peoples' Administration, 1967–*

REDDIX'S FINAL TENURE IN OFFICE, 1965-1967

The administrative officers, faculty, and staff serving with President Reddix during his final year as president were: John A. Peoples, Jr. (1964), vice president, assistant to the president; Reverend Leon Bell (1965), chaplain-student-counselor; Haskell Bingham (1965), director of public relations and information; Roland L. Buchanan, Jr. (1962), dean of students; Leonard P. Chambliss, Sr. (1952), comptroller; Lionel B. Fraser (1952), assistant dean of instruction; DeLars Funches (1948), director of admissions; Ruth K. Johnson (1962), dean of women; Ernestine A. Lipscomb (1947), head librarian; Cornelius L. Reynolds (1964), assistant professor of special education and director of freshman studies; Henry Thomas Sampson (1942), executive dean of the college and director of summer school; Wallace F. Swann, III (1960), registrar, Faculty: Margaret Walker Alexander (1949), professor of English and literature; Ida Jones Barnes (1965), instructor of English and speech; Malcolm Quincy Barnes (1963), instructor in mathematics; David C. Bass (1947), assistant professor of sociology; Willie D. Blackburn (1940), associate professor of language arts and chairman of Area of Language Arts; Allen H. Brown (1958), professor of chemistry; James Wiley Brown (1959), associate professor of humanities and social sciences; Ollie M. Brown (1958), instructor in physical education for women; E. Frenchie Campbell (1957), instructor in English and composition; Lawrence Campbell (1948), assistant professor of industrial arts; Francis Emeka Chigbo (1965), professor of chemistry; Ross C. Clay (1953), assistant professor of music; Luana Franklin Clayton (1948), assistant professor of language arts; Sam Cobbins (1964), instructor of industrial arts; Joseph W. Colen (1965), instructor in mathematics; George E. Covington (1963), assistant professor, religion and philosophy; Paul E. Covington (1964), instructor in physical education and assistant basketball coach; Thelma H. G. Crawford (1964), assistant professor of modern foreign language; George Currie (1952), professor of economics; B. B. Dansby (1940), professor emeritus of mathematics; William W. Davis (1948), assistant professor of music and director of band; Barbara C. Dease (1963), assistant professor of modern foreign languages; Marcus Douyon (1956), instructor in art and ceramics; Tellis B. Ellis, Jr. (1940), associate professor of physical education, director of athletics, chairman, Area of Physical Education, Health and Recreation; Gloria Buchanan Evans (1942), professor of English and speech, head, Department of Speech; Edward James Fisher (1963), instructor in speech and drama; Lionel B. Fraser (1952), associate professor of education; Wilbert Greenfield (1960), professor of biology, head of Department of Biology; Karl Griffin (1953), instructor in art; Emily E. Hall (1962), instructor in French and laboratory assistant; John Edward Hall (1949), professor of education; Lillian B. Hall (1949), assistant professor and assistant librarian; Homer H. Hamilton (1958), professor of education and English; Gladys S. Hardy (1940), assistant professor of biological science and science education; Joseph D. Hardy (1940), associate professor of economics; Wanda Wood Fleming Helm (1955), assistant professor of mathematics; Gladys Perry Henry (1953), instructor in music; Mayne P. Higgins (1944), associate professor of education and supervisor of students teaching on the elementary level; Lloyd Rufus Howell (1964), associate professor of sociology and educational administration; Broadus B. Jackson (1958), professor of history and chairman of Department of History and Political Science; Richard H. Jefferson (1961), professor of literature, head, Department of English and Humanities; Raymond I. Johnson (1964), assistant professor of music and choral director; Lawrence A. Jones (1949), associate professor of art and head of the Department of Art; Maria Luisa R. Jones (1949), instructor in art; Lillian Cade Lane (1944), assistant professor of education; Robert Edwin Lee (1955), assistant professor of science and mathematics; Ernestine A. Lipscomb (1947), associate professor and head librarian; Ivory C. Manning (1951), assistant professor of chemistry; Jane Ellen McAllister (1950), professor of education; Rose Embly McCoy (1944-53; 1957), professor of education; Ben J. McCullough (1950), assistant professor of education and director of Psycho-Educational Center; Calvin M. Miller (1964), assistant professor of political science; Beatrice B. Mosley (1953), assistant professor, special education; D. Antoinette Handy Miller (1964), assistant professor of music; Charles C. Mosley (1953), professor in education, director of Graduate and Saturday Division; Gene L. Mosley (1962), instructor in education and director of Department of Visual Education; Kathryn J. Mosley (1949), assistant professor of sociology; Henry Douglas Nelson (1962), instructor in music; Eli Newell (1964), instructor in mathematics; Ocie Charles Nix (1964), assistant professor of history; Herman R. Nixon (1950), assistant professor of biology and science education; Roderick R. Paige (1963), instructor in physical education and assistant football coach; Thomas J. Patterson (1964), instructor in biology, tutor for talented students; George Greshman Patton, Jr. (1959), instructor in physics; Willy Roy Patton (1947), assistant professor of industrial arts and chairman, Area of Practical Arts; William M. Peterson (1947), associate professor of English and composition; Bolton C. Price (1942), associate professor of science and chairman, Area of Science and Mathematics; Walter Lee Reed (1965), assistant football coach, instructor in physical education; Bennie L. Reeves (1964), instructor in social science; Carolyn L. Reynolds (1964), instructor in education and assistant director of teacher training; Cornelius L. Reynolds (1964), assistant professor of special education and director of freshman studies; Lelia G. Rhodes (1944), assistant professor and assistant librarian; Emma G. Robertson (1958), instructor in music; Dollye M. E. Robinson (1952), acting chairman, Area of Fine Arts, head, Music Department, associate professor of music; Oscar Allen Rogers, Jr. (1960), professor of education and social science; Julia Hubert Ruff (1962), assistant professor of English and humanities; Josiah Joseph Sampson (1963), instructor in music; John L. Shourts (1964), instructor in education and supervisor of student teaching; Allen Franklin Smith (1957), assistant professor of physical education; Cephus J. Smith (1965), instructor in English composition; Estus Smith (1962), instructor in music; Wesley Stewart (1964), assistant professor of music; Robert L. Stone (1964), associate professor of German; Ola M. Tatum (1952), associate professor of English and literature; Cleopatra D. Thompson (1946-58; 1961), professor of education; Lottie Thornton (1944), assistant professor of education; Maggie M. Little Turner (1946), associate professor of home economics, head of Department of Homemaking; John E. Uzodinma (1964), professor of biology; Harry J. Vander (1956), associate professor of geography; Willie Ward, Jr. (1965), assistant professor, business administration; Samuel E. Warren (1962), professor of economics and chairman of Area of Social Science; Dora S. Washington (1957), assistant professor of speech; George C. Washington (1957), instructor in biology; James Edward Williams (1958), associate professor of modern foreign languages; Lee E. Williams (1940), associate professor of education, director of alumni, placement and followup; Ada Lee Wilson (1950), assistant professor of home economics; Anna W. Wilson (1956), assistant professor of education; Harrison B. Wilson (1951), professor of physical education and head basketball coach; Elaine P. Witty (1963), associate professor of education and head, Department of Teacher Training; Eva Y. Woodard (1948), assistant professor of home economics; Joe Y. Woodard (1941), assistant professor of industrial arts and director of Industrial Arts Department; Oswald A. Wynter (1964), assistant professor of Spanish and French; Aurelia N. Young (1947), assistant professor of music.

Z. T. HUBERT HEALTH CENTER

R. O. Williams (1951), medical director; James Anderson (1964), assistant medical director; Minnie Armstrong (1970), practical nurse; Celestine B. Cornelius (1960), practical nurse, Hattie Dawson (1948), practical nurse; Ethel Dyson (1950), practical nurse, Lena M. Horton (1956), head nurse, Hattye Tate (1961), clerk, Health Center.

ADMINISTRATIVE STAFF

Elouise Alexander (1964), secretary, Area of Education; Peggy Lee Allen (1965), key punch operator; Aletha L. Almore (1965), secretary; Office of Student Personnel; Birdia W. Baham (1961), secretary, Office of the Registrar; Augusta Ballard (1964), secretary, Area of Language Arts; Bernice L. Bell (1953), assistant librarian; Alvin Lee Benson (1963), head resident counselor; Carvin L. Bridges (1964), inventory clerk; Dollie London Boyd (1964), secretary to purchasing agent; Earl Brown (1965), resident counselor; Vera Brown (1965), clerk, Psycho-Educational Center; Frances V. Buchanan (1963), secretary, Placement Office; William F. Calloway (1959), bookkeeper; Nannie Childs (1965), head resident counselor; Daisy B. Cobbins (1964), clerk, Registrar's Office; Isabell Coleman (1964), secretary, Special Education Program and Department of Humanities; Horice B. Colen (1965), secretary, Area of Language Arts; Sylvester Collins (1964), chief security officer; Jaccie Conyers (1959), manager, college bookstore; Ann E. Covington (1964), secretary, Area of Social Science; Fred D. Cunningham (1953), director, Department of Plant Operation; Margie F. Cunningham (1951), secretary to the executive dean; Mae Elma Curtis (1965), secretary, Office of Student Personnel; Edward L. Curtis (1964), assistant resident Counselor; Osie B. Davenport (1964), key punch operator; Lucy B. Davis (1961), clerk, Registrar's Office; Mamie E. Davis (1965), resident counselor; Princess A. Davis (1960), library assistant, William K. Dease (1963), computer technician; Walter Dillon (1965), clerk, Registrar's Office; Luce Douyon (1962), language laboratory assistant; Alma Sutton Duffy (1960), secretary, library; John W. Edon (1965), purchasing agent; Jessilynn Elliott (1962), secretary, Office of Public Relations; Margie P. Funches (1949), secretary to the comptroller; Daniel Genous (1964), resident counselor; Miriam J. Gibson (1964), secretary, Graduate Division; Floreada M. Harmon (1961), clerk, library; Robert Hill (1963), assistant football coach; Ruth C. Hutchins (1963), secretary, Area of Physical Education, Health, and Recreation; Charlotte Olevia Harris (1965), secretary, College Readiness Program; Eddie Butler Johnson (1964), cashier; James R. Johnson (1964), resident counselor; Wyvette D. Jordon (1964), secretary, Business Office; Alfred R. Junior (1963), senior accountant; Mildred B. Kelley (1957), assistant to the registrar; Matthew King (1960), accountant; Peter C. Lane (1942), director, Botanical Garden, instructor, Plant Science Department; Henry C. Lattimore (1964), assistant football coach; Ester D. Liddell (1964), secretary, Office of Admissions; Frenchie M. McDonald (1964), secretary, Audio-Visual Department; Lorea R. May (1957), dietician, assistant to food director; Orthella P. Moman (1964), clerk, library assistant; Florence R. Morris (1958), secretary to the vice president; Valmore A. Nelson (1960), director of food service; T. J. Robinson (1963), inventory clerk; Helen P. Rose (1951), resident counselor; Clara C. Smith (1961), secretary, Department of Music; Joseph M. Stewart (1965), assistant director of food service; Lula Logan Taylor (1964), library assistant; Lou Earl Teague (1964), assistant resident counselor; Murlene Terry (1960), secretary to director of plant operation; Charles L. Thomas (1965), inventory clerk; Varon O. Turner (1965), clerk-secretary to coordinator of student aid; Gwendolyn S. Wansley (1949), library assistant; Robert Knox Wansley (1955), science laboratory assistant; Mattie S. Weathersby (1965), secretary, Teacher Training Department; Hampton P. Wilburn (1958–1960), coordinator of student aid; Melita W. Woodard (1940), administrative assistant and secretary to the president; Ruth Lee Woodson (1958), student account clerk; Nellie H. Wynter (1964), secretary, Office of Student Personnel; Myrtis L. Young (1965), circulation librarian.

THE PEOPLES' ADMINISTRATION, 1977–

ADMINISTRATIVE OFFICERS
John A. Peoples, Jr., President; Lee E. Williams, Vice President for Administration; Assistant to the President; Estus Smith, Vice President for Academic Affairs; George A. Johnson, Vice President for Student Affairs; Paul W. Purdy, Vice President for Fiscal Affairs; Oscar A. Rogers, Dean, The Graduate School; Coordinator, Title III Projects; Robert H. Smith, Dean, School of Liberal Studies; Jay T. Smith, Dean, School of Industrial and Technical Studies; Beatrice Mosley, Dean, School of Education; George F. Currie, Dean, School of Business and Economics; Ivory C. Manning, Assistant Dean of the Graduate School; Haskell S. Bingham, Dean for Records and Admissions; Lonnie C. Crosby, Director of Institutional Research and Planning; Fred D. Cunningham, Director, Department of Plant Operations; Mildred Allen, Dean Student Affairs for Counseling Services; Howard Craig, Assistant to the Vice President for Fiscal Affairs and Bursar; Obra V. Hackett, Director of Development; Dennis Holloway, Assistant Dean of Academic Affairs; Walter Hurns, Acting Director, Career Counseling and Placement; Mildred Kelley, Director of Records; Hilliard L. Lackey, Director of Alumni Affairs; Melvin Miller, Director of Public Information; Bobbie N. Oatis, Dean of Student Affairs for Women; Lelia G. Rhodes, Director of the Library; T. J. Robinson, Associate Vice President for University Relations; Tommie Smith, Dean of Student Affairs for Men; Oscar C. Williams, Director of Admissions; Eugene Jackson, Director of Student Activities; Edward Curtis, Dean of Student Affairs Housing.

ADMINISTRATIVE CONFERENCE
Dr. John A. Peoples, Jr., Chairman
Dr. Lee E. Williams
  Vice Chairman
Dr. Estus Smith
Dr. Paul W. Purdy
Dr. George A. Johnson
Dr. T. J. Robinson
Dr. Mildred Allen
Dr. Haskell S. Bingham
Dr. William M. Cooley
Dr. Lonnie C. Crosby, Secretary
Mr. Fred D. Cunningham
Dr. Ivory C. Manning
Dr. Beatrice Mosley
Miss Bobbie N. Oatis
Dr. Lelia G. Rhodes

Dr. Oscar A. Rogers
Dr. Jay T. Smith
Dr. Robert H. Smith
Mr. Tommie Smith

HEADS OF ACADEMIC DEPARTMENTS—SCHOOL OF LIBERAL STUDIES
Department of Art	Dr. Grace Hampton
Department of Biology	Dr. Vernon G. Archer
Department of Chemistry	Dr. James Perkins
Department of Computer Science	Dr. Jesse C. Lewis
Department of English, Acting Head	Dr. Annie Cistrunk
Department of General Science and Physics	Dr. Charlie J. Smith
Department of History	Dr. Bennie L. Reeves
Department of Mass Communications	Dr. Johnny E. Tolliver
Department of Mathematics	Dr. Roosevelt Gentry
Department of Military Science (ROTC)	Col. Tom Adams
Department of Modern Foreign Language	Dr. Barbara Dease
Department of Music	Dr. Dollye M. E. Robinson
Department of Political Science	Dr. Leslie B. McLemore
Department of Social Science Education and Geography	Dr. Ivory Phillips
Department of Social Work	Dr. Lula King
Department of Sociology	Mr. David C. Bass
Department of Speech and Dramatic Art	Dr. Dora Washington

SCHOOL OF EDUCATION
Department of Continuing Education-Director	Dr. Norman Handy
Department of Educational Administration and Supervision	Dr. Barnes West
Department of Elementary Education	Dr. Georgia P. Napier
Department of Guidance and Counseling	Dr. Ada Cherry
Department of Physical Education	Dr. Melvin I. Evans
Department of Library Science	Dr. Cozetta Buckley
Department of Psychology	Dr. Rose E. McCoy
Department of Reading	Dr. Virgia Gambrell
Department of Secondary Education	Dr. William Rush
Department of Special Education	Dr. Reuben Gentry
Department of Health, Head	Dr. Caroline Howard

SCHOOL OF BUSINESS AND ECONOMICS
Department of Accounting — Dr. Ronald D. Niemeyer
Department of Finance & General Business — Dr. Bruce Brumfield
Department of Business Education — Dr. Eunice T. Smith
Department of Economics — Dr. John F. Hurley
Department of Management — Dr. William Cooley
Department of Marketing — Dr. Harold Lucius

SCHOOL OF INDUSTRIAL AND TECHNICAL STUDIES
Department of Industrial Arts — Mr. Willy R. Patton
Department of Industrial Technology — Dr. Jay T. Smith

DIRECTORS OF PROGRAMS AND CENTERS
Director of Admissions — Mr. Oscar C. Williams
Coordinator of the Advanced Institutional Development Program (AIDP) — Dr. Oscar A. Rogers
Associate Coordinator of the Advanced Institutional Development Program (AIDP) — Mrs. Levernis E. Crosby
Director of Career Counseling and Placement — Mr. Walter Hurns
Director of Center for Urban Affairs — Dr. Curtis A. Baham
Director of Choir — Mr. Raymond I. Johnson
Director of Computer Center — Dr. Jesse C. Lewis
Dean of Student Affairs for Counseling Services — Dr. Mildred Allen
Director of Athletics — Dr. Walter Reed
Director of Institute for the Study of History Life and Culture of Black People — Dr. Margaret W. Alexander
Director of Institutional Research and Planning — Dr. Lonnie C. Crosby
Director of Library — Dr. Lelia G. Rhodes
Director of Marching Band — Mr. Harold J. Haughton
Director of Media Center — Mr. Wendell Gorum
Director of Orchestra — Dr. Josiah J. Sampson
Director of Psychometric Services — Dr. Walter Crockett
Director of Records — Mrs. Mildred B. Kelley
Director of Student Teaching Acting — Dr. Richard Middleton, Jr.
Director of Upward Bound Program — Mr. Willie Kyles
Out-Reach Manager, Urban Affairs — Dr. Kathryn B. Weathersby
Director of Alcohol & Drugs Studies Center — Dr. Mary Benjamin
Director of Public Policy and Administration Program — Dr. Henry Hall

Administration, Faculty and Staff

COMMITTEE ON UNDERGRADUATE PROGRAM
Col. Tom Adams, Dr. Mildred Allen, Mr. David C. Bass, Chairman, Dr. Haskell S. Bingham, Dr. Bruce Brumfield, Dr. Cozetta W. Buckley, Dr. Lonnie C. Crosby, Dr. George F. Currie, Dr. Melvin I. Evans, Mr. Edward J. Fisher, Dr. John E. Hall, Dr. Norman Handy, Dr. David J. Hickman, Mr. Walter M. Hurns, Mr. Lawrence A. Jones, Dr. Dennis P. Krueger, Dr. Sinclair O. Lewis, Dr. Jesse C. Lewis, Dr. Rose E. McCoy, Dr. Leslie B. McLemore, Dr. Eunice Moore, Mr. Beatrice Mosley, Dr. Georgia Napier, Dr. Ronald Niemeyer, Mr. Willy R. Patton, Dr. James Perkins, Dr. Ivory P. Phillips, Dr. Bennie L. Reeves, Dr. Lelia G. Rhodes, Dr. Dollye M. E. Robinson, Dr. William Rush, Dr. Charles J. Smith, Dr. Estus Smith, *ex officio,* Dr. Eunice T. Smith, Dr. Jay T. Smith, Dr. John E. Uzodinma, Dr. Barnes West, Mr. Oscar C. Williams, Mr. Leon Bracey, Student, Ms. Janice Catchings, Student, Mr. Emerson Davis, Student, Ms. Beverly Schaffer, Student, Mr. Harold K. Williams, Student.

APPENDIX IV

FACULTY & STAFF UNDER DR. JOHN A. PEOPLES, JR.

ACADEMIC FACULTY

John A. Peoples, Jr., President; Emanuel J. Abston, Instructor of History; Tom Adams, Professor of Military Science; Lieutenant Colonel, United States Army; McKinley Alexander, Assistant Professor of Economics; Margaret Walker Alexander, Professor of English; Director, Institute for the Study of History, Life, and Culture of Black People; Mildred Allen, Assistant Professor of Education; Dean of Student Affairs for Counseling Services; Douglas Anderson, Instructor of Mathematics; Rosia D. Anderson, Lecturer, Department of Business Education; Johnny Anthony, Assistant Professor of Music; Robert Anthony, Assistant Professor of Biology; Mario Azevedo, Assistant Professor of History; Steve Badger, Associate Professor of Biology; Curtis Baham, Assistant Professor of Education; Director of Center for Urban Affairs; Evelyn Banks, Instructor of Art; Sarah Banks, Associate Professor of Spanish; Qazi Barkataullah, Professor of Secondary Education; Grover Duane Barnes, Associate Professor of Biology; David Bass, Assistant Professor of Sociology; Acting Head, Department of Sociology; Fred Beemon, Assistant Professor of History; Leul Belay, Assistant Professor of Business Administration; Bernice Bell, Assistant Professor of Library Science; Assistant Director of the Library; Jimmy Bell, Assistant Professor of Sociology; Coordinator for the Criminal Justice Program; Mary E. Benjamin, Professor of Sociology, Director of the Alcohol/Drug Studies Center; Rommel Benjamin, Professor of Sociology; Prem Nath Bhalla, Associate Professor of Mathematics and Statistics; Haskell S. Bingham, Assistant Professor of Education; Dean for Records and Admission; Robbie Bingham, Instructor of Library Science; Willie Dobbs Blackburn, Professor Emeritus of English; Louis Blut, Assistant Professor of Special Education; Sonny Bolls, Assistant Professor of Industrial Technology; Sandra Sue Bollinger, Instructor of Psychology; Stephen Bollinger, Associate Professor of

Psychology; Eva Mae Bowie, Instructor of Social Work; Merle James Bowling, Assistant Professor of Business Administration; Mildred J. Brackett, Assistant Professor of English; Robert Brady, Instructor of Health and Physical Education; William Brent, Musician-in-Residence; Lecturer in Music; William Brewer, Associate Professor of Industrial Technology; Sherry G. Briggs, Assistant Professor of Guidance and Counseling; Geraldine Brookins, Assistant Professor of Psychology; Mary Brookins, Instructor of Mathematics; James Brooks, Acting Head Assistant Professor of Social Work; Acting Head, Department of Social Work; Jean E. Brooks, Instructor of Social Work; William Henderson Brooks, Professor of Guidance and Counseling; Allen H. Brown, Professor of Chemistry; James Arthur Brown, Instructor of Mathematics; James L. Brown, Senior instructor, Military Science; Sergeant First Class, United States Army; Mae Eva Rainey Brown, Instructor of English; Ollie M. Brown, Assistant Professor of Health, Physical Education and Recreation; Rejohnna Brown, Assistant Professor of Elementary Education; Associate Director, ESAA Tutorial Project; Bruce Brumfield, Associate Professor of Business Administration; Head, Department of Business Administration; Nathan Brumfield, Instructor of Music; Cozetta W. Buckley, Assistant Professor of Library Science; Head, Department of Library Science; Winona W. Burns, Assistant Professor of Elementary Education; Roger D. Calcote, Associate Professor of Accounting; Joseph Cameron, Associate Professor of Biology; Lawrence Campbell, Assistant Professor of Industrial Arts; Anthony Joseph Cavell, Professor of English; Rameswar P. Chakaabarty, Associate Professor of Computer Science; Mary Green Chambers, Assistant Professor of Reading; Gwendolyn B. Chambliss, Instructor of Speech Communication; Lai-Man Chang, Professor of Economics; Ching Yuan Chao, Professor of Economics; Ada L. Cherry, Acting Head, Associate Professor of Guidance and Counseling; Francis Emeka Chigbo, Professor of Chemistry; Chung-Shing Chu, Associate Professor of Computer Science; Annie Cistrunk, Acting Head, Department of English; Associate Professor of English; Effie Clay, Instructor of Elementary Education; Luana Franklin Clayton, Assistant Professor of English; Coordinator of the University Academic Skills Center; Sam Cobbins, Assistant Professor of Technology; Ancilla M. Coleman, Professor of English; Joseph W. Colen, Assistant Professor of Mathematics; Willie Cook, Associate Professor of Art; William Cooley, Head Department of Management, Instructor of Business Administration; Della Larkin Cooper, Instructor of Business Education; Dan Russell Course, Assistant Professor of Mathematics; Miriam Covington, Instructor of Health, Physical Education and Recreation; Paul Covington, Instructor of Health, Physical Education and Recreation; Head Basketball Coach; Mamie L. Crockett, Assistant Professor of Elementary Education; Margie F. Cunningham, Assistant Professor of Business Education; George F. Currie; Professor of Economics, Head, Department of Economics; School of Business and Economics; Willie Daniel, Instructor of Health, Physical Education and Recreation; Associate Director, Therapeutic Recreation Program; Osie Davenport, Assistant Professor of Computer Science; Donald Davis, Assistant Professor of Military Science; Captain, United States Army; William W. Davis, Assistant Professor of Music; Roy James Davison,

Assistant Professor of Philosophy; James Dean, Assistant Professor of Accounting; Narah V. Dean, Instructor of Health, Physical Education and Recreation; Director of Majorettes; Barbara C. Dease, Head, Department of Modern Foreign Languages; Assistant Professor of Modern Foreign Languages; Lou Helen Devine; Instructor of Library Science; Assistant Librarian; Luce Douyon, Instructor of Modern Foreign Languages; Marcus Douyon, Associate Professor of Art; Malena Dow, Instructor of Speech Communication; Alma Duffy, Instructor of Library Science; Assistant Librarian; Edward Duplessis, Instructor of Music; Assistant Band Director; Shirley A. Elder, Instructor of Political Science; Martin L. Epps, Assistant Professor of Health, Physical Education and Recreation, Head Track Coach; Yvonne Etheredge, Instructor of Mathematics; Dora G. Evans, Instructor of English; Gloria Buchanan Evans, Professor of Mass Communications; Melvin I. Evans, Professor of Health, Physical Education and Recreation; Head; Department of Health, Physical Education and Recreation; Pius Eze, Associate Professor of Political Science; Mary J. Farrar, Assistant Professor of Guidance and Counseling; Edward James Fisher; Associate Professor of Speech Communication; Acting Head, Department of Speech and Dramatic Art; Director, Dunbar Dramatics Guild; Ethel Foreman, Assistant Professor of Education; E. C. Foster, Professor of History; Robert E. Foster, Manager of System Programming; Instructor of Computer Science; Velvelyn Blackwell Foster, Associate Professor of History and Social Science Education; Henry Calvin Frazier, Instructor of Science Education; Edward Fulton; Assistant Professor of Health, Physical Education and Recreation; DeLars Funches, Professor of Secondary Education; Margie Funches, Instructor of Special Education; Percy Edward Gambrell, Assistant Professor of Social Science Education; Virgia B. Gambrell, Head, Department of Reading; Professor of Reading; Evelyn Garrity; Professor of Chemistry; Bettye W. Gaulden, Assistant Professor of Reading; Etherlene H. Gentry; Instructor of Library Science; Assistant Librarian; Roosevelt Gentry, Head, Department of Mathematics; Associate Professor of Mathematics; Ruben Gentry; Assistant Professor of Special Education; Doris O. Ginn, Assistant Professor of English; William Gorden, Instructor of Health, Physical Education and Recreation, Assistant Football Coach; William B. Gordon, Associate Professor of Library Science; Janace Harvey Goree, Instructor of Finance and General Business; Joe E. Goree; Instructor of Music; Assistant Band Director; Marzine Green; Instructor of Mathematics; John R. Gregory, Associate Professor of Speech Communications; Patricia Grierson, Assistant Professor of English; Karl Griffin, Instructor of Art; Thomas Griffith; Assistant Professor of Psychology; Clara Groschowska, Professor of Modern Foreign Languages; Anand K. Gupta, Acting Head, Library Science Department; Assistant Professor of Library Science; Ramashwar Gupta, Assistant Professor of Accounting; Anita Hall, Associate Professor of Education, Director of Crossover Project; Henry Hall, Asistant Professor of Political Science; Director of the Public Policy and Administration Program; Jacquelyn M. Gorum, Assistant Professor of Social Work; Wendell Gorum, Head, Media Center; Phillis T. Hammond, Coordinator, Child Welfare Training Program; Instructor of Social Work; Norman Handy, Associate Professor of Secondary Education; Director of Continuing Education;

Gladys Hardy, Assistant Professor of Biology; Richard Harger, Associate Professor of Psychology; Joyce B. Harris, Assistant Professor of Reading; Shirley J. Harris, Instructor of Health, Physical Education and Recreation, Assistant Football Coach; Alferdteen B. Harrison, Acting Head, Associate Professor of History; Edward J. Harvey, Associate Professor of Biology; James C. Harvey, Professor of Political Science; Maria Luisa A. Harvey, Professor of Spanish; Harold J. Haughton, Instructor of Music; Director of Marching Band; Roland A. Havis, Assistant Professor of Psychology; Dorothy Lee Hawkins, Associate Professor of Elementary Education and Continuing Education; Wanda Wood Fleming Helm, Assistant Professor of Mathematics; Bennye Henderson, Assistant Professor of Biology; William T. Henderson, Assistant Professor of Psychology; David J. Hickman, Professor of Mathematics, Head, Department of Mathematics; Mayne Pendleton Higgins, Professor Emeritus of Education; Robert C. Hill, Instructor of Health, Physical Education and Recreation; Head Football Coach; Dennis Holloway, Assistant Professor of Chemistry; Assistant Dean for Academic Affairs; Kermit Holly, Instructor of Music; Director of Stage Band; Charles Henry Holmes, Assistant Professor of Political Science; Andrew Honeycutt, Associate Professor of Business Administration; Dr. Leon Howard, Associate Professor of Education; Dr. Caroline Y. Howard, Head, Department of Health; Professor of Health, Physical Education and Recreation; John F. Hurley, Associate Professor of Economics; Walter Hurns, Instructor of History; Director, Career Planning and Placement; Maniza Hussain, Assistant Professor of Business Education; Margaret Hutton, Professor of History; S. Sitharama Iyengar, Assistant Professor of Computer Science; Circuit Rider, Computer Center; Anita L. Jackson, Assistant Professor of Music; Jewel L. Jackson, Assistant Professor of Guidance; Quarlie Jackson, Assistant Professor of Military Science; Captain, United States Army; William Jackson, Assistant Professor of Military Science; Captain, United States Army; Dr. Clyde T. Jacob, Assistant Professor of Speech and Special Education; Jimmie James, Associate Professor of Music; Franklin Jefferson, Instructor of Social Science Education; Darwin Johnson, Assistant Professor of Psychology; George A. Johnson, Professor of Secondary Education; Vice President for Student Affairs; Joseph C. Johnson, Associate Professor of Reading and Elementary Education; Raymond I. Johnson, Assistant Profressor of Music; Director of Choir; John Paul Jones, Assistant Professor of Music; Director, ROTC Band; Lawrence A. Jones, Associate Professor of Art; Maria Louisa R. Jones, Instructor of Art; Princess Beasley Jones, Instructor of English; Willie Gertrude C. Jones; Instructor of Elementary Education; Marjorie Jordan, Associate Professor of History; Samuel C. Jordan, Assistant Professor of Mathematics; Thomas Jordan, Assistant Professor of Industrial Technology; Harold W. Joseph, Associate Professor of Accounting; Dr. Ada Karna, Professor of General Business and Finance; Ophelia D. Kelly, Instructor of Early Childhood Education; Jesse Thomas Kelly; Associate Professor of History; Joe King; Assistant Professor of Technology; Lula T. King, Head, Department of Social Work; Assistant Professor of Social Work and Sociology; Judith Karen Krabbe, Associate Professor of English; Willie D. Kyles, Instructor of Education; Counselor, Counseling Center; Director, TRIO Projects;

Dr. Gerald Lamer, Assistant Professor Department of Guidance and Counseling and Pupil Personnel Service; Lillian Cade Lane, Assistant Professor of Reading; Marvel Lang, Instructor of Geography; Raphel D. Lee, Assistant Professor of Industrial Technology; Earl C. Leggett, Associate Professor of Secondary Education; Dr. Evelyn Leggett, Assistant Professor of Reading; Howard Lett, Assistant Professor of Mass Communications; Ellistine P. Lewis, Assistant Professor of Music; Emma R. Lewis, Instructor of Music; Jesse C. Lewis, Professor of Mathematics; Chairman, Division of Natural Sciences; Head, Department of Computer Science; Director, Computer Center; Sinclair O. Lewis, Professor of Psychology; Head, Department of Guidance and Counseling; L. Frances Liddell, Instructor of Business Education; West Lindsey, Instructor of History; Robert N. List, Associate Professor of English; An-Yen Liu, Associate Professor of Psychology; Chao M. Liu, Assistant Professor of Accounting; Marshall Longmire, Assistant Professor of Science Education; Frankie Scott Loving, Instructor of English; Ally F. Mack, Assistant Professor of Political Science; Robert W. Mack, Associate Professor of Biology; Coordinator of Health Related Programs; Ivory C. Manning, Assistant Dean of the Graduate School; Zareh Maranian, Assistant Professor of Art; Houston Markham, Instructor of Health, Physical Education and Recreation; Assistant Football Coach; Ella P. Martin, Instructor of English; Jane E. McAllister; Professor Emeritus of Education; Rose E. McCoy, Professor of Psychology; Head, Department of Psychology; Flora C. McGhee, Instructor of Mass Communications; Patricia McGill, Instructor of Economics; Donald McKinney, Associate Professor of Health, Physical Education and Recreation; Patricia McKinney, Associate Professor of Health, Physical Education and Recreation; Leslie B. McLemore, Professor of Political Science; Head, Department of Political Science; Robert M. McNally, Musician in Residence, Department of Music; Sadie Magee, Instructor of Health, Physical Education and Recreation; Richard T. Middleton, Jr., Associate Professor of Secondary Education; Dr. Bryce Mitchell, Assistant Professor of English; George T. Mitchell, Assistant Professor of Political Science; Robert D. Mitchell, Associate Professor of Physics; George Moffett, Senior Instructor, Military Science; Sergeant First Class, United States Army; Iely Burkhead Mohamed, Assistant Professor of English; Orthella Moman, Instructor of Library Science; Assistant Librarian; Beatrice K. Moore, Instructor of Speech Communication; Eunice Moore, Professor of English; Head, Department of English; Inez R. Morris, Instructor of English; Beatrice B. Mosley, Dean, School of Education; Professor of Special Education; Charles C. Mosley, Sr., Professor Emeritus of Education; Kathryn Johnson Mosley, Assistant Professor of Sociology; Willie J. Mott, Instructor of Technology; Vasudeva Murthy, Assistant Professor of Economics; Julius Myers, Jr., Associate Professor of Secondary Education; Director, Student Teaching and Field Services; Lena Wright Myers, Associate Professor of Sociology; Georgia Napier, Professor of Elementary Education; Head, Department of Elementary Education; Toy Lee Napier, Associate Professor of Secondary Education; Rosie Brown Neal, Instructor of Library Science; Assistant Librarian; Fred Robert Slater Nelson, Associate Professor of Biology; Otis C. Nicols, Associate Professor of Psychology; Willie Nickelberry, Chief

Instructor, Military Science; Sergeant Major, United States Army; Dr. Ronald Niemeyer, Associate Professor of Accounting; Head, Department of Accounting; Herman R. Nixon, Assistant Professor of Biology; Gladys P. Norris, Instructor of Music; Robert E. O'Bannon, Associate Professor of Psychology; Paul J. O'Neill, Assistant Professor of Psychology; Alicia Marie O'Reilly, Assistant Professor of Business Administration; Steven J. Overman, Associate Professor of Health, Physical Education and Recreation; Yi-Chuan Pan, Assistant Professor of Mathematics; James W. Park, Associate Professor of Business Administration; Martha A. Park, Associate Professor of English; William H. Parker, Assistant Professor of Education; Coordinator of Special Recruitment; Willy Roy Patton, Assistant Professor of Industrial Arts; Head, Department of Industrial Arts; John Paul, Lecturer, Department of Music; James Perkins, Associate Professor of Chemistry; Head, Department of Chemistry; Melvin Pete, Instructor of Health, Physical Education and Recreation; Assistant Football Coach; Charles P. Phillips, Assistant Professor of Music; Ivory Phillips, Associate Professor of Social Science Education; Head, Department of Social Science Education and Geography; Mercedes Phipps, Instructor of Modern Foreign Languages; Marcel Pilate, Instructor of Mathematics; Mabel H. Pittman, Instructor of English; Samuel Polk. Instructor of Technology; Rose McInnis Portis, Instructor of English; Dr. Roland Powell, Assistant Professor of Biology(part time); Paul W. Purdy, Associate Professor of Economics; Vice President for Fiscal Affairs; Frank D. Purnell, Professor of Health, Physical Education and Recreation; Baldev Raj, Associate Professor of Biology; Prakasa Rao, Associate Professor of Sociology; Nandini Rao, Associate Professor of Sociology; Eleftherios Rasis, Assistant Professor of Industrial Technology; Walter Reed, Director of Athletics; Assistant Professor of Health, Physical Education and Recreation; Director of Intramural Sports; Bennie L. Reeves, Professor of History; Chairman, Division of Social Sciences; Head, Department of History; David Reeves; Instructor of Industrial Arts; Mary Reeves, Instructor of English; Lelia G. Rhodes, Assistant Professor of Library Science; Director of Library; Schultz Riggs, Assistant Professor of Mathematics; Dollye M. E. Robinson, Professor of Music; Chairman, Division of Fine Arts; Head, Department of Music; T. J. Robinson, Assistant Professor of History, Associate Vice President for University Relations; Oscar Allan Rogers, Jr., Professor of Social Science Education; Dean, The Graduate School; Coordinator, Title III, Advanced Institutional Development Program; Bruce E. Rosemond, Assistant Professor of Elementary Education; William Rush, Professor of Secondary Education; Head, Department of Secondary Education; Josiah Joseph Sampson, Instructor of Music; Director of Orchestra; Hosea Sanders, Instructor of Biology, Director of the Botanical Gardens; Joe Louis Sanders; Instructor of Industrial Technology; Man Mohan Sandhu, Associate Professor of Sociology; Armand M. Seguin, Assistant Professor of Industrial Arts; Balwant Sekhon, Professor of Biology; Bhupinder Sekhon, Instructor of English; Bankey W. Sharma, Assistant Professor of Economics; Ruth Lee Shirley, Assistant Professor of History; Fred L. Shore, Associate Professor of Chemistry; John L. Shourts, Assistant Professor of Secondary Education; Vaughn Sims, Lecturer, Social Work Sequence Program (Part-time); Ezzat N. Slaieh, Assistant Professor of History; Allen F. Smith, Assistant Professor of Health, Physical Education and Recreation; Head Golf Coach; Cephus J. Smith, Instructor of English; Charlie J. Smith, Professor of General Science; Head, Department of General Science and Physics; Estus Smith, Professor of Music; Vice President for Academic Affairs; Eunice T. Smith, Assistant Professor of Business Education; Head, Department of Business Education; James Robert Smith, Assistant Professor of Business Administration; Jay T. Smith, Associate Professor of Industrial Technology; Acting Head, Department of Industrial Technology; Dean, School of Industrial and Technical Studies; Leroy Terry Smith, Instructor of Social Science Education; Robert H. Smith, Professor of Sociology; Dean, School of Liberal Studies; Velsie Smith, Instructor of Library Science; Assistant Librarian; Charles Spann, Assistant Professor of Biology; Louise Spears, Associate Professor of Business Education; Willie E. Stegall, Assistant Professor of Business; Hugh Stevens, Head, Department of Art; Assistant Professor of Art; Tommie H. Stewart, Instructor of Speech Communication; William Straka, Assistant Professor of General Science and Physics; Marvin E. Stringfellow, Associate Professor of Health, Physical Education and Recreation; Richard H. Sullivan, Associate Professor of Chemistry; Rubye Sullivan, Instructor of Library Science; Assistant Librarian; Charles Suvajian, Assistant Professor of French; Thomas H. Syvertsen, Instructor of History; Sophia B. Taylor, Instructor of Special Education; Cleopatra D. Thompson, Distinguished Professor of Education; Donald Thompson, Assistant Professor of Military Science; Major, United States Army; H. McFarland Thompson, Associate Professor of Mathematics; Julius E. Thompson, Assistant Professor of History; Lottie W. Thornton, Assistant Professor of Elementary Education; Raiwan Thumchai, Associate Professor of Mathematics; Johnny E. Tolliver, Associate Professor of English; Head, Department of Mass Communications; Nellie W. Tolliver, Instructor of Library Science; Assistant Librarian; Charles H. Trottman, Associate Professor of Chemistry; Bessie L. Tucker, Instructor of Mathematics; James D. Tyson, Professor of Physics; John E. Uzodinma, Professor of Biology; Head, Department of Biology; Lius Vargus, Principal Drill Instructor, Military Science; Sergeant First Class, United States Army; Pearl Vincent, Instructor of Elementary Education; Counselor, Career Opportunities; Daniel C. Vogt, Assistant Professor of History; Segrest N. Wailes, Assistant Professor of Criminal Justice and Sociology; Dora Washington, Associate Professor of Speech; George C. Washington, Assistant Professor of Biology; W. Glenn Watts, Associate Professor of Secondary Education; Kathryn B. Weathersby, Assistant Professor of Continuing Education; Out-Reach Manager, Urban Affairs Center; Garrett Weaver, Assistant Professor of History; Robert B. Weaver, Associate Professor of Health, Physical Education and Recreation; Shih-sung Wen, Associate Professor of Psychology; Captain Benjamin Wesley, Assistant Professor of Military Science, Captain, United States Army; Barnes West, Professor of Secondary Education; Head, Department of Educational Administration and Supervision; Darnell Williams, Assistant Professor of English; Emma S. Williams, Assistant Professor of Music; Lee E. Williams, Associate Professor of Education; Vice President for Administration; Assistant to the President; Ruth M. Williams, Instructor of Social Work; Sandra Gail Williams, Instructor of Art; Tommy Williams, Jr., Instructor of Health, Physical Education; Ada Lee Wilson, Assistant Professor of Secondary Education; Roger E. Wilson, Instructor of English; Roosevelt Wilson, Assistant Professor of General Science; Russell A. Wing, Assistant Professor of Special Education; Margaret A. Wodetzki, Associate Professor of Chemistry; Melita Woodard, Assistant Professor of Business Education; Captain Lucuis Wright, Assistant Professor of Military Science, Captain, United States Army; Nellie Wynter, Instructor of Library Science; Assistant Librarian; Oswald Wynter, Assistant Professor of Modern Foreign Languages; Aurelia N. Young, Assistant Professor of Music; Michael G. Zifcak, Associate Professor of Political Science.

STAFF

Minnie L. Abdu, Teacher's Aid; Clerical Training Aide; Grace H. Adams, Assistant Counselor; Bruttie Allen, Secretary, Office of Records; Charles Sean W. Allen, Secretary, Student Financial Aid Office; Mildred Allen, Assistant Professor of Education; Acting Associate Dean of Student Affairs for Counseling Services; Jeanette Alexander, Secretary, Department of Reading; Aletha Almore, Secretary to the Vice President for Student Affairs; Clarence Anderson, Station Engineer, W.J.S.U. Radio Station; James Anderson, Chef Cook and Supervisor, Dining Hall; James Anderson, University Physician (part-time); Lueizera C. Anderson, Secretary to the Vice President for Academic Affairs; Sandria A. Anderson, Key-Punch Operator, Data Processing Center; Shirley Q. Anderson, Secretary to the Director of Athletics; Cozette W. Archie, Secretary, Department of Secondary Education; Williette Armon, Secretary, Rehabilitation Service Program; Charlotte H. Barial, Secretary, Office of Academic Affairs; Willie Barnes, Trainer and Equipment Manager, Department of Health, Physical Education and Recreation; Johnnie W. Baskin, Student Accounts Clerk, Office of Fiscal Affairs; Polly D. Battee, Secretary, Office of the President; Larry Belton, Admissions Counselor/Recruiter; Nora M. Bingham, Secretary/Cashier, Office of Fiscal Affairs; Charles E. Bishop, Coordinator of the Cooperative Education Program; Jackie T. Blackwell, Secretary, Office of Records; Rubye Blake, Secretary, Department of Industrial Arts; Leon Bland, Cashier, Bookstore; Charles Boler, Counselor, TRIO Project; Raymond Bolton, Director, New Men's Dormitory; Tommie B. Bolton, Postal Clerk; Lenora G. Bourne, Secretary to the Dean, School of Liberal Studies; Jill Brewer, Staff Assistant, Office of University Relations; Olivia Brittain, Secretary, Office of Student Affairs; John A. Brookins, Counselor, Office of Admissions; Earl B. Brown, Associate Director, Campus Union; Linda L. Brown, Secretary to the Associate Dean for Records and Admissions; Mary C. Brown, Coordinator, Special Services Program, TRIO Project; Sadie Marie Bruce, Assistant Director, Alexander East Hall; Annie Burnett, Chef Cook, Campus Union; William Calloway, Assistant Manager, University Bookstore; Deloris B. Campbell, Coordinator of Academic Skills Center, Cur-

.riculum Specialist; Ivory Campbell, Asssistant Counselor/Director, Jones and Sampson Halls; Frankie Canada, Secretary, Office of Student Affairs; Benjamin Cannon, Inventory Clerk, Plant Operations; Layuna Carson, Secretary, Library; Sylvia Catchings, Secretary to the Associate Dean of Counseling Services; Gloria Chambers, Secretary, Computer Center; Otis Chambers, Counselor, Counseling Center; Meyen Chu, Operator/Programmer, Computer Center; Ross C. Clay, Jr., Supervisor of Vending Services, Food Service Department; Linda M. Coleman, Secretary, Office of Admissions; Horice B. Colen, Secretary, Office of Admissions; Jeanette Collier, Dietician, Food Services Department; Sylvester Collins, Teaching Assistant, Department of Health, Physical Education and Recreation; Assistant Football Coach; Hiram Cooper, Chief Custodian; Robert Cooper, Director, Campus Union; Celestine Cornelius, Practical Nurse, Health Center; Walter Crockett, Director of Psychometric Services; Helen Y. Cromwell, Secretary to Director of Campus Union; Levernis Crosby, Associate Coordinator, Title III, Advanced Institutional Development Program; Mable D. Crushshon, Secretary, Division of Fine Arts; Alleane Currie, Secretary to the Director of the Institute for the Study of Life, History and Culture of Black People (part-time); Edward Curtis, Dean, Student Affairs for Housing; Varon O. Dagner, Assistant to Coordinator of Student Financial Aid; Lloyd Dale, Operators Manager/Analyst; Willie F. Daniel, Associate Director, Therapeutic Recreation Program; Instructor of Physical Therapeutic Recreation; Childa Daniels, Administrative Assistant, Therapeutic Recreation Program; Lula Davenport, Secretary, Psychometry Center; Princess A. Davis, Clerical Assistant, Library; Dorothy J. Dawson, Secretary to Director of Continuing Education; William K. Dease, Director of Data Processing Center; Connie Dixon, Secretary, Alcohol/Drug Studies Program; Otis Donald, Manager of User Service/Analyst, Computer Center; Claudette Donaldson, Accounts Receivable Clerk, Office of Fiscal Affairs; Melissa Druckrey, Secretary, Library; Rhonda Duffy, Secretary, Office of Student Financial Aid; Jennie M. Duplessis, Centrex Switchboard Operator; Ruby Durr, Supervisor, Food Services Department; Betty J. Easterling, Secretary, Office of Student Affairs; Arville Ellis, Secretary, Early Childhood Education; Edna Ellis, Lecturer, Clerical Training Program; Ora Ephrom, Secretary to the Dean, The Graduate School; Willie S. Farmer, Veteran's Affairs Coordinator, Counseling Center; Nettie Fields, Secretary to the Director, Career Planning and Placement; Bettye J. Fletcher, Associate Director, Alcohol/Drug Studies Program; Sarah Jiles Fulgram, Secretary, Office of the Director of Development; Zan Etta Funches, Secretary, Office of Admissions; Cynthia Garner, Secretary, Office of the Dean, School of Liberal Studies; Charlene Givens, Assistant Cashier, Office of Fiscal Affairs; Valerie Green, Cashier, Bookstore; Dorothy Green, Secretary, Office of Public Information; Rosie Griffin, Secretary, Library; Ruby Griffin, Secretary, Library; Edith Guston, Secretary, Department of Athletics; Rosie M. Guyton, Assistant Director, Alexander East Hall; Deborah Hardy, Department of Business Administration; Vera J. Harper, Secretary to the Director of the Center of Urban Affairs; Dorothy J. Harris, Secretary to the Purchasing Agent; Harvey Harris, Accountant and Data Machine Operator, Data Processing Center; Rose M. Hartwell,

Secretary to Federal Grants Officer, Office of Fiscal Affairs; Larry D. Haynes, Assistant Inventory Clerk; Brenda Hicks, Secretary, Preprofessional Health Careers; Annette T. Hill, Counselor, Counseling Center; Lavorn Hill, Secretary, Department of History; A. W. Holt, Assistant Director, New Men's Dormitory; James E. Hooper, Assistant Purchasing Agent; Marcella D. Hopkins, Secretary, Office of Records; Ruben Hopkins, Payroll Accountant, Office of Fiscal Affairs; Lena Horton, Head Nurse, Health Center; Roberta Horton, Secretary, Office of the Vice President for Administration; Sylvester Hosey, Director of Accounting, Office of Fiscal Affairs; Dorothy J. Huddleston, Secretary, Library; Ruby Hughes, Director of Public Information; Betty Hunt, Secretary, Department of Social Work; Mosella B. Hurst, Director, Alexander West Hall; Janet Jackson, Secretary, Office of Records; Mildred Jackson, Director of Development; Patsy L. Jackson, Secretary, Division of Fine Arts; Sondra Jacob, Associate Director of Bureau of Business and Economics Research; Pearl James, Secretary, Office of the President; Samuel Jefferson, Director of Sports Information; Susan Jefferson, Counselor/Director, Alexander North.Hall; Phyllis Jagers, Secretary, Department of Chemistry; Eddie Butler Johnson, Head Cashier, Office of Fiscal Affairs; Shirley A. Jolly, Licensed Practical Nurse; Grace D. Johnson, Secretary, Department of Social Science Education and Geography; Linda E. Johnson, Secretary to Director of Institutional Research and Planning; India R. Johnson, Secretary, Department of Special Education; Sherry A. Johnson, Graduate School Counselor; Arnell D. Jones, Purchasing Agent; Blanche Jones, Clerical Assistant, Library; Herbert Jones, Counselor, Upward Bound and Special Services Programs, TRIO Project; Ruth J. Jones, Centrex Operator; Mildred B. Kelley, Associate Director of Records; Bennie Kendrick, Secretary to Director of the Library; Leonard Kincaid, Associate Director, Alcohol/Drug Studies Program; Willie Kyles, Counselor, Counseling Center; Director, TRIO Projects; Instructor of Education; Lillian T. Lackey, Secretary, Department of Mass Communications; Wilma G. Langley, Secretary, ESSA Tutorial Project; Michael W. Langston, Heating and Air-Conditioning Maintenance Technician; Jesolyn Larry, Secretary, Media Center; Linda C. Latham, Secretary, Library; Janice Lawrence, Secretary, Department of Political Science; Betty Leemisa, Requisitions Clerk, Office of Fiscal Affairs; Curties Mary Lewis, Secretary, Department of General Science and Physics; Cozy Lewis, Programmer, Computer Center; Glenna J. Link, Course Coordinator of Freshman Career Education Courses; Victoria List, Secretary, Library; Delores J. Lockett, Assistant Director, Alexander West Hall; Shirley D. Lowery, Secretary to the Director of Publications; Barbara Luckett, Secretary, Office of Admissions; Maxine S. Lyles, Administrative Assistant, Alcohol/Drug Studies Program; Earlean Magee, Secretary, Advanced Institutional Development Program; Entricia Magee, NDSL Clerk; Jacqueline Dampier Magee, Secretary, Library; Eloise Magee, Secretary, Physical Education Department; Sadie Magee, Basketball Coach for Women; Teaching Associate, Department of Health, Physical Education and Recreation; Claudette Miller, Secretary, Department of Art; Daisy Gates Manning, Secretary, Department of Biology; Mae Robbie Manny, Clerk-Typist, Office of Records; Ernest May, Head Painter;

Bobbie N. McCoy, Secretary, Department of Student Teaching; Mary L. McGee, Secretary, Office of the Vice President for Fiscal Affairs; Rosie J. McGregg, Secretary, Office of Records; Sgt. Ronald C. Mabone, Administrative NCO Department of Military Science, Staff Sergeant, United States Army; Linda Miller, Secretary, Black Collegian Drinking Patterns; Melvin Miller, Assistant to the Director of Public Information; Lois Moncure, Dietician Cook, Early Childhood Center; Alma Moore, Secretary, Office of the President; Joyce Morgan, Secretary to the Assistant Vice President for University Relations; Florence R. Morris, Administrative Secretary to the President; John E. Morris, Youth Program Coordinator, Center for Urban Affairs; Willie Neal, Coordinator of Industry Liaison, Office of Career Planning and Placement; Valmore A. Nelson, Director of Food Services; Frances B. Newsom, Head Cashier and Assistant Hostess, Dining Hall; Robbie P. Norwood, Secretary, Alumni Affairs; Sollie Norwood, Assistant Director, New Men's Dormitory; Avis O'Neill, Programmer, Computer Center; Gwendolyn H. Owens, Secretary, Department of Accounting; Ravindra Pattar, Internal Auditor, Office of Fiscal Affairs; Cathy Patterson, Career Counselor, Cooperative Education Program; Delores Pearson, Secretary, Office of Student Affairs; Rachael E. Pittman, Secretary to Dean of School of Industrial & Technical Studies; Kimsey T. Pollard, Counselor-Recruiter, Division of Special Student Programs; Angela Porter, Key-Punch Operator, Data Processing Center; Hazel Price, Secretary, Bookstore; Jearlean T. Price, Administrative Assistant and Director of Emergency School, Assistance Act Project; Mitchell P. Purdy, Counselor, Counseling Center; Doris Quinn, Budget Clerk, Office of Fiscal Affairs; Willie P. Randle, Secretary to Career Education Data Bank; Yvonne Buchanan Ratliff, Secretary, Library; Etta D. Redmond, Licensed Practical Nurse, Health Center; Viola Reese, Secretary, Upward Bound Program; Myrtle Reid, Assistant Student Accounts Clerk, Office of Fiscal Affairs; Goldia M. Revies, Secretary, Office of Vice President for Academic Affairs; Annette Rhymes, Secretary, Office of Records; Ruby Buck Richardson, Secretary, Department of Sociology; Cynthia L. Roberts, Secretary, Health Center; Dianne Robbins, Secretary, Teaching Grants and Traineeship in Rehabilitation Counseling; Dee Lois K. Robinson, Director of Publications; Willie A. Robinson, Secretary, Office of Fiscal Affairs; Billy Allen Roby, Games Area Manager, Campus Union; Odell Roundtree, Secretary, Office of Career Planning and Placement; Myrtis R. Ross, Licensed Practical Nurse, Health Center; Daisy Sanders, Secretary, Department of Military Science; John Q. Satcher, System Analyst, Computer Center; Patricia Pettiegrew, Assistant Counselor, Alexander W.H.; Delores Pierce, Secretary, Office of Records; West Hall, Programmer, Computer Center; Deborah Seawright, Secretary, Office of Stduent Financial Aid; Myrtle R. Shields, Student Account Clerk, Office of Fiscal Affairs; John Shinall, Assistant Basketball Coach; Head, Tennis Coach; Teaching Assistant, Department of Health, Physical Education and Recreation; Emma Simpson, Secretary, Biomedical Research and Research Training Program; Alice Faye Singleton, Secretary, Department of Elementary Education; Dorothy Smith, Secretary to the Dean, School of Education; Elbert Smith, Assistant Director of Food Services; Elizabeth Smith, Secretary, Department of Health, Physical Education and Recreation; Joann Smith, Secretary, Office of

Veterans Affairs; Mildred M. Smith, Secretary, Office of Public Information; Odessa Smith, Director, Alexander East Hall; Robert Smith, Associate University Physician (part-time); Sammie L. Smith, Secretary, Office of Institutional Research and Planning; Susie Smith, Secretary, Library; Alcee Stalling, Federal Grant Officer, Office of Fiscal Affairs; Dorothy J. Stamps, Secretary to the Director of the Computer Center; Nora B. Stamps, Secretary, Advanced Institutional Development Program Supplementary; James A. Steverson, Assistant Games Area Manager, Campus Union; Allen Stewart, Coordinator of Student Financial Aid; Barbara Straka, System Analyst/Programmer, Computer Center; M. R. Stringer, Captain and Director, Security Force; Patricia Strong, Secretary, Library; Rubye Sullivan, Assistant Librarian; Instructor of Library Science; Earlene Sutton, Key-Punch Operator, Data Processing Center; Ernestine D. Talbert, Career Counselor, Office of Career Planning and Placement; Arthur J. Taylor, Secretary, Library; Curtis Taylor, Head Carpenter; Janice L. Taylor, Secretary, Counseling Center; Shirley J. Taylor, Secretary, Office of the Assistant Vice President of University Relations; Murlene Terry, Secretary to the Director of Plant Operations; Charles L. Thomas, Assistant Director, Department of Plant Operations; Vera Thomas, Secretary, Library; Delores Thompson, Secretary, Library; Naomi W. Thompson, Secretary, Student Financial Aid Office; William P. Ting, Social Science Computer Specialist; Ollie Tolliver, Secretary, Office of Records; David Tope, Supply Sergeant, Military Science; Staff Sergeant, United States Army; Daisy Trammel, Secretary, Office of the Center for Urban Affairs; Evelyn Trottman, Dietician, Food Services Department; Vera Turner, Secretary, Office of Records; Willie Turner, Director, Stewart Hall; Murdell W. Varnado, Television Production Specialist, Media Center; Florence Veal, Hostess and Assistant Dietician, Dining Hall; Steve D. Walker, Recruiter Counselor, Office of Admissions; Gwendolyn Wansley, Laboratory Associate, Curriculum Laboratory, School of Education; Robert Wansley, Teaching Associate and Laboratory Assistant, Division of Natural Sciences; Monty C. Ware, Army Unit Supply Specialist, Military Science; Specialist 4, United States Army; Cathy Weaver, Secretary to Director of Food Services; Lue Della Wells, Secretary, Department of Economics; Tien-Pao Wen, System Analyst/Programmer, Computer Center; Delores White, Secretary, Department of Business Education; Lillie P. White, Secretary, Counseling Center; Mary M. White, Secretary to the Director of Institutional Research and Planning; Sheron White, Cashier, Bookstore; Robert Whiting, Psychometrist, Psychometry Center; Bertha K. Williams, Secretary, Office of Dean, School of Education; Calvin Williams, Food Service Manager, Campus Union; Assistant to Food Services Director; Debra Williams, Secretary, Department of English; Mary L. Williams, Secretary, Career Planning and Placement Office; Mary Jean Wilks, Secretary, Department of Plant Operation; Rosie Williams, Secretary, Office of Associate Dean of Student Affairs for Counseling Services; Lillian Wilson, Secretary, Library; Mary E. Winford, Secretary, Department of Political Science; Carolyn Wolfe, Secretary, Departments of Guidance and Counseling and Administration and Supervision; Christine Young, Key-Punch OPerator.

APPENDIX V

JACKSON STATE UNIVERSITY ALUMNI

National Alumni Association Chapter Presidents, and Slate of Officers, 1978–1979

CHAPTER PRESIDENTS 1978-79

Mr. Kenneth Hamilton
JSU Atlanta, GA Chapter
Mr. Robert Tyler
JSU Brookhaven, MS Chapter
Mr. Alphonzie Morgan
JSU Carthage-Leake County Chapter
Mr. Dewitt Ginn
JSU Central Mississippi Chapter
Mr. Melvin Jackson
JSU Chicago, IL Chapter
Mrs. Ceola Holston
JSU Clarke County Chapter
Mr. Charles Dockery
JSU Cleveland, OH Chapter
Mr. Walter Johnson
JSU Coahoma County Chapter
Mr. Kermit Dilworth
JSU Columbus-Lowndes Chapter
Mr. Tommie D. Jackson
JSU Copiah County Chapter
Ms. Patricia A. Hayes
JSU Corinth, MS Chapter
Mr. Lamar Walton
JSU Dallas, TX Chapter
Mr. Franch Jackson, Jr.
JSU Davenport, Iowa Chapter

Ms. Gloria D. Allen
JSU Dayton, OH Chapter
Mr. John T. Floyd
JSU Detroit, MI Chapter
Mr. Chester Hughes
JSU Flint, MI Chapter
Mr. Elwood Lumpkins
JSU Gary, Indiana Chapter
Mr. Edward Richardson
JSU Greenville, MS Chapter
Mr. C. J. Ollie
JSU Greenwood-Leflore Chapter
Mr. Johnny M. Cook
JSU Grenada, MS Chapter
Mr. Perry J. Love
JSU Gulfport, MS Chapter
Mrs. Mary B. London
JSU Hattiesburg, MS Chapter
Mr. Leland Redmond
JSU Houston, TX Chapter
Mr. R. C. Bendord
JSU Humphrey County Chapter
Mr. Booker Rankin
JSU Huntsville, AL Chapter
Mr. Franch Jackson, Jr.
JSU Illowa Chapter

Mr. Timothy Ray Williams
JSU Indiana Chapter
Mr. James W. Robinson
JSU Indianapolis, IN Chapter
Mrs. Bobby Rushing
JSU Indianola-Sunflower Chapter
Mr. Thomas J. Hill
JSU Jackson County Chapter
Mr. Robert Funches
JSU Jackson-Hinds Chapter
Mr. Ernest Byrd
JSU Jasper County Chapter
Mr. William White
JSU Kosciusko, MS Chapter
Mrs. Coe Alice Stirgus
JSU Lucedale, MS Chapter
Mrs. Lillie Johnson Kline
JSU Las Vegas, Nevada Chapter
Mrs. Olevia W. Jones
JSU Laurel, MS Chapter
Mrs. Maude Winston
JSU Lawrence County Chapter
Ms. Clarice Johnson
JSU Los Angeles, CA Chapter
Mr. Harrel L. Cargin
JSU Louisville, KY Chapter
Ms. Joyce Stepney
JSU Marion-Walthall Chapter
Mr. Eugene Sargent
JSU Memphis, TN Chapter
Mrs. Billy L. Sykes
JSU Meridian, MS Chapter
Mr. Roger Morris
JSU Mid-Delta Chapter
Mrs. Darcus Denton
JSU Milwaukee, WI Chapter
Mr. Malcolm Stevens
JSU Muskegon, MI Chapter
Mrs. Beverly B. Smith

JSU Natchez, MS Chapter
Mr. Bobby Morris
JSU New Orleans, LA Chapter
Mr. Walter Ramsey
JSU New York Chapter
Mr. Albert Ford
JSU Northern California Chapter
Mr. T. D. Thompson
JSU Northern California Chapter
Mr. Tommie Shelby
JSU Oxford-Lafayette County
Mr. Melvin O. Harris
JSU Pike County Chapter
Mr. Watson Lee Jackson
JSU Scott County Chapter
Mrs. Gladys D. Smith
JSU Simpson County Chapter
Mr. Robert Henry Elsy, Sr.
JSU Southeast Louisiana Chapter
Mr. Robert Sanders
JSU South Eastern Michigan Chapter
Dr. Jacob W. Deering
JSU Tampa, FL Chapter
Mr. Bobby Mason
JSU Tri-State Chapter
Mr. George Allen
JSU Twin-Cities Chapter
Mr. McArthur Bell
JSU Tunica County Chapter
Atty. James Ford
JSU Tupelo, MS Chapter
Mr. George Smith
JSU Vicksburg, MS Chapter
Mr. Thomas C. Tolliver, Jr.
JSU Wilkinson County Chapter
Mr. Lloyd Whitley
JSU Winston County Chapter
Mr. Edward Neal
JSU Yazoo City, MS Chapter

ALUMNI CHAPTERS AND SLATE OF OFFICERS*

JSU Central Mississippi Chapter
Tchula, Mississippi
    President   Mr. Dewitt Ginn

*As submitted to the author in response to questionnaires to Alumni chapter presidents, 1976.

Vice President   Mrs. Gladys Walker
Secretary   Miss Johnnie Ruth Jackson
Assistant Secretary   Mrs. Genola Redd
Reporter   Mrs. Claree Brown
Chaplain   Mrs. Hattie Brown

Outstanding Alumnus
    Mr. Jacob J. McClain
        1. Mississippi and NEA Meritorious Service Award, 1972
        2. White House Invitation from President Lyndon B. Johnson to the Congressional Medal of Honor Ceremony

JSU Clarke County Chapter
Enterprise, Mississippi
Founding Date: October 30, 1970
Officers:
    President   Mrs. Geola E. Holston
    Vice President   Mrs. Birtha C. Cameron
    Secretary   Mrs. Hattie J. Coleman
    Treasurer   Mrs. Annie L. McGowan
    Chaplain   Mrs. Pearlie H. Hoze
    Reporter   Mrs. Eunice O. Edmonson
Distinguished Members:
    Charles Pugh
        U.S. Department of Labor
        Washington, D.C.

JSU Clarksdale-Coahoma Chapter
Coahoma, Mississippi
Founding date: Fall of 1954
Officers:
    President   Walter Johnson
Outstanding Alumni:
    Ms. Zee A. Barron
        Founder of Coahoma Jr. College
    Mr. Marion Reid
        Former Coahoma Jr. College Registrar
    Dean Mary G. Whiteside
    Retired Educator (Deceased 1978)
    Frank McCune (Deceased 1977)
        Long time educator and coach
        Asst. Superintendent of the Clarksdale Public Schools

Robert S. Willis
   Principal
Bennie S. Gooden
   Community Leader
Walter Johnson
   Chapter President
Johnny Lewis
Ms. Martha L. Jackson
   Former Miss Jackson State College
Ms. Elizabeth Bowie Wilson
   Former Miss Jackson State College
Troy Catchings
   Community Leader
Dr. McKinley Martin
   Director of Continuing Education at Coahoma
   Jr. College and Civil Rights Activist

JSU Cleveland, Ohio Chapter
Cleveland Heights, Ohio
Founding Date: July 1, 1974
Officers:
   President   Charles Dockery
   Vice President   William Olowu
   Secretary   Louise Goodwin
   Assistant Secretary   Bertha Collins
   Treasurer   Arthur Lawson
   Reporter   Mildred Gardner
   Financial Secretary   Nellie Johnson
   Business Manager   Will R. Collins
   Chaplain   Ruffin Goodwin
Outstanding members:
   Arthur J. Lawson, '64
   James A. Easterling, '63
   Will Roy Collins, '64
   Henry L. Caston, '63
   Abiodum Dayo Olowu, '71
   James Alley, '63
   Charles Dockery, '61
   William H. Abshaw, '63
   Thomas D. Wilson, '64

JSU Detroit, Michigan Chapter
Detroit, Michigan
Founding Date: 1947
Founded By: Dr. Estemore A. Wolfe
Officers:

President	John T. Floyd
Vice President	Joe Clay
Recording Secretary	Myrtle Compton
Corresponding Secretary	Henrene Swan
Treasurer	John Floyd
Pianist	Edward Nobles
Reporter	Ida Floyd
Chaplain	Katie Young
Custodian	Henry Wolfe

JSU Houston, Texas Chapter
Houston, Texas
Founding Date: October 10, 1976
Officers:

President	Leland Redmond
1st Vice President	Marilyn Weakley
2nd Vice President	Evalia Jones
Treasurer	Mabel Scott
Secretary	Pearl Porter
Reporter	Milton Austin
Assistant Secretary	Rose Austin

JSU Illowa Chapter
Davenport, Iowa
Founding Date: April 22, 1977
Officers:

President	Franch Jackson, Jr.
1st Vice President	Winston C. Mikel
2nd Vice President	Charles Robinson
Secretary	Ella Swaggard
Assistant Secretary	Margaret Deere
Correspondence Secr.	Mary Jackson
Treasurer	Julious J. Johnson
Chaplain	Jimmy Horton
Parliamentarian	Joan Jackson
Editor of Newsletter	Sally Mikel

JSU Indianapolis Indiana Chapter
Indianapolis, Indiana
Founding Date: October, 1974
Officers:
    President   James W. Robinson
    Vice President   Percy Griffin
    Secretary   Elnora Woods
    Treasurer   Melvin L. Woods
    Corresponding Secretary   Anna Young
Outstanding Alumni:
    Melvin Woods
    Elnora Woods
    James W. Robinson

JSU Jackson—Hinds County Chapter
Jackson, Mississippi
Founding Date: 1940
Officers:
    President   Robert Funches
    Vice President   Harold Haughton
    Secretary   Ruth Moore Harris
    Assistant Secretary   Shirley P. Buckley
    Treasurer   Curlee Stowers Wilson
Outstanding Alumni:
    Mrs. Mayne Higgins   Mrs. Curlee Wilson
    Mrs. Mable Bankston   Dr. E. C. Foster
    Mrs. Louise Owens   Dr. T. J. Robinson
    Mrs. Geneva Nelson   Mr. Earl Brown
    Mr. Hillard Lackey   Mrs. Jerutha Steptoe
    Mr. Emanuel Reeves   Mr. James Stevenson
    Mr. Leon Bland   Mr. James Garner
    Mr. Jerry Daniels   Mr. Obra V. Hackett
    Mr. Willie Farmer   Mr. Will T. Chambliss
    Mrs. Shirley P. Buckley   Dr. Paul W. Purdy
    Mr. Robert Funchess   Mr. Paul Covington
    Mr. Bob Hill   Dr. Mildred Jackson
    Mr. Robert Braddy   Mrs. Doris Smith
    Mrs. Elizabeth Blank Owens Mrs. Myrtle Cowherd
    Mrs. Dorothy Williams   Mrs. Betty Hunt
    Mr. John Morris

JSU Laurel, Mississippi Chapter
Laurel, Mississippi
Founding Date: September 1926
Officers:
    President   Mrs. O. W. Jones
    Vice President   Mrs. Dorothy Peppers
    Secretary   Ms. Betty Jenkins
    Assistant Secretary   Mrs. Barbara Brumfield
    Treasurer   Mrs. Willie M. Oldham
    Member-at-Large   Mrs. Esther M. Rayford
Charter members include:
  Mrs. H. V. J. McInnis (founder)
  Dr. Harvey L. Brown (deceased)
  Mr. Joe Booth (deceased)
  Mrs. Mary Laws Booth
  Mrs. Drucille Reid Byrd
  Mrs. Bessie Beale Dittaway
  Mrs. Bobby O. Reid Dukes (deceased)
  Mrs. Lucy Beale Jones
  Mr. Ulysses S. McInnis (deceased)
  Mrs. Legertha Beale Mott

JSU Leflore County Chapter
Itta Bena, Mississippi
Founding Date:
Officers:
    President   Charles T. Ollie
    Vice President   Mrs. Diane Wilson Jones
    Secretary   Ms. Charlotte Patterson
    Assistant Secretary   Ms. Alice Holmes
    Treasurer   Ivory Loggins
    Business Manager &
      Reporter   Mrs. Catherine G. Pearson

JSU Los Angeles Chapter
Los Angeles, California
Founding Date: 1954
Officers:
    President   Clarice Clayton Johnson
     1st Vice President   Sylvannus Lloyd
     2nd Vice President   Ms. Mary Spell

Recording Secretary — Mrs. Phyllis Norwood
Corresponding Secretary — Ms. Betty Allen
Financial Secretary — Miss Alta F. Ellis
Treasurer — Luther Williams
Parliamentarian — Wiley White
Chaplain — Mr. Julius Inge
Publicist — Ms. Frankie Mitchell
Sargent-at-arms — Mrs. Florida C. Hyde
Historian — Mrs. Lillian Inge

JSU Marion-Walthall Chapter
Columbia, Mississippi
Founding Date: October, 1950
Founded By: Mrs. Eunice Martin
　　　　　　Miss Iris Johnson
　　　　　　Willie S. McLaurin (President)
Officers:
　President — Joyce H. Stephney
　Vice President — Leslie Peters
　Secretary — Miss Hazel Abram
　Treasurer — Mrs. Mary Oatis
　Reporter — G. S. Owens
Outstanding Alumni:
　Mrs. Sallie Thompson Pittman
　Jewel Ginn
　Helman Johnson
　Roosevelt Oatis
　Mrs. Olivette Johnson
　Fred Idom

JSU Memphis, Tennessee Chapter
Memphis, Tennessee
Reinstated: October 1975
Officers:
　President — Eugene Sargent
　Vice President — Maurice Sargent
　Secretary — Mattie Byrd
　Assistant Secretary — Helen Brown
　Treasurer — Carl Brown
　Reporter — Ella M. McNeamer

JSU Meridian, Mississippi Chapter
Meridian, Mississippi
Founding Date: 1952
Officers:
    President — Billy L. Sykes
    Vice President — Fletcher Ludgood
    Recording Secretary — Miss Rellie Williams
    Correspondence Secretary — Mrs. Marjorie Cole
    Treasurer — Mrs. Estella G. Young
    Advisor — Mr. W. A. Reed, Jr.

JSU Minneapolis, Minnesota Chapter
Minneapolis, Minnesota
Founding Date: 1974
Officers:
    President — Dr. Velma McLin Mitchell
    Vice President — Abraham McCarty
    2nd Vice President — George Allen
    Secretary — Selottie Barnes
    Treasurer — John Barnes
    Program Chairperson — Barbara McCarty
    Reporter — Dorothy Michael
    Public Relations — Emerson David
    Abraham McCarty
    Willia J. Dennis

JSU Natchez, Mississippi Chapter
Natchez, Mississippi
Founding Date: 1958
Chapter Presidents:
    Samuel Young
    Charlie Jones
    Jerome Dickey
    Dr. E. C. Foster
    Pauline Pearson Fields
    Oscar Kelly Reed
    Beverly Barnes Smith

JSU Oxford-Lafayette Cos. Chapter
Oxford, Mississippi
Officers:
    President — Mr. Tommie Shelby

1st Vice President	Dorothy Henderson
2nd Vice President	Tommie Shelby
Secretary	Leon Buford
Treasurer	Almelia Frierson
Reporter	Eva Joyce Goliday
	Myrtle Parker

JSU Simpson County Chapter
Mendenhall, Mississippi
Founding Date: 1952
Officers:

President	Gladys Durr Smith
Vice President	Mrs. Roberta Lee
Secretary	Doris N. Perkins
Assistant Secretary	Joyce Gray White
Treasurer	Kathryn Black Weathersby
Chaplain	Odis B. Smith
Parliamentarian	Mack Nichols, Jr.
Chairman, Program Committee	Mary McLaurin
Committeemen	Velma Payne
	Cleo Fletcher
	Carrie Pickerning
	Myrtis Smith
	Elma Curry

Outstanding Alumna:
  Gladys Durr Smith

JSU Wilkinson County Chapter
Woodville, Mississippi
Founding Date: October 16, 1975
Officers:

President	Thomas C. Tolliver, Jr.
Vice President	George Wilkinson, Jr.
Secretary	Gladys E. C. Hines
Assistant Secretary	Bessie Jefferson
Treasurer	Mrs. A. A. H. Lewis
Chaplain	Virginia C. Wilkinson
Reporter	Olivia L. Smith
Business Manager	William Ward
Parliamentarian	Henry L. Tolliver

APPENDIX VI

JACKSON STATE UNIVERSITY ATHLETICS

TEAM CHAMPIONSHIP AWARDS, 1949 TO 1976

1976
Martin Luther King Basketball
  Tournament
Southwestern Athletic Conference
  Indoor Track
Southwestern Athletic Conference
  Cross-Country Track
NAIA District 30 Indoor
JSU Men's Invitational Track Meet

NAIA National Track Meet
Southwestern Athletic Conference
  All-Sports Trophy
NAIA District 30 Baseball
JSU Women's Invitational Basketball
  Tournament
Orange Blossom Classic Basketball
  Tournament

1975
Southwestern Athletic Conference 20
  Champion
Southwestern Athletic Conference
  Basketball
Southwestern Athletic Conference
  Cross-Country Track
NAIA National Track Meet
South-West Recreational Track Meet
JSU Women's Track Meet

Prairie View Women's Track Meet
Southwestern Athletic Conference
  All-Sports Trophy
Southwestern Athletic Conference
  Indoor Track Meet
Southwestern Athletic Conference
  Golf Tournament
NAIA District 30 Track Meet

1974
State Mutual Magnolia Classic Football
MEAC-Southwestern Athletic
  Basketball Classic
Magnolia Classic Basketball
  Tournament
Southwestern Athletic Conference
  Basketball Tournament

NAIA District 30 Track Meet
Southwestern Athletic Conference
  Indoor Track Meet
Southern College Track Meet
Southwestern Athletic Conference
  Track

TEAM CHAMPIONSHIP AWARDS (CONTINUED)

1973
Southwestern Athletic Conference
  Football
NAIA District 27 Track Meet
University of Nebraska/Omaha
  Basketball Tournament
NAIA District 27 Indoor Track Meet
Fort Worth Park Track Meet

JSU Indoor Meet (Men)
Southern Collegiate Meet
Southwestern Athletic Conference
  All-Sports Trophy
Southwestern Athletic Conference
  Baseball

1972
Southwestern Athletic Conference
  Football Co-Champion

Magnolia Classic Basketball
  Tournament
Invitational College Relays (Track)
Southwestern Athletic Conference
  Baseball

1971
NAIA District 27 Baseball
NAIA District 27 Basketball

1970
Southwestern Athletic Conference
  Basketball

1969
NAIA District 27 Basketball

1968
NAIA District 27 Basketball
Southwestern Athletic Conference
  Basketball

Southwestern Athletic Conference
  Baseball

1967
Georgia Invitational Basketball
Southwestern Athletic Conference
  Basketball

1966
Southwestern Athletic Conference
  Basketball
Georgia Invitational Basketball

1964
Southwestern Athletic Conference
  Basketball

1962
Southwestern Athletic Conference
  Football
All-American Bowl Football

Orange Blossom Classic National
  Champions

1961
Southwestern Athletic Conference
  Football

TEAM CHAMPIONSHIP AWARDS (CONTINUED)

1957
Mid-Western Athletic Conference
  Co-Champion Football

1956
Mid-Western Athletic Conference
  Basketball Classic

1953
Tri-State Basketball Tournament
Mid-Western Athletic Conference
  Basketball Classic

1951
South-Central Athletic Conference
  Track

1949
South-Central Athletic Conference
  Track

Mid-Western Athletic Conference
  Basketball Tournament

Football Records and Coaches

YEAR	WON	LOST	TIED	HEAD COACH
1946	4	3	1	T. B. Ellis
1947	4	4	0	T. B. Ellis
1948	3	5	0	T. B. Ellis
1949	7	3	0	T. B. Ellis
1950	7	2	1	T. B. Ellis
1951	6	4	0	T. B. Ellis
1952	3	5	1	John Merritt
1953	5	4	0	John Merritt
1954	2	6	1	John Merritt
1955	5	4	0	John Merritt
1956	6	2	0	John Merritt
1957	6	2	0	John Merritt
1958	6	2	1	John Merritt
1959	5	5	0	John Merritt
1960	6	4	0	John Merritt
1961	9	1	0	John Merritt
1962	10	1	0	John Merritt
1963	4	5	0	Edward Clemons
1964	6	4	0	Roderick Paige

Jackson State University Athletics

FOOTBALL RECORDS & COACHES (CONTINUED)

YEAR	WON	LOST	TIED	HEAD COACH
1965	5	3	0	Roderick Paige
1966	5	3	0	Roderick Paige
1967	5	4	0	Roderick Paige
1968	3	6	0	Roderick Paige
1969	2	6	0	Ulysses McPherson
1970	4	7	0	Ulysses McPherson
1971	9	1	1	Robert Hill
1972	8	3	0	Robert Hill
1973	8	2	0	Robert Hill
1974	7	3	0	Robert Hill
1975	7	3	0	Robert Hill
1976	5	4	0	Robert Hill, W. C. Gorden

Football All-Time Professional Athletes*

YEAR	NAME	POSITION	TEAM
1956	Robert Hill	RB	Baltimore Colts
1960	Frank Dorsey	RB	Los Angeles Rams
1963	Harold Cooley	OG	New York Giants
	Roy Curry	DB	Chicago Bears
	Willie Richardson	WR	Baltimore Colts
	Albert Grier		Detroit Lions
1964	Leslie Duncan	DB	Washington Redskins
	Ben McGee	DT	Pittsburgh Steelers
1965	Coy Bacon	DT	Los Angeles Rams
	Verlon Biggs	DE	Washington Redskins
	Bennie Crenshaw	DB	New York Giants
	T. B. Ellis, III	DB	Green Bay Packers
	Roy Hilton	DT	Baltimore Colts
	Frank Molden	DT	Philadelphia Eagles
	Gloster Richardson	WW	Dallas Cowboys
	Elbert Vaughn	DB	New York Giants
1966	Taft Reed	DB	Philadelphia Eagles
	Thomas Richardson	SE	New England Patriots

*Players drafted or signed as free agents.

FOOTBALL ALL-TIME PROFESSIONAL ATHLETES (CONTINUED)

YEAR	NAME	POSITION	TEAM
1967	Willie Turner	DB	New York Giants
	John Walker	DB	Atlanta Falcons
	Lem Barney	DB	Detroit Lions
	James Jackson	DB	Cleveland Browns
	Cladius James	WR	Green Bay Packers
	Robert Hughes	DT	Atlanta Falcons
1968	Douglas Chatman	DE	New York Giants
	Sidney Ellis	DB	Cincinnati Bengals
	Tommy Funches	OT	Houston Oilers
	James Hartfield	KOS	Los Angeles Rams
	Jimmy Holifield	DB	New York Giants
	Cephus Jackson	LB	Los Angeles Rams
	Harold Jackson	WR	Los Angeles Rams
	John Outlaw	DB	New England Patriots
	Edgar Whipps	DB	Cleveland Browns
	Eugene Wren	DB	Detroit Lions
1969	Monroe Alexander	RB	Cleveland Browns
	Jimmy Carr	DT	Detroit Lions
	Richard Harvey	DB	New Orleans Saints
	John Hughes	DE	Detroit Lions
	Leroy Mason	DB	Dallas Cowboys
	Booker Wilson		Chicago Bears
1970	Richard Castor	DE	New York Jets
	John Shinall	DB	New York Giants
1972	Jerome Barkum	FB	New York Jets
	Edgar Handy	OG	San Diego Chargers
	Ed Whimbly	DB	Chicago Bears
1973	Leon Gray	OT	Miami Dolphins
	Emanuel Zanders		New Orleans Saints
1974	Raymond Key	P	Chicago Fire
	James Marshall	DB	Dallas Cowboys
	Donald Reese	DE	Miami Dolphins
	John Tate	LB	New York Jets
	Roscoe Word	DB	New York Jets
	Douglas Baker		New Orleans Saints
1975	Walter Payton	RB	Chicago Bears
	Robert Brazille	LB	Houston Oilers
	John Tate	LB	New York Giants
	Ricky Young	FB	San Diego Chargers
	Matthew Norman		
	Charles James	CB	New York Jets
	Rodney Phillips		New Orleans Saints

Basketball Season Record Since 1951

YEAR	WON	LOST
1951–52	22	9
1952–53	23	4
1953–54	20	6
1954–55	23	5
1955–56	29	4
1956–57	24	1
1957–58	22	4
1958–59	19	7
1959–60	22	4
1960–61	20	6
1961–62	19	7
1962–63	17	7
1963–64	20	5
1964–65	21	7
1965–66	24	5
1966–67	20	9
1967–68	24	3
1968–69	19	8
1969–70	26	5
1970–71	23	7
1971–72	15	11
1972–73	21	7
1973–74	22	5
1974–75	25	4
1975–76	18	11
TOTAL	538	151
PERCENTAGE	780	

All-Time Professional Athletes*

YEAR	NAME	POSITION	TEAM
1972	Brown, Marvin	F	Baltimore Bullets
1960	Buchner, Cleveland	F	New York Knicks
	Golden, Russell	F	Phoenix Suns
1970	Herndon, Louis	G	Chicago Bulls
1969	Holt, A. W.	F	Dallas Chaparals
1954	Ingram, McCoy	C	Minneapolis Lakers
1970	Johnson, Glenn	G	Chicago Bulls

*Players drafted or signed as free agents.

BASKETBALL ALL-TIME PROFESSIONAL ATHLETES (CONTINUED)

YEAR	NAME	POSITION	TEAM
	Jones, Glendale	G	New Orleans Jazz
1965	Leflore, Lyvonne	F	Baltimore Bullets
1967	Manning, Edward	F	Baltimore Bullets
1970	Sellers, Aaron	F	San Diego Rockets
1970	Shinall, John	G	Atlanta Hawks
1975	Short, Eugene*	F	New York Knicks
	Ward, Henry	F	San Antonio Spurs
1970	Walls, David	F	Denver Rockets
1970	Warner, Cornell	F	Buffalo Braves
1972	Watkins, Ben	F	Baltimore Bullets
	Yarborough, Jerry	F	Chicago Bulls

*Eugene Short became the first JSU player to be drafted in the first round when the New York Knicks selected him first in the 1975 draft.

APPENDIX VII

COFOUNDERS, BOARD OF TRUSTEES, & ADMINISTRATORS

Selective Supportive Personnel in the Development of Jackson State University

CO-FOUNDERS
    Baptist Missionary Convention
    American Baptist Home Mission Society

EARLY PHILANTHROPISTS
    Baptist Missionary Convention
    American Baptist Home Missionary Society
    Rosenwald Fund
    Slater Fund
    Southern Education Board
    General Education Board

CORPORATE BOARD OF TRUSTEES, INCORPORATION 1938
    Mr. W. F. Bond, State Superintendent of Education, Jackson, Miss.
    Dr. C. L. Barnes, Practicing Dentist in Jackson
    Mr. J. W. Dixon, Treasurer, Jackson College Alumni
    Mr. W. W. Blackburn, Executive Secretary, Negro State Teachers' Association
    Mr. J. H. Coates, President, Universal Life Insurance Company
    Rev. C. A. Greer, Pastor, Farish Street Baptist Church
    Mr. P. K. Lutken, President Lamar Life Insurance Company
    Mr. W. B. McCarty, President, McCarty-Holman Wholesale Grocery
    Dr. J. W. Provine, Educator and Baptist Leader
    Dr. S. D. Redmond, Real Estate and Lawyer Broker

Judge J. Morgan Stevens, Prominent Lawyer in Mississippi
Miss Fannie Traylor, Executive Secretary, Women's Missionary Union
Mr. E. W. Banks, Businessman
Miss F. O. Alexander, Educator and Teacher Trainer of the State Department of Education

PRESENT BOARD OF TRUSTEES OF STATE INSTITUTIONS OF HIGHER LEARNING

Verner S. Holmes, M.D., M.D., President
E. E. Thrash, Executive Secretary & Director
Bobby L. Chain, Vice President
R. C. Cook
Robert W. Harrison, Jr., D.D.S.
Charles C. Jacobs, Jr.
John R. Lovelace, M.D.
Travis E. Parker
Neal Denton Rogers, Jr.
Robert L. Shemwell, Jr.
W. M. Shoemaker
Mirian Q. Simmons
Boswell Stevens
Betty A. Williams

PRESIDENTS

Charles Ayer, 1877-1894
Luther G. Barrett, 1894-1911
Zachary T. Hubert, 1911-1927
B. B. Dansby, 1927-1940
Jacob L. Reddix, 1940-1967
John A. Peoples, Jr., 1967-

VICE PRESIDENTS

Vice President for Administration
Lee E. Williams (1940) B.S. Jackson State University; M.S. Ohio State University; Ed.S., George Peabody College for Teachers; LLD Tougaloo College

Vice President for Academic Affairs
Estus Smith (1962), B.S. Jackson State University; M.M.E. Indiana University; Ph.D. University of Iowa: Fellow, American Council on Education Academic Administration Internship Program

Vice President for Student Affairs
   George A. Johnson (1970) A.B. Tougaloo College; M.S. Indiana University; Ed.D. Mississippi State University
Vice President for Fiscal Affairs
   Paul W. Purdy (1967) B.S. Jackson State University; M.A. Purdue University; Ed.D. University of California at Los Angeles
Associate Vice President for University Relations
   T. J. Robinson (1963-65; 1966-72; 1974-) B.S. Jackson State University; M.A. Eastern Michigan University; Ph.D. Southern Illinois University

DEANS—THE GRADUATE SCHOOL
   Augustus C. Blanks, First Director of Graduate Studies
   Dr. Charles C. Mosley, Director of Graduate Studies
   Oscar Rogers (1960), A.B. Tougaloo College; S.T.B., Harvard Divinity School; N.A.T. Harvard University; Ed.D., University of Arkansas; Post Doctoral, University of Washington
   Ivory C. Manning (1951) Assistant Dean of the Graduate School B.S. Jackson State University; M.S. Northwestern University; Ph.D. University of Minnesota

SCHOOL OF LIBERAL STUDIES
   Robert H. Smith (1973-)
   B.S. Southern University; M.A. University of Illinois; Ph.D. Florida State University

SCHOOL OF EDUCATION
   Cleopatra D. Thompson (1946-58; 1961-1977)
   B.S. Alcorn A & M University; M.A. Atlanta University; Ed.D., Cornell University; Post Doctoral Fellow, State University of Iowa
   Beatrice B. Mosley (1965-67; 1968-)
   B.S. Tougaloo College; M.S. Indian University; Ed.D., University of Southern Mississippi

SCHOOL OF BUSINESS AND ECONOMICS
   George F. Currie (1952)
   B.A., Wilberforce University; M.A., Ph.D., University of Illinois
   William Cooley (1978-)
   B.S. Tuskegee Institute; M.S. University of North Dakota; D.B.A. Mississippi State University

SCHOOL OF INDUSTRIAL AND TECHNICAL STUDIES
    Jay T. Smith (1973)
    B.S., Alcorn A & M University; M.S. Bradley University; Ed.D., University of Missouri

DIRECTOR OF ADMISSIONS/REGISTRAR (SINCE 1940)
    B. B. Dansby (1940) 1942-49
    DeLars Funches (1948) 1949-69
    Wallace F. Swann, III (1960) 1969-76
    Mildred B. Kelley (1957) 1977-
    Oscar C. Williams (1968) Director of Admissions
    Dr. Haskell S. Bingham, Dean for Admissions and Records

ACADEMIC DEANS OF THE INSTITUTION (SINCE 1940)
    Florence O. Alexander (1940) 1940-43
    H. T. Sampson (1942) 1945-67
    Lionel B. Fraser (1952) Assistant Dean 1953-67
    Haskell S. Bingham (1965) Assistant Dean 1967-69
    Wilbert Greenfield (1960) 1967-73
    Estus Smith (1962) 1973-

BUSINESS MANAGER/COMPTROLLER (SINCE 1940)
    Harold Jacobs 1940-43, 1947-49
    J. A. Welch 1945-46
    C. A. Christophe (1945-46)
    Robert Henry Beasley (1948) 1949-59
    Leonard P. Chambliss, Sr., (1952) Asst. Comptroller 1955-59; Comptroller, 1959-69
    Frederick D. Jones (1969) 1969-72
    Paul W. Purdy (1967) 1972-

DEAN OF STUDENTS & COUNSELOR OF MEN
    Richard T. Middleton 1947-49
    William S. Edmonds (1949) Counselor of Men 1949-50
    Walter O. Gill (1956) 1961-63
    James R. Johnson (1964) Assistant Dean 1967-69
    Tommie Smith (1968) Associate Dean of Students for Men 1971-73; Associate Dean of Student Affairs for Men 1973-75; Dean of Student Affairs for Men 1975-

DEAN OF STUDENTS & COUNSELOR OF WOMEN
    Odessa H. Waters 1949-50

Ruth K. Johnson (1961) Assistant Dean 1967–69
Bobbie Nell Oatis (1967) Assistant Dean 1969–71; Associate Dean 1971–73; Associate Dean of Student Affairs for Women 1973–75; Dean of Student Affairs for Women 1975–

DEAN OF STUDENTS
William S. Edmonds (1949) 1951–53
D. W. Wilburn (1951) 1953–57
Walter O. Gill (1956) 1957–61
Oscar A. Rogers 1960–61
Wallace A. Higgins (1962) 1963–65
Roland L. Buchanan, Jr., (1962) 1965–69
Tommie Smith (1968) Acting Dean 1969–71
George A. Johnson (1970) Dean of Students 1971–73; Dean of Student Affairs, 1973–75; Vice President for Student Affairs, 1975–
Edward L. Curtis, Dean of Student Affairs for Housing

CHAPLAINS
Rev. A. L. Rice (1946) 1947–59
Rev. James Wiley Brown (1958) 1959–63
Rev. George E. Covington (1963) 1963–65
Rev. Leon Bell (1965) 1965–69
Rev. A. W. Crump (1977) 1977–

OFFICE OF PUBLIC RELATIONS
DeLars Funches 1949
Bennie J. Cole (1949) 1949–53
W. O. Robinson (1950) 1953–65
Ivory C. Manning 1956–59 Director of Extension
William M. Bailey (1959) Assistant Director 1961–63
Haskell S. Bingham (1965) 1965–67
Alvin Lee Benson (1963) 1967–71
Stanley Johnson (1971) 1971–73
Obra V. Hackett (1973) 1973–77
Melvin Miller (1976) Director of Public Information

COLLEGE PHYSICIANS
Dr. W. E. Miller 1945–50
Dr. A. M. Hall 1951–59
Dr. C. B. Christain 1959–65
Dr. R. O. Williams 1965–69
Dr. James Anderson 1967–
Dr. Robert Smith

DIRECTOR OF THE LIBRARY (SINCE 1940)
    Sara Jane Watts-Lovelace 1940-46
    Ruby E. Stutts Lyells 1945-47
    Ernestina A. Lipscomb (1947) Head Librarian 1947-76
    Lelia G. Rhodes (1944) 1976-

BAND DIRECTORS
    Kermit W. Holly (1943) 1943-46
    William W. Davis (1948) 1948-71
    Dollye M.E. Robinson 1961-62 Assistant Band Director
    Harold Haughton (1965) Assistant Band Director 1967-71;
       Director of the Marching Band 1972-
    Estus Smith (1962) Assistant Band Director 1967-69
    Jimmie James (1966) Assistant Band Director 1969-73
    John Paul Jones (1969) Director ROTC Band 1973-
    Edward Duplessis (1970) Assistant Band Director 1975-
    Joe E. Goree (1970) Assistant Band Director 1975-

CHOIR DIRECTORS (SINCE 1940)
    Ariel M. Lovelace 1940-47
    Aurelia Young 1947-49
    Kermit Holly
    E. Rogie Clark (1948) 1949-53
    Sara Booker Turner
    Robert Henry
    Emma Goldman Lewis
    Raymond I. Johnson (1964) 1965-

*Date in parenthesis indicates initial employment

Chronology of Academic Deans
in the History of
Jackson State University since 1911

NAME	TITLE	DATE
B. B. Dansby Morehouse College 1906; Head, Department of Mathematics, Florida Baptist College 1907; Graduate Student, University of Chicago 1911; Jackson College since 1911	Dean of the College	1911-23

Cofounders, Board of Trustees & Administrators

NAME	TITLE	DATE
A. R. Reeves Mathematics, Morehouse College A. B. 1898; Teacher of Mathematics and Science Arkansas Baptist College, 1898–1912; Teacher of Mathematics, State Norman School, Pine Bluff, Arkansas, 1912–20, Jackson College, since 1920 Acting Dean of the College	Acting Dean of the College	1924–25
Adolph L. Rice, A.M. Theology—Language, A.B., University of Nebraska, B.D. Chicago University; Assistant Pastor, Mt. Helm Baptist Church; Jackson College since 1924 Dean of the College	Dean of the College	1926–33
A. A. Latting,	Head Teacher	1932–33
A. L. Perkins	Acting Dean	1939–40
Henry T. Sampson A.B., Morehouse College; M.S., University of Chicago; Graduate Study, University of Chicago	Dean of the College Dean of Instruction Executive Dean of the College and Director of Summer School	1933–38 1942–55 1955–67
Florence O. Alexander B.S., Hampton Institute; A.B., Hunter College; A.M., Columbia University; Study (Graduate) University of Cincinnati; Jackson College since 1918	Director of Instruction	1940–43
Lionel B. Fraser B.S., Hampton Institute; Ed.M., Harvard University Further Study University of Wisconsin, University of Chicago	Assistant Dean of Instruction Acting Dean of Instruction	1955–67 1967–68

298 *Jackson State University 1877–1977*

NAME	TITLE	DATE
Charles C. Mosley, Dr. A.B. Eureka College; M.A. in Education, University of Illinois; Ed.D., Indiana University	Director of Graduate Studies Acting Asst. Dean for Graduate Studies	1959–67 1967–69
Haskell Bingham B.S., Jackson State College; M.A., University of Denver; Ph.D., George Peabody College for Teachers	Assistant Dean of Instruction Assistant Dean of Academic Affairs Dean of Admissions & Records	1967–70 1971–72 1973–
Wilbert Greenfield B.S., North Carolina A & T State University; M.S., Ph.D. State University of Iowa	Dean of Instruction Dean of Academic Affairs	1967–70 1971–72
Estus Smith B.S., Jackson State College; M.Ed. Indiana University; Ph.D. University of Iowa Fellow, American Council on Education, Academic Administration Internship Program 1971–72	Associate Dean for Liberal Studies Dean, Liberal Studies Vice President for Academic Affairs	1969–70 Dec. 1972 July 30, 1973 1973–
Oscar A. Rogers A.B., Tougaloo College S.T.B., Harvard Divinity School; M.A.T., Harvard University; Ed.D., University of Arkansas; Post Doctoral Tri-University Fellow in Social Science-Social Studies University of Washington, 1968–69	Acting Assistant Dean for Graduate Studies Dean of Graduate Studies Dean of the Graduate School	1969–70 1971–72 1973–
Augustus C. Blanks	Director of Graduate Studies	1959

Cofounders, Board of Trustees & Administrators 299

NAME	TITLE	DATE
Cleopatra D. Thompson B.S., Alcorn College; M.A. Atlanta University; Ed.D. Cornell University Post-Doctoral Fellow, State University of Iowa	Associate Dean of Education & Technical Studies Dean, School of Education & Technical Studies Dean, School of Education	1968-70 1971-72 1973-77
Mosley, Beatrice B. B.S. Tougaloo College M.S. Indiana University Ed.D. University of Southern Mississippi	Dean, School of Education	1977-
Robert H. Smith B.A., Southern University; M.A., University of Illinois; Ph.D., Florida State University	Dean, School of Liberal Studies	1973-
Jay T. Smith B.S., Alcorn A & M College M.S. Bradley University; Ed.D. University of Missouri	Dean, School of Industrial and Technical Studies	1973-
George F. Currie B.A., Wilberforce University M.A., Ph.D., University of Illinois	Dean, School of Business and Economics	1973-78
William Cooley B.S., Tuskegee Institute; M.S., University of North Dakota; D.B.A. Mississippi State University	Dean, School of Business & Economics	1978-

APPENDIX VIII

CENTENNIAL COMMITTEE MEMBERS

CENTENNIAL COMMITTEES
Dr. John A. Peoples, Jr., Chairman, Ex officio
Dr. Lee E. Williams, Chairman
Dr. Estus Smith, Vice Chairman
Dr. Paul W. Purdy, Secretary
Mr. Hilliard L. Lackey, Centennial Coordinator

CENTENNIAL STEERING COMMITTEE
Dr. Lee E. Williams, Chairman
*Mrs. Dee L. Kincaid Robinson
†Dr. Estus Smith
Mr. Hilliard L. Lackey
Mr. E. S. Bishop, Sr.
Dr. E. C. Foster
Mr. Leopolian Gentry
Dr. Clara Grochowska
Mr. Obra V. Hackett
Mrs. Esther S. Marshall
Dr. Rose E. McCoy
Mr. Edwin Mullen
Dr. John A. Peoples, Jr.
Dr. Paul W. Purdy, Secretary
Dr. Lelia G. Rhodes
Dr. Dollye M. E. Robinson
Dr. T. J. Robinson
Mrs. Lottie W. Thornton
Dr. Estemore A. Wolfe
Mrs. Aurelia N. Young

CENTENNIAL COMMITTEE
Dr. Lee E. Williams, Chairman
*Mrs. Sandra E. Walker
Dr. Margaret Walker Alexander
Dr. Mildred Barksdale
Mr. E. S. Bishop, Sr.
Dr. Emmett C. Burns
Mr. Hiram D. Bullock
§Dr. B. Baldwin Dansby (Deceased)
Mrs. Lelia Davis
Dr. E. C. Foster
Dr. DeLars Funches
Mr. Leopolian Gentry
Mr. Karl Griffin
Dr. Elwyn Grimes
Dr. Clara Grochowska
Mr. Obra V. Hackett
Reverend Daniel Heath
Reverend Isiah Henderson
Mrs. Lillian W. Inge
Mr. James Johnson
Mr. Hilliard L. Lackey
Mrs. Emma G. Lewis
Dr. Rose E. McCoy
Mrs. Esther S. Marshall
Mr. Edwin Mullen
Mr. Roosevelt Oatis

Centennial Committee Members 301

Dr. John A. Peoples, Jr., *ex officio*
Mrs. Mary G. Peoples
Dr. Paul W. Purdy
Dr. Leroy Ramsey
Mrs. Daisy S. Reddix
Dr. Lelia G. Rhodes
Mr. Willie Richardson
Mrs. Frances D. Robertson
Mrs. Dee L. Kincaid Robinson
Dr. Dollye M. E. Robinson
Mr. James W. Robinson
Mrs. Rose Howard Robinson
Dr. T. J. Robinson

Attorney Alix Sanders
Dr. Charlie J. Smith
Lt. Willie Smith
Dr. Raymond Stewart
Dr. Cleopatra D. Thompson
Mrs. Lottie W. Thornton
Mrs. Nellie Winter Tolliver
Mrs. Bertha Drungole West
Dr. Calvin S. White
Dr. Lucius Williams
Miss Mildred Williams
Dr. Estemore A. Wolfe
Mrs. Aurelia N. Young

HONORARY CENTENNIAL COMMITTEE MEMBERS—THE $1,000 CLUB
PAID MEMBERS:

Mr. Earl W. Banks
Mr. John M. Black
Mr. Robert Brazile
Mrs. Paralee W. Burgs
Mrs. Vera Chambers
Mr. & Mrs. Robert B. Cooper
Mrs. Gustava M. Gooden
Dr. James Harvey
‖ Dr. Maria L. Harvey
Mrs. Mayne P. Higgins
Dr. Margaret Hutton
Mrs. Florida C. Hyde
Mrs. Lillian W. Inge
Dr. Marjorie W. Jordan
Mr. & Mrs. Steve Matthews
Dr. Rose E. McCoy
Mr. & Mrs. B. J. McCullough
Mr. & Mrs. Fred McDowell
Mrs. Sadye W. Montgomery
Mt. Helm Baptist Church

Mrs. Dessie Newton
Dr. John A. Peoples, Jr.
Mrs. Mary G. Peoples
Ms. Bobbie N. Oatis
Mr. Walter Payton
Mrs. Lula E. Pendleton
Dr. Estus Smith
Mrs. Gladys Durr Smith
Dr. & Mrs. Robert H. Smith
Mr. Robert L. T. Smith, Jr.
Ms. Curlee Stowers
Ms. Jerutha Stowers
Mr. & Mrs. H. M. Thompson
Mrs. Lottie W. Thornton
Mr. Leroy Weathersby
Mrs. Alice B. Weathersby
Dr. & Mrs. Lee E. Williams
‖ Dr. Estemore A. Wolfe
Mrs. Sadye M. Womack
Ms. Nettie Stowers

PLEDGED MEMBERS:
Mr. Leroy Akon
**Mr. A. A. Alexander
**Miss F. O. Alexander
Mr. Lawrence Aldridge
Mr. & Mrs. Willie T. Allen
Miss Aletha Almore
Mr. Thelman L. Anderson

*Staff Person
†Co-Chairperson
‡Student
§Deceased
‖ Contributors of $2,000

Mr. Robert Anthony
Ms. Mary Bacon
Mr. Vera P. Bailey
Mr. Fred Baker
Mrs. Zee A. Barron
Mr. John L. Bayne
Mrs. Glynell W. Beard
Mr. Edward S. Bishop, Jr.
**Mr. Edward S. Bishop, Sr.
Mr. & Mrs. Stanley Blackmon
Mr. Robert L. Braddy
Mr. Robert Bradley
Mr. James A. Brookins
Mr. Bonnie Brown
Mr. & Mrs. Earl B. Brown
Mr. Gotrea Brown
Mr. & Mrs. Jimmie D. Brown, Jr.
Mrs. Martha L. Brown
Mrs. Mary M. Brown
Dr. T. B. Brown
Dr. Bruce Brumfield
Mr. & Mrs. Luther B. Buckley
**Dr. & Mrs. Emmett C. Burns
Mr. Ralph E. Burns
Ms. Mattie D. Byrd
Mr. & Mrs. Orestes Carmicle
Mrs. Lillian B. Carter
Mr. F. D. Casher
** Mr. & Mrs. Troy Catchings
**Mr. Will T. Chambliss
Mr. Albert Chatman, Jr.
Dr. Chung-Shing Chu
Dr. Annie Cistrunk
Mr. Robert G. Clark
Mr. Ross C. Clay, Sr.
Dr. & Mrs. Sam Cobbins
**Mrs. Margie W. Cole
Mr. & Mrs. Chester Coleman
Mr. Paul E. Covington
Mr. William L. Cross
Mr. & Mrs. Edward L. Curtis
Ms. Charlestine Dillon
Mrs. Pearl M. Draine
Ms. Alta Faye Ellis
Mrs. Gertrude Ellis

Mr. Martin Epps
Mr. James Ford
Dr. E.C. Foster
Mr. & Mrs. Jimmie Franklin
Attorney Hillman T. Frazier
Mr. Lee A. Frison
Mrs. Nanie L. Gaines
Mrs. Lorraine B. Gayden
**Dr. & Mrs. Roosevelt Gentry
**Dr. & Mrs. Ruben Gentry
Mr. & Mrs. C. Gilleylan
**Mrs. Beatrice Ginn
Ms. Doris O. Ginn
Mr. & Mrs. Curtis Gray
Mr. & Mrs. James E. Griggs
**Mr. & Mrs. Obra V. Hackett
Mr. Lee Hammond
Mr. Alfred N. Handy, III
Dr. Alferdteen Harrison
Mr. Richard Harvey
Mr. Harold J. Haughton
Mr. Robert C. Hill
** Mr. J. Herman Hines
Mr. Walter Hurns
Mrs. Mosella B. Hurst
Ms. Bobbie B. Jackson
Mr. Eugene Jackson, Sr.
Mr. Joe Louis Jackson
Dr. Mildred C. Jackson
Mr. & Mrs. T. D. Jackson
Mr. Tom C. James, Jr.
Mr. & Mrs. Vernon J. Jasper
Ms. Bessie L. Jefferson
Mr. A. P. Johnson
Mr. James R. Johnson
Mrs. Marion D. Johnson
Mr. Roland Johnson
Mr. & Mrs. Walter L. Johnson
Ms. Bergie Jones
Mrs. Bertha T. Jones
Ms. Ollie M. Jones
Mrs. Pearl Jones
Ms. Vera Baskin Jones
Mr. & Mrs. George Jordan
Mrs. Mildred B. Kelley

Centennial Committee Members

Mr. James C. Kinney
Mr. & Mrs. Willie D. Kyles
Mr. Hilliard L. Lackey
Mr. & Mrs. Douglas Langston
Dr. Ralph Lee
Ms. Patricia A. Lewis
**Mr. & Mrs. Edward L. Lipscomb
Ms. Christine Lloyd
Mr. Percy Lowe
Ms. Annie M. McGee
Mrs. Ella M. McNearmer
Dr. & Mrs. Robert Mack
Ms. Fern Martin
**Ms. Queen E. Mims
Ms. Alice Minor
Mr. & Mrs. Bobby Morris
Dr. Georgia Napier
Dr. Lee Napier
Mr. Wallace Neely
Mr. V. A. Nelson
Dr. & Mrs. Robert Nixon
Mr. & Mrs. Roosevelt Oatis
Mrs. Mary Ruth Ousley
Mr. & Mrs. William Overton
Mrs. Eunice Patton
Mrs. Freda R. Powell
Reverend Albert Price
Mr. Charles E. Pugh
**Dr. & Mrs. Paul W. Purdy
Mr. Nolen Zeno Qualls
Dr. Walter L. Ramsey
Mr. L. V. Randolph, Sr.
Mrs. Bertha L. Redfield
**Mrs. Birdie Redmond
Dr. & Mrs. Walter Reed
Mr. W. A. Reed, Jr.
Dr. & Mrs. Bennie L. Reeves
**Mr. & Mrs. John D. Rhodes, Sr.
Mrs. Frances D. Robertson
Dr. Dollye M. E. Robinson
Mr. James R. Robinson
**Dr. & Mrs. T. J. Robinson
Mr. Billy A. Roby
Mr. Alfred R. Ross
Mr. Bobby L. Rushing

Mrs. Lillie S. Russ
Mr. & Mrs. Maurice Sargeant
Ms. A;ma Scott
Ms. Marie Scott
Mrs. Evelyn H. Silas
Mr. & Mrs. Webster E. Silas
Dr. James W. Simmons
Dr. & Mrs. Charlie J. Smith
Ms. Delores Smith
Mr. Tommie Smith
Mrs. Mary H. Stamps
Mrs. Jerutha Steptoe
Mr. & Mrs. James A. Steverson
Mr. Peter Stewart
Mrs. Ora L. Strong
Mr. John D. Sullivan
§Mr. John L. Sullivan
Mr. & Mrs. Horace Tate, Jr.
Mr. Will Taylor
Mrs. Bertha Thames
Ms. Katherine Thames
Mr. Charles L. Thomas
Mrs. Katie B. Thomas
Mr. & Mrs. James Tillman
Mr. & Mrs. James L. Todd
Dr. & Mrs. Johnny L. Tolliver
Mr. Thomas C. Tolliver
Ms. Kathleen Turner
Mrs. Lillie Turner
Mr. Robert Tyler
Mr. George Ward
Ms. Bettye J. Washington
Mr. Edward Watters
Dr. Shing-sung Wen
Dr. Barnes M. West
Mrs. Bertha D. West
Miss Mary G. Whiteside
Mr. Lawrence Wilder

---

*Staff Person   **Paid Members
†Co-Chairperson
‡Student
§Deceased
‖Contributors of $2,000

Mrs. Virginia C. Wilkinson
§Mrs. Beulah Williams
Mr. James F. Williams
**Mr. & Mrs. Luther Williams
Ms. Mildred Williams
Mr. Oscar C. Williams
**Mrs. Rellie M. Williams
Mrs. Shirley P. Williams
Mr. Timothy Ray Williams
Mrs. Clinton Wilson, Jr.
Ms. Eargie Winters
Mr. & Mrs. Jack P. Witty
**Mrs. Estelle Young
§Attorney Jack Young, Sr.
Mrs. Mardis Young
**Dr. Michael Zifcak

BOARD OF DIRECTORS—
JACKSON STATE UNIVERSITY DEVELOPMENT FOUNDATION

Mr. A. A. Alexander
Mr. Earl W. Banks
Mr. Leon Bracey
Mr. Edward S. Bishop, Sr.
Mr. Tom Bowen
§Dr. B. Baldwin Dansby
Dr. E C Foster
Dr. DeLars Funches
Ms. Ethel Green
Attorney Carsie Hall
Mr. Robert Holmes
Mr. J. Herman Hines
Mrs. Florida C. Hyde
Dr. Mildred C. Jackson
Mr. James Johnson
Mr. Hilliard L. Lackey
Mr. R. Benjamin Lampton
Mr. Edward L. Lipscomb
Mr. Donald Lutkin
Mr. Richard McRae
Dr. John A. Peoples, Jr.
Dr. Paul W. Purdy
Mrs. Daisy S. Reddix
Dr. T. J. Robinson
Mr. Robert L. T. Smith, Jr.
Dr. Lee E. Williams
Dr. Estemore A. Wolfe

JACKSON STATE UNIVERSITY NATIONAL ALUMNI ASSOCIATION PRESIDENTS

§Mr. Edgar T. Stewart, 1938-44
Mr. A. A. Alexander, 1944-48
Mrs. Lottie W. Thornton, 1948-50
Mrs. Estelle Young, 1950-54
Dr. Lee E. Williams, 1954-66
Mrs. Frances D. Robertson, 1966-72
Mr. Edward S. Bishop, Sr., 1972-76
Dr. Estemore A. Wolfe, 1976-

JACKSON STATE UNIVERSITY "ALUMNUS OF THE YEAR" RECEPIENTS

Dr. Estemore A. Wolfe, 1960
§Mr. John W. Dixon, 1961
Dr. Lee E. Williams, 1962
Mrs. Hattie J. McInnis, 1963
Mrs. Lottie W. Thornton, 1964
Mrs. Beulah R. Williams, §1965
§Attorney Jack Young, Sr., 1966
Mrs. Frances D. Robertson, 1967
Dr. John A. Peoples, Jr., 1968
Representative Robert G. Clark, 1969
Mr. & Mrs. John L. Sullivan, §1970
Mr. John M. Black, 1971
Mrs. Gladys Durr Smith, 1972
Dr. Lelia G. Rhodes, 1973
Mr. A. A. Alexander, 1974
Mrs. Gustava M. Godden, 1975
Mr. Edward S. Bishop, Sr., 1976

Centennial Committee Members

NATIONAL ALUMNI ASSOCIATION CHAPTER PRESIDENTS 1975-1976

Ms. Gloria D. Allen/Dayton, Ohio
Mr. Will T. Allen/Grenada
Mr. James Bacchus/Memphis, Tennessee
Mr. McArthur Bell/Tunica
Mr. R. C. Benford/Beizoni
Mrs. Eva Bishop/Corinth
Mr. Stanley Blackmon/Grand Rapids, Michigan
Mr. Robert Carr/Chicago, Illinois
Dr. J. W. Deering/Tampa, Florida
Mr. Kermit Dilworth/Columbus
Mr. James E. Easterling/Cleveland, Ohio
Mr. Robert Elsey, Sr./Ponchatoula, Louisiana
Mr. Calvin Ford/Huntsville, Alabama
Attorney James Ford/Pontotoc
Attorney Hillam T. Frazier/Jackson
Ms. Lucindy Greene/Milwaukee, Wisconsin
Mr. Dewitt Ginn/Durant
Mr. Kenneth Hamilton/Atlanta, Georgia
Mr. Andrew Hardmon/Greenville
Mr. Melvin O. Harris/Magnolia
Mr. Harrison Harvard, Jr./Vicksburg
Mrs. Dorothy Henderson/Oxford
Mr. Thomas J. Hill/Moss Point
Ms. Ceola Holston/Enterprise
Mr. Freddie Jackson/Flint, Michigan
Mr. Tommie D. Jackson/Hazlehurst
Mr. Watson Lee Jackson/Forest
Mr. Walter Johnson/Clarksdale
Mrs. Lillie Johnson Kline/Las Vegas, Nevada
Mrs. Mary R. London/Hattiesburg
Mr. Percy J. Love/Gulfport
Mr. Elwood Lumpkins/Gary, Indiana
Mr. Bobby Mason/Washington, D.C.
Dr. Velma McLin Mitchell/Minneapolis, Minnesota
Mr. Clifton Moore/Detroit, Michigan
Mr. Alphonzie Morgan/Carthage
Mr. Bobby Morris/New Orleans, Louisiana
Mr. Roger B. Morris/Mound Bayou
Mr. C. J. Ollie/Greenwood
Mr. Eugene Owens/Laurel
Mr. Walter Ramsey/West Hempstead, New York
Mr. Bobby L. Rushing/Indianoia
Mrs. Gladys Durr Smith/Mount Olive
Ms. Beverly B. Smith/Natchez
Ms. Joyce Stepney/Columbia
Mrs. Coe Alice Stirgus/Lucedale
Mr. B. L. Sykes/Meridian
Mr. Joseph Thomas/Yazoo City
Mr. Thomas C. Tolliver/Woodville
Mr. Robert Tyler/Brookhaven
Mr. William White/Kosciusko
Mr. Lloyd Whitely/Louisville
Mr. Timothy Ray Williams/Fort Wayne, Indiana
Ms. Maude L. Winston/Silver Creek

STUDENT GOVERNMENT ASSOCIATION PRESIDENTS

Mrs. Lottie W. Thornton, 1943-44
Mr. Bennie J. Cole, 1945-46
Mr. L. V. Randolph, 1946-47
Mr. Leroy Weathersby, 1947-48
Dr. John A. Peoples, Jr., 1948-49
Dr. John A. Peoples, Jr., 1949-50
Dr. Joe L. Cain 1950-51
Mr. David R. Williams, 1951-52
Mr. Sidney L. Moore, 1952-53
Mr. Lee H. Virgil, 1954-55
Mr. Lavatus Powell, 1955-56
Dr. Haskell Bingham, 1957-58

*Staff Person
†Co-Chairperson
‡Student
§Deceased
‖Contributors of $2,000

Mr. Aaron Jones, 1958-59
Mr. Joe Louis Jackson, 1959-60
Attorney Walter Williams, 1960-61
Dr. Arthur L. Williams, 1961-62
Mr. William Brassfield, 1962-63
Dr. Elwyn Grimes, 1963-64
Mr. Emmett K. Morris, 1964-65
Mr. Miller C. Taylor, 1965-66
Attorney Hermel Johnson, 1966-67
Mr. Charlemagne Payne, 1967-68
Mr. Eddie Pate, 1968-69
Mr. John Brookins, 1969-70
Attorney Warner Buxton, 1970-71
Mrs. Sandra M. Hawthorne, 1971-72
Mr. Kenneth Hamilton, 1972-73
Lt. Joseph C. Phillips, 1973-74
Mr. Anthony Adefemi, 1974-75
Mr. Leon Bracey, 1975-76
Mr. Samuel Jones, Jr., 1976-77

JACKSON STATE UNIVERSITY SENIOR CLASS PRESIDENTS

Mrs. Mayne P. Higgins, 1930-31
§Mrs. Mollie Young Sims, 1932-33
Mr. Frank B. McCune, 1938-39
Dr. DeLars Funches, 1939-40
Mrs. Ruth M. Williams, 1941-42
Mrs. Rose H. Robinson, 1943-44
Mrs. Frances L. D. Robertson, 1944-45
Mrs. Dorothy W. S. Johnson, 1945-46
Mr. George Swann, 1946-47
Mr. Solomon Frelix, 1947-48
Mr. Johnny Edwards, 1948-49
Mr. Edwin Mullen, 1949-50
Mr. Billy Sykes, 1950-51
Dr. Barnes M. West, 1952-53
Mr. Robert Anthony, 1953-54
Mr. James Johnson, 1954-55
Mr. Leroy W. O'Quinn, 1955-56
Mr. Nolen Zeno Qualls, 1959-60
Mr. Esley Ambrose, 1960-61
Dr. Paul W. Purdy, 1961-62
Mr. Roosevelt Fitzgerald, 1962-63
Mr. Thomas Wilson, 1963-64
Mr. Harrison Woods, 1964-65
Mr. James Felton, 1965-66
Dr. Ruben Gentry, 1966-67
Mr. Tyree Irving, 1967-68
Mr. Freddie Henderson, 1968-69
Mr. Marvel Lang, 1969-70
Mr. Joseph T. Hardy, 1970-71
Mr. Phillip Pittman, 1971-72
Mr. James Macon, 1972-73
Mr. Felix Caston, 1973-74
Ms. Betty Bush, 1974-75
Mr. George Foster, 1975-76
Mr. George Smith, 1976-77

FORMER JACKSON STATE UNIVERSITY QUEENS:
"MISS JACKSON FAIR" AND "MISS JACKSON STATE"

Helen L. Washington Griffin, 1933-34
Linnell Geeston Thigpen, 1935-36
Louise Kerns Catchings, 1946-47
Grace Townes Oatis, 1947-48
§Jennie V. Carr, 1948-49
Nora Morgan Jones, 1949-50
Joyce Williams, 1950-51
Inez Morris Wilson, 1951-52
Dorothy Jean Lee Gray, 1952-53
Dorothy Jean Lee Gray, 1953-54
Mertha Lockett Jackson, 1954-55
Elizabeth Bowie Wilson, 1955-56
Robbie Barnes Bingham, 1956-57
Gladys M. Dennis, 1957-58
Lynda F. Lyons Beverly, 1958-59
Dorothy Jean Miller Coleman, 1959-60
Doris Nichols Smith, 1960-61
Joyce Thomas Holly, 1961-62
Lois A. Savage Nixon, 1962-63
Beverly Ann Bowser Robinson, 1963-64
Brenda Joyce Lang, 1964-65
Vivian Leigh Hilley Dotson, 1965-66
LaVerne Wallace, 1966-67
Mamie Hanshaw Barnes, 1967-68

Tommie Harris Stewart, 1968-69
Mary Ellen Coleman, 1969-70
Eddie Jean McDonald Carr, 1970-71
Martha Anderson, 1971-72
Emma Jean Brown Smothers, 1972-73

Jacqueline Bacchus, 1973-74
Gwendolyn Durham, 1974-75
Ethel Green, 1975-76
JoAnn Durham, 1976-77

CENTENNIAL ACTIVITIES COMMITTEES

CENTENNIAL ALUMNI DAY COMMITTEE

Mr. Hilliard L. Lackey, Chairman
‡Mr. Phillip Brewer
Mr. John Brookins
Mr. Robert B. Cooper
Dr. Maria L. Harvey
*Mr. Walter Hurns

Mrs. Mildred B. Kelley
Mr. Edwin Mullen
Miss Robbie N. Oatis
‡Mr. Purvis Short
‡Ms. Shelia Sims
Mrs. Jerutha Steptoe

CENTENNIAL ALUMNI NEWSLETTER COMMITTEE

Mr. Hilliard L. Lackey, Chairman
Mr. Henry Banks
Ms. Virgia Brock
*Mrs. Daisy Cobbins
Dr. Gloria B. Evans
*Ms. Thelma C. Hickman

Ms. Rubye K. Hughes
Mr. Walter Hurns
‡Mr. Warren Lampkin
Mrs. Flora C. McGee
Dr. Ivory C. Manning
Mrs. Bruce Mitchell

CENTENNIAL ALUMNI SEMINAR COMMITTEE

Mr. Hilliard L. Lackey, Chairman
Dr. Mildred Allen
*Mr. Charles Bishop
Mr. Edward S. Bishop, Sr.
Dr. Emmett C. Burns
‡Ms. Mary Evans
Attorney Hillman T. Frazier
‡Mr. John Hardy
Mrs. Mayne P. Higgins

Dr. Mildred C. Jackson
‡Mr. Eddie James
Mrs. Ophelia R. Kelley
Mrs. Louise B. Owens
Mrs. Mitchell P. Purdy
Mrs. Sophia B. Taylor
Mrs. Lottie W. Thornton
Mrs. Ruth M. Williams

CENTENNIAL ATHLETIC COMMITTEE

Dr. Walter Reed, Chairman
†Mr. Robert Braddy
Mr. Allen H. Brown
Mr. Robert B. Cooper
‡Ms. Faye Cornelius
†Mr. Paul Covington
*Mr. T. B. Ellis
†Mr. Martin Epps
Dr. DeLars Funches

†Mr. Robert C. Hill
Mr. Hilliard L. Lackey

*Staff Person
†Co-Chairperson
‡Student
§Deceased
‖Contributors of $2,000

Mr. Roosevelt Oatis
Mr. Willy R. Patton
Dr. Paul W. Purdy, *ex officio*
Dr. T. J. Robinson
†Mr. John Shinault

†Mr. Allen F. Smith
Mr. Alcee Stalling
Dr. Robert B. Weaver
Dr. Lee E. Williams, *ex officio*

CENTENNIAL ATHLETIC BANQUET COMMITTEE
Mr. T. B. Ellis, Chairman
Mr. Allen H. Brown
Mr. Robert B. Cooper
Dr. DeLars Funches
Mr. Shirley Harris
‡Ms. Bertha Hardy
*Mr. Samuel Jefferson
Mr. Hilliard L. Lackey

‡Ms. Mary Alice Moore
Mr. Roosevelt Oatis
Mr. Willy R. Patton
Dr. Walter Reed
Mr. Alcee Stalling
Dr. Robert B. Weaver
Dr. Lee E. Williams, *ex officio*

CENTENNIAL BOOK FAIR COMMITTEE
Mrs. Gladys Johnson, Chairwoman
‡Ms. Tanya Barnes
‡Mr. Willie Carr
‡Ms. Jean Clayton
‡Mr. Dwayne Duffy
‡Mr. Michael Lampton

‡Ms. Deborah Mingo
*Mrs. Orthella P. Moman
‡Ms. Gloria Neal
Mrs. Rosie B. Neal
Mrs. Mable Pittman
Mrs. Nellie Wynter

CENTENNIAL BUDGET COMMITTEE
Dr. Estus Smith, Chairman
Mr. Hilliard L. Lackey
*Mr. Walter Hurns

Dr. Paul W. Purdy
Mr. Leopolian Gentry
Dr. T. J. Robinson

CENTENNIAL CHRISTMAS CONCERT COMMITTEE
Dr. Dollye M. E. Robinson,
    Chairwoman
Mr. Harold J. Haughton
*Mrs. Mabel Crushshon
Mr. Raymond I. Johnson

Dr. Anita Jackson
Dr. Jimmie James
Mrs. Gladys P. Norris
Mrs. Aurelia N. Young

CENTENNIAL CITATION COMMITTEE
Dr. T. J. Robinson, Chairman
Mr. Obra V. Hackett
Mr. Hilliard L. Lackey

Dr. John A. Peoples, Jr., *ex officio*
Dr. Paul W. Purdy
Dr. Lee E. Williams

CENTENNIAL COMMENCEMENT COMMITTEE
Dr. Lee E. Williams, Chairman
*Ms. Roberta Horton

‡Mr. Michael Allen
‡Mr. Leon Bracey

Centennial Committee Members 309

*Mr. Robert B. Cooper
Dr. Haskell Bingham, Ex officio
‡Mr. George Foster
Mr. Henry Frazier
Mr. Obra V. Hackett
Mr. Hilliard L. Lackey
Mr. West Lindsey
Dr. Richard T. Middleton
†Ms. Evelyn Mims
Dr. William Parker

Mr. Willy R. Patton
Mrs. Mable Pittman
Mrs. Dee L. Kincaid Robinson,
  ex officio
Dr. Oscar A. Rogers, Jr.
Dr. William Rush
Mr. Hosea Sanders
Dr. Charlie J. Smith
Major Donald Thompson

CENTENNIAL CORONATION COMMITTEE

Mrs. Tommie Harris Stewart,
  Chairwoman
*Ms. Aletha Almore
Mr. Emanuel Abston
Ms. Jacqueline Bacchus
Mr. Lawrence Campbell
Mrs. Gwendolyn B. Chambliss
Mrs. Levernis Crosby
Mr. William W. Davis
Mrs. Vivian H. Dotson
Mrs. Malena W. Dow
Mr. Edward J. Fisher
Mrs. Margie Funches
Mr. Obra V. Hackett
‡Mr. Ronnie Hicks
Mrs. Joyce T. Holly
Mr. Kermit Holly
Ms. Rubye K. Hughes

Ms. Mertha L. Johnson
Dr. George Johnson
Mr. Raymond I. Johnson
Mrs. Beatrice K. Moore
Ms. Bobbie N. Oatis
Mrs. Grace T. Oatis
‡Ms. Jean Redmond
Mr. David Reeves
Mr. Hosea Sanders
Mr. Tommie Smith
Ms. Murlene Terry
Dr. Charles Trottman
‡Ms. Annette Wells
‡Ms. Antoinette Wells
Mrs. Eva Y. Woodard
Miss JSU & Court
SGA Officers

CENTENNIAL DISTINGUISHED ALUMNI PERFORMERS COMMITTEE

Mr. William W. Davis, Chairman
Dr. Jimmie James
*Mrs. Henrietta McMillan

Mr. Lawrence A. Jones
Mr. Harold J. Haughton
Mr. Freddie Waites

CENTENNIAL DISTINGUISHED ARTISTS SERIES COMMITTEE

Mrs. Gladys P. Norris, Chairwoman
*Mr. Eugene Jackson
‡Mr. Michael Allen
Dr. Ben Bailey
Mr. Henry Banks
Mrs. Tommie Bolton
‡Mr. Leon Bracey
‡Ms. Ethel Green

*Staff Person
†Co-Chairperson
‡Student
§Deceased
‖Contributors of $2,000

Mr. Harold J. Haughton
Dr. Dorothy L. Hawkins
Dr. Anita Jackson
Mr. Raymond I. Johnson
Mrs. Maria L. Jones
‡Ms. Evelyn Mims
Mrs. Mildred B. Kelley
Mrs. Ophelia R. Kelley

Mrs. Emma G. Lewis
‡Ms. Bobbie Mallett
Ms. Bobbie N. Oatis
‡Ms. Olivia Smith
Mr. Charles Phillips
Mr. Oscar C. Williams
Dr. Dollye M. E. Robinson
Dr. Oscar A. Rogers, Jr.

CENTENNIAL ECUMENICAL FORUM COMMITTEE

Dr. Bennie L. Reeves, Chairman
*Mr. Allen Stewart
Mr. Grover D. Barnes
Mrs. Eva M. Bowie
Dr. William Brewer
Mr. Earl B. Brown
Dr. T. B. Brown
Mrs. Marie S. Bruce
Mrs. Effie Clay
Mr. F. D. Cunningham
Mrs. Yvonne Etheredge
Dr. Clara Grochowska

‡Ms. Patricia Houseworth
Mr. Walter Hurns
Mr. Richard T. Middleton, Sr.
Dr. Geraldine B. Mohammed
‡Ms. Patricia Peagues
Mrs. Mercedes Phillips
Mr. Samuel Polk
Reverend Albert Price
Dr. Fred Shore
Father Lawrence Watts
Mrs. Mamie D. Taplin
Mrs. Sophia B. Taylor

CENTENNIAL FESTIVAL OF THE ARTS COMMITTEE

Mrs. Malena Dow, Chairwoman
‡Ms. Lillian Amos
Mr. Earl B. Brown
Mrs. Ollie Brown
Mrs. Luana F. Clayton
Mr. William W. Davis
‡Mr. Lawrence Evans
†Mr. Edward J. Fisher
‡Ms. Sharon Fleming
‡Ms. Vivian Fleming
‡Ms. Mwanda Gilbert
Dr. Richard Harger
Dr. Alferdteen Harrison
‡Mr. Morris Henderson

‡Ms. Annette Hill
Mr. James Hooper
†Dr. Anita Jackson
Mr. Raymond I. Johnson
‡Mr. Warren Mason
‡Mr. Sherwin Maynor
‡Mr. Robert Merchant
Mrs. Gladys P. Norris
‡Ms. Patricia Quinn
Dr. Dollye M. E. Robinson
Mrs. Tommie Harris Stewart
Ms. Myriam Talbert
‡Mr. Olger Twyner, III
‡Mrs. Aurelia N. Young

CENTENNIAL FOUNDERS' DAY COMMITTEE

Mrs. Cozetta Buckley, Chairwoman
Mr. Emanuel Abston
‡Ms. Carolyn Baird
Mrs. Bernice Bell
Mr. Edward S. Bishop, Sr.

Mr. Robert B. Cooper
‡Ms. Peggy Dixon
Mrs. Alma Duffy
Dr. Anita Jackson
Mr. Raymond I. Johnson

Centennial Committee Members 311

*Mrs. Orthella P. Moman
Mrs. Francis G. Morris
Dr. Lelia G. Rhodes
‡Ms. Patricia Robertson

‡Ms. Dianne Smith
Mrs. Susie Smith
Dr. Lee E. Williams, *ex officio*

CENTENNIAL HISTORICAL EXHIBITS COMMITTEE

Dr. E C Foster, Chairman
Ms. F. O. Alexander
Dr. Margaret Walker Alexander
Mr. Earl W. Banks
Mrs. Bernice Bell
Mrs. Ruth B. Campbell
§Dr. B. Baldwin Dansby
Mr. John W. Dixon
Mr. William Dyson
‡Mr. Dean Foster
Dr. Velvetyn B. Foster
Dr. Jimmie Franklin
Mr. Percy Greene
Dr. Frederick D. Hall
*Dr. Richard Harger
Dr. Alferdteen Harrison
Mr. Giles A. Hubert
Dr. Margaret Hutton
Ms. Janice S. Jackson
Mr. Samuel Jefferson

Mrs. Eddie B. Johnson
Mr. Hilliard L. Lackey
Mrs. Ernestine A. Lipscomb
Mrs. Esther S. Marshall
Dr. Rose E. McCoy
Mrs. Hattie J. McInnis
Dr. Leslie B. McLemore
Mr. George Mitchell
Dr. Charles C. Mosley, Sr.
Dr. Ivory Phillips
Mr. Leroy Ramsey
Mrs. Daisy S. Reddix
Dr. Bennie L. Reeves
Dr. Lelia G. Rhodes
Mrs. Tommie Harris Stewart
Mr. Hugh Stevens
Dr. Julius Thompson
‡Mr. Olger Twyner, III
Mrs. Estelle Young

CENTENNIAL HOMECOMING COMMITTEE

Mr. L. T. Smith, Chairman
*Mrs. Edith Guston
Mr. L. T. Smith, Chairman
*Mrs. Edith Guston
*Miss Charlene Mims
‡Mr. Michael Allen
Mrs. Evelyn Banks
Mr. Earl B. Brown
Mr. Lawrence Campbell
Mr. Ronald Coleman
Mrs. Miriam Covington
‡Mr. Brel Clark
‡Mr. Carl Clark
Mr. T. B. Ellis, *ex officio*
Mr. Martin Epps
Mr. Karl Griffin
Mr. Obra V. Hackett

Mr. Harold J. Haughton
Mr. Eugene Jackson
Mr. Cornell Johnson
Captain Donald Jones
Mr. Lawrence A. Jones
Mr. Hilliard L. Lackey
Dr. Walter Reed
Mr. David Reeves
Mrs. Mercedes Phillips
‡Mr. Joe Whitfield
‡Ms. Ann Winter

*Staff Person
†Co-Chairperson
‡Student
§Deceased
‖Contributors of $2,000

312 Jackson State University 1877-1977

CENTENNIAL HOMECOMING DANCE COMMITTEE
Mr. Harold J. Haughton, Chairman
*Mrs. Cathy Patterson
Dr. Williams Brooks
Mr. Edward Duplessis, Jr.
Mr. A. D. Jones
Mr. Hilliard L. Lackey
Mrs. Earnestine Talbert

CENTENNIAL HONORS NIGHT COMMITTEE
Dr. Maria L. Harvey, Chairwoman
*Mrs. Charlotte Barial
Dr. Mildred Allen
Mr. David C. Bass
Mrs. Cozetta Buckley
‡Ms. Angelita Currie
‡Ms. Jimmie A. Dampier
Lt. James E. Davis
Dr. Melvin I. Evans
‡Ms. Velma L. Evans
‡Mr. Calvin Fraley
Mr. Edward J. Fisher
Dr. John E. Hall
Dr. Norman Handy
Dr. David J. Hickman
Mr. Walter Hurns
Mr. Lawrence A. Jones
Dr. Jesse C. Lewis
Dr. Sinclair O. Lewis
‡Ms. Doris O. McGee
Dr. Leslie B. McLemore
Dr. Rose E. McCoy
Dr. Georgia Napier
Dr. Ronald Niemeyer
Mr. Willy R. Patton
Dr. James Perkins
Dr. Ivory Phillips
Mrs. Mitchell P. Purdy
Dr. Bennie L. Reeves
Dr. Dollye M. E. Robinson
Dr. William Rush
Dr. Charlie J. Smith
Dr. Eunice T. Smith
Dr. Johnny L. Tolliver
Dr. Johnny L. Tolliver
Dr. John E. Uzodinma
Dr. Barnes M. West
‡Ms. Deborah Wilson

JACKSON STATE UNIVERSITY APPRECIATION WEEK COMMITTEE
Mr. Obra V. Hackett, Chairman
*Mrs. Dorothy Green
‡Ms. Jeanette Conquista
Mr. James Hooper
Mrs. Thelma C. Hickman
Ms. Rubye K. Hughes
‡Ms. Doretha Presley
Mr. Hilliard L. Lackey
Mrs. Dee Kincaid-Robinson
Dr. T. J. Robinson
‡Mr. Roger Solis
Dr. Johnny L. Tolliver

JOHN A. PEOPLES' DAY COMMITTEE
Dr. Lee E. Williams, Chairman
*Mrs. Florence Morris
Mrs. Bernice Bell
Mr. Lonnie C. Crosby
Dr. Robert List
Dr. Rose E. McCoy
Mrs. Dee Kincaid-Robinson
Dr. T. J. Robinson
Mr. Ray Self
Dr. Estus Smith
Mrs. Lottie W. Thornton
Mrs. Murdell Varnado
Dr. Lucius Williams

Centennial Committee Members 313

CENTENNIAL LECTURE SERIES COMMITTEE
Dr. Anthony J. Cavell, Chairman
Mrs. Luana F. Clayton
Dr. Margaret Walker Alexander
Dr. Curtis Baham
Mrs. Malena W. Dow
Mrs. Emma G. Lewis
Mrs. Beatrice K. Moore
Mr. John Morris
Miss Bobbie N. Oatis

CENTENNIAL LEGISLATIVE DAY COMMITTEE
Dr. Mildred C. Jackson, Chairwoman
*Dr. Curtis Baham
*Mr. Willie Neal
Mr. A. A. Alexander
Mr. Edward S. Bishop, Jr.
Representative Robert G. Clark
Mr. Lonnie C. Crosby
Mr. Edward Curtis
Dr. E C Foster
Dr. DeLars Funches
‡Mr. Eddie James
Mr. Clark Johnson
Dr. George A. Johnson
Dr. Marjorie Jordan
Dr. Freda Judge
Hilliard L. Lackey
Mr. E. L. Lipscomb
‡Ms. Sarah Malone
Mr. V. A. Nelson
Miss Bobbie N. Oatis
Mr. Samuel Polk
Dr. Paul W. Purdy
Dr. Estus Smith
Dr. Kathryn Weathersby
Mr. Calvin Williams

CENTENNIAL MEDIA—BLITZ COMMITTEE
Mr. Obra V. Hackett, Chairman
*Mr. Willie Farmer
‡Mr. Coolidge Anderson
Mr. E. S. Bishop, Sr.
‡Ms. Jeanette Conquista
Mr. Robert B. Cooper
Mr. Cliff Farrier
Dr. John Gregory
Ms. Rubye K. Hughes
Dr. Robert List
Mr. Bruce Payne
‡Ms. Doretha Presley
Mr. Walter Sadler
‡Mr. Roger Solis
Mres. Murdell Varnado
Mr. Michael Weems

CENTENNIAL MULTI-MEDIA PRESENTATION COMMITTEE
Dr. Johnny L. Tolliver, Chairman
‡Dr. E C Foster
*Mr. Willie D. Kyles
*Mr. Tommie Smith
Dr. Margaret Walker Alexander
Mrs. Willie D. Blackburn
Mr. William W. Davis
Mr. John Dixon
Dr. Gloria B. Evans
‡Mr. Calvin Fraley
Dr. John Gregory
Mrs. Gustava M. Gooden
Dr. Alferdteen Harrison
Mrs. Mayne P. Higgins
Mr. Walter Hurns
†Ms. Judy Jefferson
Mr. Samuel Jefferson

---

*Staff Person
†Co-Chairperson
‡Student
§Deceased
‖Contributors of $2,000

Mrs. Lillian Lackey
Mrs. Lillian C. Lane
Dr. Robert List
Mrs. Flora C. McGee
Mrs. Annie M. B. McGhee
Dr. John Paul

Dr. Lelia G. Rhodes
‡Mr. Don Thigpen
Mr. Michael Weems
Dr. Lee E. Williams
Mrs. Melita W. Woodard

CENTENNIAL MURAL COMMITTEE
Mr. Lawrence A. Jones, Chairman
*Mrs. Murdell Varnado
Dr. Margaret Walker Alexander
Mr. Robert B. Cooper
Mr. F. D. Cunningham

Dr. E C Foster
Dr. Leslie B. McLemore
Dr. John A. Peoples, Jr.
Dr. Lelia G. Rhodes
Dr. Lee E. Williams

CENTENNIAL OPERA/SOUTH COMMITTEE
Dr. Dollye M. E. Robinson, Chairwoman
Dr. Margaret Walker Alexander
*Mrs. Murdell Varnado
Dr. Ben Bailey
Mrs. Rosia Crister

Miss Narah Dean
Mr. Raymond I. Johnson
Dr. Estus Smith
Mrs. Tommie Harris Stewart
Dr. Louis Stokes

CENTENNIAL PICNIC COMMITTEE
Mr. V. A. Nelson, Chairman
*Ms. Ruby Durr
Mr. Earl B. Brown
Mrs. Jeanette Collier
Mr. Willie F. Daniels
‡Ms. Deborah Davis
Mrs. Yvonne Etheredge
Mrs. Etherlene Gentry
Mr. William Gordon
Mrs. Ophelia R. Kelley
Mr. Hilliard L. Lackey

Dr. Raphael Lee
Mrs. Frances Liddell
‡Mr. A. W. McPherson
Mrs. Frances G. Morris
Dr. Walter Reed
Mr. Joseph Sampson
Mr. Elbert Smith
Mrs. Velsie L. Smith
‡Mr. Carlos Tillman
Mrs. Bessie L. Tucker
Mrs. Florene Veal

CENTENNIAL PICTURES AND ARTIFACTS COMMITTEE
Dr. T. J. Robinson, Chairman
Mr. A. A. Alexander
Mr. Earl W. Banks
Mrs. Willie D. Blackburn
Mrs. Miriam D. Johnson
Mrs. Thelma C. Hickman
Mrs. Mayne P. Higgins
Mr. Luther J. Marshall

Dr. John A. Peoples, Jr., *ex officio*
Dr. Lelia G. Rhodes
Mrs. Dee L. Kincaid-Robinson
Ms. Dorothy Dean Smith
Mr. W. A. Reed, Jr.
Mrs. Lottie W. Thornton
Dr. Lee E. Williams

Centennial Committee Members

CENTENNIAL PROCLAMATIONS COMMITTEE
Dr. T. J. Robinson, Chairman
Ms. Rubye K. Hughes
Mr. Willie Farmer
‡Mr. Calvin Fraley
Mr. Hilliard L. Lackey
Mr. Obra V. Hackett
Dr. Charles Holmes

CENTENNIAL PROGRAM COMMITTEE
Dr. Dollye M. E. Robinson, Chairwoman
*Mrs. Mabel Crushshon
Dr. Ben Bailey
Mrs. Zee A. Barron
Mrs. Willie D. Blackburn
Mr. Edward J. Fisher
Dr. Jimmie Franklin
Dr. Lelia G. Rhodes
Mrs. Tommie H. Stewart
Mrs. Lottie W. Thornton
Mrs. Aurelia N. Young

CENTENNIAL RECORDS OF PROCEEDINGS COMMITTEE
Mrs. Dee L. Kincaid-Robinson, Chairwoman
*Ms. Shirley Dianne Lowery
Dr. Anthony J. Cavell
Ms. Rubye K. Hughes
Dr. Judith Krabbe
Mrs. Flora C. McGee
Dr. Paul W. Purdy
Mrs. Pearl M. Vincent
Mr. Michael Weems
Dr. Lee E. Williams, *ex officio*

CENTENNIAL SKIT (HISTORICAL) COMMITTEE
Mr. Edward J. Fisher, Chairman
Mr. A. A. Alexander
Mrs. Bernice Bell
Ms. Doris O. Ginn
Mr. Harold J. Haughton
Mrs. Annie M. B. McGhee
Dr. Velma McLin Mitchell
*Mrs. Beatrice K. Moore
Dr. Dollye M. E. Robinson
Mr. Julius Thompson
Mrs. Aurelia N. Young

CENTENNIAL SONG FESTIVAL COMMITTEE
Dr. Dollye M. E. Robinson, Chairwoman
*Mr. John Brookins
Mr. Harold J. Haughton
Dr. Anita Jackson
Dr. Jimmie James
Mr. Raymond I. Johnson
Mrs. Gladys P. Norris
Mrs. Aurelia N. Young

CENTENNIAL SOUVENIRS AND MEMENTOES COMMITTEE
Dr. T. J. Robinson, Chairman
*Ms. Rubye K. Hughes
Mrs. Evelyn Banks
Mr. Edward S. Bishop, Sr.
Mr. William Calloway
Ms. Thelma C. Hickman
Mr. James Johnson
Mr. Hilliard L. Lackey
Dr. Paul W. Purdy

*Staff Person
†Co-Chairperson
‡Student
§Deceased
‖Contributors of $2,000

SPORTS HALL OF FAME COMMITTEE
Ms. Bobbie N. Oatis, Chairwoman
*Mr. T. B. Ellis
Mr. Allen Brown
‡Mr. Richie Cousin
Mrs. Malena W. Dow
‡Ms. Jean Farrar
‡Ms. Virginia Jackson
Dr. Robert List
Mrs. Nellie Tolliver
‡Ms. Saint Mary Topps
Mr. Calvin Williams

CENTENNIAL SYMBOL AND FLAG COMMITTEE
Mr. Obra V. Hackett, Chairman
*Mr. Lonnie C. Crosby
Mr. Willie D. Kyles
Dr. Robert List
Dr. T. J. Robinson, *ex officio*
Mrs. Pearl M. Vincent

CENTENNIAL SYMPOSIUM COMMITTEE
Dr. Oscar A. Rogers, Jr., Chairman
*Mrs. Levernis Crosby
Dr. George F. Currie
Dr. Jay T. Smith
Dr. Robert H. Smith
Dr. Cleopatra D. Thompson
Mrs. Pearl M. Vincent
Dr. Katheryn Weathersby

CENTENNIAL THEME COMMITTEE
Mr. Edwin Mullen, Chairman
Dr. E C Foster
Dr. Lelia G. Rhodes
Dr. Dollye M. E. Robinson
Dr. John A. Peoples, Jr.
Dr. Estus Smith
Mrs. Lottie W. Thornton
Dr. Lee E. Williams

CENTENNIAL TREE COMMITTEE
Mrs. Beatrice K. Moore, Chairwoman
Mr. F. D. Cunningham
Mrs. Etherlene Gentry
Mr. Peter C. Lane
Mr. Hosea Sanders
*Mr. Willie Scott
Mrs. Eva Y. Woodard

CENTENNIAL YEARBOOK COMMITTEE
Dr. George A. Johnson, Chairman
Mrs. Evelyn Banks
*Mr. Karl Griffin
Ms. Rubye K. Hughes
Mr. Eugene Jackson
Mr. A. D. Jones
Dr. Robert List
Mrs. Frankie Loving
Mrs. Flora C. McGee
Mrs. Mable Pittman
Mrs. Rose M. Portis
Dr. John A. Peoples, Jr., *ex officio*
Mrs. Dee L. Kincaid-Robinson
Mr. Bankey L. Sharma

---

*Staff Person
†Co-Chairperson
‡Student
§Deceased
‖Contributors of $2,000

APPENDIX IX

PUBLIC SCHOOLS IN JACKSON

NAMED FOR GRADUATES OR FORMER STUDENTS

DEVA LINCOLN BROWN (1881-1952) graduated from Jackson College in 1935. Began teaching in the Jackson Public Schools as first grade teacher at Jim Hill Elementary School where she taught for fifteen years and was later transferred to Reynolds Elementary School. She gave 31 years as first grade teacher in the Jackson Public Schools.

GEORGIA BEATRICE DAWSON (1902-1962) was born August 25, 1902 in Jackson, Mississippi. Her early education began at Smith Robertson. In 1928, she was appointed to the W. H. Lanier High School. She completed the teacher training program of Jackson College in 1940 and received her Bachelor of Arts degree from Tougaloo College in 1954. Miss Dawson retired from the Public School System in 1961 after completing thirty-three years of teaching.

EMMA LEE ISABLE (1882-1939) was born February 16, 1882. She attended the Bowman Public School in Vicksburg, Mississippi. She attended the Hirsch's School of Stenography Haven Institute and in 1920, the University of Chicago. She enrolled in Jackson College in 1930 and in 1934, received the Bachelor of Arts degree. Beginning in the Jackson Public Schools as a substitute during the 1918-1919 following employment in the Vicksburg Public Schools,

Mrs. Isable was appointed to teach in the Hill School on Lynch Street where she taught second and fourth grades from 1921 to 1923 and third grade from 1923 to 1936. She was transferred to the Reynolds Elementary School in 1936 and remained there until her death in 1939.

MARY STEWART JOHNSON (1871-1944) graduated 1891 from Normal Department of Jackson College. In 1935, she received the Bachelor of Arts degree. In 1920 she was employed by the Jackson Public Schools as first grade teacher of Hill School. She remained there for two years. In 1922, she was transferred to Martin School as teacher of the primary grades. Subsequently, she was assigned as first grade teacher and remained in that position for 22 years. A few days prior to the beginning of the academic school year, 1944-45, she was stricken with a fatal heart attack. She died September 8, 1944.

MARY LOTTIE WILLIAMS MORRISON (1882-1956) received the Bachelor of Arts degree from Jackson College in 1936. From 1918 to 1936, Mrs. Morrison taught eighth grade and served as assistant principal at Robertson School. From 1936 until her appointment in 1941 as principal in the Martin Elementary School, she served as teaching principal at Reynolds School. She retired from the Jackson Public Schools June 15, 1954.

SALLIE RATHER REYNOLDS (1872-1931) was born December, 1872 in Holly Springs, Mississippi five years before Natchez Seminary was founded. She attended Canton Normal, Jackson College, and Alcorn. In 1902, she was employed in the Jackson Public Schools as a teacher of the third grade at the Robertson Elementary School. Her teaching career spanned a period of twenty-five years. Reynolds was closed in 1971 as a part of a Court Order. It was reopened in August, 1972 as a Day Care Center.)

WILLIAM HOWARD WALTON (1897-1958) received the high school diploma from Jackson College in '26 and the Bachelor of Arts degree in 1927. He also obtained a Bachelor of Arts degree from Lane College in Jackson, Tennessee. He served as principal of a rural elementary school in Silver Creek, Mississippi. Subsequently, he taught social studies at Jim Hill then located on Lynch Street. When Hill was moved to its new site in 1939, he was assigned to teach science, a capacity he served in until his death.

LETTIE E. FOOTE YOUNG (1877-1944) received all of her education in Jackson. She attended Jackson College from 1895-1898 and Jackson College Normal Schools in 1915. She began teaching in the Jackson Public Schools in 1922 at the Smith Robertson School where she taught for two years before being transferred to Martin School. She was not there very long before she was reassigned to Robertson School where she taught for nine years. She completed twenty-two years of service to the Jackson Public Schools serving the nine years at Reynolds where she took a leave-of-absence from her teaching duties in 1944. She passed away July 6, 1944. Lettie Young School was closed by an administrative decision in 1969.

RETIREES

If education means the training of the intellect to perceive the truth and forming of the will to choose the good, then the retired faculty may claim with pride that the academic mission of their lives lives on in the lives of thousands of students who grew in wisdom and godliness because of their genuinely personal commitment to the teaching profession. It was undoubtedly men and women like the following: Blackburn, Willie Dobbs, 1934-1974; Clay, Ross, 1953-1974; Ellis, Tellis B., 1940-1977; Fraser, Lionel B., 1952-1967; Hall, John Edward, 1949-1977; Hall, Lillian, 1949-1974; Higgins, Mayne, 1944-1974; Jones, Lawrence, 1949-1978; Lane, Peter C., 1942-1975; Lee, Robert Edwin, 1955-1968; Lipscomb, Ernestine, 1947-1976; McAllister, Jane E., 1950-1968; McCullough, Ben J., 1950-1976; Mosley, Charles C., Sr., 1953-1973; Peterson, William, 1946-1967; Price, Bolton C., 1942-1972; Thompson, H. M., 1964-1978; Thompson, Cleopatra, 1946-1978; Turner, Maggie Little, 1946-1966; Warren, Samuel, 1962-1967; Woodard, Eva, 1947-1976; Young, Aurelia N., 1947-1977.

President Peoples had in mind when he describes the good teacher in his inaugural address: "Let it be understood that a good teacher at Jackson State College cannot be a peaceful man. He must be a man at war against the forces of ignorance and tyranny of the mind and spirit." Truly, the retired faculty at Jackson State University were the marathon torch-bearers of the truth that makes men free.

While these men and women nurtured in the students truth and goodness, men like Peter C. Lane, 1941-1975 cultivated the environment with an eye for aesthetic freshness that lent beauty to a mid-city campus. Additional staff persons to retire are: Davis, Lelia C., 1941-1953; Johnson, Ruth, 1961-1968; and Reddix, Daisy Shirley, 1940-1965. To Mrs. Daisy Shirley Reddix was left the task of publishing her husband's memoirs, *Voice Crying in the Wilderness*, that tell of his life and effort of twenty-seven years in making Jackson State the school it was from 1940-1967.

SELECTED CURRENT UNIVERSITY PUBLICATIONS

Blue and White Flash—Student Government Association Publication

Jackson State University Alumni: Newsletter—Published quarterly by Alumni Affairs Office, Hillard Lackey, Editor

Jackson State University Catalog

Jackson State University Faculty News

Jackson State University Graduate Catalog

JSU Now—Office of Publication

Jackson State University Review—Office of Faculty Research and Publications

Jacksonian—Student Government Association Publication

Scope—Office of Publication

Student Handbook

The Tiger

APPENDIX X

JACKSON STATE UNIVERSITY PUBLICATIONS

Faculty, Staff, and Students

Akponwei, Patrick S., Ph.D., *Lesions of the Central Nervous System and the Levels of Motor Functions so Affected*. Loughborough, Leicester, U.K.: University of Nottingham, 1957.

Alexander, Margaret Walker, Ph.D., *For My People*. New Haven: Yale University Press, 1942.

———, *Jubilee*. Boston: Houghton Mifflin, 1966.

———, *Prophets for a New Day*. Detroit: Broadside Press, 1970.

———, *How I Wrote Jubilee*. Chicago: Third World Press, 1972.

———, *October Journey*. Detroit: Broadside Press, 1973.

Alexander, Margaret Walker and Nikki Giovanni, *A Poetic Equation, Conversations Between Nikki Giovanni and Margaret Walker*. Washington, DC.: Howard University Press, 1974.

Barkatullah, Qazi M., Ph.D., *Islam: The Religion for Mankind*. Jackson: Hederman Brothers Press, 1972.

———, *Introduction to Educational Measurement and Evaluation*. Chicago: Cube Press, 1971.

———, *Jesus Son of Mary*. Philadelphia: Dorrence and Company, Inc., 1973.

———, *Education During the Middle Ages Under the Muslims*. Los Angeles: Crescent Publications, Inc., 1974.

———, *The Lady Mary, Ahmaditth Movement in Islam*. Washington, D.C.

Calcote, Roger, D., Ph.D., *An Application of Marginal Economics Theory to Financial Statement Analysis*. Grambling, Louisiana: Grambling College, 1975. (monograph)

Cavell, Anthony J., Ph.D., *Corpus of Belearic Inscriptions Up to the Arab Conquest.* Classical Folia.

―――――, Editor, *Jackson State Review.*

Cavell, Anthony J., Ph.D., Editor, *Jackson State University Review,* 1974-75.

Chao, Ching, Y., Ph.D., *Production Economic.* Taiwan: National Compilation Committee, 1969.

Clayton, Luana F., Farrell, H. Alfred, and Johnson, Edward S., *The Administration of a Curriculum Experiment.* Institute for Services to Education, Inc., 1974.

Covington, Matilda N. *A Brighter Tomorrow; How to Live Better in Every Area of Human Endeavor.*

Dansby, B. Baldwin, *A Brief History of Jackson College,* Jackson: Jackson College, 1953.

Dease, Ruth Roseman, *Scan-Spans.* New York: Vantage Press, 1967.

Ferris, William R. Jr., Ph.D., *Mississippi Black Folklore: A Research Bibliography and Discography.* Jackson: University Press of Mississippi, 1971.

Fletcher, Tom. *100 Years of the Negro in Show Business.* New York: Burge & Co., 1954.

Foster, E. C., D.A., *The Americana: A History.* New York: Holt, Rinehart & Winston, 1970, Textbook, Revised Edition 1975.

―――――, (Coauthor), *The New Social Studies for the Slow Learner: A Rationale for Junior High School American History Course.* American Heritage, 1969.

Foster, Velvelyn B., D.A., *The Americans: A History of the United States.* New York: Holt, Rinehart & Winston, 1970 Revised 1975.

―――――, *Living in Urban America.* New York: Holt, Rinehart & Winston, 1974.

―――――, (Coauthor) *The New Social Studies for the Slow Learner: A Rationale for Junior High School American History Courses.* American Heritage, 1969.

Gaulden, Betty W., Ph.D., *Good Ideas for Teaching mathematics.* State Department of Alabama, 1973.

Gupta, Anand K., Neelameghan, A., and Ranganathan, S. R., Editors, *Free Book Service for All: An International Survey.* Bombay, India, 1969.

Harvey, James, Ph.D., *Civil Rights During the Kennedy Administration.* Hattiesburg: University Press of Mississippi, 1971.

―――――, *Black Civil Rights During the Johnson Administration.* Hattiesburg: University Press of Mississippi, 1973.

Harvey, Maria Luisa Alvarez, Ph.D., *Cielo y Tierra en la Poesia Lirica de Manuel Altolaguirre.* University Press of Mississippi, 1972.

―――――, *Pasos Negros: Black Footsteps.* Second Year Spanish Reader in preparation.

———, *But Here You Would Have Your Black Kids*. Now in preparation.
Holly, Joyce Cheriner Thomas. *Exploring Matter & Energy*. (bibliographic listing incomplete)
Jackson, Joseph Harrison. *Unholy Shadows and Freedom's Holy Light*. Nashville: Townsend Press, 1967.
———, *Many but One;* the Ecumenics of Charity. New York: Sheed & Ward, 1964.
Additional publications include *Stare in the Night* and *The Eternal Flame*.
Kelly, J. Thomas, Ph.D., *Thorns on the Tudor Rose: Monks, Rogues, Vagabonds and Sturdy Beggars*. University Press of Mississippi, 1977.
Ladner, Joyce A., *The Death of White Sociology*. New York: Random House, 1973.
———, *Tomorrow's Tomorrow: The Black Woman*. New York: Doubleday & Co., 1971.
List, Robert N., Ph.D. *The Joyce/Ellison Connection*. Jackson: University Press of Mississippi. (In preparation).
Mercer, Walter A., *Teaching in the Desegregated School: Guide to Intergroup Relations*. New York: Vantage Press, 1971.
———, *Humanizing the Desegregated School: Guide for Teachers and Teacher Training*. New York: Vantage Press, 1975.
Meredith, James. *Three Years in Mississippi*. Bloomington: Indiana University Press, 1966.
Myers, Lena W. Ph.D., "Black Women & Self Esteem," in *Another Voice: Feminist Perspectives on Social Life & Social Science*, edited by Marcia Millman and Rosabeth Kanter. New York: Anchor/Doubleday Publishers, 1975.
Overman, Steve, Ph.D., *Students in Medieval Times and Today*. Portland, Maine: J. Weston Walch, 1976. (Work text)
Phillips, Ivory, Ph.D., *White Racism and Black Powerlessness: Past, Present and Future*.
Pittman, Mabel Hall, Ph.D., (Coauthor), *Outlooks Through Literature*. America Reads Series. Scott Foresman & Company. 1973.
Farrell, Edmund J.; Pierce, James L.; Pittman, Mable H.; and Wood, Kerry M. *Traits & Topics: An Anthology of Short Stories*. Fountainhead Series. Glenview, IL: Scott, Foresman & Company, 1975.
———, *Comment: An Anthology in Prose*. Fountainhead Series. Glenview, Illinois: Scott Foresman & company, 1976.
———, *Upstate/Downstage: A Theater Festival*. Fountainhead Series. Glenview, Illinois: Scott, Foresman & Company, 1976.
Ramsey, Leroy, L., *The Trial and the Fire*. New York: Exposition Press, 1967.
Reddix, Jacob L., *A Voice Crying in the Wilderness, the Memoirs of Jacob L. Reddix*. Jackson: University Press of Mississippi, 1974.

Rogers, Oscar, Ed.D. *My Mother Cooked My Way Through Harvard With These Creole Recipes.* Jackson: University Press of Mississippi, 1972.

Simmons, James W. *Thoughts From the Mind.* New York: Exposition Press, 1967.

_____. *Poetical and Philosophical Expressions.* New York: Exposition Press, 1971.

_____. *Relationship of Esteem Values With Intelligence Quotient and Grade Point Average.* San Francisco, California: R. & W. Research Associates, January, 1977.

Thompson, Cleopatra D., Ed.D., *The History of the Mississippi Teachers Association.* Washington, N.E.A. Teachers Right, 1973.

Thompson, Julius Eric, Ph.D., *Hopes Tied Up in Dreams.* Philadelphia: Dorrance & Co., 1970.

_____. *Blues Said: Walk On.* (bibliographic information incomplete), April 1977.

Thumchai, Rawiwan, Ed. D., *Arithmetic Textbook, Grades 1-4.*

_____, *How to Help Children Learn Mathematics.*

_____, *Health Education in High School.*

_____, *The Evaluation of Entrance Examination.* Thailand: University in Thailand.

Warren, Samuel E., *The Teacher and Other Poems.* Houston, Texas, 1953.

Williams-Burns, Winona W., Ph.D. *Art of Black Africa.* Portland, Maine: J. Weston Welch.

_____, *Themes in Black American Art.* Portland, Maine: J. Weston Welch, Summer 1978. (Slide and Tape Commentary)

_____, *Selection Criteria for Records, Filmstrips and Films for Young Children.*

Williams, Lee E. & Williams, Lee E., II. *Anatomy of Four Race Riots.* Hattiesburg: University Press of Mississippi, 1972.

NOTES

Notes For Chapter I

1. Dunbar Rowland, *History of Mississippi: The Heart of the South* (Chicago: S. J. Clark Co., 1925) II, 469.
2. American Baptist Home Mission Society Annual Report 1875 p. 12.
3. *Mississippi Journal of Constitutional Convention, 1865* (Jackson: E. M. Yerger State Printers, 1865), 148.
4. *Journal of the Proceedings in the Constitutional Convention of the State Of Mississippi, 1866* (E. Stafford Printers), 33-34, *Jackson Daily Clarion*, April 8, 1868.
5. Stuart G. Noble, *Forty Years of Public Schools in Mississippi, with Special Reference to the Education of the Negro.* (New York: Teachers College, Columbia University, 1918), 28-32, 43.
6. *Vicksburg Daily Times*, October 28, 1869.
7. Julius Kendel, "Reconstruction in Lafayette County," *PMHS* (XIII), 258.
8. *Hinds County Gazette*, October 12, 1870.
9. Patrick H. Thompson, *The History of Negro Baptists in Mississippi* (Jackson, Mississippi: W. H. Bailey Printing Co., 1898), 49.
10. *Ibid.*, 60.
11. *Ibid.* 607.
12. *Ibid.* 61.
13. *Ibid.*, 62.
14. *Ibid.*, 62-65.
15. *Ibid.*, 78.
16. *Ibid.*, 86-87.
17. *Ibid.*, 84.
18. *Ibid.*, 108-11.
19. *Ibid.*, 116-24.
20. *Ibid.*, 135.
21. *Ibid.*, 136, 142.
22. *Ibid.*, 140.
23. The Consolidated American Baptist Missionary Convention to the Mississippi Baptist Convention, Brooklyn, July 22, 1875, quoted in *Ibid.*, 19.

Notes For Chapter II

1. American Baptist Home Mission Society Report, September 13, 1877.
2. Excerpt from the First Report of the Supervisory Surgeon General of the Marine Hospital Service for the fiscal year 1872, p. 2.
3. A letter to Nathan Bishop, J. B. Hoyt, and others, Finance Committee of the American Baptist Home Mission Society, Jersey City, October 9, 1875.
4. American Baptist Home Mission Society, Minutes, January 15, 1876.
5. The Memorial of the American Bap-

tist Home Mission Society to the Senate and House of Representatives of the United States in Congress, Assembled April 3, 1876, praying for legislation authorizing the Secretary of the Treasury to confirm to said Society the sale of the Marine Hospital Building at Natchez, MS. April 5, 1876, p. 2.

6. A letter from Justin Morrill, Chairman of the Committee of Public Building and Grounds, April 17, 1876, page 2.

7. Ibid.

8. *U. S. Statue at Large of the U. S. of America from December 1875 to March 1877* Vol. XIX, Washington Government Printing Office 1877, p. 202.

9. Ibid.

10. Ibid.

11. American Baptist Home Mission Society Reports, 1876.

12. Thompson, *The History of Negro Baptists in Mississippi*, 142.

13. Dansby, *Brief History of Jackson College*, 2-3.

14. *The First Half Century of Madison University, 1819-1869, or the Jubilee Volume containing sketches of Eleven Hundred Living and Deceased Alumni with Fifteen portraits of Founders, Presidents and Patrons.* (New York: Sheldon & Co., 1872), 93, 293.

15. American Baptist Home Mission Society Reports, Sept. 13, 1877.

16. *The Journal of Negro History* (Washington, D.C.: The Association for the Study of Negro Life and History, 1969), 237-38; William J. Simmons, *Men of Mark: Eminent Progressive and Rising* (New York: Arno Press and New York Times Reprint, 1968; Cleveland, Ohio; Geo M. Rewell & Co., 1887), 474-80.

17. Simmons, *Men of Mark*, 474-80.

18. Ibid., 476.

19. Interview with Dr. B. B. Dansby who knew Page personally.

20. Logan, *Howard University*, 37.

21. *Natchez Seminary Catalogue, 1877*, 4.

22. American Baptist Home Mission Society, Board Minutes December 1879.

23. *Natchez Catalogue, 1879-80*.

24. American Baptist Home Mission Society Board Minutes December 1880.

25. *Jackson College Catalog, 1903-04*, 27.

26. *Natchez Seminary Catalogue, 1882-83*, 15-16.

27. Charles Ayer, "Natchez Seminary for Freedmen," *Natchez Post*, 1877.

28. *Catalogue of the Natchez Seminary: one of the Eight Institutions founded and sustained by the American Baptist Home Mission Society... Natchez, Mississippi, 1879-80, 11*.

29. Ibid., 10.

30. Ibid., 10-11.

31. Natchez Seminary Catalog 1878-79, p. 3.

32. Report of the American Baptist Home Mission Society Educational Committee Report, October 8, 1878

33. Baptist Signal Circular, 1878; American Baptist Home Mission Society Reports, 1878.

34. Annual Report of the Board, American Baptist Home Mission Society, 1883, p. 47.

35. American Baptist Home Mission Society Board Minutes Handwritten, December 11, 1882, pp. 352, 362.

36. American Baptist Home Mission Society, Board Minutes, February 12, 1883, p. 386.

37. American Baptist Home Mission Society Board Minutes, Finance Committee, October 24, 1884, p. 507, April 26, 1883, p. 431.

38. American Baptist Home Mission Society Board Minutes, Finance Committee, July 30, 1884

39. Annual Report, 1884.

40. Minutes of the American Baptist Home Minutes of the American Baptist Home Mission Society, January 8, 1883, October 8, 1883.

41. Annual Report of the Board, American Baptist Home Mission Society, 1883; Mary C. Reynolds, *Baptist Missionary Pioneers Among Negroes*, (New York: NY) p. 86.

42. Dansby, *Brief History of Jackson College*, 27-28.

43. Thompson, The History of Negro Baptists in Mississippi, 31-33.

44. Board Minutes, July 14, 1884.

45. Dansby, *Brief History of Jackson College*, 28; Interview with Dr. B. Baldwin Dansby, August 1971.

46. *Jackson College Catalog, 1890-91*, 10.

47. Thompson, *The History of Negro Baptists in Mississippi*, 229.

48. *Jackson College Catalogue, 1890-91*, 11, 13.

49. *Jackson College Catalogue, 1893-94*, 8-9.

50. Ibid., 13.

51. *Jackson College Catalogue, 1890-91, 15*.

52. *Jackson College Catalogue, 1890-91,* 13-14.
53. Thompson, *The History of Negro Baptists in Mississippi,* 12-13.
54. *Ibid.,* 12.
55. Thompson, *The History of Negro Baptists in Mississippi,* 12.
56. *Jackson College Catalogue, 1887-88,* 2-3.
57. *Jackson College Catalogue, 1892,* 2.
58. Thompson, *The History of Negro Baptists in Mississippi,* 13.
59. *Richmond Theological General Catalog,* "Theological4', 1892, 35.
60. *Jackson College Catalogue, 1930-31,* 72.
61. *Jackson College Catalogue,* 1893–94, 90.
62. *Jackson College Catalogue, 1889-90.*
63. *Jackson College Catalogue, 1886,* 16.
64. *Natchez Seminary Catalogue, 1897-98,* 16.
65. *Jackson College Catalogue, 1886,* 16.
66. *Jackson College Catalogue, 1891-92,* 16.

Notes For Chapter III

1. Dansby, *Brief History of Jackson College,* 31.
2. Interview with Dr. B. B. Dansby, August 1971.
3. Reynolds, *Baptist Missionary Pioneers Among Negroes,* 91.
4. Dansby, *Brief History of Jackson College,* 34.
5. American Baptist Home Mission Society Board Minutes, Education Committee's Report July 15, 1901, Ledger p. 304.
6. American Baptist Home Mission Society Board Minutes, August 12, 1902.
7. *Jackson College Catalogue, 1901-02,* 10; *Jackson College Catalogue, 1902-03,* 9.
8. Interview with Dr. B. B. Dansby, June 1970.
9. Reynolds, *Baptist Missionary Pioneers Among Negroes,* 92.
10. Deed recorded, Hinds County, State of Mississippi, 28th day of February 1903, Book 39, p. 276.
11. Reynolds, *Baptist Missionary Pioneers Among Negroes,* 92.
12. Deed recorded, Hinds County State...of Mississippi 28th day of February 1903, Deed Book.
13. Interview with Miss F. O. Alexander, February 15, 1872; Miss Alexander graduated from Jackson College in 1912.
14. Reynolds, *Baptist Missionary Pioneers Among Negroes,* 91.
15. American Baptist Home Mission Society, Minutes of the Finance Committee, February 1903.
16. *Ibid.,* March 1903.
17. *Jackson College Catalogue, 1903-04,* 21.
18. Annual Report of the Board, 1904, 130.
19. American Baptist Home Mission Society, Board Minutes, March 11, 1907.
20. *Jackson College Catalogue,* 1895–96, 4.
21. Interview with Dr. B. B. Dansby.
22. Thompson, *The History of Negro Baptists in Mississippi,* 346.
23. *Ibid,* 347.
24. *Ibid,* 348-49.
25. *Ibid,* 350.
26. *Jackson College Catalogue, 1897-98,* 20.
27. Thompson, *The History of Negro Baptists in Mississippi,* 356.
28. *Jackson College Catalogue, 1899-1900,* 3.
29. *Ibid.,* 22
30. Dansby, *Brief History of Jackson College,* 41.
31. *Jackson College Catalogue, 1906-07,* 20.
32. Interview with Dr. B. B. Dansby.
33. *Jackson College Catalogue, 1910-11,* 24.

Notes For Chapter IV

1. American Baptist Home Mission Society Minutes, May 8, 1911.
2. Dansby, *Brief History of Jackson College,* 58.
3. American Baptist Home MIssion Society, Minutes of the Board Meeting, February 1911.
4. *Ibid.*

Notes for Chapter V

5. American Baptist Home Mission Society, Minutes of the Board Meeting, May 8, 1911.
6. *Jackson College Catalogue, 1911–12*, unpaged.
7. *Jackson College Catalogue, 1912–13*, 3.
8. *Jackson College Catalogue 1913–14*, 39.
9. Interview with Dr. B. B. Dansby.
10. Dansby, *Brief History of Jackson College*, 63.
11. *Jackson College Catalogue, June 1927*, 14.
12. Interview with Annie Mae Brown McGhee.
13. *Jackson College Catalogue, 1913–14*, 11.
14. *Jackson College Catalogue, 1920–21*, 7.
15. Zachary T. Hubert to Dr. Wallace Buttrick, president of the General Education Board, June 19, 1919; Hubert to Dr. George R. Hovey, superintendent of education, New York, American Baptist Home Mission Society's representative for Jacksgn College, June 28, 1919.
16. Minutes of the Board of Trustees, Jackson College, March 8, 1923.
17. Correspondence to President Hubert from the Secretary of Education, March 5, 1925.
18. Correspondence from President Zachary T. Hubert.
19. Schedule amount of salaries, etc., contributed to Jackson College from the American Baptist Home Mission Society sent to Dr. B. B. Dansby from H. Kummann, Assistant Treasurer, American Baptist Home Mission Society, February 28, 1947.
20. *Jackson College Catalogue*, 1925–26, 21.
21. Cited in Jackson College's Official College Song.
22. Dansby interview.
23. *The Jacksonian*, 1925, unpaged.
24. *The Jacksonian* Foreword.
25. *Jackson College Catalogue, 1895–1896*, 17.
26. *Jackson College Catalogue*, 1912–13.
27. *Jackson College Catalogue, 1918–1919*, 4.
28. Interview, E. W. Banks, January 1, 1976, Peoples Funeral Home.
29. American Baptist Home Mission Society, Minutes, Committee on Education September 19, 1927.
30. *Jackson College Bulletin*, vol. 19, no. 1. (August 1938), 5–6.
31. Dansby, *Brief History of Jackson College*, 86.

Notes For Chapter V

1. American Baptist Home Mission Society, Committee on Education, September 19, 1927.
2. ABHMS Board Minutes, October 10, 1927. (As recommended by the Board of Trustees of Jackson College.)
3. *Ibid.*, 97.
4. *Ibid*, 98.
5. Dr. George Hovey's response of August 24, 1928 to Professor O. A. Combs' letter regarding non-appointment.
6. Correspondence B. B. Dansby, November 26, 1929.
7. William Tyler to Dr. George Hovey, secretary of education, August 10, 1929.
8. N. C. Newbold Report in Committee on Teacher Training for Negro Students in Mississippi, to Dr. George Hovey, secretary of education, New York, N.Y., January 4, 1930, p. 1; hereinafter cited as Newbold Report.
9. Dr. George R. Hovey to N. C. Newbold, superintendent of public instruction, Raleigh, N.C., January 9, 1930.
10. Newbold Report, 1.
11. Dansby, *Brief History of Jackson College*, 100.
12. *Ibid.*, 110.
13. *Jackson State Catalogue, 1928–29*, 11.
14. *Jackson State College Catalogue, 1929–30*, 9–10.
15. Interview with Dr. Dansby.
16. Dansby, *Brief History of Jackson College*, 107.
17. Board Minutes Committee on Education, January 16, 1933.
18. Typewritten transcript, interview with Charlotte Capers, David Watts, Mississippi Department of Archives and History, and Paige Ogden.
19. Interview with Attorney Latting, Memphis, Tennessee, February 10, 1972.

20. Interview with President Dansby.
21. Dr. B. B. Dansby to Dr. Frank Padelford, executive secretary, Board of Education, Northern Baptist Convention, January 6, 1936.
22. B. B. Dansby to Dr. Frank Padelford, March 31, 1936.
23. W. F. Bond to Dr. Frank Padelford, April 9, 1936.
24. P. H. Easom, "The Greatest Educational Need in Mississippi Today" Mississippi Educational Journal, XVI. No. 4, (January, 1940), 78-79.
25. B. B. Dansby to Dr. Frank Padelford, March 30, 1938.
26. See appendix.
27. Minutes, Finance Committee, Board of Managers, American Baptist Home Mission Society, June 20, 1938.
28. *Ibid.*
29. Interview with B. B. Dansby.
30. Dansby, *Brief History of Jackson College*, 134.
31. *Ibid.*, 136-137.
32. E. E. Thrash, executive secretary and director, Board of Trustees of State Institutions of Higher Learning, State of Mississippi.
33. John A. Peoples, Jr., Memorial Address, College Hill Missionary Baptist Church, November 22, 1975.
34. *Ibid.*

Notes For Chapter VI

1. Interview with President Reddix, June 1971.
2. Jacob L. Reddix, *A Voice Crying in the Wilderness* (Jackson, Miss.: University Press of Mississippi, 1974), 132-33.
3. *Ibid.*, 136.
4. Charles H. Wilson, *Education for Negroes in Mississippi Since 1910* (Boston: Mender Publ. Co., 1947), 292.
5. Mabel Carney, "Doctoral Dissertations and Projects Relating to the Education of Negroes," *The Advanced School Digest*, VII no. 3. (February 1942), 1.
6. Warranty deed signed by David H. Sims, president of the Board of Trustees, J. P. Campbell, and James A. Thornton, secretary of the Board of Trustees, notorized 29th day of April, 1963 as recorded in Book 1424, p. 377.
7. P. H. Easom and J. A. Travis, "Status of Negro Schools in Mississippi, 1939" *Mississippi Educational Journal*, XVII, No. 3, (December, 1940), 49.
8. *Jackson College for Negro Teachers Bulletin, 1949-50*, 9.
9. Dean of Instruction Report, 1950-51.
10. *Ibid.*
11. *Jackson State College Catalog, 1951-53*, 118-19, 125-26.
12. *Ibid.*, 96, 131-32.
13. *Ibid.*, 51, 56-57, 103.
14. *Jackson College Bulletin, 1953-55*, 9-10.
15. Role and Scope Study of Jackson State College, 1966. Introduction Dean H. T. Sampson.
16. Mississippi Laws, 1956, Chapter 293-94, p. 371; Minutes of the Board of Trustees, February 16, 1956, p. 4.
17. *The Annual Report*, Executive Dean, 1961, p. 6.
18. *Jackson State College—Division of Graduate Studies Bulletin* (Jackson Mississippi: Jackson State College, 1964), 4.
19. *Jackson College Bulletin, 1955-57*, 159-60.
20. Minutes of the Board of Trustees, December 17, 1959, p. 2.
21. *Jackson State College Bulletin, 1961-63*, 10-11.
22. John E. Brewton, "Higher Education in Mississippi: Digest of the Survey Report, 1954," 43, 56-59.
23. Mississippi Study of Higher Education, 1945, p. 84.
24. *Ibid.*, 90.
25. Dansby, *Brief History of Jackson College*, 96.
26. Willie Dobbs Blackburn, Dedication of the H. T. Sampson Library, Ninety-fourth Founders' Day Convocation, Jackson State College, Oct. 25, 1973.
27. Cleopatra Davenport Thompson, "The Jackson State College Graduate in American Society, A Follow-up Study of 306 Students, 1944-1953"-unpublished thesis, presented to the faculty of the graduate

school of Cornell University for the Degree of Doctor of Education, September 1930.
28. *Ibid.*, 3, 150-51.
29. Elaine Paige Witty, "A Proposed Master's Degree Program in Elementary Education at Jackson (Mississippi) State College," George Peabody College for Teachers, (June 1965), 158.
30. *Ibid.*, 3, 149.
31. Reddix, *A Voice Crying in the Wilderness*, 143-144.
32. *Ibid.*, 163-64.

Notes for Chapter VII

1. President Peoples' Inaugural Address, March 8, 1968.
2. *Ibid.*
3. William W. Scranton. Chairman. Report of the President's Commission on Campus Unrest, (New York: Discus Books/Published By Avon, 1977) 417-436
4. *Ibid.*, 432.

Data were obtained via interviews with President Peoples, administration, faculty, students, alumni, examination and analysis of official university publications, and author's emperical observations and research as a member of the faculty since 1945.

INDEX

The index is necessarily selective. An individual listing of Boards of Trustees, faculty, administrators, staff, distinguished alumni, and Centennial Committees would result in such an interminably long index that its usefulness would be considerably diminished.

The appendices include: Documentary and Legal Records; Proclamations of the Centennial Celebration; listing of Faculty and Staff during Reddix's Final Tenure in Office; listing of Faculty and Staff under Dr. John A. Peoples, Jr.; Jackson State University Alumni; Jackson State University Athletics; Cofounders, Board of Trustees and Administrators; Centennial Committee Members; Public Schools in Jackson Named for Graduates; and Jackson State University Faculty Publications.

The listing of class presidents and deans reflects a few inaccuracies, but are cited from the most accessible sources of information.

Academic Courses (curricula, early); 23, 24, 29-31, 44-46, 55. *See also* respective section

Academic Faculty (Reddix, 254, Peoples 262)

Academic Vice President—Establishment of office, 155

Act of Congress incorporating Jackson College 1890 (See Appendix Legal Documents) 236-240

Advanced Institutional Development Program (AIDP); goals of, 182-83; career programs, 183-84; Office of Publications, 185; Office of Institutional Research and Planning, 185-86; University Industry Cluster, 186-87; Criminal Justtice and Correctional Services Program, 188

Agricultural program, 55-56

Alexander, A. A., 195, 213, 214

Alexander, Florence Octavia, 49, 54, 70, 83, 93, 106-107, 115, 139, 140
Alexander, Margaret Walker, 132, 140, 141, 144, 171-74, 175, 199
Alexander, Mildred, 103
Alexander, Will W., 103
Allen, W. Clyde, 54
Allied Health Professions, 163
Alma mater. See "Jackson Fair"
Almore, Aletha, viii
Alumni. See Jackson State University alumni
Alumni Association. See Jackson State University Alumni Association
"Alumnus of the Year," 214, 304-305
Ambrose, Theodore, 68
American Baptist Home Mission Society: enters field of black education, 3-4; seeks school site, 10-11; collaborates with Baptist Missionary Convention in founding school for freedmen, 12; buys Marine Hospital, Natchez, 15-18; original mission of, 18; opens Natchez Seminary, 18-19; relocates school, 25; withdraws support, 86-87
American Church Institute for Negroes, 78
Anderson, J., Jr., 42
Anderson, Ruth W., 54
Appropriations (State), 165-166
Archer, Stevenson, 10-11
Ardoyno, Delores, 175
Asheim, Lester, 124
Athletics, 68-69, 135-36, 192-98
Ayer, President Charles: educational background of, 18; as head of Natchez Seminary, 18-19; moves school to Jackson, 26-28; salary of, 27; curriculum under, 29-31; results of administration, 33; resignation of, 33; Ayer Hall named for, 40; mentioned, xiv, 20, 25, 32, 34, 40, 46, 107
Ayer, E. A., 28, 107
Ayer, Mrs. Charles, 20, 26, 27-28, 107

Baham, C. A., 188
Bailey, Ben, 175
Bailey, Thomas H., 43
Band. See Jackson State University Marching Band

Banks, Earl W., 68, 73, 93, 195
Baptist Messenger, 33, 70
Baptist Missionary Association Convention: organizational meeting, 6-8; H. P. Jacobs elected president of, 7; first annual convention, 7-8; seeks to found school for training of ministers and teachers, 8; charge to ministers, 8-9; proposes site for school, 9-11; financial problems of, 11-13. *See also* American Baptist Home Mission Society
Barlow, W. W. J., 82
Barnes, C. L., 92, 96
Barrett, Ella M. (Mrs. Luther), 37, 41
Barrett, President Luther G.: appointed president of Jackson College, 34; educational background of, 34; seeks relocation of college, 35-39; Barrett Hall named for, 40; expands curriculum, 43-46; resigns from college, 47-48; mentioned, xiv, 33, 40, 46, 50, 52, 70
Barron, E. M., 105
Barron, Zee Anderson, 73, 105, 207
Barton, Nathan B., 43
Battle, A. V., 116
Baugh, Atha, vii
Bell, Bernice, viii
Bell, Leon, 140
Benton, Barbara Zenobia, 84
Berry, George, 82
Betts, Velena W., 85, 207
Bible Institutes, 73
Bicentennial (U. S.), xvi, 198
Bicentennial Campus, 198-200
Bingham, Haskell, 294, 298
Bishop, Edward S., 195, 214
Black, John M., 214
Black, Moses, 6, 11
Black and Tan Convention, 5, 8
Blackburn, Benjamin A., 198
Blackburn, W. W., 93, 96
Blackburn, Willie Dobbs, 105, 116, 131, 141
Black Studies, 171-74
Blanks, Augustus, 154
Blodgett, John T., 43
Blue and White Flash, 137, 203
Board of Trustees, x, 193, 292
Bolton, Horace, 69

Bolton, Roy, 68
Bond, W. F., 85, 89, 91, 92, 93, 94, 96
Bontemps, Arna, 132, 144
Boothe, Joe, 68
Braddy, Robert, 198
Bragg, Jubie B., 52
Brazille, Robert, 195
Brown, Benjamin, 138-39
Brown, Samuel W., 42, 43
Brown, Sterling A., 131
Brown, T. B., 195, 212
Bryant, Emma O., 52
Buchanan, C. A., 42
Buck, John T., 43
Buffkin, Archie, 212
Burns, Emmett, 217-18
Burroughs, Margaret G., 173
Burrows, Vinie, 173
Buttrick, Wallace, 59
Byrne, Tony, 200

Campbell College, 78, 79, 108
Campbell, J. A. P., 25, 108
Campus Unrest, 137-39, 176-80
Carnegie Foundation, 162
Catchings, Troy, 277, 302
Casey, Hubert D., 40
Cates, Ed, 178-79
Cavell, Anthony, 204
Centennial, xiii, 200-206, 217-18
Centennial Committee Members, 300-316
Center for Urban Affairs, 187
Chapman, John H., 43
Chivers, E. E., 40
Christmas, J. B., 43
Clark, Bessie, 52
Clark, E. Roger, 132
Clark, Robert G., 195, 211-12, 214
Clark, W. W., 140
Clayton, Luana Franklin, 132
Clemons, Harvey A., 54
Clubs, *See* student activities
Coates, J. H., 93, 96
Coates, Patricia, 204
Cobb, Bessie C., 52
Cochran, Thad, 201-203
Coleman, Alvin, 136-194, 198
Coleman, Ancilla, viii
Coleman, Fonzie, 177

Colegate-Rochester Divinity School, vii
College Hill Baptist Church, 41
Collins, Sylvester, 198
Combs, Oswell A., 54, 78
Committee of Eighty-two, 192
Conservatory of Music, 62-63, 64
Conyers, John, Jr., 171
Corporate Board of Trustees, 92-93, 291-2
Courtney, Beulah, 54
Courtney, Howard, 69
Covington, Paul E., 196-97, 198
Crompton, Helen G., 52
Crosby, Lonnie, 204
Curriculum, 23-24, 29-33, 43-46, 104, 113-21
Currie, George F., 156-158
Curtis, Florence, 85
Custard, C. R., 42

Danner, Margaret, 173
Dansby, President Budey Baldwin: appointed dean of men, 52; appointed president of Jackson College, 75; educational background of, 75-76; initiates extension programs, 76-77; inherits debt, 77; cricitism of, 78; financial difficulties of, 80-82, 86-93, 98; introduces quarter system, 83-84; retires, 99; death of, 99-100; mentioned, xiv, 55-56, 74, 85, 96-98, 105, 132, 135, 141, 143
Dansby, Mammie Granderson (Mrs. B. B.), 92, 101
Davis, Ossie, 172
Davis, Russell C., 178, 200
Davis, Tuwaine, 177
Davis, William W., 132
Declaration of Independence, xvii
Dee, Ruby, 172
Depression. *See* Great Depression
Development Foundation, 192
Diamond Jubilee, 131-32
Diggs, James J., 28
Dixon, John W., 93, 96, 214, 304
Doctorates, holders of, 209-10
Documents. *See* Legal Documents
Dodson, Owen, 132
Dorr, Donald, 175
Drake, Anetta, 37-38
Drake, St. Clair, 144, 171, 172

DuBois, William Edward Burghart, 50, 172
Easom, P. H., 88, 94-95, 113, 116
Edwards, Necie E., 54
Elementary and Secondary Education Act (ESEA), 125
Ellis, Tellis B., 105, 135-36, 146, 194, 195, 198
Embly, Rose. *See* McCoy, Rose Embly
Engles, Bernice, 148
Enrollment, *See* student enrollment
Epps, Martin, 198
Evans, Gloria Buchanan, 132, 145
Evans, James C., 132
Evans, Mari, 174
Evans, S. R., 143
Everett, Frances, 39
Evers, Charles, 177

Faculties, *see* appendix
Faculty Senate, 158, 201
Farish Street Baptist Church, 140
Farm Security Administration, 103
Fighting Parsons, 34
Finch, Brenda, 197
Finch, The Honorable Cliff, 200
Ford, Ola Tatum, 132
Ford Foundation, 125, 132, 162
Ford, Helen, 192
Foreign Students, 214-15
Founders Day: Golden Anniversary, 72; Diamond Jubilee, 131-32; Centennial Celebration, 200-06
Fraser, Lionel B., 123, 140
Fraternities, 189
Frederick Hall Music Center, 167, 168
Freedmen's Bank, 12-13, 18
Freedmen's Bureau, 3, 6, 12
Freeman, Maude Fagain, 215
Frisby, C. W., 82
Fugitive Slave Law, 7
Fulgham, F. L., 43
Funches, DeLars, 123, 295

Gaithright, T. S., 6
Gaston, Mrs. Fred A., ix
George, Henrene, vii
Gibbs, Phillip, 177
Gilliam, Joe, 136, 194, 198

Gillian, Raymond, 195
Giovanni, Nikki, 173-74
Glover, M. G., 69
Goitein, David, 132
Gooden, Gustava M., 63, 64, 214, 304
Gorden, W. C., 196, 198
Gorum, Wendell, 204
Gowdy, 38-39
Graduate School: establishment of 152; deans, 293
Graduate Studies, 110, 119, 23, 129, 154-55
Great Depression, 78, 207
Green, Ethel, 198-99
Green, James Earl, 177
Green, Stephen, 43
Greene, Percy, 68, 69
Greene, Rollin P., 132
Greenfield, Wilbert, 156
Greer, C. A., 93, 96
Gregory, John M., 25
Griffin, Rosie, viii
Griffin, Rubye, viii
Griffin, William E., 54
Grisham, Milton H., 103
Grochowska, Clara, viii, 204
Gunther, R. B., 96

Hackett, Obra V., Director of Office of Development, 277, 279, 302, 316
Haley, Alex, 171
Hall, Frederick D., 62, 63, 64, 203
Hardaway, A. H., 82
Hardy, Joseph D., 105, 116
Harrison, Alferdteen, 199
Harrison, Robert W., 181
Harvey, Maria Luisa Alvarez, 192
Hastie, William H., 132
Hathaway, Frank R., 36
Haughton, Harold, 199
Hayden, Robert, 132
Hayes, Charles, 144
Hederman, Tom, 98
Henderson, A. C., 145
Henderson, J. H., 31
Henry T. Sampson Library, 130-31, 168-9
Heslip, Jesse S., 54
Higgins, Commodore Dewey, 64, 73, 195, 207

Higgins, W. H., 42, 43, 195
Hightower, W. H., 42
Hill, Robert, 196, 198
Hilliard, Elbert, vii
Hilt, Zack, 103
Holloway, Dennis, 212
Home Mission Society. *See* American Baptist Home Mission Society
Hovey, George, 60, 78-82
Howard, O. O., 19
Howe, William, 15
Hubert, Giles, 195
Hubert, Marietta E., 52, 54
Hubert, President Zachary T.: appointed president of Jackson College, 51; educational background of, 51; faculty under, 52-55; upgrades curriculum, 53, 55-58; expands physical plant, 58-61; criticism of, 73; resigns, 74; mentioned, xiv, 64, 68, 71, 72, 75, 78
Hubert, Z. T., Jr., 69
Hudson, Richie A., 69, 70, 73
Hughes, Langston, 132
Hunter, Charlayne, 174
Hutchins, Edna M., 52-53
Hutson, Jean Blackwell, 172
Hutton, James Buchanan, 48
Hutton, Margaret, vii

Illinois Central Railroad, 39
Institute for the Study of History, Life and Culture of Black People, 171-74
Institutional Reaffirmation of Accreditation, 180-182
"Iron Thirteen," 68-69

Jackson, Andrew, 26
Jackson, Battle of, 27
Jackson, Eugene, 199
Jackson, Joseph, 73
Jackson, Juanita G., 105
Jackson, Maude Alexander, 73
Jackson, Preston J., 53
Jackson College: founding of, 25-27, first faculty, 27-28; curriculum of, 29-31; relocation of, 35-39; black control of, 41-43; reorganization of curricula, 43-46; program of studies upgraded, 55; baccalaureate program, 57-58; student regulations (c. 1926), 71-72; financial problems of, 77-93; 1933 budget, 86-87; changes name to Mississippi Negro Training School, 103. *See also* Natchez Seminary
Jackson College for Negro Teachers, 110-21, 135. *See also* Mississippi Negro Training School; Jackson State College
"Jackson Fair," 65, 203, 206
Jacksonian, 69-70, 132
Jackson State College, xviii, 121, 131-32, 135. *See also* Jackson State University
Jackson State Review, 174
Jackson State University: purpose of, xvii; "founding father" of, 8; evolution of name, 134-35; academic program under Peoples, 151-55; gains university status, 155; administrative reorganization of, 155-58; Black Studies at, 171-74; and Opera/South, 175-76; 1970 riots at, 176-80; as Bicentennial campus, 198-200; centennial of, 200-206; alumni of, 206-14; foreign students at, 214-15; mission of, 216-17
Jackson State University alumni, 206-14 320
Jackson State University Alumni Association, 71, 213-14
Jackson State University Industry Cluster, 186-87
Jackson State University Marching Band, 176
Jackson State University Media Center, 169-71
Jacobs, H. P.: first elected president of Baptist Missionary Convention, 7; life of, 7; attends Black and Tan Convention, 8; serves in Mississippi Legislature, 8; addresses Baptist Convention, 8-9; elected secretary of convention, 13; mentioned, 6-14
James, Leonard, 105
Jeer, 28-29
Jobe, E. R., 214
John F. Slater Fund, 32
Johnson, Amos M., 42, 43
Johnson, Climmie, 177
Johnson, Florence E., 39
Johnson, George A., 156
Johnson, Henry, 68

336 Index

Johnson, Hermel, 140, 141
Johnson, Horace, 68
Johnson, Miriam Dansby, 101, 106
Johnson, The Honorable Paul B., Jr., 167
Johnson, The Honorable Paul B., Sr., 98, 103, 104, 115
Johnson, Raymond I., 199
Jones, E. B., 42
Jones, Harry, 46, 212
Jones, Lawrence A., 172
Jones, Samuel, 204
Jones, Wede, 212, 215
Jordan, June, 173-74
JSU Now, 203
Julius Rosenwald Fund, 60, 102, 103, 104, 105, 127

Kaiser, Ernest, 172
Kelly, Tom, 178
Kempton, Alvan A., 41
Kendrick, Bennie, viii
Kenter, Leroy, 177
King, Vera I., 73
King, Wyla, 212
King Solomon Baptist Church, 6, 8, 13
Kirksey, James, 55
Klay Industrial Mission, 46
Krabbe, Judith, 174
Kuhlman, A. F., 130

Lackey, Hilliard L., 203, 213, 214
Laevell, Halvert O., 103
Latham, Etta L., 52
Latham, M. J., 48
Latham, William J., 71
Latting, Augustus A., 91-92
Lawrence, Joyce Whitsitt. *See* Wangara, Malaika Ayo
Lawson, V. V., 69
Legal Documents, 224-246
Lewis, Curties Mary viii
Lewis, Jesse C., 158
Liberal Arts Program, 56, 116, 118-19, 123, 129
Library, 22, 30, 40, 43, 59, 80, 84-85, 126-30. *See* Henry T. Sampson Library
Lincoln, C. Eric, 171
Lipscomb, Ernestine Anthony, 127, 169, 172

List, Victoria, viii
Literary Arts Festival, 131
Loach, Annie M., 49
Logan, Rayford, 172
Lovelace, Ariel M., 105
Lovett, Florence S., 53
Lowery, William Tyndal, 40
Lutkin, P. K., 93, 96
Lyells, Rubye Stutts, 126
Lynch, Street John R., 120, 137-38, 178

McAllister, Jane Ellen, 106-108, 123, 125-26, 139
McAllister, Robert, 27, 45
McCarty, W. B., 93, 96
McCoy, Rose Embly, 140, 145, 204
McCullough, Ben J., 123
McCune, Frank, 195
McDaniel, Joseph M., 132
McDonald, Hazel B., 73
McGee, Ben, 198
McGhee, Annie Mae Brown, 54, 57, 58
McInnis, Hattie Jones, 213
McIntosh, Mary E., 41
McKinney, Henderson, 26, 28-29, 46, 53, 212
McKinney Missionary Society, 33, 46, 70
McLaurin, A. J., 72
McLendon, R. D., 120
McPherson, Ulysses, 196
MacVicar, Malcolm, 41
MaGee, Sadie, 197
Mallory, W. M., 82
Manning, Ivory C., 158
Marine Hospital. *See* United States Marine Hospital
Markham, Houston, 198
Marshall, Luther, 68
Marshall Field Foundation, 107
Marston, Sylvester Witt, 25
Mayhorn, Gloria, 177
Maxwell, Green C., 54
Maxwell, Irene B., 54
Media Center, 169-71
Merrill, Lott W., 16
Merrit, John A., 136, 194, 198
Miller, Melvin, 295
Millsaps, Reuben Webster, 28, 36
Millsaps College, 25, 27-28, 30, 35, 37

Ministers' Institute, 46, 73, 82
Miss Black America, 172
Missionary Baptist Education Academy, 12
Missionary Baptist General Association, 21
Mississippi College, 85
Mississippi Legislature, 8, 10, 32, 93, 95, 98, 103
Mississippi Negro Training School, 102-103, 110, 134-35. *See also* Jackson College; Jackson College for Negro Teachers
Mississippi State Department of Education, 75, 88, 94, 104, 106, 113, 117, 139, 140
Mitchell, Lucius, 212
Moman, Orthella, viii
Moore, L. V. Rouser, 32
Mora, Elizabeth Catlett, 172
Morehouse, Henry L., 38-39
Morgan, T. T., 41, 42
Morrill, Justin S., 16-17
Morris, A. E., 24, 25
Morris, John, 188
Mosley, Charles C., 122-23, 154
Mosely, Kathryn B., 172
Mt. Helm Baptist Church, 27, 31-32
Mt. Olivet Association and Sunday School Convention, 31
Music Department, 24, 30, 46, 56, 62. *See also* Conservatory of Music; Frederick Hall Music Center

NAIA (National Association of Intercollegiate Athletics) 194, 197, 284-85
NASM (National Association of the School of Music) 181
NCAA (National Collegiate Athletic Association) 194, 197
Natchez, xvii, 7, 10, 13, 15, 17, 20, 25-26
Natchez Seminary: founding of, 15-19; finances of, 20-21; regulations of, 21-22; courses of study, 23-24; problems of, 25; moves to Jackson, 25-26; mentioned, xiv, xviii, 6, 8, 12
National Archives, vii
National Council for Accreditation of Teacher Education, 181, 220
National Ministers Institute, 82

National Science Foundation, 125, 162
Newbold, N. C., 82
Normal Department, 24, 29-32, 43-44, 55
Norris, Edward P., 198
Norris, Gladys P., 199

Office of Public Relations, 295
Oldfield, Jack, 199
Olive, A. L., 69
Opera/South, 175-76
Overstreet, J. J., 82
Owens, C. H., 42
Owens, George, 175

Padelford, Frank W., 93
Page, Inman E.: family background of, 19; educational background of, 19-20; accepts post at Natchez Seminary, 20; resigns, 20; subsequent career of, 20
Paige, Roderick, 196, 198
Patton, Joseph T., 78
Pawley, Thomas D., 64, 65, 68, 203
Payton, Walter, 192, 196
Peoples, President John A., Jr.,: as SGA president, 137; inaugurated president of Jackson State, 142-44; educational background of, 144-50; academic programs under, 151-55; administrative reorganization under, 155-58, develops Faculty Senate, 158-59; and SUNY-Binghamton-Jackson Project, 160-61; devises Thirteen College Curriculum Program, 161-62; gets federal grants, 163-64; building program under, 167-69; and riots of 1970, 176-80; starts Advanced Institutional Development Program, 182-88; heads Bicentennial campus, 198-200; celebrates JSU centennial, 200-206, 218; mentioned, 99-100, 141, 175, vii, xiii- xv
Peoples, Mary Galloway (Mrs. John A.), 149, 150
Perkins, Addison L., 105
Perkins, R. Roy, 41
Pete, Melvin, 198
Peyton, J. J., 42, 43
Phillips, D. W., 19-20
Pierce, W. W., 96
Pine Street Baptist Church, 7

Pinkett, John R., 52, 68, 69, 71
Pollard, Randle, 6, 13
Porter, Dorothy Burnett, 172
Porter, J. E., 106
Powers, Ridgely C., 5
Practice School, 45, 85
President's Commission on Campus Unrest, 137, 138, 176-78
Price, Bolton C., 116
Proclamations, Centennial (see appendices)
Proctor, Samuel D., 204
Project LAMP, 174
Provine, J. W., 93, 96
Public Schools in Jackson—Named for Graduates, 317-319
Purdy, Paul W., viii, 156, 158, 203, 212
Purnell, A. D., 83

Quarter System, 83

Ramsey, Leroy, 195
Rashied, Raja, viii
Reconstruction Period, 4-5
Reddick, Lawrence, 172
Reddix, Daisy Shirley (Mrs. Jacob), 141
Reddix, President Jacob L.: assumes presidency of Mississippi Negro Training School, 102-103; background of, 102-103; recommendations to the Board of Trustees of State Institutions of Higher Learning, 104-105; faculty under, 105-108; building program under, 108-10; revamps curriculum, 113-20; establishes graduate program, 120-23; enlarges library, 126-30; attitude toward intercollegiate sports, 136; administration overview, 139-40; death of, 141; relation with J. A. Peoples, 146-51; mentioned, xiv, 132, 134, 137, 143, 192-93
Redmond, S. D., 93, 96
Reed, W. A., Jr., 69
Reese, Andrea, 177
Reeves, Bennie L., viii, 199
Reid, M. M., 64
Retirees, 319-320
Reynolds, Mary C., 38
Rhodes John D., ix
Rhodes, Lelia G., vii-ix, xiii, 141, 190, 210, 214

Rice, Greek L., 96
Richards, Ernest, 68
Riddell, Tally D., 123
Riots of 1970, 176-80
Robert R. Moton Foundation, 163
Roberts, Benjamin F., 106
Robertson, Frances D., 214
Robinson, Dollye M. E., 175, 180-81, 210, 217
Robinson, T. J., 156, 212
Rodgers, Carolyn, 173
Rogers, Oscar Allan, 154, 156, 158
Roosevelt, Eleanor, 103
Rose Hill Baptist Church (Natchez), 11, 21
Rosenwald Fund, 102-105, 127
Rowe, A. V., 43
Russell, Francis, 132

Saint's Baptist Missionary Association, 6
Sampson, Calvin T., 17-18
Sampson, Henry Thomas: appointed dean of Jackson College, 77; supports Dansby, 78; inaugurates two-year program, 83; and graduate program, 121; library dedicated to, 130-31; mentioned, 91, 123, 145, 148
Sanders, Lou Helen, viii
Sanders, Patricia Ann, 177
Sanderson, Eli, 28
Sawyer, Granville, 181
Scholarships, 190-92
School of Business and Economics, 152
School of Education, 152
School of Industrial and Technical Studies, 152
School of Liberal Studies, 152
Scope, 203
Self-Help Opportunity Center (SHOC), 125
Shiloah Baptist Church (Columbus), 11
Shirley, Gladys D., 105
Shirley, Ruth, 199
Shirley, William A., 73
Shockley, Ann, 172
Simmons, Juanita G., (Mrs. T. C.), ix
Simmons, Rev. T. C., ix
Simms, Rhoda L., 52
Simons, Kathleen H., 55, 79-80

Simpson, O. J., 196
Slater Fund, 32, 94
Slavery, xviii, 4, 9, 19
Sloan Foundation, 163
Smith, Allen Franklin, 198
Smith, Estus, viii, 156, 158, 175, 203, 212
Smith, Frank, 86, 89
Smith, Gladys Durr, 214
Smith, Jay T., 156
Smith, Jesse Carney, 171
Smith, Robert H., 156
Smith, Rose, 28
Snodgrass, A. D., 42
Snyder, Perry A., 199
Social Sciences, 115-16, 137
Sororities, 189
Southern Association of Colleges and Schools, 180-182
Southern Association of Colleges and Secondary Schools, 87, 114, 126
Southern Educational Foundation, 107
Southwestern Athletic Conference (SWAC), 194-98
Spinks, Stella, 177
Sports Hall of Fame, 195
Sproles, Henry F., 43
Stanley, Frank L., 84
Stanley, Sarah O., 52
Stansel, Mrs. Horace S., 103
Stevens, J. Morgan, 93
Stevenson, M., 24
Stewart, Edgar T., 68, 213
Stowers, Curlee, 301
Stowers, Jerutha, 301
Stowers, Nettie, 301
Student Activities, 136-37, 188-89
Student Enrollment, 19, 21, 24, 28, 33, 37, 40, 48, 188
Student Government Association, 136-37, 140, 189-90
Sullivan, John L., 195, 207, 214
SUNY-Binghamton-Jackson State Project, 160-61
Sykes, B. L., 140

Tate, Pearl R., 105
Tatum, Elbert L., 116
Tatum, Ola M., 132
Taylor, Arthur, viii

Temple, R. J., 42
Theology Department, 30-31, 73
Thirteen College Curriculum Program, 161-62
Thomas, A. J., 55, 80
Thomas, W. P., 55
Thompson, Benjamin, 13
Thompson, Cleopatra D., 133, 156
Thompson, Era Bell, 132
Thompson, J. Young, 31
Thompson, Julius E., 200
Thompson, Lonzie, 177
Thompson, Patrick H., 7, 31-32, 41, 42, 53
Thompson, William J., 55
Thornton, Lottie Lorene Williams, 110, 137, 141, 190, 213, 214
Tigerettes, 197
Tillinghast, S. R., 85
Tilton, A. V., 28
Tolliver, Johnny, 176, 199
Tolson, Melvin, 132
Tomlinson, E. T., 72
Topp, E. B., 28-29, 42, 53, 212
Tougaloo College, 88, 125
Travis, J. A., 113
Traylor, Fannie, 93
Tubb, J. M., 140
Tubb, T. J., 123
Tuitions, 20-21, 84
Tyler, William, 80

United States Marine Hospital (Natchez), 13, 15-17, 26
University Publications, Faculty, 203, 321-324

Vanderpool, Shirley A., 141
Varnado, W. L., 82
Vashon, George B., 19
Vicksburg, 4, 6, 8, 43

Walker, Matthew, 144
Waller, The Honorable William, 155
Walton, William Howard, 69
Wangara, Malaika Ayo, 173
Ware, Marie, Y., 105
Washington, Booker T., 50
Washington Addition, 38

Waters, Odessa Howard, 147
Watson, Clarence, 195
Watts-Lovelace, Sara Jane, 106, 126
Weakley, Vernon Steve, 177
Weatherall, Melita A., 106
Weathersby, Kathryn, 188
Welch, W. Bruce, 115
West, A. S., 24
Westbrook, C. D., Jr., 69, 73, 195
West-Peyton, Anges S., 26
Wheatley, Phillis, 172-74, 199
White, Charles L., 72
White, The Honorable Hugh L., 93, 94, 96
Whiteside, Mary G., 69, 70, 73, 105
Whitfield, H. L., 40
Whitney, S. Leon, 140
Wilburn, D. W., 123
Wilcher, J. B., 69
Williams, Betty, 212
Williams, Beulah R., 214
Williams, C. C., 55
Williams, Dan, 172
Williams, The Honorable John Bell, 167
Williams, Lee E., viii, 106, 115, 123, 133, 140, 150-51, 156, 203, 206, 212, 214
Wilson, Charles, 106
Wilson, Harrison B., 136, 194
Wilson, Herbert A., 195
Wilson, Redd, Jr., 177
Witty, Elaine Paige, 133-34
WJSU, 176
Wolfe, Estemore A., 201, 214
Wolfe, Robert L., 195
Woodard, Joe Y., 106
Woodard, Willie, 177
Wooster, Edson Gaius, 20, 25
Wright, Arthur D., 64, 68

Yazoo Mississippi Valley Railroad (YMV), 38, 97
Yellow Fever Epidemic, 25
Young, Aurelia N., 140
Young, Estelle, 213
Young, H. H., 69
Young, Jack, 214
Young Men's Christian Association (YMCA), 46, 70
Young Men's Lyceum, 46
Young Men's Temperance League, 46
Young Woman's Christian Association (YWCA), 46, 70
Young Women's Temperance League, 46

Zuber, Etta Augusta, 106
Zuber, J. D., 72

www.ingramcontent.com/pod-product-compliance
Lightning Source LLC
Chambersburg PA
CBHW080633230426
43663CB00016B/2847